Why Liberalism Works

Why Liberalism Works

*How True Liberal Values
Produce a Freer, More Equal,
Prosperous World for All*

Deirdre Nansen McCloskey

Yale
UNIVERSITY PRESS
NEW HAVEN AND LONDON

Chapter 25 was first published by the Institute of Economic Affairs, London, 2016.
Chapter 35 was first published by *Prospect* magazine, March 2016.

Yale University Press books may be purchased in quantity for educational, business, or promotional use.
For information, please e-mail sales.press@yale.edu (U.S. office) or sales@yaleup.co.uk (U.K. office).

Set in Fournier MT Std type by Westchester Publishing Services.
Printed in the United States of America.

Library of Congress Control Number: 2019937532
ISBN 978-0-300-23508-1 (hardcover: alk. paper)

A catalogue record for this book is available from the British Library.

This paper meets the requirements of ANSI/NISO Z39.48-1992 (Permanence of Paper).

10 9 8 7 6 5 4 3 2 1

Contents

Preface

By the time you finish this book, I hope I will have persuaded you of the case for a new, and old, liberalism. The L-word is not taken to mean US "liberalism," the distressingly anti-liberal, lawyer-driven politics of increasing governmental planning and regulation and physical coercion. It is instead the rest of the world's "liberalism," economist driven, "the liberal plan," as old Adam Smith wrote in 1776, "of [social] equality, [economic] liberty and [legal] justice," with a modest, restrained government giving real help to the poor.[1] True modern liberalism.[2]

I am arguing for the continuing desirability of a liberalism conceived in the eighteenth century (so original and up to date am I), an idea slowly implemented after 1776, with many hesitations and false turns. I began to realize around 2005 or so that a liberal "rhetoric" explains many of the good features of the modern world compared with earlier and illiberal régimes— the economic success of the modern world, its splendid arts and sciences, its kindness, its toleration, its inclusiveness, its cosmopolitanism, and especially its massive liberation of more and more people from violent hierarchies ancient and modern. Progressives and conservatives and populists retort that liberalism and its rhetoric also explain numerous alleged evils, such as the reduction of everything to money and markets or the loss of community and God or the calamity of immigration by non-whites and non-Christians. But they are mistaken.[3]

From the Philippines to the Russian Federation, from Hungary to the United States, liberalism has been assaulted recently by brutal, scare-mongering populists. A worry. Yet for a century and a half the relevance of liberalism to the good society has been denied in a longer, steadier challenge, by gentle or not-so-gentle progressives and conservatives. Time to speak up.

It is an optimistic book, piercing the sky-is-falling gloom which seems always to command a ready market. The pessimism is expressed innocently, even proudly, by good-hearted scholars and editorial writers. But then it is appropriated by bad-hearted tyrants in order to push people around. First, absolutely terrify the people. The terrorists are coming. Even my good friends the good-hearted—the slow socialists and moderate conservatives—call up pessimisms about the economy or the environment or the greatness of the nation, with similar consequences. Look at American politics after 9/11 or during Trump, or look as far back as British politics in the Gordon Riots or in the age of the French Revolution. Terrorism works with more than guns and bombs and guillotines.

The point here is to convert you to a "humane true liberalism," which you probably harbor anyway. Modern liberalism. You don't *really* favor pushing people around with a prison-industrial complex, or with regulations preventing people from braiding hair for a living, or with collateral damage from drone strikes, or with a separation of toddlers from their mothers at the southern US border, do you? I'll bet not. As someone put it: Do unto others as you would have them do unto you.

I try here to follow also another old rule for liberalism, an intellectual version of the Golden Rule, articulated in 1983 by Amélie Oksenberg Rorty— to listen, really listen, to your questions and objections.[4] The book includes therefore interviews by journalists and other earnest doubters, who sometimes put forward well-intentioned but often illiberal objections to a free society.

The origins of the essays in varied audiences leave a residue of repetition, which I hope does not excessively grate. I've tried to keep forward motion despite the repetition. And some of the repetitions are healthy, things you really, really need to know—chiefly that according to the scientific consensus in economic history, the much-maligned "capitalism" has raised the real income per person of the poorest since 1800 not by 10 percent or 100 percent, but by over 3,000 percent. Cheap food. Big apartments. Literacy. Antibiotics. Airplanes. The Pill. University education. The increase is a factor of *thirty*. That is, 30 minus the original, miserable, base of 1.0, all divided by the base is 29/1, to be multiplied by 100 to express it per hundred—or a 2,900 percent increase over the base, 3,000 near enough. I will keep saying it, and keep dazzling you with my prowess in arithmetic, until you feel it on your pulse. It is the greatest, yet regularly overlooked, fact about the modern world. Most people by actual questionnaire think that since olden days the real capacity of poor people to buy goods and services has increased maybe 100 percent, at the outside 200 percent, a doubling or a tripling. They're quite wrong.[5] The increase has been much, much greater. If we appreciate it, the appreciation will transform all our politics. For example, the fact of the Great Enrichment is a crucial element in showing that humane true liberalism of the modern sort I advocate here is good and enriching, in every sense.

The Great Enrichment doesn't mean, of course, that there's nothing more to do in helping the poor, especially by ending the numerous, monstrous, and yet politically popular policies that in fact damage them worldwide. But it does mean that it is mischievous to attack, as many political theories do, a "capitalism" that has done more than anything else to help the poor. The Great Enrichment doesn't mean that little bits of other systems—a soupçon of socialism for worthy public projects, a cup of Christian charity for the poor, a tablespoon of encouragement to worker-owned cooperatives, such as law and accounting firms—are to be scorned. But it does mean that replacing "the system" as a whole would be disastrous for the poor, as it has been shown to be in the USSR after 1917, in Venezuela after 1999, and over and over again in between.

The book was not through-written, unlike my economic-historical trilogy backing up many of the factual claims made here. To make consecutive reading smoother I've arranged the whole into a moderately coherent argument, the skeleton of which you can discern by reading slowly through the table of contents. Notice that part III is a detailed inquiry into the leading illiberal worry nowadays, the alleged rise of inequality, just to show that detailed inquiries are possible and yield liberalism-favoring results. Part IV deals in less detail with various other illiberal worries. Part of the thrilling drama of the present book is watching the rather obvious liberal ideas retailed here, peddled by me in essays from a miscellany of newspapers and magazines over the past few decades, seep into my slow-thinking economist's mind. The seeping took place during my mad, program-less life from my early fifties on, changing gender, becoming a progressive Christian, embarking on explaining the nature and causes of the wealth of nations, seeing the eighteenth-century light.

Except for the long, introductory part I, which has circulated a bit in a shorter version as "Manifesto for a New American Liberalism," most of the essays are "occasional," that is, occasioned by this or that invitation to sound off. The variety of audiences I was asked to address makes the prose not uniform in tone, though I've edited it here and there to approach uniformity. I have included a couple of my more open-handed academic pieces defending the foundations of a free society, from *The Bourgeois Virtues: Ethics for an Age of Commerce* (University of Chicago Press, 2006), the first volume of the Bourgeois Era trilogy on history, economics, and literature. I've written a good deal for the *Wall Street Journal*, the *New York Times*, and the *Financial Times*, but most of the journalistic pieces here are from *Reason* magazine, because *Reason* is the leading voice of true liberalism in the United States. You need to know it, and to subscribe. Get woke, and reasonable.

In other words, each chapter has its own little arc of argument and often its own style, about political philosophy or gay rights or economic history or economic policy or Thomas Piketty. The beginning of each provides a sentence or two of context. The endnotes and bibliography give sources for the quotations, and the backing for many of the facts and ideas. When an assertion is made in the text without a reference you can usually assume either that it is referenced elsewhere in the book or that I am taking the assertion to be obvious on its face, or obvious in light of current economic and historical knowledge. The book is not an academic tome, but it tries earnestly to sustain a serious standard of truth telling, based on actual facts and coherent ideas. Well . . . you judge.

If there's anything erroneous here, I blame the people who have advised me. The wretches should have saved me from my errors. But, seriously . . . I thank Professor Jason Briggeman for brilliant editorial advice. My editors at Yale, Seth Ditchik in acquisition and Karen Olson in production, as well as copy editor Kelley Blewster and Brian Ostrander of Westchester Publishing Services, gave me more advice, most of which I followed. So I get unwarranted credit for their good ideas. Katherine Mangu-Ward, the editor of my beloved *Reason* magazine, played a similar role in many of the essays, though most are revised from their published form. The blog of my friend the liberal economist Donald Boudreaux, *Café Hayek,* has provided scores of leads to true liberal thinking, which I have boldly stolen. In the Bourgeois Era trilogy I thanked in more detail the embarrassingly large number of people on whom I have depended in slowly getting my science right and then realizing my true and modern liberalism.

I urge you to reconsider your politics, as I did, by listening, really listening, to new facts and ideas, or reconsidering the old ones. Staying open minded is usually a good plan. The economist and true liberal Bryan Caplan asks, "Who ever made an enemy by contradicting someone's belief about what is wrong with his car?" Yet enemy-making is commonplace in our debates about politics, such as about abortion or the minimum wage or trade protectionism. Caplan continues: "For practical questions [such as auto repair], standard procedure is to acquire evidence before you form a strong opinion, match your confidence to the quality and quantity of your evidence, and remain open to criticism. For political questions [such as whether we should be left or right or liberal], we routinely override these procedural safeguards."[6]

I want you to become less self-satisfied in your progressivism or your conservatism or even your relaxed middle-of-the-road-ism—a political identity, whatever it may be, acquired at age twenty or so and never seriously questioned thereafter. I want you to realize that the conventional opinions all depend on turning the government's monopoly of coercion on your good neighbors, and then on yourself. Often enough—to revive a useful word, a favorite of the eighteenth-century essayist and conversationalist Samuel Johnson—the conventional opinions are mere "cant," which is to say routinely repeated yet unexamined ethical claims, often wrong or bad. Johnson would say, "My dear friend, clear your mind of cant!" Good advice.

I want you to espouse modern liberal rhetoric, sweet talk, peaceful exchange, toleration of the other, and to see their good consequences. I want you to become much less certain that The Problem is "capitalism" or the Enlightenment; or that liberty can be Taken Too Far; or that hating other people is jolly good fun; or that governmental programs of war, socialism, expropriation, protection, subsidy, regulation, nudging, and prohibition are usually innocent exercises by our wise mothers and fathers in government to better the lives of us all.

With an open mind and a generous heart, dear friends, I believe you will tilt toward a humane true liberalism. Welcome, then, to a society held together by sweet talk among free adults rather than by coercion applied to slaves and children.

PART ONE

You Should Become a Humane True Liberal

1. Modern Liberals Recommend Both Golden Rules, That Is, Adam Smith's Equality of Opportunity

I make here the case for a modern and humane version of what is often called "libertarianism." It is not right wing, reactionary, or some scary creature out of dark money. It stands in the middle of the road—recently a dangerous place to stand—being tolerant and optimistic and respectful. It's true liberal, that is, anti-statist, opposing the impulse of people to push other people around. It's not "I've got mine," or "Let's be cruel." Nor is it "I'm from the government and I'm here to help you, by force of arms if necessary." It's "I respect your dignity and am willing to listen, really listen, helping you when you wish, on your own terms." When people grasp it, most like it. Give it a try.

It depends on and nourishes ethics. Ethics has three levels, the good for self, the good for others, and the good for the transcendent purpose of a life.[1] The good for self is the prudence by which you self-cultivate, learning to play the cello, say, or practicing centering prayer. Self-denial is not automatically virtuous. (How many self-denying mothers does it take to change a lightbulb? None: I'll just sit here in the dark.)

The good for a transcendent purpose is the faith, hope, and love to pursue an answer to the question "So what?" The family, science, art, the football club, God give the answers that humans seek.

The middle level is attention to the good for others. The late first-century BCE Jewish sage Hillel of Babylon put it negatively yet reflexively: "Do *not* do unto others what you would *not* want done unto yourself." It's masculine, a guy-liberalism, a gospel of justice, roughly the so-called Non-Aggression Axiom as articulated by libertarians since the word "libertarian" was redirected in the 1950s to a (then) right-wing liberalism. Matt Kibbe puts it well in the title of his 2014 best seller, *Don't Hurt People and Don't Take Their Stuff: A Libertarian Manifesto*.[2]

On the other hand, the early first-century CE Jewish sage Jesus of Nazareth put it positively: "Do unto others as you would have them do unto you." It's gal-liberalism, a gospel of love, placing upon us an ethical responsibility to do more than pass by on the other side. Be a good Samaritan. Be nice.

In treating others, a humane libertarianism attends to both Golden Rules. The one corrects a busybody and coercive pushing around. The other corrects an inhumane and soul-destroying selfishness. Together they are the other-ethics of modern liberalism. What we do not need is the reactionary version, the old spoof of the Golden Rule, namely, "Those who have the gold, rule." Nor do we need to follow the Florida football player on the eve of the Florida–Florida State game, "I follow the Good Book: 'Do unto others before they do it unto you.'" Neither is non-aggressive or nice.

The Golden Rule in either formulation, note, is radically egalitarian. In the Abrahamic religions you are to treat *every* human soul the way you would wish to be treated. You are to honor your one God and keep His day holy, but the rest of the Ten Commandments are about treating other humans as you would wish to be treated in matters such as truth telling or adultery. By contrast, in the theism of the Hindus or in the civic religion of the Confucians you are to treat the Brahman or the emperor as superior souls. An Untouchable or a peasant or a woman or a younger son is not to expect equal, reciprocal treatment. Of course, it was not until the bourgeois societies of late eighteenth-century Europe that anyone but an early Christian radical or a late Muslim saint thought to carry out in any large society the sweetly other-regarding theory of Abrahamic egalitarianism. Until Tom Paine or Adam Smith, a duchess was still a duchess, a sultan still a sultan, King Herod still Great.

In most of the world the word "libertarianism" is still plain "liberalism," as in the usage of the middle-of-the-road, deregulating, anti–"illiberal democracy" president of France elected in 2017, Emmanuel Macron, with no "neo-" about it.[3] That's the L-word I'll use here. But either "libertarianism" or "liberal" will do if understood to follow in modern fashion the real

Golden Rules. The sainted Tom Palmer of the liberal Atlas Network has it right. "Chances are almost 100 percent that you act like a libertarian. You don't hit other people when their behavior displeases you. You don't take their stuff. You don't lie to them to trick them into letting you take their stuff, . . . or knowingly give them directions that cause them to drive off of a bridge. . . . You're a civilized person. Congratulations. You've internalized the basic principles of libertarianism."[4] And of true liberalism.

The American economist Daniel Klein calls the three-hundred-year-old tradition that he and I praise "Liberalism 1.0," being Hillel of Babylon's negative version of the Golden Rule, Kibbe's and Palmer's don't hit people.[5] Channeling the C. S. Lewis book on the minimum commitments of faith, *Mere Christianity* (1952), Dan also calls it "Mere Liberalism." I push it along a little here, more in line with Jesus of Nazareth's version, to Liberalism 2.0. Maybe 1.5. Eamonn Butler of the Adam Smith Institute in London has written two splendid short books, *Classical Liberalism: A Primer* (2015) and *An Introduction to Capitalism* (2018). I wish Eamonn had left off the "classical," and had abandoned the misleading word "capitalism." David Boaz of the liberal Cato Institute in Washington wrote a lucid guide, *Libertarianism: A Primer* (1997), reshaped in 2015 as *The Libertarian Mind*. I wish David had called it *The Modern Liberal Mind*.

In Britain they call it "Orange-Book Liberalism." In a desperate summary for Americans, humane liberalism 2.0 is pre-Trump grown-up in trade policy and in civil discourse; post-Obama tolerant in social policy; post-Clinton responsible in federal deficits; post-LBJ democratic in civil rights; pre-McKinley non-interventionist in foreign policy; and pre-Lincoln or even pre-Jackson hands-off in economic policy. The complications are necessary. The economist Arnold Kling notes that identity politics on the left and Trumpism on the right means that it is no longer enough to say of true liberals in the United States that they are traditionally Democratic on social rights and traditionally Republican on economic rights.[6]

The Blessed Adam Smith recommended in 1776 "the liberal plan of equality, liberty, and justice."[7] The first in Smith's triad is a hoped-for equality in social standing, which he favored. Contrary to the attitude of the country club, and contrary to the pride of some of the men wearing Adam Smith ties, and contrary to a leftist's assumptions about Smith when she has not actually read a whole page of him with attention, Smith was an egalitarian. A man's a man for a' that.[8]

The second item that Smith hoped for in his liberal plan—equal liberty—is the economic right he wanted you to have, equal to anyone else's, to open a grocery store or enter an occupation. Especially occupations. Smith was outraged by the licensing and passports and other restrictions on the ability of a working man to use his powers harmlessly, or indeed helpfully. He would have been appalled, for example, by the fine-enforced rule in Oregon nowadays that you cannot publish remarks about engineering matters, such as the timing of traffic lights, without being a duly *government*-licensed engineer, even if you are in fact fully trained as an engineer.[9]

The third hoped-for item, justice, is seen by Smith the liberal as another equality, your standing equal to any other person before the powers of the government and before the courts of the government if used by other people against you. Smith was concerned with what philosophers call "commutative" justice—the justice in the procedures for getting stuff, and then protecting it and one's person. The contrast is with "distributive" justice, namely, how the stuff and personhood, after it is gotten, will be "distributed," as it were (the very word "distributed" is an illiberal metaphor, because the distribution is imagined as being achieved by coercion, not by commutative, voluntary agreement—it's not a deal but a draft). Smith's commutative justice is summarized in the modern idiom by Klein and Boaz and other liberals as the just procedure of "not messing [without consent, a right to say no] with other people's stuff," or persons.[10] We should all be so constrained in justice, equally.

The theme in liberalism, you see, is equality—derived it may be from the equal natural rights of each, or from the somewhat self-contradictory ruminations of utilitarians, or from the analogy with exchange among equals embodied in contractarianism, or from the implied equality under a community of Catholic conservatives or leftish communitarians, or from the consequences of equality for the survival of societies, or, as seems best to me, from the modest "analytical egalitarianism" so characteristic of eighteenth-century social thought in Scotland. Analytical egalitarianism was labeled and explored in 2008 by the economists and intellectual historians Sandra Peart and David Levy, with numerous examples.[11] A fault in Friedrich Hayek's famous liberal book *The Constitution of Liberty* of 1960 is that he depends on consequential reasons for liberty, such as economic productivity or community survival. Likewise, the economist Jeffrey Myron of Harvard and of the liberal Cato Institute in Washington articulates, most ably, a "consequentialist" libertarianism, by which he means that one can often show that liberty achieves higher utility in terms of output than slavery. The War on Drugs, for example, had bad effects on US income, not to speak of Colombia's or Mexico's. The trouble is that such utilitarian reasoning can also justify the worst tyrannies, as the tyrants regularly claim. It seems better to justify free human life through the natural and equal and analytically modest dignity we should all learn in our adulthood, to have and to grant to others, regardless of payoff.[12] Such equality is what Huck Finn gradually discovered on the raft about Jim, for whom he was willing then to suffer Hell's fire.

So I am taking back the word "liberal," used strangely in the United States, and nowhere else, to mean "leftish statist." (In Latin America it has been the conservatives and their cousins, not the socialists and their cousins, who have stolen the word "liberal," to mean "rightish statist.") Recently the US "liberals" have become frightened by the L-word, and now call themselves "progressives." Let them have the word "progressive" (supposing they don't mind being associated with the excesses of US Progressivism, such as compulsory sterilizations).

Then we real and modern liberals get to keep the good old L-word.

2. Liberalism Had a Hard Coming

In the eighteenth century the liberal idea aborning was that every person regardless of age or gender or ethnicity or position in the hierarchy should have equal rights. Such an idea of equality was still to most people shocking. About gender, for example, it was inconceivable even to the Founding Brothers. In earlier centuries of agriculture and its accompanying hierarchy, topped by the stationary bandits in charge, a liberal equality was held in fact to be absurd and dangerous. Justice was a matter of treating a duke as a duke and a plowman as a plowman, with the differing respect owed in justice to each—but certainly not *equality*. You bowed low to a duke. And you did not murder a plowman, unless provoked.

In 1381 the Lollard priest John Ball was drawn and quartered for asking "When Adam delved and Eve span, / Who then was the gentleman?" In 1685 Richard Rumbold, an English Leveler condemned to the scaffold under James II, declared—doubtless to the amusement of the crowd standing by to mock him—"I am sure there was no man born marked of God above another, for none comes into the world with a saddle on his back, neither any booted and spurred to ride him."[1] In 1685 such an egalitarian notion was deemed madness, except by a few weirdos such as the Quakers, who shook hands instead of bowing or curtseying or doffing their hats, and who allowed even women, of all absurd practices, to testify in the meeting to the Holy Spirit. In northwestern Europe a century or so after Rumbold the idea that no man was born marked of God above another was well on its way to becoming a commonplace, at any rate among advanced radicals and a few Old Whigs. Smith and his avant-garde allies of the long eighteenth century from

John Locke and Voltaire to Thomas Paine and Mary Wollstonecraft advocated a new, voluntaristic egalitarianism. They were in a word liberals.

And they were persuaders, not enforcers. They favored sweet talk, not
guns. Well, perhaps a *few* guns, at the Boyne and Saratoga and Valmy, in aid
of equal liberty for free male, adult, well-to-do citizens, especially those es-
pousing approved religious and political ideas. After all, it is the long eighteenth century we are talking about, and liberalism was young. But mainly
when the new liberals heard the word "guns" they reached for their rhetoric.
Even in foreign policy they did. The Founding Brother who does not have a
hip-hop musical about him, James Wilson, wrote in 1791 that "it may, perhaps, be uncommon, but it is certainly just, to say that nations ought to love
one another."[2] A hard Realpolitik in foreign policy implemented with bombs
and guns is not liberal.

Such a liberalism, I hope to persuade you, is the best version of being
an inclusive, democratic, pluralistic, and persuadable human, such as has been
the best theoretical ideal of, for example, an American since 1776. The liberal ideal has only very gradually been fulfilled anywhere, and nowhere perfectly. It has always been under contestation, often violent. The revolutionary
socialist or the revolutionary theocrat wants to overturn liberalism and es-
tablish a heaven on earth, now, by first cowing or jailing or murdering those
who demure, putting the selected men of the Party or the Revolutionary
Guard in charge. And the mere thugs like Putin or Orbán or Mugabe likewise take the liberals as their chief enemies. Nativist fascists of a more theoretical bent, too, object illiberally to immigrants moving toward economic
opportunity, your tired, your poor, / The wretched refuse of your teeming
shore. And Southern US trees, in aid of subordination, bore a strange fruit.

By contrast, the African-American poet Langston Hughes sang in 1935:
"O, let America be America again— / The land that never has been yet— /
And yet must be—the land where *every* man is free."[3] Free to move, to invent, to persuade, to offer a dollar, with no master in charge. The result of
liberal democracy's partial, imperfect fulfillment has been a slow but in the
end spectacular approach worldwide to flourishing, in which fewer and fewer
people are pushed or bossed around without their voluntarily given consent
or contract.

In its fitful development such a liberalism—from Latin *liber*, long understood by the slave-holding ancients as "possessing the social and legal status of a free man (as opp. to slave)," and then *libertas* as "the civil status of a

free man, freedom"—came to mean the theory of a society consisting *entirely,* if ideally, of free people.[4] No slaves at all. Equality of status. No pushing around. Sweet talking. Persuasive. Rhetorical. Voluntary. Minimally violent. Humane. Tolerant. No racism. No imperialism. No unnecessary taxes. No domination of women by men. No casting couch. No beating of children. No messing with other people's stuff or persons. The government, said the German sociologist Max Weber in 1919, can with justice claim "the monopoly of the legitimate use of physical constraint/force/violence/coercion" ("das Monopol legitimen physischen Zwanges").[5] Liberalism recommends that the monopoly be used gingerly. It recommends a maximum liberty to pursue your own project, if your project does not use your own or the government's physical coercion to interfere with other people's projects. It is a noble vision, suited to free men and women.

Yet, alas, late in the nineteenth century in France and Germany and even in the original-liberal Anglo-and-Dutch sphere a clerisy of artists and journalists and professors commenced railing against such splendidly sweet and productive liberalism, and its bourgeois carriers. (The word "clerisy," which I'll use often, is of German origin, and is how Samuel Taylor Coleridge and I refer to the intelligentsia, journalists, ministers, professors, novelists, and the rest of the scribbling tribe.) Gustave Flaubert wrote to George Sand in 1867, "Axiome: la haine du bourgeois est le commencement de la vertu," which is to say, it is an axiom that hatred of the bourgeois man is the beginning of virtue.[6] About the same time in Latin America "Positivists" à la Comte were pressing the case for rationalist social engineering, mixed to be sure with a conservative version of liberalism.[7] The Great Enrichment we have experienced since 1800 didn't come fast enough, the anti-liberals complained. It was a project of our vulgar and commercial fathers. It was not governed by our preconceived rational patterns. Dark money is behind it. Let us use the government's monopoly of legitimate coercion to better the poor, or to glorify the nation. Let us take from Peter to give Paul capabilities, or to buy tanks and jets for him. And then vice versa.

By the time in 1942 that the Austrian-American economist Joseph Schumpeter (1883–1950) wrote *Capitalism, Socialism, and Democracy* most of the clerisy expected comprehensive socialism to prevail. Even Schumpeter, a liberal enthusiast for a business-respecting civilization, did so. And most of the clerisy had long welcomed the prospect. In 1919 the American journalist Lincoln Steffens, returning from the nascent Soviet Union, declared, "I have seen the future; and it works."[8] By 1910 at the latest, as I said, the New Liberals in Britain and the new Progressives in America, for what they assured us were the best of motives, had redefined the L-word to mean its opposite, a slow socialism. I take "socialism" in a baggy sense to mean the proposal to use the government's powers of coercion to achieve social as against individual ends, ranging (beyond the minimalist assurances of liberalism) from a little coerced redistribution all the way to massively coerced central planning. (The various post–Great War soviet and spartacist uprisings in Bavaria, in wider Germany, northern Italy, and Russia, Hungary, Bulgaria, and others were the *fast* sort of socialism, that is, communism, fascism, and national socialism.)

Understand that I am not saying that government has no role. But I am saying that we have in the past century fallen into thinking that it's usually a good idea to make its role larger and larger. What do you call an economy in which the share of governmental expenditure has gone from single digits to large double digits, and a polity in which politicians compete to make the digits larger and larger? I suggest that it should be called double-digit socialism (not 100 percent, you see), and needs to be reduced in scope. The slow and partial socialism of FDR in 1933 and Clement Attlee in 1945 was supposed to raise up the working man by slow compulsion of law, backed by the government's monopoly of coercion, slowly expropriating the economic royalists. Businesspeople were imagined not as bringers of news from owners of inputs and buyers of their products but as extracting for themselves tons of gold in the back room. The gold could be appropriated endlessly for the benefit of workers by improving conditions endlessly. The eight-hour day. Paid vacations. Health care. Surely the sum of cash wages and good working conditions, our friends the slow socialists claim, is determined not by economic productivity but by the outcome of the struggle over who gets that gold.

The New Deal in the United States and Clause Four Socialism in the United Kingdom did not recommend the sanguinary violence urged by the hard-left and hard-right socialists in a hurry. But the beautiful ends were pretty much the same, as were some of the means, such as seizure of capital without compensation, or its equivalent in taxation. Two years after the Bolshevik Revolution the British legal scholar A. V. Dicey wrote disapprovingly that "revolution is not the more entitled to respect because it is carried through not by violence, but under the specious though delusive appearance of taxation imposed to meet the financial needs of the State."[9]

On the left, our friends (listen up, Jack, Arjo, Nancy) would do well to reflect on the authoritarian cast of European social democracy c. 1900 and of American Progressivism c. 1910 and of American High Liberalism c. 1960 and of the American social democracy of Bernie or of the British hard-line socialism of Jeremy c. 2019. Our friends on the right, too, should reflect on the authoritarian cast of their conservatism or Republicanism, most extreme in the capture of the GOP by Trump.

I ask you merely to reflect.

3. Modern Liberals Are Not Conservatives, Nor Statists

Modern liberals do not sit anywhere along the conventional one-dimensional right-left spectrum of governmental coercion. The spectrum stretches from a violently compelled right-conservative policy of imperial wars to a violently compelled left-US-"liberal" policy of class warfare. Along the spectrum the question is merely in which direction the massive coercion is to be applied, and neither rightist not leftist pauses to question its massiveness. The wind is toward the left, Olaf Palme, the socialist prime minister of Sweden, is supposed to have said. Let us make sail. Anywhere along the spectrum the government exercises compulsion backed by police. Nowadays such policies penetrate unusually deeply into people's lives. To be governed under such a régime is to be ruled, bossed, taxed, drafted, redistributed, questioned, rousted, coerced, beaten, watched, overseen, inspected, judged, nudged, prohibited, licensed, regulated, expropriated, propagandized, pushed, gassed, tasered, shot, jailed, and executed. Yes, occasionally benefited, too. But at whose cost in compulsion and corruption?

The true liberal, by contrast, sits up on a second dimension, the non-policy apex of a triangle, so to speak. That is, we liberals 1.0 or 2.0 are neither conservatives nor socialists. The liberal economist and political philosopher Hayek argued in "Why I Am Not a Conservative" that both conservatives and socialists believe, with most lawyers and soldiers and bureaucrats, that "order [is] . . . the result of the continuous attention of authority."[1] In a word, they advocate statism. The extravagant modern growth of law as legislation, to be contrasted with the older notion of law as the discovered good or bad customs of our community, embodies such a belief.[2] Both ends of the conventional spectrum of massive governmental coercion, and the middle, too, Hayek continued, "lack faith in the spontaneous forces of adjustment."

Many writers and politicians conventionally classified on right or left join in fact the true liberals perched on the apex. On the "right" in the United States one thinks of David Brooks, George Will, Andrew Sullivan, or Jonah Goldberg (some of whom, by the way, have occasionally said nice things about my work, such as Goldberg 2018; brilliant and tasteful gentlemen, all of them). On the US "left" nowadays it's harder to find true liberals, especially among the clerisy, but one thinks at least of the comedian-commentator Bill Maher and maybe the Democratic Freedom Caucus, and a few other politicians such as Senator Cory Booker. What they have in common is a worry about a busybody or coercive government.

The modern liberal economist Donald Boudreaux writes that "many people believe that we human beings left undirected by a sovereign power are either inert blobs, capable of achieving nothing, or unintelligent and brutal barbarians destined only to rob, rape, plunder, and kill each other until and unless a sovereign power restrains us and directs our energies onto more productive avenues."[3] That's why the statists left or right think they need massive coercion, in order to compel the barbarians and blockheads to get organized.

Long ago the picture had some plausibility, enough in the minds of its painters, for example, to justify slavery as helping the darkies to do something useful, or to hold Indonesians in Dutch apprenticeship for another century or two. When the Irish were illiterate and the Italians superstitious, a masterful state seemed to make sense. I don't actually think so, but you can at least see why the masters would favor a picture of inert blobs or brutal barbarians. But the theories look a lot less plausible in an age in which the Irish and the Irish Americans have among the highest educational attainments in the world, and the Italians, despite some strange voting recently, are far from barbaric and superstitious. In other words, modern liberalism fits the modern world of high human capital better than the old rightish model of dim-witted peasants properly led by the aristocracy or the old leftish model of gormless proletarians properly led by The Party. If ever there was a time to let people go, and to have a go, it is now, when they are so obviously ready for a liberal autonomy. Yesterday, one might put it, was the time for the aristocracy or the state. Now is the time for liberalism.

The conservative/reactionary believes that social customs, even if long-lived, are terribly fragile in the face of the irritating changes we see daily, such as a falling away from religious belief or the coming of gay marriage. And on the other end of the spectrum the progressive/socialist believes that nothing will happen to bad customs unless she makes a law to change them. She is confident that she knows what the future laws will bring. I mean, it says so right here in the law that, say, poor people's wages can be raised by passing a minimum wage. Fifteen dollars. Twenty. Heck, why not one hundred?

"The [real] liberal," by contrast, Hayek wrote, "accept[s] changes without apprehension, even though he does not know how the necessary adaptations will be brought about."[4] No one in 1960 anticipated the internet. No one in 1900 anticipated that autos could safely whiz past each other a few feet apart on two-lane roads at a combined speed of 120 miles per hour. Almost no one in 1800 anticipated the Great Enrichment (amounting, the economic historians have discovered, I noted, to some 3,000 percent per person.) Almost no one in 1700 anticipated liberalism. Yet, like evolution in animals or in art or in language or in science, the necessary adaptions were brought about, with few if any visible hands of extraction and governance.

People did it, not the governments. The Nobel economist Vernon Smith expressed the point this way: "The early 'law-givers' did not make the law they 'gave'; they studied social traditions and informal rules and gave voice to them, as God's, or natural, law. The common lawyer, Sir Edward Coke, championed seventeenth-century social norms as law commanding higher authority than the king. . . . Mining claims were defined, established, and defended by the guns of the mining clubbers, whose rules were later to become part of public mining law."[5] Donald Boudreaux commenting on Smith's passage writes, "No myth is responsible for as much mischief . . . [as the one] that proclaims that social order must be designed. . . . And no particular instance of this myth is worse than that which insists that law—the rules that govern human interactions—is and can only be the product of the state."[6]

A conservative admires such spontaneous evolution up to a couple of decades before the present, yet is angry and fearful about any recent or, God help us, future evolution. Adoption of children by gay couples, say. Yuk. A social democrat, on the other hand, does not admire many of the evolutions up to the present, and is confident she can lay down a better future by com-pelling you to give up your stuff and your liberty—for your own welfare, dear. Industrial policy, say. The true liberal person, by contrast, admires some old evolutions—English common law, for instance, though not its en-slaving doctrine of *femme couverte*—and looks with a cheery confidence to a future of unforced evolutions by liberated if constitutionally and especially ethically constrained adults, whatever in the world the evolutions might turn out to be.

At root, then, a true liberal, and the minority of liberals among Repub-licans and Democrats, Tories and Labourites, believes that, as much as pos-sible, no one should push people around, standing over them with a gun or a fist to force them to do his will. It is an ethical conviction. The modern lib-eral, I have noted, abhors hierarchies of men over women, masters over slaves, politicians over citizens. The great American liberal philosopher David Schmidtz argues that each person's "right to say no" is vital, "the backbone of cooperation among self-owners."[7] Said Bartleby the scrivener in Melville's tale of 1853, "I would prefer not to."[8] As a free man and no slave, he could say no, whether or not it was good for him. He was an adult, and as an adult he was owed respect for his preferences, if not a paid job.

The nineteenth-century English liberal Herbert Spencer noted in 1891, when such liberal ideas had come under assault from the left (as they long had been assaulted from the right), that the only alternative to contract or agree-ment or free will is the coercion of superior status and pushing around: "As fast as the régime of contract is discarded the régime of status is of necessity adopted. As fast as voluntary co-operation is abandoned compulsory co-operation must be substituted. Some kind of organization labor must have; and if it is not that which arises by agreement under free competition, it must be that which is imposed by authority."[9] The American journalist, lexicog-rapher, and liberal 1.0 H. L. Mencken wrote in 1922, "The ideal government of all reflective men, from Aristotle to Herbert Spencer, is one which lets the individual alone—one which barely escapes being no government at all."[10] "The key functions of the legal system," writes the liberal legal theorist Rich-ard Epstein, "can be neatly summarized in four words: aggression no, ex-change yes."[11] As Boaz puts it at the outset of *The Libertarian Mind*, "In a sense, there have always been but two political philosophies: liberty and power."[12]

Boudreaux notes that nowadays "it is believed that the beneficent sovereign power must be 'the People,' usually in the form of democratic majorities."[13] The philosopher Jason Brennan and the economist Bryan Caplan, with numerous others back to Burke and Hobbes and Plato, note that *il populo* commonly make wretched decisions about governing.[14] Well, if so, we had better keep the decisions modest in scope, and constrained by a constitution and by *stare decisis,* and constrained especially by liberal ideology and by liberal ethics. We should have, that is, a policy of as little coercive policy as we can manage— liberty not power.

The liberal economist Klein draws attention to the distinction Adam Smith made between the passive and the active sentiments.[15] An emotion is passive, a passion is active. An emotion comes during our first, unreflective moment, and sometimes it suffices ethically. We see a child about to fall down a well. Anyone, even a gorilla, is moved to intervene.[16] But such passive emotions—what the orthodox economists call in their strange way "maximizing utility"—are not enough to make us fully human. After all, grass maximizes its utility, unreflectively, passively, seeking light and nourishment. So do pigeons. By contrast, *human* action, to use the "Austrian" economic term, is not merely reactive to constraints and utility functions but active and creative, the exercise of the free and creative and (some of us think) God-given will that can say yes, or no.

Smith noted in 1759 that contemplating the mass extermination of the Chinese would give one less emotional pain of the immediate, unreflective, utility-maximizing sort than the loss of a little finger. But on such an occasion the passive emotion is on reflection "so sordid and so selfish" that it cannot satisfy our ethical opinion of ourselves. In his egalitarian and liberal way, Smith draws attention to "the real littleness of ourselves . . . and the natural misrepresentations of self-love."[17] True, sober reflection on facts and reasoning is painful to our little selves. But it is needful for a human life beyond reaction, impulse, utility-maximization. The noble and generous path, of deciding to care more about the mass of Chinese than about one's little fingers, requires an active passion, in this case a passion for justice. In practice it will entail human action, as for example in the steady humility of the scientist before facts.

But wait. Klein draws the liberal conclusion against the coercive spectrum from left to right: "The governmentalization of social affairs throws us into the passive position. That is what [true] liberalism understands." We need, Smith and Klein and I believe, to get off the spectrum entirely, and into the noble and generous and reflective and un-coerced place of a liberal apex suitable to free adults. We need to be scientists in human ethics as much as in natural philosophy. We need passionately to reject the unreflective little-fingerism of massive government, a government inviting us to be emotional pigs motivated only by passive self-interest, oinking pseudo-scientists grubbing for careers instead of seeking truth, with governmental farmers to feed us maximally with slop.

The liberal philosophers Tomasi and Brennan call themselves "neoclassical liberals," contributing to a lively website created by the philosopher Matt Zwolinski, Bleeding Heart Libertarians.[18] "Bleeding heart" refers to the conservative sneer against weepy leftists, and indeed to the Christian pity for Our Savior on the cross, and His wounds. We modern liberals say we should all have hearts—not stony hearts but bleeding, for the pity of mortal lives.

Which is to say that *humane* and modern liberals 2.0 believe that people should help and protect other people when they can. Contrary to the left's conviction that classical liberals favor pushing the poor off the road in aid of some crazy Social Darwinist scheme, we want the poor to prosper. Really. (And we classical, and modern, liberals have accumulated massive evidence that the left's and the right's policies do *not* allow the poor to prosper.) We liberals care. Do unto others, we say. Help people in a flood. Feed the poor in the church basement. Let young men on Chicago's West Side get real, profit-making jobs aside from drug running—as the policies of slow socialists and moderate conservatives do not let them. Let the poor and persecuted into the United States or Britain or Germany. Stop the Rwandan massacre, through coercion if necessary, as President Clinton in 1994 did not. Protect the Muslim adult males of Srebrenica, according to the sworn duty of honorable soldiers, by coercion if necessary, as the Dutch Brigade in 1995 did not.

That is, we humane liberals do not stand against poor people, as leftists routinely charge without looking into it much. (They say, "Why should we *listen* to Koch Institute or Mont Pelerin Society evil?" Therefore, Nancy MacLean and Phil Mirowski do not realize that the Institute and the Society are strongly opposed to corporate welfare and to American imperialism and to the prison system and to the drug laws.) We humane liberals are not ungenerous, or lacking in ruth. Nor are we strictly pacifist, willing to surrender in the face of an invasion by Canada, or a cyberattack by Russia.

But we believe that in getting such good things as effective help for the poor and effective security for the nation, the government should not turn carelessly to coercion at home or abroad. People should not use pushing other people around as a first choice, for either leftish or rightish purposes, risking the permanent infantilization of the poor or a clueless policing of the world. People should depend chiefly on voluntary agreements among adults, such as commercially tested betterment, or peaceable treaties of free trade, or agreements for self-protection, or civil conversation, or soulful charity, or the gift of grace, with the dignity of majority voting constrained strictly by the dignity of civil liberties for the minority. Above all people should respect the other person by respecting her liberty to say no.

4. Liberals Are Democrats, and Markets Are Democratic

True and modern liberalism especially is democratically inclusive, fulfilling at last in social and economic practice the egalitarianism of Abrahamic religions. In the mid-nineteenth century John Stuart Mill and Alexis de Tocqueville were the first liberals in a young movement who felt the need to assume the existence of thoroughgoing political democracy, and to worry about it. Much later the pioneering management theorist of the 1920s, Mary Parker Follett, who coined "win-win," defined democracy not merely as majority voting—and then after the voting a bit of pushing the losers around—but as a true-liberal program of discovering win-win solutions.[1]

For collective decisions, I say again, a liberal democracy often results in poor choices. Such is life. In reaction, Jason Brennan puts forward a bizarre suggestion for a rule exclusively by the well-informed, with college degrees, and Hayek a bizarre suggestion for age restrictions on voting. But even such undemocratic policies would probably not result in much better choosing—besides stripping away the equal human dignity for everyone that is the core belief in the liberalism both men advocate. Their proposals sacrifice their true liberalism to a utilitarian fancy that smart or old people know what to do. The liberal Stephen Davies argues persuasively that although smart people think they know it all, in fact the wisdom of crowds or of invisible hands commonly works better.[2] The smart and old and well-informed, after all, led the United States to invade Iraq and Vietnam, to jail Japanese-Americans, to sterilize the poor, and to justify slavery. The core problem is that any government enslaves a little or a lot, which is to say that it bosses people with coercion. That, after all, is its admitted business. Putting smart people in charge of such a business is not always going to be a good idea. Better to have people who respect your autonomy, such as commercial businesses sweet talking you into win-win by buying its shoes or ships or sealing wax. Let's do less government and more business.

The private rule of win-win has public uses. It will properly recommend closing an enterprise that is not paying its way, in order to open an enterprise that earns more for the community than it costs. As has been accepted in socialist high theory since the 1930s, an omniscient central planner would do exactly the same thing in closing the unprofitable enterprise. Ludwig von Mises was the first to say so, in 1920, and engaged in a fierce debate for many years with the theorists of central-planning socialism. In the end the two sides roughly agreed in theory. Ideal socialism, they concluded, imitates ideal commerce. Oskar Lange, a socialist economist and communist functionary of note, declared that for Mises's role in making the point clear, "a statue of Professor Mises ought to occupy an honorable place in the great hall of the Ministry of Socialization or of the Central Planning Board of the socialist state."[3] The planner, that is, would aim at the same economic betterment for the community—at the extra cost under socialism of literally pushing people around by command from the Central Planning Board instead of letting the people respond to prices cast up by voluntary human interactions, in the manner of art or language.[4] (The theoretical discussion assumed that postproduction distribution could be adjusted in any way we wished by lump-sum transfers out of surplus value or profits, whether earned by the government or by private companies. It was crazy, but both sides theorized this way. They were trying to separate questions of production from questions of distribution.)

In other words, the prices in a liberal economy set by supply and demand would achieve the same desirable reallocation that an omniscient economic planner in a socialist utopia would recommend, though without the socialist fist of gulags and government. Breakfast porridge with blueberries at the Perfectionists' Café in Terminal 2 of Heathrow Airport costs £5.50. The price sends a signal to the traveler that if she buys and eats it she takes from somewhere else in the economy £5.50 worth of other goods and services. She chooses to pay the price if her pleasure in eating exceeds the price. She thereby earns a species of profit, which economists call "consumer's surplus." (By no means is it only producers who earn profit, as to the contrary the old Marxists claimed, because they did not have the benefit of 1870s economics.) We can admit that allocation by prices does not achieve nirvana. But the highly plausible claim by the liberal is that prices negotiated in markets are better at inducing the consumer's surplus for us all than the system of being ordered about under threat of coercion by central planners—planners who could not possibly know how much the traveler in Heathrow would willingly pay that frosty morning.

The practical implication of such ruminations is that the complaint of populists and many good-hearted leftists that, say, Hungarian farmers or West Virginia coal miners are losing out to something called "neoliberalism" is misdirected. The farmers and miners are losing out, yes, but to economic betterment that all of us would wish to go forward. The problem is not neoliberalism but progress, whether directed by the price system or by the commissar (and I just told you why the direction would be the same). What is being complained about is change, and as it happens desirable change. If Hungarian farming is no longer a good idea, or West Virginia mining, then it should stop, regardless of what politics we espouse— "capitalist" or socialist—assuming we want the betterment, for the benefit of the poorest among us. We may want to help out the farmers or the miners in some generous way. All right, though such changes are so pervasive in a progressing society that the generous impulse to do so is in fact impractical, if we attend to every person disturbed by progress. There are too many, because no one is an island, entire of herself, each a piece of the continent, a part of the main. But keeping people in unprofitable jobs is anyway a bad way to proceed. Profits are a signal of general worthiness.

A liberal system of prices does the best we can in this vale of tears for achieving our ends. It is the simplest means of social cooperation, arising spontaneously in every human community from the caves to the present. Like language, it does not need to be forced or designed. And like language there is no simple alternative available. The proposals from the seventeenth century on to produce artificial languages stripping away the inconvenient messiness of natural languages embody the same utopianism as does central planning. It is no surprise to find Francis Bacon proposing central planning of both language and science. Uncoerced prices, like languages, have the latent function of persuading, tempting, suggesting, with no person arranging, pushing, threatening, beating with planners and police. As the Blessed Adam Smith said, "The offering of a shilling, which to us appears to have so plain and simple a meaning, is in reality offering an argument to persuade one to do so and so, as it is for his interest."[5] The buyer gains and the seller does, too. It is win-win, the best of democracy.

John Tomasi, to distinguish his (and my) views from the strange American usage of "liberal," calls true or classical or modern liberalism's alliance with modern democracy the liberalism of the common man.[6] It is not the faux "liberalism" recommended by a leftish or rightish clerisy with college degrees who want you to be forced into specific patterns they have imagined of outputs, prices, and incomes. It is not, that is, the left or right illiberalism of comfortable or obedient servility to a government or church run by our masters. Our masters won't let us say no. *Heel! Good* dog!

Tomasi's modern liberalism of the common man reminds one of Walt Whitman, singing long ago about the democratic and liberal person, "Of every hue and caste am I, of every rank and religion, / A farmer, mechanic, artist, gentleman, sailor, Quaker, / Prisoner, fancy-man, rowdy, lawyer, physician, priest. / I resist any thing better than my own diversity, . . . / I am large, I contain multitudes."[7] Such ordinary people, it was discovered by cautious experiments in the nineteenth and then especially in the twentieth century, actually do contain multitudes, without much help from a government devoted chiefly to servicing wealthy special interests or restricting immigration or enforcing racial segregation or giving jobs to a new aristocracy of spoil-takers and college graduates. That is to say, we discovered by trying it out that ordinary Dutch and British and American and then numerous other people, Swiss and Irish and Mexican, when left largely to themselves by government, did in fact contain multitudes of abilities for self-government and for economic and spiritual progress, formerly untapped. They could now run a clothing cart on Maxwell Street. They could watch out from the tenement window for the kids playing stickball in the street. They could move to a better job on the railways. They could rise from the factory floor to CEO at Whirlpool.[8] They could invent intermittent windshield wipers.[9] They could operate a food truck.[10] They could immigrate from Italy to make the first self-sustained nuclear reaction before the Germans did.

Like liberty unsupervised in the arts and sciences, or in music and journalism, such modern liberty unsupervised in the economy worked wonders. The old hierarchies began to retreat, though sometimes replaced by new governmental hierarchies of experts and Party cadres. Mainly, the ordinary people, when freed, ventured out, and showed their un-ordinariness. In the 1790s Haydn, absenting himself from his decades-long subordination in livery to the aristocratic house of Esterházy, took two long visits to London, selling music to the enlarging bourgeoisie there and becoming rich by providing his commercially tested betterments, his innovations. He liked it, and so did his paying audiences. The son of a wheelwright and a cook contained multitudes.

The abilities of ordinary people are routinely undervalued by conservatives and progressives, by right Tories and left Labourites. Our friends both on the right and on the left wish to use governmental power to judge people or to nudge them. If the judgers and nudgers are economists of an illiberal tendency, they believe that the ordinary economy of supply and demand and the ordinary psychology of common sense are overwhelmed by scores of appalling imperfections grievously obstructing the social good, which the economists can discern so much more accurately than the mere consumers and businesspeople.[11] The conservatives and progressives, in other words, view ordinary people as barbarians or blockheads, as children unruly or ignorant, to be tightly governed.

We modern liberals don't.

5. Liberals Detest Coercion

Liberalism is liberty from physical coercion by other humans, and in particular a liberty from coercion by masters or governments or gangsters, or masterful governmental gangsters. The great liberal Robert Higgs writes that the liberal "should never concede the moral high ground to those who insist on coercively interfering with freedom: the burden of proof should always rest on those who seek to bring coercion to bear against innocent people."[1]

But yes, I admit it: *some* imposition by governmental coercion is necessary. Not all laws are bad. Not all taxes, either. Got it. But perhaps then we can move to the question of exactly *how much* law, *how much* taxation, *how much* coercion. A big, modern government, which takes a third to a half of the national product for its purposes, depends too much on coercion—taxing its citizens, bombing foreigners, jailing pot smokers, protecting favored occupations and Whirlpool stockholders, seizing property by eminent domain for private projects, breaking into homes and offices at dawn to enforce the worst of the tax laws. A little, non-modern government depends on it, too.

Any government tends to, because of the tempting monopoly of coercion, which after all is the most direct way to results. Coercion requires no tiresome dialogue, such as in courts for Central Americans petitioning for asylum guaranteed in US law under the 1951 Refugee Convention and its 1967 Protocol. The economist Yoram Barzel calls even a rule-of-law government the "violence-wielding enforcer."[2] It is easier to *force* people directly to stop polluting than to, say, *charge* them for it by establishing property rights in clean air, and letting the law of contract and tort argued in a court of law do the rest, or to *persuade* people by discussion about it in a free press, encouraging individual and corporate responsibility for the environmental. It is so much easier to bring in the police to fine and jail people than to reason with them. The word usual for policy in the time of the Blessed Adam Smith was "police."[3] That's right. Policy, police. It's the impulse of the lawyer and legislator, and the tyrant, and of some economists.

By contrast, as the liberal sort of economist notes, the market for goods, like the (often unpriced) markets for art and science and ideas, relies on persuasion, sweet talk. Fully a quarter of labor income is earned by sweet talk on the job, and all of private national income, of course, by the offers expressed in money, a still more pervasive form of sweet talk.[4] In a non-slave society the boss has to work largely by persuasion, seldom using even market discipline, and never physical coercion legally. "John, would you please take over drill press 10 today? Harry is out sick." "Sure, boss." Or at arm's length the offers of money: "Here's $3." "Thank you, ma'am. Here's your decaf caramel macchiato grande." Or: "Let me make a painting by dripping colors on a big canvas and see if you like it." "Wow! A late Jackson Pollock! I'll gladly give you $32,645,000 for it."[5] Or: "Liberty is the theory of liberalism." "Oh, I get it." Sweet talk. There's no pushing around. It is mutual benefit, positive sum, win-win.

A liberal, to put it another way, really, really does not like the sometimes necessary monopoly of coercion, even if exercised in aid of a democratic majority. Though she readily admits that a little coercion is required for some limited purposes of government, she is an ardent friend of the non-governmental and voluntary order of art or market or science or journalism— trade, invention, and persuasion. She dislikes the necessarily violent and police-heavy policy of the feudal order, or of the bureaucratic order, or of the military-industrial order. As put by the Hungarian-born British economist P. T. Bauer, a lonely voice during the 1950s and 1960s against, for example, foreign aid to incompetent or murderous régimes, we should eschew "policies or measures which are likely to increase man's power over man; that is, to increase the control of groups or individuals over their fellow men."[6] He was recommending a liberty defined as freedom from violent human interference.

The illiberal order of a large government is thick with orders from the hierarchy, on the top of which our masters perch, justified by thousands of laws passed in each legislative session, and sub-regulations in stunning numbers issued annually by the bureaucracy. A deep student of these matters, the economist and liberal Veronique de Rugy, writes that "Americans would be horrified if they knew how much power thousands of unelected bureaucrats employed by federal agencies wield."[7] The humane liberal belongs instead, as Hayek declared, to "the party of life, the party that favors free growth and spontaneous evolution," against the various parties of right and left that wish "to impose [by coercion] upon the world a preconceived rational pattern."[8]

We liberals, whether plain vanilla 1.0 or leaning more toward humane 2.0, want a society that relies chiefly on the much-misunderstood word "rhetoric." The Roman rhetorician Quintilian quoted Cato the Elder defining its perfection as "the good man skilled at speaking."[9] Liberalism is deeply a matter of such rhetoric, the discovery (as Aristotle said) of the available means of (non-violent) persuasion in each case, how to engage in "sweet talk."[10] The Latin *suadeo*, "I persuade," has the same Indo-European root as English "sweet." Ethics, goodness, the Golden Rules make for sweetness.

The study of the art of rhetoric, after being for two millennia the basis of education in the West, and having parallel forms in much of the East and South, came to be despised by the self-described tough, realistic, and logical European intellectuals of the seventeenth century, such as Bacon and Descartes, Hobbes and Spinoza. Bewitched by Euclid, they were certain they could discern The Truth independent of merely human skillful speech.[11] Ever since, rhetoric has been disreputable—as though there is some other path to truth outside of good humans talking skillfully. Indeed, the skillful talk in advanced mathematics during the nineteenth century caused geometries to proliferate, radically undermining old Euclid and the easy unity of Truth. Gödel did more. We were driven back to the liberal conversation of humankind, as in the end we always are. There is no Archimedean point.

Rhetoric is in fact a practice anciently fitted since the Sicilian lawyers of the early fifth century BCE to a free society. We have only two ways of initiating change in the behavior of others, violent threats or amiable sweet talk. The sweet talk is usually better. It is not always so, and not recommended for Al Capone or Stalin, but is usually better for free adults raised to follow Hillel and Jesus, with good self-cultivation and a good transcendent purpose. Rhetorical sweet talk, for example, is what I'm doing for you now. *For* you, understand, not *to* you. It is a gift, not an imposition. (Glad you appreciate it.)

Adam Smith's first paid job was teaching rhetoric to fourteen-year-old Scottish boys, and he retained his belief that "everyone is practicing oratory on others through the whole of his life."[12] A liberal society practices oratory—constrained, as Smith noted, by the impartial spectator, one's conscience, the active sentiment, the ethical passion, the person within the breast, ultimately God. The alternative is physical coercion applied to others in aid of mastery. The Patriots of the American Revolution were very willing to tar and feather Loyalists.[13] And the Patriot leaders we call the Founding Fathers assumed that men such as they, high in the social hierarchy of an agricultural society, would continue to rule, continuing to be the fine gentlemen ruling over the mere commoners, as masters over their slaves.[14] The ruling men of the eighteenth century routinely beat their slaves, wives, children, apprentices, servants, soldiers, and sailors. Then the liberal evolutions after 1776 increasingly stayed their hands, right down to the #MeToo movement.[15]

6. Liberalism Had Good Outcomes, 1776 to the Present

Such a humane liberalism—contested as it has been always by authoritarians of left and right, both of them inspired by the ur-anti-liberal Hegel—has for two centuries worked on the whole astonishingly well.[1]

For one thing, it produced increasingly free people, a product which we moderns hold as a great good in itself. We hold it most passionately if we are humane true liberals. In succession the slaves, lower-class voters, non-Conformists, women, Catholics, Jews, Irish, trade unionists, colonial people, African-Americans, immigrants, socialists, pacifists, women again, gays, people with disabilities, and above all the poor from whom most of us descend have been increasingly allowed since 1776 to pursue projects consistent with not using physical coercion to interfere with other people's projects. As someone put it, in the eighteenth century kings had rights and women had none. Now it's the other way around.

An ancient justice-as-unequal-hierarchy was replaced gradually by a new eighteenth-century theory of justice-as-equal-standing. The replacement reached philosophical maturity in the 1970s with two books by philosophers at Harvard. John Rawls declared in *A Theory of Justice* (1971) that justice was fairness, that is, equality of outcome, such as a pizza coercively divided by the government equally among friends, or strangers. Robert Nozick counter-declared in *Anarchy, State, and Utopia* (1974) that justice was equal liberty, such as allowing the friends, without coercive supervision by government, to divide it as they saw fit and then to trade a share or two for an extra beer—and allowing the wandering stranger to buy in, too. Both men were liberals, descended from eighteenth-century models against hierarchy. But Rawls descended from the French and statist tradition of Rousseau and Helvétius, leading at the worst to the Finland Station and Lenin's Russia. Nozick descended from the Scottish and voluntarist tradition of Hume and Smith, leading at the best to the Midwest farm and Willa Cather's Nebraska.

And quite surprisingly, an unanticipated if very welcome consequence, the liberalism of the nineteenth century—by inspiriting for the first time a great mass of ordinary people to have a go—produced a massive explosion of economic betterments for ordinary people. Moderns and especially liberals rate the Great Enrichment high, against elevating the servicing of kings and gods. The common people contained multitudes of gifts for us all, mechanical harvesters to the modern novel.

How massive? How great? What multitudes? Liberalism resulted, as I have said (and will keep saying until you embrace it as the great fact of the modern world), in a fully *3,000* percent increase in the goods and services for the poorest among us. Listen to it. Out of liberalism, economic historians can tell you (there is no scientific debate about its rough magnitude, though there is debate about its causes), came a three *thousand* percent betterment. The liberal plan gave voice and permission to the Ben Franklins and Isambard Kingdom Brunels and Nikola Teslas and Albert Einsteins and Coco Chanels and Willa Cathers, otherwise mute and inglorious, to innovate. And it gave permission to have a go to the ordinary worker, able in liberty to get a new job; or to the ordinary shopkeeper, able in liberty to open her own shop. The liberating gave us steam, rail, universities, steel, sewers, plate glass, forward markets, universal literacy, running water, science, reinforced concrete, secret voting, bicycles, automobiles, free speech, cardboard boxes, airplanes, washing machines, air conditioning, antibiotics, the pill, containerization, free trade, computers, and the cloud. And it gave us the less famous but crucial multitudes of free lunches prepared by the alert worker and the liberated shopkeeper pursuing their own little projects for profit and pleasure. Sometimes, unexpectedly, the little projects became big projects, such as John Mackey's one Whole Foods store in Austin, Texas, ending with 479 stores in the United States and the United Kingdom, or Jim Walton's one Walmart in Bentonville, Arkansas, ending with 11,718 stores worldwide. It has given us too a startling rise in the ability to seek, too, the transcendent in Art or Science or God or Baseball.[2]

It was a stunning Great Enrichment, material and cultural, well beyond the classic Industrial Revolution of 1760–1860, which had merely doubled income per head. Such doubling revolutions as the Industrial had been rare in history but not unheard of, as for example in the surge of northern Italian industrialization in the Quattrocento.[3] The goods and services available to even the poorest rose dramatically, in a world in which mere doublings, rises of merely 100 percent, had been unusual and temporary, as in the commercial glory of fifth-century Greece or the commercial vigor of the Song Dynasty. In every earlier case the industrial revolutions had eventually reverted to a real income per head in today's prices of about $2 or $3 a day, the human condition. Even the domestication of plants and animals in nine locations worldwide, 8,000 BCE to 2,000 BCE, had not seen a permanent rise of income per head—though the larger populations now supportable had felicitous effects in the founding of city life and literacy, from Mesopotamia to Mesoamerica. But for Malthusian reasons, real income per head in agricultural economies had always reverted to $2 or $3 a day.

It didn't after 1800, or 1860, or 1973, or now, and it's not going to. Huzzah.

Consider living on $2 or $3 a day. Many people still do—though since 1973 their number has fallen like a stone.[4] The Green Revolution after the 1960s made India a grain exporter. Liberalization after 1978 in China made its cities modern. And, as I just said, after 1800, or 1973, or whatever recent year you care to choose, there has been no hint of reversion. In every one of the forty or so recessions since 1800 in the United States, the nation's real income per head has promptly, usually in two or three years, exceeded what it had been *at the previous peak*.[5] No exceptions. Up, Rup, up.

Even including the $2 a day still earned by people crushed by their illiberal governments, exercising monopolies of coercion, or by outlaws, exercising oligopolies of coercion, *world* real income per head during the past two centuries has increased by a factor of ten—and by that factor of thirty in countries such as Hong Kong, South Korea, Finland, Botswana which have fully used the liberal opportunity. The material and cultural enrichment bids fair now to spread to the entire world.[6] Hallelujah.

And the enrichment has been massively equalizing. It is a myth, though a persistent one, that the Great Enrichment entailed the pursuit of riches at the expense of equality. The truly unequal societies have been those in which land and the sword ruled, or in recent times those in which a violent gang has seized governmental power, the Russian Federation under Putin, for example, or Malaysia under Najib Razak. A market system is in fact egalitarian, letting entry erode excess profits from innovation, for the benefit from the innovation of the poorest, who get running water and electric lights. Every modern technological change from telephones to computers has aroused fears of a "digital gap." Yet because of entry at the smell of profit, it's never persisted. In the third act the poor get smartphones, cheaply. Every time.

The poorest since 1800 have been the greatest beneficiaries of commercially tested betterment, whose ideology was liberalism or, shall we say (instead of the misleading "capitalism"), "innovism." The rich got some additional diamond bracelets. All right. Meanwhile the poor for the first time got enough to eat. Nowadays in places like Japan and the United States the poorest make more, corrected for inflation, than did, say, the top 10 percent two centuries ago. Boudreaux makes a plausible case that the average poor woman in the United States is richer even than John D. Rockefeller was.[7] She now has antibiotics and air conditioning and five hundred channels of rubbishy TV, all of them unavailable to poor old John D. Likewise, Jane Austen (1775–1817) certainly lived in material terms more modestly and with less medical security than does now the average resident of East Los Angeles. Our Jane died at forty-one of some disease—Addison's (President Kennedy's disease), Hodgkin's, tuberculosis, we are not sure—probably easily cured or at least managed today. Equality of real comfort for the poor in adequate food, housing, clothing, education, health, entertainment, and most other important goods and services has steadily increased peak to peak since 1800. It does yet. In countries fully experiencing the Great Enrichment, such as Germany and Japan and Singapore, the average real income in today's prices (and with it the median and the comforts of the poorest) has increased from the $3 a day in 1800 to over $100 a day.[8]

As Schumpeter put it in 1942, "Queen Elizabeth owned silk stockings. The capitalist [or 'innovist'] achievement does not typically consist in providing more silk stockings for queens but in bringing them within the reach of factory girls in return for steadily decreasing amounts of effort. . . . The capitalist process, not by coincidence but by virtue of its mechanism, progressively raises the standard of life of the masses."[9] By now the standard of life for the American masses is four times higher than in the early 1940s, when American real income per person averaged about what it is now in Brazil. Ordinary Americans now have washing machines, anti-depressants, cheap air travel, a bedroom for every child, an advanced education for many. In the early 1940s, they did not. In the early 1840s, such items were inconceivable.

Recently in China and India a new economic liberalism has enriched the poor in spectacular fashion. China and India are still very poor on average by European standards. But wait for a generation or two. Later in the present century—and sooner if conservatives and socialists will abandon their illiberal schemes for pushing people around—everyone on the planet will be US or Finnish rich. The museums and concert halls will be filled, the universities will boom, a full life will be open to the poorest. Modern liberalism will enrich us all.

7. Yet After 1848 Liberalism
Was Weakened

I do *not* mean, I have already said, "liberalism" as the word is used in the United States, as *social* democracy, or more boldly democratic socialism, in which the government is assigned ever-widening powers of pushing people around, and in which people are to be held in the wrong jobs perpetually, under an imagined *"social* contract" inconsistent with liberty and flourishing.[1] Among the social democrats—most of my good friends, actually—the use of French-derived "liberty" and especially its Anglo-Saxon synonym "freedom" seem to me confused. (I will, by the way, refer frequently, as I already have, to "my friends" on the left or right or middle. I do not by this intend to sneer or condescend. I do in fact have many friends on the left and on the right and in the middle. I love them and respect their opinions, mistaken though they so often are. I stand ready to help them discover their true liberalism. You're welcome.)

The classic definition of liberty/freedom is the condition of being liberated/free from physical interference by other human beings. It means, as I said, not being a slave. It means not being pushed around under threat of physical coercion. It means being allowed to set up a food truck or move to Birmingham. The implementation of liberty/freedom, as Robert Hayden, the U.S. poet laureate in the 1970s, put it, has been the "way we journeyed from Can't to Can."[2] As Mill said in 1859, the issue in avoiding enslavement is "the nature and limits of the power that society can legitimately exercise over the individual," such as governmental subsidies demanded by a trade union and extracted from others to keep unprofitable coal mines open, or the slave owner demanding socially granted power to whip Silas back into Can't.[3]

After a century of a steadily more fully articulated liberalism, though, the New, or Social, Liberalism of T. H. Green in the 1880s and later Leonard Hobhouse began a slow turn to social democracy in liberal England, followed after 1890 by progressives in the United States and anticipated by the few Continental socialists after 1848. The nature and limits of the power exercised by the society over the individual mine owner or worker were greatly extended. Extended coercion by government was justified by the claim that in the struggle between capital and labor the poor were anyway being coerced, requiring what John Kenneth Galbraith much later called a "countervailing power." In Britain the legal scholar Dicey saw by 1919 that "the main current of legislative opinion from the beginning of the 20th century has run vehemently towards collectivism."[4] The liberal vision from Smith to Bastiat of a society of free people entering into mutual agreements was replaced by a socialist vision from Marx to Mao of a society of classes locked in conflict. While the economists were developing a theory of wages based on productivity, the politicians were developing a theory based on power.

Why the illiberal turn? Dicey gives reasons in 1919, but admits its roots are earlier. Perhaps it was caused by the fall of literal serfdom and slavery, a liberal triumph in the British Empire, in Russia, in the United States, and at last in Brazil, a triumph which turned the clerisy by analogy to less dramatic absences of individual consent and contract. Every case of poverty was then redefined as slavery, "wage slavery." Let us do with wage slavery what we did with actual slavery: pass a coercive law.

Perhaps, too, the evident triumphs of physical (and much later biological) sciences inspired a physics-envious yet self-satisfied program to apply Science to society, by pushing people around. Perhaps the new patina of democracy after 1867 in Britain and Prussia and Switzerland, and earlier in France and the Americas, gave the New Liberals the conviction that the age of the General Will had in fact arrived. We voted for the government, they said, so how could it be tyrannical? Such was the political logic of the plebiscite in France in 1850 that established Napoleon III as emperor, as of its recent spawn in Russia and Turkey. In Switzerland it had been used more genially for centuries in the *Landsgemeinde,* a direct democracy analogous to town meetings in New England. It appeals to what the French liberal

Benjamin Constant in 1819 called "ancient" freedom, the freedom assigned to free male citizens (alone) to participate in a polis, even if the polis then overrules individual consent and contract with coercive drafts and taxes and punishments, even for the free male citizens.[5] Love it or leave it.

Perhaps the newly successful nationalisms and imperialisms put liberals in a mood to carry on pushing other people around—for their own good, you see. The elite was already using the government to push around the dusky lesser breeds without the law, so why not extend it to home? The early Protestant missionaries in Britain preached to the unchurched in the big industrial cities as much as to overseas heathens. And anyway the upper and upper-middle classes were long accustomed to reaching down to help the poor, on the old upper crust model of Lady Bountiful, or in the nineteenth-century bourgeois version, to reform them, on the new model of Major Barbara and the Salvation Army.

Perhaps a Protestant Christianity, lately under challenge, was redirected to secular purposes. The anti-slavery agitation had been such a redirection. Mine eyes have seen the glory of the coming of the Lord. Later in the nineteenth century a startlingly high percentage of American Progressives, such as Woodrow Wilson, were the children of Protestant ministers.[6] Likewise, back in England T. H. Green and Leonard Hobhouse were the sons of Anglican pastors. Perhaps, at least in the United States, post-millennialism in theology gave American Protestants a program of establishing heaven on earth.[7] (The Catholics and Jews and European Protestants were more realistic.)

Perhaps the rise of independent newspapers consequent on the invention of cheap paper and the steam rotary press, capable of enormous press runs and therefore profitable advertising, amplified the call for statism. The classical liberal Herbert Spencer noted as early as 1853 two of the major templates for modern news stories, still in vigorous use today: "Take up a daily paper and you will probably find a leader exposing the corruption, negligence, or mismanagement of some State-department. Cast your eye down the next column, and it is not unlikely that you will read proposals for an extension of State-supervision."[8] Perhaps even the rise of photography in the newspapers, as it had started to do in the coverage of war, and still does in the television coverage of famines and refugees, made charitable people vividly aware of how the other half lives. The thousands of photographs by Lewis Hine early in the twentieth century, such as the famous one of the little girl tending her machine in the Whitnel Cotton Mill in North Carolina, challenged the presumption of free contracting.

Or perhaps the New Liberal sons, freed from mere work to attend Oxford and Yale, were rebelling against their fathers, who had made their fortunes in a vulgar trade. In Henry James's novel of 1903, *The Ambassadors*, it is never revealed what vulgarity back in Connecticut supported the leisure of the American expatriates in Europe. Perhaps, perhaps. In truth, the causes of the illiberal turn in the late nineteenth century by self-described liberals are mysterious. Yet the turn came.

The result was that by around 1900 even in the liberal Anglosphere the left had added a "freedom" of being liberated (so to speak) from any constraint whatsoever, as for example liberated from the law of gravity, or from the law of scarcity, or of unintended consequences, and especially liberated from the law of social accounting—the law, whether liberal or socialist, that if an enterprise is unprofitable it should be closed, for the benefit of us all. The additional "freedom" seemed plausible, as the next step, as I said, after ending literal slavery. We can make the world anew, the new "liberals" believed, in their scientistic confidence, by repealing the irritating old laws, and putting a new law of governmental planning and protection and compulsion in their place. If one could fly like Superman, one would be "free" as a bird. Let's do it. If one could improve the race by sterilizing the third generation of imbeciles, or jailing a thousand British homosexuals a year, we would be "free" from defect. Let's do it. If one could benefit from the third of Roosevelt's four "freedoms" in his speech of 1941, one would be adequately rich by taking from others.[9] Let's do it. "Freedom," the New Liberals argued, is the same thing as being adequately rich or pure or powerful, which desiderata, they said, the government can arrange with ease and justice. Let's do it.

In High Liberalism, to put it another way, the equal and individual liberty I have to make a voluntary arrangement with you was extended to a novel and socialized "freedom/liberty" of mine to seize your goods, through the government's monopoly of coercion, in order to give to me or to a group favored by me a set of "positive" freedoms. I am to have a freedom/liberty from want, for example, regardless of my supply of goods to you. "Every man a king," said Huey Long of Louisiana in 1934, and his method was that of both Bad King John and his enemy Robin Hood, characteristic of the feudal order and later the socialist or fascist or welfare-state order, under a theory of zero sum, win-lose. "It is necessary to scale down the big fortunes," said Huey, "that we may scatter the wealth to be shared by all of the people."[10] Scale down by coercion the one person's legitimate earnings by trade and betterment in order to give money to another voter for Huey, and all will be well.

Under High Liberalism, as under feudal hierarchy or crony capitalism or fascist nationalism or conservative reaction or any number of illiberal régimes, I am to have especially a liberty to regulate, through the government's monopoly of coercion, your behavior in ways beneficial to me or to my assigns. I am to have for example a liberty to prevent your entry into my trade, forcibly backed by police. My customers would be benefited by such an entry, but I can stop it, thank God. For example, I am to have a liberty to stop Juan Valdez from coming to my country to trade peaceably with me, by a law forcibly backed by ICE. Juan's entry would benefit my fellow citizens, but I don't like people like him, and with the help of the government I can stop him. And so forth, by law and regulation. "We" are to have a liberty to impose tariffs on imports that prevent you from buying where you wish. "We" are to have a liberty to prevent foreign doctors from practicing freely in the United States, or for that matter preventing anyone who wants to set up as a doctor to set up. "We" are to have a liberty to wage an offensive war for king and country, or a war to end all wars, financed by your goods or your body appropriated for the purpose. It is a socialized "we."

Such, then, is "liberalism" as misdefined in these latter days in parts of the Anglosphere. Boaz quotes Schumpeter's witticism about the theft of the word "liberal": "As a supreme, if unintended, compliment, the enemies of the system of private enterprise have thought it wise to appropriate its label."[11] The appropriation was not "mere" rhetoric. It illustrates the non-mere-ness of how we talk to each other. The historian Kevin Schultz has written a dual biography of that odd couple, William Buckley the conservative (1925–2008) and Norman Mailer the radical (1923–2007), *Buckley and Mailer: The Difficult Friendship That Shaped the Sixties* (2015). Schultz documents how both men rebelled against the High Liberalism of the 1950s and 1960s. Yet the Establishment of High Liberalism has in policy won, with a good deal of approval from the Conservative Establishment. It has crowded out the old and adult projects of a free people, such as families as ethical schools or the self-provision for old age or a trade-union insurance for unemployment or a prudent wariness about foreign entanglements. Mailer and

Buckley, each in his own flamboyant fashion, sought civil discourse in a liberty-loving society. They failed.

The left-right quarrel has yielded at last the fact-free dogmatisms of left and right we hear daily, even among otherwise adult and benevolent folk. The left fears and despises the rich, such as bankers. The right fears and despises the poor, such as Hispanic immigrants. And the middle believes fairy tales from both, in particular the tales that governments are omni-competent and that private free choice is highly defective. One hears from nice leftists like the economist Joseph Stiglitz remarks summarizable as: "If there is *any* spill-over, then the government of the United States or Britain should step in with police powers to stop it." Or one hears from not-so-nice rightists such as the political scientist Paul Wolfowitz remarks summarizable as: "If there are *any* bad people in the world, then the government of the United States, with British help, should drop bombs on them." When someone asked Michael Bloomberg, the brilliant businessman and three-time mayor of New York City, what he thought about legalizing marijuana, he brought out the fact-free dogma that marijuana is a gateway drug.[12] When someone challenged Lindsey Graham, the brilliant senior senator from South Carolina, about America's over-reach abroad, he brought out the fact-free dogma that if we don't fight them in Syria, we'll have to fight them in Charleston.[13]

The slow-socialist, High, or Progressive "liberals" of the late nineteenth and early twentieth centuries such as Lloyd George and Woodrow Wilson, and then also their supposed enemies the Burkean Conservatives such as, recently, Boris Johnson and Lindsey Graham, seized what they imagined to be the ethical high ground. It entailed widening coercion by governmental violence. The New Liberals and the Progressives have been declaring since around 1900—joining in this the Conservatives since Thomas Carlyle who had long made a similar declaration—that "Our motives for widening the scope of governmental coercion are pure and paternalistic. Our policy of physical coercion is designed to help the pathetic, childlike, unruly poor and women and minorities, so incapable of taking care of themselves, or behaving themselves. To leave the business of the citizens to themselves and to their peaceful markets would be highly dangerous, unlike our lovely proposals for coercion at home and abroad. You so-called Modern Liberals 2.0 criticize our splendid policies. We progressives conclude that you must hate the poor and women and minorities, or indeed all the ordinary citizens, and must love only the rich, by whose pay by Koch we know you are corrupted to speak so hatefully. And we conservatives, likewise, conclude that you do not sufficiently love our king and country, the land of hope and glory, the home of the brave and the land of the free. We progressives and conservatives join in crying, 'For shame, for shame!!' Why should we listen to such evil people?"

The essence of humane true liberalism, to the contrary, is a small government, honest and effective in its modest realm, with a hand up for the poor. Mainly leave people alone to pursue their non-violent projects voluntarily, laissez-faire, laissez-passer. Yet do not ignore the disadvantaged, or disdain them, or boss them around with judges or nudges, or refuse loftily to help them, issuing a country-club sneer of "I've got mine, you losers." Humane liberalism is not atomistic and selfish, contrary to what the High Liberals believe it to be—and as some misled (self-identified) libertarians sometimes talk in their boyish way, as if they believed it, and weren't raised by mothers. Humane true liberalism is, on the contrary, an economy and polity and society of equal dignity.

8. The "New Liberalism" Was Illiberal

The New Liberal/Statist/Progressive believed in a very particular theory of the economy. She has believed down to the present that the economy is above all *easy* to administer, and that therefore intentional action by wise folk having no business experience does the trick, quite easily. She does not believe that knowledge of what we should do and how to do it is distributed locally among the people, accessible only by unregulated markets. People in fact, she believes, get better housing and the eight-hour day from governmental plans and compulsions, such as the Wagner Act facilitating excellent industrial unions, or rent controls providing wonderfully cheaper housing, or an entrepreneurial government coming up with brilliant ideas.[1] John R. Commons (1862–1945) of the University of Wisconsin was the American sage of such statism, described at length in the Irish poet Micheal O'Siadhail's astounding epic in 2018, of which Quartet 2, still more astoundingly, sings accurately of, believe it or not, economics and its intellectual history. Says O'Siadhail (oh-sheel, by the way) of Professor Commons: "Empiricist, you purged the harsh / And gilded age with labour law / And compensation, chose to side / With plans to practice price controls; Protectionism too you saw / As trammeling a too-free trade."[2]

Betterment, the statist says, especially if she is a labor lawyer or a labor historian inspired by Commons, had little or nothing to do with private agreements in commerce directed by profits earned both by producers and consumers, and yielding therefore an increasingly enriched working class, which could with its higher marginal product get beyond houses without central heating or twelve-hour work days without rest. "Don't be silly," the statist retorts to the true liberal account of enrichment. "We New Liberals and Continental socialists came in the nineteenth century to see 'intentionality' [to use a word favored in New Liberal public theology] as crucial to making a just society—easily in law though a struggle in politics. After intentional struggles on the picket line and intentional votes in Parliament, the just and rich society was finally achieved. None of your mythical invisible hand about it." The just and rich society did not occur, she is saying, through enrichment from creative trade and innovation, allowed to better us, down in the farmers' market or the auto dealership—but by pure hearts and coercive regulations. In the 1950s the young New Dealers intent on justifying a more active government—among them Arthur Schlesinger Jr. and my father, Robert Green McCloskey—looked back for precedents, such as into the age of Jackson and of Henry Clay, and its splendid, compelled "internal improvements."[3] Their students still do.[4] Thus we achieved, they have been saying, a new freedom.

Quite apart from the factual and economic problems with such a leftish history of the fruits of intentionality in the economy, the philosophical problem is that we already have words for such "freedoms"—namely, adequate comfort, great wealth, considerable power, unusual physical abilities, central heating, subsidies from taxes. To use the freedom-word to mean all these other good things, such as in the economist Amartya Sen's and the philosopher Martha Nussbaum's vocabulary of "capabilities," confuses the issue.[5] Capabilities are good. We should work to assure that every person on the planet has them, chiefly if not only by letting a free economy enrich ordinary people, as it has regularly done. Adam Smith declared, when a nascent economics was shifting attention away from the glory of the king toward the flourishing of the people, that "no society can surely be flourishing and happy, of which the far greater part of the members are poor and miserable."[6] That's the humane part of humane liberalism, expressed in its goal of higher real income per head, and greater flourishing of the heads, especially the poor ones. But developing such good things is not in itself "freedom," unless we want to smoosh into the one word all good things under the sun.[7]

To put it another way, Smith and I do claim emphatically that development is the *consequence* of freedom, the obvious and simple plan of natural liberty. But development—contrary to one of Sen's book titles—is not the *same thing* as freedom. A cause is not the same thing as its consequence. No one would deny that it's good to be developed to the extent of being adequately rich. In 1937 Beatrice Kaufman advised a friend, "I've been poor and I've been rich. Rich is better!"[8] Yup. Yet we still need a word for a distinct "freedom from physical constraint by others." The constraint in political terms is called "tyranny" (Greek *tyrannos*, "master"), its opposite "liberty/freedom." We need to watch out for tyranny, and its consequences in poverty. And beyond money and poverty, we need to watch out for the consequences of tyrannical unfreedom in preventing other sorts of human flourishing. Tyranny is bad for the human soul. Now as much as in 1776 or 1789 we need to watch out for the tyranny of the king, husband, slave owner, chief, village elder, bureaucrat, police. Watch and ware.

My friends the social democrats appear to believe that in Stockholm and Boston there is no longer a special problem of tyranny as such, because we got rid of tsars and wife beaters, and after all we *vote* for the mayor who bosses us around ("ancient" freedom again), taxing us by the fist of coercion to give out good things to others, such as the mayor's good supporters, regardless of whether the supporters, according to their abilities, do anything for the rest of us. The general will reigns, which was Rousseau's bizarre solution to the problem of maintaining liberty yet giving power to the government to regulate property.[9] So let's smoosh the word "freedom." I would gently remind my friends that the Russian Federation has acquired a new tsar, and Turkey a new sultan, voted by the *volonté générale* onto their thrones. And even in Stockholm and Boston, lovely as those places are, it is a mistake to believe that wife beating is over, or taxation utterly harmless, or politicians altogether free from tyrannical tendencies.

To put it still another way, among social democrats "freedom" has come to mean simply, in the jargon of economists, "having a money budget constraint far from the origin," that is, being rich. We do want such capabilities, I said. And of course in the short run Paul can readily get an enriched budget constraint by seizing money from Peter, or getting Huey Long or Amartya Sen to do it. But consider the long run. Being free in the original and usefully differentiated sense of being free from violent constraint by tyrants large or small has regularly in fact resulted, after a time of commercially tested betterment encouraged by the liberty, in money budget constraints *far* from the origin, with the whole society enriched, and not merely Paul at the expense of Peter. Such a positive sum is what the New Liberals or the Old Conservatives have never really believed. In the long run, they intone, we are all dead. Meanwhile, income rains down like manna, they say, with no incentive or opportunity cost, and should be distributed according to our needs, or in olden times given to the lord for his castle.

The rescue of the Germanic/Anglo-Saxon word "freedom" or the Latin/French word "liberty" from the care of social democrats and democratic socialists hostile to commerce or of conservatives and reactionaries hostile to equality is not a "mere" matter of definition, to be set aside in serious discussions as pettifogging. If we are to avoid slavery, we need a word for non-slavery—or so we all supposed before Rousseau-Green-Sen-Nussbaum spoke out loud and bold, telling us that the general will discerned by the polis *is* freedom.

If "freedom" is shifted to the utilitarian definition of Rousseau-Green-Sen-Nussbaum to mean "income," then any particular coercion by the government might after all be a good thing, so long as the gain is greater than the pain. And the social democrats or their brethren the unalloyed socialists believe that a big part of the so-called pain contemplated should in (social) justice be discounted, as an irritating and inconsequential desire of ordinary adults for the dignity of autonomy. In the United States the nudgers, as they call themselves, such as Cass Sunstein and Richard Thaler and Robert Frank, wish to use behavioral economics to deprive people of autonomy, for their own good, to manipulate them to a higher utility contour—rather than to alert or educate them and then let them choose for themselves. To hell with liberty.

In 1881 T. H. Green spoke of liberty "properly understood"—the usual locution, in the nineteenth century, as Tom Palmer has observed, during the shift from liberty as freedom from human constraint to liberty as freedom from any constraint.[10] It becomes what you, in the opinion of the clerisy, "would" want to do, what in the style of Plato your true, higher self would order up. T. H. Green continued: "we do not mean merely freedom from restraint of [human] compulsion. . . . We mean a positive power or capacity of doing . . . anything worth doing," by the lights of the clerisy.[11] In 2018 the British left, in honor of Marx's bicentenary, declared that British local governments should build more council houses, to be rented out at favorable rates to favored folk. The government should not, that is, pay attention to the silly and capitalist and inegalitarian desire of the British working class to be owners of their own homes. They need instead to live as residential pets, something they "would" want.

Such declarations, well-meaning or not, are how social democracy proceeds by small steps from a liberal society of responsibility and self-cultivation, with a non-entangling safety net, to an acceptance of widening governmental coercion and economic engineering, with a coercive clerisy arranging an economy of obedient slaves. It is not a conspiracy, understand, but a natural consequence of the widening right to vote and the desire for security rather than liberty. We are made into secure slaves and children and pets, not a free people. The state of New Hampshire has the motto on its auto license plates "Live Free or Die." In 1974 a motorist who wanted to live free decided on religious and political grounds that he didn't like the motto, and covered it up on his plates with tape. He was arrested, and served fifteen days in jail.[12] Thus pethood. *Bad* dog!

In short, the New or High or Progressive "liberal" woman, however one names her, together with her husband the hierarchical conservative irritated by the uppity poor, advocate a régime of pushing people around, as for example prohibition of alcohol in the United States, and then of drugs (T. H. Green, predictably, favored prohibition of strong drink). As implemented in the twentieth century, her progressive régime, not to speak of her husband's reactionary régime mixed in with hers, had little of voluntary agreement about it, and a good deal of coercively illiberal rhetoric, with a disdain for the pitiable or irritating poor, a zero-sum economics, and not much of a search for win-win among responsible adults in charge of their own choices.

The liberal economist the late Leland Yeager argued that "the principled approach to economic policy recognizes that the task of the policymaker is *not* to [use governmental coercion exercised by planning experts to] maximize social welfare, somehow conceived, and *not* to achieve specific patterns of outputs, prices, and incomes. It is concerned, instead, with a framework of institutions and rules within which people can effectively cooperate in pursuing their own diverse ends."[13] Diversity. I like knitting, you like model trains. Let's allow people to have both.

Freedom/liberty, empirically speaking, that is, usually does yield win-win. Look to the long-run outcome of giving un-slavery to people since 1800. By contrast, tyranny, empirically speaking, usually yields zero or negative sum. Not always. It's not a matter of pure reason, *der reinen Vernunft*, but a matter of documented history.[14] It's what the history of true liberalism has pretty much shown, with few exceptions, as has the contrasting history of true socialism, in East Germany as against West, for example, or of North Korea as against South, or recently of Venezuela as against Colombia.

And beyond matters of budget constraints and money riches—in this, I repeat, respectfully contradicting my socialist and conservative friends—freedom/liberty, understood as the condition of not being humanly coerced, has on the whole resulted in the rest of human flourishing, in culture and in self-cultivation. Again it doesn't have to be so by sheer logic, whether proffered by the left or the right. Maybe in the extreme a boot stamping on a human face forever would yield, say, great art. But in historical fact it is liberalism that has yielded wider, non-economic flourishing. Socialism or reaction have not. Take Italian fascist literature or Russian socialist realism painting. Please. The liberal societies are highly creative, and reasonably virtuous. The societies that are socialist or reactionary or heavily regulated or in the extreme boot-stamping are stifled—ranging from being merely somewhat dull to being very nasty indeed.[15]

After 1945 the colony of Hong Kong, for example, was free from a good deal of human coercion by planners. It was more or less laissez-faire in its economy (though as a British Crown colony it had no political rights whatsoever, zero ancient freedom—but it did have English common law, an advantage for modern, individual freedom). Despite massive immigration from the mainland, it developed in two generations from a Somalia level of poverty to an income per head only a little below that of the United States. By contrast, I reiterate, the old and repeated experiments in making humans in economic matters into clients or pets or slaves of the government, ordered about by police or planners, without the right to say no, have regularly resulted in budget lines hugging the zero origin, as in Mao's China or Maduro's Venezuela, or indeed in the closed corporate village of conservative nostalgia.[16] And the great artistic ages, such as fifth-century Greece or fifteenth-century Italy or the fifties in the United States, were built on commerce, yielding freedoms to trade, to innovate, to think, to speak, and yielding for more and more people all the other freedoms and flourishings.

9. The Result of the New Illiberalism Was Very Big Governments

In 1913 the total expenditure in GDP of all levels taken together of American government, local, state, and federal, according to the economic historian Robert Higgs, was about 7.5 percent.[1] Therefore the shocking corruptions of many governments at the time—for instance, Chicago's or Boston's—didn't matter much to the wide economy. But by 1996 the share of total American governmental expenditure at all levels had risen to 32 percent, and governments regulated more and more of the rest, by way of what Higgs labels the increasing "scope" of government. The figure is still higher in most other rich countries. In the United States the scope of government had been leashed a bit in the 1970s and 1980s by deregulation, as for airlines, and in Britain by Margaret Thatcher's brief flirtation with true liberalism, and in Sweden after the crisis of the 1990s. But later the regulation drifted up again, commonly in response to democratic pressures of the sort we spoof in Chicago as the city's motto, "Ubi meus?" Where's mine? All levels of government became more and more regulatory. Thatcher in Britain, for example, centralized K–12 education.

The prevalence of big government arises in part from a belief that the market and competition are by nature importantly imperfect—for which economists have gathered surprisingly little evidence, though many of them hold most passionately to the belief.[2] The belief in imperfection was made concrete in twentieth-century economics by the expanding scope of enforced "policies" to counteract the allegedly important imperfections (their importance, I repeat, regularly undocumented), such as engineering spillovers and

47

natural monopolies and the rest. At the federal level the EPA, the FDA, the FTC, the FCC, the FPC are such ideas institutionalized.

The belief in market imperfections has been allied to a belief that government, which is of course flawless when staffed by the very economists claiming that markets are significantly imperfect, can itself easily counteract the imperfections (most of which, a liberal would point out, the government itself caused). There's the "easy reform" lemma in the New Liberalism. Bring on the economists, say the anti-liberals, and bring on the lawyers and politicians, too. They are well known to be perfectly wise and incorruptible.

The result in France, for example, is that the government's share of national expenditure is 55 percent. French monopolies and regulations proliferated steadily until Macron. Jean Tirole, that noble country's most recent Nobel in economics (2016), noted wryly that the French "are perhaps more distrustful than any other nationality of the market and competition," and correspondingly more charmingly trustful of *l'État*.[3] The composition of bread has been strictly regulated in Paris since the Middle Ages, and Parisian rents have been frozen since the First World War. In 1999 another French economist caused a national outcry by the mere mention of the common sense of the so-called public-choice school of economics in the United States pioneered by the true liberal economist James Buchanan (Nobel 1986)—that politicians and economic and legal officials might sometimes after all have also their own interests in mind, interests sometimes imperfectly correlated with the public good. I mean, maybe. As Geoffrey Brennan and James Buchanan put it, "In all practically relevant cases, governments—or more accurately the individuals involved in governmental process—do possess the power to coerce. They do exercise genuinely discretionary power, and it is both empirically reasonable and analytically necessary to assume that over some range they will exploit that power for their own purposes, whatever these may be."[4] Maybe their purposes arrive at the public interest. But the betting is not. And, the public-choice economists say, the politicians and economic and legal officials may in fact not know even approximately what to do for the public good. The French clerisy was outraged by the mere mention of such a crazy, liberal, Anglo-Saxon idea.

The increase in governmental scope, even aside from the proliferating schemes of the economists offering themselves as expert economic engineers, has happened of course with popular support. It expresses a tyranny of the majority, which has haunted democracy since the Greeks. "Let the government," cry the winners of the last election, the majority voters in, say, Hungary or Turkey in 2018, "devise programs to help nice people like us. And by all means let us tightly regulate those other, not-so-nice, people"—people of color, say, or Kurds, or Jews, or immigrants on their way to the German or Texan border, or secularists, or city dwellers, or new entrants competing with favored monopolies of doctors and lawyers and cotton farmers. "All this will assure our own safety and riches here in the suburbs, or in the thankfully over-represented countryside. We are angry and terrified," and made so by populist politicians of the Orbán-Trump sort raising false alarms about immigrants and Jews and Muslims. "Keep us safe, with a big, heavily armed government," enforcing a War on Black Drugs, or a War on Hispanic or Syrian Immigrants. "Regulate even ourselves, because we admit to being childlike and fearful, boohoo. In order to keep restaurants from poisoning us, for example, do not rely on the fake-news press and the wretchedly elite judiciary," and the conse-quent if imperfect protection from tort and fraud. "Set aside all those, and for good measure murder the journalists and depose the judges, as enemies of the nation. Instead, appoint an inspector with police powers" and the favor of the ruling elite, to swing by the restaurant once a year, with a hand extended for a bribe, which action will immunize the actually poisoning restaurants from fur-ther prosecution. "Let us, in short, be safe and poor rather than free and rich," dependent rather than autonomous, children rather than adults. People de-mand it. Many of them don't mind being slaves. We liberals urge them to be-come free.

It's symmetrical, left and right, because both the Dems and the GOP, Labour and the Tories, want the government to be really, really big, without regard to free choice, and to follow majoritarian opinion really, really closely, without regard to minorities. We Modern True Liberals stand against them both, opposing the tyranny of the majority on either side of the usual spec-trum. Hip, hip, hurray for Smith, Wollstonecraft, Thoreau, Bastiat, Mill and their descendants.

By contrast, if you are on the left or the right, a Democrat or a Republican, a red Labourite or a blue Tory, you view the government as an instrument for doing the glorious public things that good folk want, such as the Hoover Dam, or the National Park System, or Her Majesty's Prisons. You will probably object to Weber's definition of the government as a monopoly of coercion. You will certainly object to Tolstoy's definition, in 1857, of the government as "a conspiracy designed not only to exploit, but above all to corrupt its citizens."[5] And you will object vehemently to the more recent definition along the same lines by the anarcho-capitalist economist Murray Rothbard (1926–1995), of the government as "the most extensive criminal group in society."[6] Murray used to say that the government is a band of robbers into whose clutches we have fallen. Will Rogers used to thank God that we don't get the government we pay for. Especially you will object to such cynicism if you are among the minority of the world's population living under tolerably honest governments, a citizen of Göteborg, Sweden, perhaps, or of St. Paul, Minnesota. Surely this talk of "coercion" and "corruption" and "criminality" as the basis for government, you will complain, is over the top.

Unhappily, no, not as a general rule. Few in human history would have thought to dispute the cynical definitions, before the upsurge in the late nineteenth century of an optimistic, Rousseau-and-Hegel-inspired nationalism-socialism claiming that governments are quite nice, and do happily express the general will, which after all is surely your own will—and that the dangerously nasty actors are international corporations and other institutions of voluntary exchange, or the minorities annoyingly objecting to a general will that justly imposes Jim Crow laws and persecution of gays. In 1853 Herbert Spencer asked, "Which will be the most healthful community—that in which agents who perform their functions badly, immediately suffer by the withdrawal of public patronage; or that in which such agents can be made to suffer only through an apparatus of meetings, petitions, polling-booths, parliamentary divisions, cabinet-councils, and red-tape documents? Is it not an absurdly utopian hope that men will behave better when correction is far removed and uncertain than when it is near at hand and inevitable? Yet this is the hope which most political schemers unconsciously cherish."[7]

Correspondingly, a socialist, whether democratic or not, believes to her core that The Problem is not such a government, but private and profitable property (threatened daily by the withdrawal of public patronage). It is why we always identify enterprises as "non-profit" if we wish to commend them, with the implication that profit-making is inherently corrupting—and as though no non-profit had ever allowed an Irish priest to abuse a child sexually or led an official from Oxfam to seek sexual favors from his clients. If the socialist is not simultaneously a sweet anarchist, such as Prince Peter Kropotkin (1842–1928), she will naturally turn to the government, as the most obvious tool against such evil profit and property, to fix things up. Let us have a dictatorship of the proletariat. Let us have "radical markets" uprooting the right to say no, turning everyone into a slave of other people's wills, in order to achieve a utilitarian paradise.[8] Surely the government or other people's will can do better with my life and goods than I can. Mill noted in 1859, during the rush of self-government in those post-1848 days, that many people had come to believe that the rulers' power "was but the nation's own power, concentrated, and in a form convenient for exercise."[9] We have already, they said, a perfect government of the people, by the people, for the people, the general will. Mill did not believe it worked quite that way, not reliably, not yet. Nor, for that matter, did Lincoln. Better the right to say no.

To test your belief that the government is your own (good) will generalized, and to test in particular your disbelief in the centrality of coercion in government, I suggest an experiment on April 15 of not paying your US income taxes—perhaps giving voluntarily a few contributions in strict proportion to the share of the government's budget you judge to be effective and ethical. Whether you tend toward left or right on the conventional spectrum, you will have plenty of corrupting items in mind *not* to give to. The new fighter jet that doesn't work. The corporate subsidy that does.

Then try resisting arrest. Then try escaping from prison. Then try resisting re-arrest. After release, if ever, you will note the contrast with the non-policy, non-police arenas of commerce or persuasion. Try buying an iPhone rather than a Samsung. Nothing happens. Try not agreeing with McCloskey. Ditto. You will observe a sharp difference from your experience with the entity possessing the monopoly of coercion, even in Göteborg or St. Paul.

10. Honest and Competent
Governments Are Rare

Economists are strangely obsessed with offering to the rest of us their utilitarian advice on policy, advice which routinely disregards liberty. They are un-self-conscious about it, assuming that they have the right and duty to tell you what to do and to recruit the monopoly of coercion to make you do it. Utility is thereby maximized, they will say. The contrast with scholars in other social sciences, such as sociology or anthropology or even most of political science, is sharp. Naturally, for a policy to have an effect, whether intended or not, it has to be implemented. If there is resistance it must be implemented through physical coercion, legitimately exercised by the police ("police *force*"; "military *forces*"). Every piece of advice from economists that is not the removal of previous policy requires people to be pushed around, or at best tricked.

Taxes, for example, even if we voted for them, are not voluntary—considering that any rational person would like to be exempted, if she could arrange it on the side without shame or penalty. The trickery is that taxes are voted quite separately from the expenditures they enable, giving everyone the impression, as Bastiat said once, that they can live at everyone else's expense. Nor are other laws voluntary, many of which we would all agree are desirable, such as laws in favor of vaccination, or against private force and fraud, or for that matter against public force and fraud. If a bad citizen or politician could steal with impunity, he would do it. After all, he's bad. Better use the police to stop him. No scandal there. Such a monopoly, if we agree on its legitimacy and accept its authority, is not on its face evil. We would hardly prefer competing *oligopolies* of physical coercion, mafiosi running around leaning on shopkeepers and construction firms and lemon growers, a war of all against all.

And of course we do need the police to handle the numerous mafiosi, thieves, murderers, con men, rapists, extortionists, amoral politicians, and other private or public users of force and fraud. As the founding liberal, the Dutch-influenced Englishman John Locke, said in 1689, "The depravity of mankind [is] such that [some] had rather injuriously prey upon the fruits of other men's labors than take pains to provide for themselves."[1] And we need armies to prevent invasion by, say, the terrifying Canadians or the appalling French, or to prevent visitations of missiles from Russia or North Korea. And we need an FBI or an MI5 foiling clumsy plots to influence domestic elections or to poison people in the park. When the guardians do their guarding with integrity, as in the reasonably liberal and well-managed countries they mostly do, the police and soldiers and prosecutors and judges and jailers do a noble job. No objection there, either. They deal daily with the depravity of human-kind. Thank God for their dirty and dangerous labors to protect us from the depraved. Thank you for your service. Serve and Protect. *Semper fi*. Hurrah for the guardians.

But *quis custodiet ipsos custodes?* Who guards the very guardians? We do. We need to watch them closely, with an apparatus of meetings, petitions, polling booths, parliamentary divisions, cabinet councils, and red-tape doc-uments, even in the liberal and well-managed countries. After all, the guard-ians are armed.

And in the world at large there are many exceptionally bad guardians, murdering journalists and dismembering them, say, or running phony elec-tions in which the present government gets 95 percent of the vote. The "lib-eral and well-managed countries," in which the monopoly of coercion is exercised with reasonable justice and competence, under suitable guarding of the guardians, are in human experience extremely rare. Before 1800 there were a handful of them, ever, anywhere, locally. Nowadays, look at the 176 countries in the world ranked in 2016 by Transparency International for its Corruption Perceptions Index, ranging from Denmark and New Zealand at the top to Zimbabwe and North Korea at the bottom. Suppose, generously, that we reckon the top 30 or so to be reasonably honest—worthy, say, of fresh infusions of taxpayer dollars, and anyway worthy of a degree of trust in their politicians and guardians.[2] Portugal in 2016 was the marginal case of the 30, ranked 29th. Italy, by contrast, though in many ways liberal, or indeed anarchistic, was ranked at 60th out of the 176, just below Romania, which is highly corrupt, and Cuba, which is highly illiberal, and just above Saudi Arabia, which is both. Despite many upstanding Italian judges, prosecutors, and police, no wise Italian (of which there appear to be too few) wants to give the extant government more power.

The prime minister in liberal Spain (ranked 41st) arranged to build a hugely expensive high-speed train from Madrid to his small home city.[3] It wouldn't happen in Denmark or New Zealand, though in some US states quite similar corruptions do occur. In my own state of Illinois, for instance, a proposed third airport for Chicago was corruptly placed. In the state I grew up in, Massachusetts, a corrupt Big Dig in Boston buried a highway, making richer the rich friends of the politicians. (I focus here on self-interested corruption alone, setting aside economic incompetence without notable venality, such as the half-built high-speed rail between San Francisco and Los Angeles.) The United States overall ranks 18th. But some of its constituent states and cities would rank much lower. The politicians and guardians in such places lack full integrity or competence, as for example the city government of Chicago covering up torture and murder of African-Americans by the police.[4]

Ask, then: what percent of the world's population was governed in 2016 by the better governments, taking countries as a whole and following the relaxed, better-than-Portugal standard, such as Japan (20th) or France (23rd)? What is the weight in present-day human experience of honest and competent government? Answer: 10 percent. That is, fully 90 percent of the world's population suffered in 2016 under governments agreed on all sides to be disgracefully corrupt and incompetent, and mostly illiberal, being notably worse than Portugal's.

Yet right and left along the usual spectrum, contrary to the modern liberals perched above it, want to give such governments—among them the worst portions, too, of the United States and the United Kingdom (10th)—more money and more powers of physical coercion. For example, in both the United States and the United Kingdom the government, with considerable popular support, wishes to deport law-abiding and hardworking immigrants in response to a scientifically bankrupt economic notion, which is anyway unethical, that immigrants take jobs away from natives, or a scientifically bankrupt sociological notion, also unethical, that their children will never become properly American or British. The Italians—who considering the longstanding depravity and incompetence of their masters should all be at least *liberali,* if not *anarchisti*—regularly vote governments back into power that spend taxes still more carelessly and make off with public money still more brazenly and push people around still more enthusiastically. Thus the election in 2018 in Italy of neo-fascist populists.

My friends the statists imagine, in their twentieth-century naïveté, that the government has the capacity to "regulate" markets with justice and efficiency. It was recently proposed in Italy, for example, to introduce strict governmental licensing, enforced by the police, for the men who literally hold the welfare of the nation in their skilled hands, pizza cooks. The first question a modern journalist asks of any new industry or any new misfortune is: Where is governmental regulation of the business and of entry into it? Where was our mother the government? The presumption is that a complex modern economy will need and can get and should have complex regulation, enforced from above, which will protect us from the bad actors.

In June of 2018 the humane true liberal David Brooks put the reply to such feelings this way: "Statist social engineering projects cause horrific suffering because in the mind of statists, the abstract rule is more important than the human being in front of them. [Thus the Trumpians cried, 'We enforce the law,' while boldly violating US laws of refugees and habeas corpus and human dignity.] The person must be crushed for the sake of the abstraction. This is exactly what the Trump immigration policies are doing. Families are ripped apart and children are left weeping by the fences constructed by government officials blindly following a regulation."[5] You go, David.

Regulator, regulate yourself. A retired Italian judge, who had courageously fought the Mafia in the Clean Hands prosecutions in the early 1990s, emphasized at a gathering of four thousand people curious about liberalism at Porto Alegre, Brazil, in April 2018 that even the strikingly incompetent Italian government mainly needed first to attend to the urgent task of . . . regulating *private* monopoly.[6] Of pizza cooks, say. Yet 90 percent and more of the world's people live under governments such as Italy's that exercise with venality and clumsiness the *master* monopoly, the government's monopoly of legitimate coercion. The government, as economists have found, is the source of all seriously oppressive private monopolies, such as those of taxis or electricity or broadcasting or, once, telephones.[7] If entry is eliminated, the customers have nowhere to go. The government, paid off by the monopolists in possession, is put in charge of entry. Hmm. In dispensing and supporting such monopolies, the governments put forward as "regulators" have not regulated their own corruptions. *Custodes, custodite ipsos*: guardians, guard your very selves. It seems at least strange for the Italian judge to suppose that governmental regulators—in Italy, of all places—have the capacity to protect us from the private monopolies that they themselves have created. As James Madison wrote in *The Federalist*, "In framing a government which is to be administered by men over men, the great difficulty lies in this: you must first enable the government to control the governed; and in the next place oblige it to control itself."[8]

At the same session in Porto Alegre a modern liberal Italian professor of political philosophy teaching in Brazil noted that a society with a minimal government and with correspondingly wide private enterprise would have no public corruption, because there would be no regulator with police powers to corrupt. (I speak here of corruption alone, setting aside the question of whether markets are mostly good on other counts.) A narrow scope for the monopoly of coercion, the professor pointed out, implies a narrow scope for diverting the coercion to private profit, which is what public corruption means. By contrast a society with minimal private enterprise and massive government would consist almost entirely of corruptions, that is, of the shifting of purchasing power by physical force (*physischen Zwanges*) to a favored group—because that by definition is how all things are allocated in such a régime. Thus, in its theory, North Korea. (Yet even in North Korea a black market exists, and has recently expanded, which undercuts some of the reallocations by its unhinged, coercion-addicted government.[9])

The point is that in a market, whether black or white, both sides have to agree, or else the deal does not go through. Markets may not achieve nirvana, as I have already conceded. (I told you I am for the moment setting that issue aside.) But at least in the activities governed by markets there can be no use of the monopoly of coercion to shift resources from one person to another, absent mutual consent, because market activities *are* by mutual consent.

Yet the right wing argues with approval, and the left wing with disapproval, that mutual deals *are* violent, that an employment relationship is like the master-slave relationship. It's not. Exit can be exercised, however miserable the options. Neither voice nor loyalty figures.[10] A poor person can exit a wretchedly paid job for another job a little less wretched. But she cannot do so if under assignment by a government with its master monopoly, enforcing a gulag of slaves. Draftees can go AWOL but then get physically punished for it by the government. The sharecropper, by contrast, can move to the North, and the landlord cannot bring him back from Chicago as though a fugitive slave. A market is a device, that is, for non-violent, non-physically-coerced choice. Even a consumer facing a monopolist can choose to say no. Refusing to buy the goods that the governmentally sponsored monopolist offers, such as a telephone in the old days, might well be highly inconvenient to the buyer. But at least the offer *can* be refused. Do without a phone. Go to a phone booth. Don't take the monopolized taxi. Walk. An offer you literally can*not* refuse under threat of prison or death, such as paying taxes or serving in the military draft, entails monopoly-with-muscle, which is to say mafia-like or government-like coercion.

Buchanan put it this way: "The economy that is organized on market principles effectively minimizes the number of economic decisions that must be made politically, that is, through some agency that acts on behalf of the collective unit."[11] (Or at least it "acts on behalf" ideally.) If we make voluntary deals, by contrast, we don't need to call on the government and its police and muscle to exercise direct decisions. Buchanan continued: "In practical terms, we may say that an economy organized on market principles minimizes the size and importance of the political bureaucracy." The market minimizes the prevalence of the (few, we hope) civil servants who would take advantage of their position for unjust personal or party gain. It restrains the wielders of involuntary transactions backed by the threat of coercion, "the long arm of the law," as we say. Markets in India doubtless have "imperfections." But its government, everyone agrees (ranked in 2016 at 79th, lower even than Italy), has more. From 2006 to 2012 the regulators of the liquor markets of India extracted large bribes for letting Jim Beam sell whiskey there.[12] It was so even though India has since 1991 been leaving more and more decisions to the market, many more than it did under its socialist governments 1948–1991.[13] The leaving-to-markets has been good for poor Indians escaping the long arm of the License Raj.

In other words, Weber's violent if legitimate monopoly—when applied to an expansive agenda of policies designed to judge the barbarians or to nudge the blockheads—has dangers. It has dangers even in the few and mainly small countries that are well managed, and has much more so in the numerous and often populous countries that are badly managed.

The historian Thomas Babington Macaulay railed in 1830 against Robert Southey's proto-socialism: Southey would suggest that "the calamities arising from the collection of wealth in the hands of a few capitalists are to be remedied by collecting it in the hands of one great capitalist, who has no conceivable motive to use it better than other capitalists, the all-devouring state."[14] In 1917 Lenin imagined the left's vision of the transition to communism: "This control will really become universal, general, and popular; and there will be no getting away from it, there will be 'nowhere to go.' The whole of society will have become a single office and a single factory, with equality of labor and pay."[15] What neither Southey nor Lenin understood was one of Adam Smith's few wholly original teachings—he has often been accused, with some justice, of getting his ideas from the tiny group of French liberals. Smith taught that allowing people to have somewhere to go, instead of enserfing them to the all-devouring state or to one all-devouring slave master, raises the working person. If you can exit, you do not need to exercise voice on the picket line or loyalty to the Party. Take this job and stuff it.

The very word "liberty" in the rhetoric of both left and right has reverted to its medieval and coercive meaning, in the plural, "liberties"—"a liberty," such as "the liberty of the City of London," being a special and distinct privilege for this or that person or group, enforced against any who would presume to claim it for herself without the gracious permission of the government of London. The economic historian John Wallis notes that some liberal countries shifted in the nineteenth century from personal to general law. They moved away from, for example, enclosure of open fields or incorporation of businesses through one-by-one special action of the legislature to a general enclosure act (1801 and especially 1836 in the United Kingdom) or a general incorporation act (in the United States as early as 1795, in North Carolina).[16] The reign of person-specific as against general liberties is seen for example in the government-enforced and grossly unequal protection for tire companies in Ohio or the relaxed policing of drugs in white suburbs or the outlawing of private schools lest anyone get a better education.

It contradicts the core liberal criticism of the old "liberties" articulated, it is commonly believed, by Thomas Paine, giving to every other human being every chance and right he claims for himself (it in fact is due to "the Great Agnostic," Robert G. Ingersoll [1833–1899]).[17] Whoever articulated it, it's the Golden Rule again. The pseudo-Paine formula works for "negative" liberties—the right to say no—but not for so-called positive liberties—the "right" to take from others for the benefit of other others. If everyone claims such positive liberties, everyone is impoverished, by taking and taking and taking. Look at extractive governments such as Zimbabwe's, or any war of all (or of those in charge) against all.

The slow socialism of High Liberalism, egged on by the slow fascism of nationalism, has long recommended, and has eventually achieved, I have noted now repeatedly, an astonishingly high share of national income spent by the government out of coerced taxes. The share is often higher than the most appalling tyrannies of the past. Slow socialism has achieved also, as I just noted, medieval standards of "liberties" regulating one's stuff, imposed by experts on more and more people, more governmental intervention in this or that wage bargain, more eugenic sterilization of undesirables, more economic "protection" offered to this or that favored group, more police-enforced licensing of this or that occupation, more electronic inspection of the residents, more obstructions to the mobility of labor, more nudging of the unruly poor, more nationalizations of the means of production, more ignorant armies clashing by night. Large government in practice has been grotesquely inegalitarian, and resulted in the stagnant growth of the 1970s in the United Kingdom or the clumsy policing of the world since 1945 by the United States. The slow-socialist motto is, "I'm from the government, and I'm here to help you—by messing with someone's stuff . . . maybe yours." Or, "Don't tax him, / Don't tax me: / Tax that man / Behind the tree." The slow fascist mottos are much the same. Statism, both.

Anyone not bewitched by Rousseau's and Lenin's and Mussolini's proposition that a general will discerned by the Party is trumps, or even the gentler versions in Green and Hobhouse and the two Roosevelts, will admit that power to coerce has dangers. The great (American-definition) liberal Lionel Trilling wrote in 1948 that "we must be aware of the dangers that lie in our most generous wishes," because "when once we have made our fellowmen the objects of our enlightened interest [we] go on to make them the objects of our pity, then of our wisdom, ultimately of our coercion."[18] Every mother knows the dangers. And when she loves the beloved for the beloved's own sake, she resists them.

11. Deirdre Became a Modern Liberal Slowly, Slowly

The progressives and the conservatives kindly left the word "libertarian," a redirection of the word becoming common by the 1960s, for the mere liberals, who against a statist age remained loyal to Smith and John Stuart Mill, Tocqueville and Bastiat, Lord Acton and Macaulay. The mere liberals were people like the economists Hayek (1899–1892) and Milton Friedman (1912–2006) and James Buchanan (1919–2013) all their adult lives, the philosopher Robert Nozick (1938–2002) in his early middle age, and the economic historian Deirdre Nansen McCloskey (1942–) in her maturity. Deirdre's father (1915–1969), I have noted, was an eminent political scientist, a New Deal Democrat drifting rightward. She vividly remembers him around 1960 using "libertarian" as a term of contempt. For a long time it kept her from taking humane liberalism seriously.

Eventually she did. The story is shared with tens of thousands of leftish members of the clerisy in twentieth-century Europe and its offshoots who moved in life from socialism to liberalism 1.0 or 2.0. Some few even became conservatives. Vanishingly few went the other way. (I leave it to you to draw the moral.) As the old joke has it, anyone who by age sixteen is not a socialist has no heart. Anyone who by age twenty-six is still a socialist has no brain. I just made the cut.

As so many upper-middle-class adolescents are for a while, I was at age sixteen or seventeen entranced by the socialist vision of justice as fair shares, a Joan Baez socialism, with the singing of labor songs. I dreamt I saw Joe

Hill. I wanted to help the poor and disadvantaged—which remains my sole political objective, as it is for all of us modern liberals (though we want to *actually* help, rather than rest at virtue-signaling how superior in pity we conceive ourselves to be). Therefore, I majored in economics and became a standard-issue Keynesian. I was making my fellows the object of my pity, then of my newly acquired wisdom, ultimately of my coercion.

One of us three college roommates, 1961–1964, a brilliant electrical engineer who later became a professor of physiology at the State University of New York at Buffalo, used to read the liberal Ludwig Mises's *Human Action* (1949) in breaks from examining second-order differential equations. I remember David leaning perilously back in his swivel chair, his feet up on the desk, smoking unfiltered Gauloises cigarettes, with Castro's speeches from Cuba via shortwave set at low volume to serve as a droning background, the old tan-bound Yale Press edition of Mises perched upon his knees. The other roommate and I, both leftish Democrats, both studying economics à la Harvard College out of Paul Samuelson's Keynesian textbook in those happy days, scorned the engineer's non-orthodox, voluntaristic, and "conservative" economics. Derek and I favored instead a pity-driven coercion in the style of Keynes, Samuelson, and Stiglitz. Yet in reading Mises during work breaks, our David learned more of the economics of a free society than the two of us did attending hundreds of hours of classes in Keynes and slow socialism.

A couple of years later, in 1964, beginning in graduate school, still at Harvard, I intended to join the other self-defined elite economists down in Washington as a *social* engineer, "fine-tuning" the economy, as we put it. At the time only a handful of graduate programs in economics, such as those at UCLA, the University of Washington, the University of Virginia, and above all the University of Chicago, doubted the Ivy League slow-socialist and utilitarian theory of expertise, which down to the present retains an iron grip on economic thought.[1] Yet a year or two into my graduate studies at Harvard it began to dawn on me what the core of economics said—Mises's *Human Action* and its Liberalism 1.0. The core denied the premise of utilitarian social engineering, left and right, the premise that a social engineer (as again the Blessed Smith put it) "can arrange the different members of a great society with as much ease as the hand arranges the different pieces upon a chessboard."[2] In the mid- to late 1960s the most prominent piece of social engineering on display, the American invasion of Vietnam, didn't seem to be working out as planned. By the time in 1968 I got my first academic job, ironically at that same anti–Ivy League Department of Economics at the University of Chicago, a version of humane liberalism as against coercive social engineering was beginning to make sense.

Chicago economics was then notorious at Harvard for being "conservative." (We of the left did not distinguish liberals 1.0, or 2.0, from conservatives. The left still does not. Come on, guys: get a *little* serious about political theory.) Back as a senior in college, in the fall of 1963, still a vaguely Keynesian leftie, I had not so much as considered applying to Chicago's large and distinguished graduate program in economics, then early in its twenty-year reign as the most creative department of economics in the world. Why listen to such evil people? My undergraduate essays in economics were denunciations of the Chicago School for its lack of pity, and for its idiotic misunderstanding of the theory of monopolistic competition devised by my teacher of microeconomics at Harvard, Edward Chamberlain.

Yet a dozen years after spurning the Department of Economics at the University of Chicago, and now tenured at the very place, I became its director of graduate studies. A textbook on Chicago-style microeconomics that I wrote in 1982—after discerning in 1980 that the Department of Economics at Chicago did not value me as highly as I thought my due, and shaking the dust of the place off my sandals and moving to the University of Iowa (go Hawks!)—contains a chapter showing that monopolistic competition is self-contradictory. As the Dutch say, "Van het concert des levens krijgt niemand een program." In the concert of life no one gets a program. You're telling me.

By the late 1960s and early 1970s, by age thirty or so, that is, I had become a thoroughly Chicago School economist, and in the uses of supply-and-demand analysis I remain one. As a rough guide to the liberal flourishing of ordinary people in market economies such as those of Denmark or Japan or the United States, the supply-and-demand arguments have never been scientifically overturned as empirical approximations, despite what you may have heard from Paul Krugman or Robert Reich.[3] My earliest big paper in economic history, entitled "Did Victorian Britain Fail?" (1970), was an early "supply-side" rejection of using the Keynesian demand-side economics for the long run. Krugman might want to have a look at it. Another paper a few years later, "New Perspectives on the Old Poor Law" (1973), distinguished the distorting effects of intervening in the wage bargain from the effects of giving a tax-supported cash subsidy to the poor to bring them up to a respectable standard. Reich might want to have a look at it. The cash subsidy, as against the numerous ill-advised interventions in the wage bargain since the coming of New Liberalism, is what economists left and right have been calling since the 1950s the "negative income tax," or nowadays the "earned income tax credit," such as the $9 a month the Indian government proposed in 2016 to replace its hundreds of corrupt and cumbersome subsidies.[4] The negative income tax, as for example Oportunidades in Mexico and the Bolsa Família in Brazil, has been widely adopted in Latin America, with pretty good results.[5] It is liberalism 1.0, made "Christian" (or Hindu or "bleeding heart" or humane) by a preferential option for the poor.

12. The Arguments Against Becoming a Liberal Are Weak

The routine arguments against a modern true liberalism are, as I gradually came to realize after the 1960s, startlingly weak. For example, it is not true, as earnest and amiable slow socialists argue, as I have noted, that the taxation and spending and regulation by big governments are innocuous because, after all, they are voted on by "us" and anyway "give back services." The modern liberal will in response inquire gently of the High Liberal: Did you vote for each of the 81,640 pages of new regulations promulgated by the federal government during 2016? Or the 70,000 pages of the Internal Revenue Code? Did your representatives in Congress or the White House know even roughly what was in them? Did you or they properly understand the economic consequences, as against what the lawyers and lobbyists will have claimed the taxes and regulations were "designed" to do? Design is good for dresses and furniture and automobiles—and such commercial designs, after all, face the salubrious test that the people pay for them directly and therefore value them at least at their price, which they in justice voluntarily pay. If the designs are governmental, however, the people do not get to value them item by item. Every two years or so they get to vote on the whole menu. Remember Spencer and the cookery of meetings, petitions, polling booths, parliamentary divisions, cabinet councils, and red-tape documents. Do you really want the exact fixed-price menu of national parks and governmental licensing requirements and local schools and corrupt road building and aggressive foreign policy that government now provides? Or would you rather order à la carte, at a lower price and higher quality?

Another weak objection to laissez-faire, even in some true liberal theory, is the notion that the government is composed of ethical philosopher monarchs, who can therefore be trusted to run a government kindly, giving us most wisely the monarch-chosen stuff out of taxes—the taxes gently, sweetly, democratically extracted from the stuff we make. When the commissioner of the US Food and Drug Administration Margaret Hamburg retired in 2015, she was introduced on National Public Radio as having regulated fully a fifth of the American economy.[1] The statistic is startling, yet accurate.[2] Food. Drugs. Was Ms. Hamburg a Wonder Woman—a wholly ethical and wholly wise philosopher queen? It seems unlikely, though I am sure she is very nice. Therefore the early-stage cancer treatment that works in Berlin, Germany may not be accessible to you in Houston, Texas, because the treatment still awaits a certified finding by America's FDA affirming that the drug or procedure or medical appliance has "efficacy," tested unethically by "gold standard" double-blind experiments guided by meaningless tests of statistical significance, and going far beyond the original brief of the FDA to test merely for safety, not for an elusive efficacy, an efficacy anyway regularly modified in the clinic by discoveries by doctors trying out the drug or appliance off-label.[3] That last was the history of Rogaine (minoxidil), originally an FDA-restricted heart drug, now an over-the-counter treatment for male-pattern baldness—"over-the-counter" because the politicians responded to the middle-aged men demanding that it be made easily and cheaply available, despite the FDA. But not cancer drugs for women.

A supposition that government is in the hands of philosopher kings and queens seems on its face naïve, which is what Buchanan's notion of public choice economics avers. The naïveté is well illustrated by the perils of the US Constitution, from the Alien and Sedition Acts of 1798 down to Trumpism. Wise or not, the governor, whoever she is, has a weak incentive in prudence to be careful with other people's money, or with other people's lives. She is insulated by infrequent elections and by the power and prestige of massive modern governments. As Higgs puts it in a Facebook comment on October 28, 2018, "Imagine people who are free to lie without adverse repercussions because, first, no one expects members of their group to tell the truth as a rule and, second, no one can hold them to account. . . . You recognize, I suppose, that I am describing typical politicians and government functionaries."

John Locke opined that "the one only narrow way which leads to Heaven is not better known to the magistrate than to private persons, and therefore I cannot safely take him for my guide, who may probably be as ignorant of the way as myself, and who certainly is less concerned for my salvation than I myself am."[4] Yet Margaret Hamburg of the FDA waxes proud of her "program" to spend your money to coerce you, and she waxes proud, too, of her power to enforce her decisions concerning one-fifth of the US economy by violence. Power, you might say, tends to corrupt.

Trilling wrote in 1948 that the danger is that "we who are liberal and progressive [or indeed Burkean and conservative] know that the poor are our equals in every sense except that of being equal to us."[5] The "us" are the natural governors, graduates of Columbia University, New York, or of Trinity College, Dublin, or of Sciences Po, Paris. After 2016 such arrogance among the elite was detected and punished by the Trump voters, and worldwide by populists from Britain to Brazil. High Liberals and conservatives suppose that the poor and the rest are incompetent to manage their own affairs. Therefore, we of the clerisy—a regiment of which Boaz calls "court intellectuals" gathered in the District of Columbia, with another lively regiment of Eurocrats stationed in Brussels—are supposed to guide the poor and the mere citizens. The clerisy strolls proudly in the glittering courts of Washington or Brussels, in Springfield, Illinois, or Chicago's City Hall.[6] "We will do so much better," they say to each other, "than the poor or the mere citizens can do for themselves in their pathetic homes and markets."

As Paine wrote in the liberal birth year of 1776, "Government, even in its best state, is but a necessary evil; in its worst state, an intolerable one."[7] Better keep the power to coerce modest. By 1849, at the first maturation of liberalism 1.0, Henry David Thoreau declared, "I heartily accept the motto, 'That government is best which governs least'; and I should like to see it acted up to more rapidly and systematically."[8] In that same year in far Torino a liberal economist of Italy, Francesco Ferrara, wrote that "taxation is the great source of everything a corrupt government can devise to the detriment of the people. Taxation supports the spy, encourages the faction, dictates the content of newspapers."[9] In 1792 even in a quasi-liberal Britain the government owned secretly over half of the newspapers.[10] As Boudreaux wrote recently, "The only sure means of keeping money out of politics is to keep politics out of money."[11] Small government. The bumper sticker on my little Smart car read, "Separation of Economy and Government."

We modern liberals are accused of being uncharitable, as ignoring the poor and wanting the rich to be lazily rich. Not so. Look at what Liberals 1.0 and 2.0 actually do. And anyway the indictment from the left depends on an implausible psychological theory. It supposes that a whole class of political thinkers claim disingenuously that it does have the poor chiefly in mind, but secretly wants to make the rich even richer out of rents. But why would anyone want such an outcome? What would be one's motive to wish that Liliane Bettencourt gets more yachts? Corrupting pay from the corporations? Fellowships from a humane-liberal billionaire? Profitable association with a constitutional-liberal professor? The privilege of joining the Mont Pelerin Society, all in order to impoverish the poor and enrich the rich?

If that's how psychology works, as a simpleton's version of an economic and social cash nexus, consider the pay from the government to teachers in governmental schools and universities, or fellowships from the sweet slow socialist George Soros, or profitable alliance with the hard leftists Naomi Klein or Jane Mayer or Nancy MacLean. On such a psychological theory, all such associations would be corrupting.

But surely not. Instead of making up dark conspiracies posited on a juvenile, marxoid theory of why people say what they say, let's listen, really listen, to the arguments of our supposed enemies, and consider their logic and evidence. Nancy MacLean, a historian at Duke University, won't. She refuses to reply to criticism about her book, hailed on the left, assaulting the liberal economist James Buchanan. She has announced that she will not speak to anyone who has gotten Koch money, or she adds, to anyone at any university that has. Her own university has gotten such money. Perhaps it is because she forbids herself to speak to herself that the book is so startlingly ignorant.

Admittedly, a certain strain of conservatives, and the more brotherly as against the more sisterly liberals, exhibit just such a lack of sympathy for the disadvantaged. It is part of a larger pattern of self-regarding. The modern liberal columnist for the *Chicago Tribune*, Steve Chapman, observes that "the familiar criticism of libertarians is that they have a selfish obsession with their own rights and no regard for how the exercise of those rights injures others," such as the deadly spillover from children not vaccinated for measles on children whose immune system is compromised.[12] The exclusive self-regard, I repeat, has parallels at the country club. And it is paralleled on the left in a patronizing attitude toward the pitiable poor. None of these is sensible or honorable. William Buckley's appalling defense back in the 1960s of the tyranny directed at the poor among African-Americans exhibited one version of it.

But a lack of concern for the less fortunate of our brethren is by no means intrinsic to modern liberalism. On the contrary. Dr. Adam Smith was much given to acts of secret charity, and did not sound a trumpet before him. John D. Rockefeller, a believing Baptist, gave substantial shares of his income to charity right from his beginnings in Cleveland. Andrew Carnegie on his death gave all of it. A lack of unself-regarding concern for others is not at all implied by humane true liberalism, or by Christian libertarianism, or by neoclassical libertarianism, or by a modern liberalism 2.0 of the bleeding heart.

Many conservatives or communitarians or Greens or Catholic social teachers believe that liberalism entails a retreat from society altogether. Patrick Deneen's *Why Liberalism Failed* (2018) is a recent example, but the genre has a long, even tedious, history—from Michael Sandel's *What Money Can't Buy* (2012), right back to the originals on the left and right, such as Marx's eloquence about the cash nexus or Carlyle's about the dismal science (dismal, it needs to be known, because the liberal political economists, such as Carlyle's friend John Stuart Mill, irritatingly, *opposed* the sweetly medieval system of slavery in the British Empire, which Carlyle un-dismally and eloquently supported).[13] Liberalism, intones Deneen, entails "the loosening of social bonds" (bonds such as slavery in the British Empire), "a relentless logic of impersonal transactions" (so unlike the transactions of pious Israelites selling lumber to Egyptians, say), and the proposition that "human beings are thus, by nature, non-relational creatures, separate and autonomous" (as for example in the non-relational exploration of human relationships in the bourgeois and liberal English novel since 1700).[14]

Ayn Rand had here a bad effect, with her masculinist doctrine of selfishness, and her uniformly male, reckless, and self-absorbed heroes in her illiberal-posing-as-liberal novels, ever popular with college freshmen. Especially fresh-men. Senator *Rand* Paul in his run for the Republican presidential nomination in 2016 got disproportionately fewer votes from women than from men. Yet his policies of stopping the drug war on Black and on Hispanic families, and of reducing the flow of bags filled with the bodies of Appalachian boys fighting distant wars, like most of his proposals, were the most family friendly on offer from any candidate, including (in their actual as against their "designed" effects) the proposals from the frankly socialist

Bernie Sanders. As for charity, and aside from his ill-considered views on compulsory vaccination for measles, Dr. Paul regularly contributes his skill as an eye surgeon to sight-saving operations in poor countries. One wonders what Senator Sanders, or his slow-socialist ally Thomas Piketty, does in that line. I urge Dr./Senator Paul, for the good of our shared modern liberalism, to ditch that misleading "Rand," and change his first name to, say, Adam.

13. We Can and Should Liberalize

Even at this late hour, it is practical to reduce a bit the size and power of government, letting free people have a go (in the sportsmanlike phrase of the British). The reduction is achievable by parts whether or not a Painean or Thoreauesque or Ferrarite ideal is finally achieved. We do not need to go as far as what Jeffrey Myron calls "Libertarian Land," that is, a United States of the 1890s without Pinkertons killing unionists, and with votes for women. Nor do we need to implement a version of the 1790s without slavery, and also with votes for women—with no large army, no FDA or FCC, no massive state and local interventions in the economy. Jeff and I would like such worlds, true. But we urge you to calm down, and not rest with doubting that such utopias are achievable in a modern democracy. Consider what we can nonetheless do to make the economy and society richer and more just.

To consider, for example, another weak argument against laissez-faire, our coercion-minded friends are mistaken that the more complicated an economy is, the more regulatory attention it needs from the governors. It is a lawyer's view of how an economy works. The professor of law Eric Posner, defending the massive delegation of powers to federal agencies such as the FTC and the FDA, claims that "detailed regulation . . . is necessary to keep a modern economy humming."[1] To the contrary. Likewise, a correspondent of Boudreaux complained that to offer the counsel "Let the market handle it" is simplistic and Pollyannaish. Boudreaux replied, "Quite the opposite. To let the market handle matters is to allow as many creative minds as are willing to put their own efforts and resources on the line in their quests to address whatever problems exist, and it is to use the most effective and reliable of tests—market competition—to judge and to monitor the efforts. What *is* simplistic and pollyannaish is to say 'Let the government handle it.'"[2] Let the highly ethical philosopher monarchs handle it. Let Margaret Hamburg govern one-fifth of the American economy.

A complicated economy far exceeds the ability of even a government-sized collection of human intellects to govern it in detail. By her own intellect, a person's own life is properly so governed, or her little household, or maybe even her big company—though any adult knows that even little societies are hard to plan in detail, offering endless surprises. You get no program. But governing in great detail from the capitol the trillions of plans shifting daily by the nearly 330 million individuals in the American economy, much less nation building abroad, is a fool's errand, and yields the opposite of "humming"—because, as Smith again put it, "in the great chess-board of human society, every single piece has a principle of motion of its own."[3] The principles of motion are idiosyncratic. People are motivated in varying proportions by prudence, temperance, courage, justice, faith, hope, and love, together with the corresponding vices. By way of such principles of motion, you and I pursue our endlessly diverse projects, knitting and model railroading. Such a liberal plan fits well a society in which people are taken as free and equal—equal even to the Columbia/Trinity College/Sciences Po graduates of the clerisy.

What to do, then, in leashing the power to coerce? The practical proposals are legion, because illiberal policies by now are legion, as they were also during the feudalism that the eighteenth-century liberals overturned. True, it takes an idea to kill an idea. Most theories of vested interests, as the economists Wayne Leighton and Edward López point out, imply that the vesting is irreversible (as indeed it was supposed to be for medieval monks "vested," that is, ceremonially dressed for the first time in their official robes).[4] Gordon Tullock, the co-founder of public-choice theory, noted in 1975 that gifts to favored folk—such as the restrictions on entry to owning taxis, the low-cost grazing on governmental land, the home-mortgage deduction on personal taxes, and the hundreds of other favors and handouts enforced by the monopoly of coercion, such as the public protection of slave capital in the United States before the Civil War—get capitalized into the prices of the assets to which they are attached.[5] The secondhand buyer of taxi medallions, Western ranches, private houses, or American slaves gets no supernormal profits. Slaves were not a "cheap source of labor," as is commonly said. Southern slave owners had paid for the future expected productivity of the slaves capitalized into the price, and subsequently earned nothing supernormal.

Yet each favor and handout and protection of vested interests shifts the direction of capital and labor artificially, resulting in over-investment in, say, mortgaged houses, or over-investment in corruption to get and maintain restrictions on entry to, say, ownership of taxi medallions, or over-investment in a war to protect slavery. Of course, any proposal to drop the mortgage-interest deduction or to let Uber and Lyft compete freely with medallioned taxis raises political storms. Or a Civil War. Meanwhile the social loss in misallocation of investment will last as long as the protection lasts. The mortgage-interest deduction alone wastes every year nowadays 1 percent of GDP.[6] It doesn't take many such over- and under-investments to yield an economy-wide stagnation.

But it seems unjust, if globally efficient in utilitarian terms, to impose a capital loss on people who have innocently bought medallions or houses. It was unfair, slave owners said, to impose a capital loss on those who had bought slaves. (Yet neither would they accept compensated emancipation.) And whether just or not, according to Tullock the withdrawal of regulation seldom happens. The political storms create a "transitional gains trap." We're stuck. The theory of political history proposed by Douglass North, John Wallis, and Barry Weingast in 2009 has the same structure.[7] How does a society get out of an equilibrium of vested interests if vested interests, as against honest argument and liberal ideology, are the only way the politics operates? In a Dilbert cartoon, Dilbert's boss declares, "History repeats." Dilbert innocently asks, "Then how does something new ever happen?"[8] Up to 1800, after all, liberalism and economic growth had been routinely opposed, throttled, starved, in the interest of rent-seeking elites. Then something new happened.

Yet protectionist policies do occasionally change, sometimes startlingly quickly. The changes can give us hope that history is not stuck, that we are not doomed to a future, to quote the ending of *1984* again, of a governmental boot stamping on a human face forever. Leighton and López give the example of the deregulation of many important sectors of the American economy, beginning in the 1970s under President Carter and continuing under President Reagan. In 1977, two years after Tullock's article showing why such change was impossible, except maybe in the very long run, "fully regulated industries accounted for 17 percent of GNP. But by 1988 that share had dropped to 6.6 percent."[9] Leighton and López remark dryly that "deregulation was a surprise to some, especially to public choice theorists." The monk sometimes does cast off his vestments and take a wife. Luther did. And his wife was a former nun.

There seems to be something amiss in the equilibrium theories, with their materialist opposition to speech, ideas, free will, rhetoric, human action, ideology as historical forces. In 1775 the equilibrium was mercantilism. By 1875, after the rise of a liberal ideology, mercantilism and feudal regulation had receded, at any rate in Britain and in the countries of new settlement, and even some in France. By 1975 an ideology of mercantilism and feudal regulation had crept back, with its accompaniment of vested interests. Then it was quickly overturned by a liberal ideology. By now it has crept back yet again. Why such changes, whether for good or ill?

North, Wallis, and Weingast want to be seen as tough materialists, but when they seek explanations of the "transition proper" toward liberal "open access societies," they fall naturally into speaking of a rhetorical change. Two crucial pages of their 2009 book speak of "the transformation in thinking," "a new understanding," "the language of rights," and "the commitment to open access."[10] In a word, ideology. Buchanan, the public-choice theorist, once noted how important ideology was: "From war to trade to love . . . agreement on the rules by which we shall live, one with another, domestically and internationally, is, of course, informed by scientific inquiry and understanding. But, at base, the problem is not one of involving technological application of scientific discoveries, and it seems a mark of folly to treat it as such, that is, as an engineering problem."[11] It is ideology that changes.

That is, although North, Wallis, and Weingast appear to believe that they have a materialist explanation, informed by scientific inquiry and understanding, of the liberal rise of "open access to political and economic organizations," in fact their explanation for why Britain, France, and the United States for a while tipped into open access is ideational.[12] It's not an engineering problem. Ideas change because of sweet or nasty talk as much as because of good or bad material interests. What actually happened was an ideological, ethical, rhetorical change toward liberalism around 1800, and again with Carter's chairman of the Civil Aeronautics Board in the 1970s. He brought technical economics to bear on regulated airlines, but under auspices of a new ideology. And then came Reagan's numerous modern liberal deregulators.

An ideology of liberalism, that is, has occasionally won out against ideologies of pushing people around. We can do it again. Cut the seven thousand units of corrupt government in Illinois. Kill off the large programs of corporate welfare, federal and state and local, as many liberal billionaires propose, against their own financial interests. The vicious Jones Act protecting US shipping is a case in point. The Import-Export Bank is another. Higgs described the bank as "another contrivance to shift wealth from the politically weak and alienated to the politically strong and connected, while sanctifying the transfer with incantations of economic humbug."[13]

To move toward liberalism, that is, close the agricultural programs, which allow high-income farmers such as my grand uncle Oliver in Watseka, Illinois, to farm the government, as he put it, instead of the land. Sell off public assets such as roads and bridges and street parking, which in an age of electronic transponders can be better priced by private enterprise. Close the American empire. Welcome immigrants. Abandon the War on Drugs. Give up eminent domain for developers, and civil forfeiture and armored personnel carriers for police departments. Implement the notion in Catholic social teaching of "subsidiarity," placing modest but existing and essential governmental responsibilities such as trash collection or fire protection down at the lowest level of government that can handle them properly. Then outsource to profit-making firms the trash collection and the fire protection. Then, with transparency and journalism, watch the outsourcing as vigilantly as one watches the government.

To finance K–12 education, and especially nursery school through elementary school, N–8—socially desirable but often out of reach of the poor—give families vouchers to cash in at private schools, such as Sweden has done since the 1990s and as Orleans parish in Louisiana has done for poor families since 2008. To achieve such universal K–12 or N–8 education, and a select few of other noble and otherwise privately un-fundable purposes, such as carbon taxes against global warming or defensive armaments in a war of survival, by all means tax or regulate you and me, not only the man behind the tree. But eliminate the inquisitorial income tax and regulation, replacing it with a tax on personal consumption declared on a one-page form, as has long been proposed by economists such as Robert Hall and Arthur Laffer. Still better, use only an equally simple value-added tax on owners of businesses, to reduce if not eliminate the present depth of inquisition. Eliminate entirely the so-called corporate income tax, because it is double taxation and because economists have, scientifically speaking, after many decades of earnest inquiry, achieved no consensus about which people end up paying it. (The old bumper sticker of the 1970s, "Tax corporations, not people," when you think about it, doesn't make a lot of sense.) Give a poor person cash in emergencies and for disabilities, out of those modest taxes on you and me. Quit inquiring into whether she spends it on booze or her children's clothing. Leave her and her family alone. Stop pushing people around.

A government does of course "have a role"—as in indignant reply to such proposals my progressive and conservative friends put it to me, predictably, relentlessly. George Romney, the automaker and conventional 1950s Republican, opposing the liberal 1.0 and conservative Barry Goldwater in 1964, declared, "Markets don't just *happen*," that there must be "*some* role for government."[14] Well, yes, of course, government has "*some* role," though contrary to Romney's assertion most markets do in fact "just happen," because people find them mutually beneficial, with or without governmental action. Markets just happen, to cite two extreme cases, inside jails and prisoner-of-war camps, with no governmental action to enforce the deals made. Markets just happened among pre-contact Australian aborigines buying their boomerangs from better-skilled bands hundreds of miles distant.[15]

Anyway, only briefly, at age fifteen or so, if you care, did I think of myself as a literal "anarchist" (which properly does not mean "bomb-throwing nihilist" but *an-archos*, Greek for "no ruler"). Government has an essential role in those wars of survival, for example, in which a focused, single purpose of repelling the invaders from Canada is exactly what's required, and can be achieved for the duration with justified if often over-applied coercion. Then after the victory we can hope that we can get rid of the coercion coming from the expanded role for government—without a great deal of hope, actually, as Higgs has shown.[16]

And yes, by all means let us have a government, a small one, to protect us from force and fraud by fellow Americans—though of course such private arrangements as door locks and high-reputation suppliers and competition in markets achieve the protections in most cases much better and at a much larger economic scale, to speak quantitatively, than does their alleged "ultimate" backing by governmental courts and police and inspectors. The English Court of Chancery is no more "ultimate" than private arrangements for the transmittal of property, or the private gates with guards protecting it. In London in the eighteenth century a wealthy person hired armed guards if he intended to walk across town. The legal scholar Tom W. Bell argues in detail that most countries have private sub-governments in which in numerous ways the writ of the government's law does not run, a private law expanding rapidly.[17] Protect us, we pray, especially from government itself, from its habit of suspending the right to habeas corpus or abridging the right to vote or spying on civil-rights leaders or enforcing bedroom and bathroom norms or beating up on sassy citizens.

14. For Example, Stop "Protection"

Governments claim to protect, when on their good behavior, and not, say, interning Japanese-Americans. But the government should leave off giving *economic* "protection," such as President Trump provided against the nefarious plot by Chinese and Mexicans to sell us at low prices very long ties for men and very good parts for cars. Let us have instead a separation of economy and government.

It is not really "protection" anyway. It's favoring. As in Mafia usage, governmental "protection" is regularly corrupted for the favoring of the rich. It is a tax on the enterprises that provide cheap goods and services for poor people. It violates the equal liberty of people—Americans or foreigners or non-mafiosi—to compete without physical coercion in offering good deals to American consumers. Such taxation is of course the very purpose of the Mafia, extracting an income of protection money by making an offer you can't refuse. And it is the purpose, too, of the Chicago City Council, encouraged by well-placed bribes . . . uh . . . campaign contributions to prevent by ordinance the poor-person-supplying Ikea or Walmart from opening in town. Extortion and favoring and rent-seeking by elites, exercising the monopoly of coercion, puts a drag on betterment, stopping people with new ideas from competing for our voluntary purchases. In the extreme it stops economic growth cold, as it did during the grinding millennia of poverty before 1800, and before open-access liberalism.

Would you want governmental "protection" from new ideas in music or science or cooking? Probably not. Would you always "buy American" in spices or medical innovations? No. Suppose you believe that an embargo on evil anti-American nations such as Iran or North Korea is a good idea. Then why do you want to impose a self-applied embargo on Americans themselves by the American government—which is what "protection" by tariff is? Tariffs do not protect. They take and they favor. They are taxes on some citizens of the government imposing them, in order to favor other, more powerful citizens.[1]

And if you really do think favoring some Americans and buying exclusively from Americans is a good idea, to be enforced by tariffs and jail terms, why not still better buy Illinoisan or Chicagoan or even Printer's-Row-ian? That way your neighborhood will be enriched. Or for that matter why not make everything you want yourself in your own home, achieving thereby true self-sufficiency and plenty of "jobs"? Grow your own wheat. Make your own accordion. Invent your own economic theory. Bravo.

Our rightist or leftist and anyway statist friends will ask in irritated reply, concerning for instance the Russian interference in elections via Facebook, "Can Facebook regulate itself in the public interest? Obviously not," they say. No business, they suppose, has ever acted in the public interest. Profit is a sign of sin. Bring on, therefore, the experts and their police from Washington or Whitehall. Does Whirlpool in the United States falter in the washing-machine business? All right, persuade the government to erect tariff barriers against competition from foreigners such as LG and Samsung.

Most people in an illiberal age approve of such "protection of US jobs." They don't realize that the protection takes from Peter to pay Paul, and then from Paul to pay Peter. A tariff on washing machines might protect a thousand Americans from hurtful competition, at the cost of eliminating their incentive to improve, and distorting the pattern of investment. But it directly hurts a hundred thousand other Americans with higher prices and lower quality, in magnitudes that substantially reduce national prosperity on net. It has happened every time it's been tried. Consult populist Argentina, 1946 to the present. Or Trump's experiments in 2018.

The economist Maximiliano Dvorkin of the Federal Reserve Bank of St. Louis reckoned that between 2000 and 2007 the United States lost from competition with China about 800,000 jobs (a tiny fraction, by the way, of the jobs "lost" from what we all agree is desirable technological change, such as the demise of video stores and the myriad other jobs moved or made obsolete; they amounted during the same seven years to scores of millions, not 0.8 million). But according to Dvorkin the trade with China gained on the same account a similar number of *other* jobs, for a net effect on jobs of zero (the same is true on a much larger scale of so-called technological unemployment). And as a result of the lower prices from such reallocation and competition in the China trade, "U.S. consumers gained an average of $260 of extra spending per year for the rest of their lives."[2] Expressed as a capital sum discounted to the present, the free trade with China was like every consumer getting a one-time check for about $5,000. Pretty good.

Do you so fear instead the multinational corporation—which is trying in its evil way to sweet-talk you into buying its running shoes—that you are willing to erect a comprehensive socialist monopoly, backed by guns, to prevent you from getting any shoes but government-issue or government-regulated? Do you expect such regulation-on-steroids to be less corrupt than dark money from corporations?

Consider that you may be mistaken. Witness the third of the world ruled once by communism, or the recent history of Venezuela, or the dismal history of modern Egypt with its army-run economy. As an Italian liberal, and anti-fascist, Benedetto Croce, put it in 1928, "Ethical liberalism abhors authoritarian regulation of the economic process [equally from the left as from the right, from socialism as from fascism], because it considers it a humbling of the inventive faculties of man."[3] In order to protect the US Postal Service's monopoly, inspectors in trench coats used to go around in December putting the arm on little children distributing Christmas cards for free in neighborhood mailboxes. In Kentucky by law nowadays, as in Illinois and many other states formerly, to open a new company for moving furniture—two men and a truck, say—you must get permission from . . . wait for it . . . the existing moving companies.[4] George Will noted, after blasting "certificates of need" such as those required by the moving-company law (also for MRI machines in hospitals, automobile dealerships, and on and on), that "the sprawling, intrusive, interventionist administrative state—a.k.a. modern government—that recognizes no limits to its competence or jurisdiction is inevitably a defender of the entrenched and hence a mechanism for transferring wealth upward."[5] You go, George.

And of course much worse. The communist, fascist, and national socialist régimes dating from 1917, 1922, and 1933, all of them versions of socialism inspirited by nationalism, left upwards of one hundred million people dead in their pursuit of planning rationality and national honor. Maybe you don't want to be a socialist, fast or slow.[6] Consider the evidence.

The sweet if culpably naïve theory, again, as I have noted, is that the implementers of slow socialism are wise and ethical philosopher kings and queens. The theory is imagined on the blackboards of Cambridge or New Haven or Princeton, and, without the lovely mathematics, on the political stump nationwide. Yet economic protection/favoritism as implemented regularly hurts the helpless more than it helps them. And it always favors the few protected, who are easy to see up on the stage, to be favored over the unseen multitudes damaged offstage. Protect *this* job, even though each year in the United States up to 14 percent of jobs disappear, as must be the case in a dynamic economy enriching of the poor.[7] In 2000 over a hundred thousand people worked in video stores. Now, as I noted, none but a very few hardy and nostalgic souls. In the late 1940s there were hundreds of thousands of manual telephone operators working for AT&T alone. In the 1950s elevator operators by the thousands lost their jobs to passengers pushing buttons and listening to sweetly recorded messages announcing the floors, with, in many hotel elevators, maddening TV shows to boot. Typists have vanished from offices—the lawyers or their assistants write the briefs directly on their computers. And the biggest, worldwide example is farming. In 1810, about 80 percent of Americans lived or worked on farms; now it's 1 percent and falling.[8] Yet the farm-state senators demand protection, such as a law to make gasoline from corn, and to protect sugar at twice the price it could be purchased from Brazil. The tiny group favored will have given a nice contribution to a congressperson's welfare, or anyway given a vote. Thus we get useless military tanks and planes to stop the coming Canadian invasion, built with parts made in every congressional district, and garnering votes for every sitting congressperson.

Tariff protection, for example, which pushes up profits and wages in American-made steel, will of course at the same time, if offstage, hurt American consumers of steel. Obviously. It did in 2018 for makers of thousands of steel products from cars to nails. That is what it was designed to do, and—unusually for "designed" policies—what it actually achieved, a self-inflicted embargo, as I have said. (Let us pass over in silence the hurt to foreigners who want to sell us oil and auto parts at prices we agree to. Yet since when is a cosmopolitan concern for foreigners not to be recommended ethically? And what sort of childish nationalism thinks that hurting Canadians or Mexicans is good for Americans?)

Regularly, I also said and will keep saying until you get it, such offstage damage imposed on the *un*protected Americans is many times larger in economic terms than the onstage favor granted to the few protected Americans. In 2017 the American government agreed with Mexican sugar producers to restrict imports of Mexican sugar. The agreement kept the price of sugar at the high, long-protected American price.[9] But the jobs saved in US sugar production by the high price enforced by the restriction were a tiny fraction of the jobs destroyed in sugar-using production. Candy producers in Chicago have been shutting down or moving to Mexico for a long time. When it comes to protecting sugar growing, the four senators from cane sugar–growing Florida and Louisiana are very, very interested, with the six from Texas, Hawaii, and (beet sugar–growing) North Dakota also expressing a forceful opinion on the matter. Strange, yes?

When in the early 1980s the American government imposed quotas on Japanese automobiles, the additional cost each year to American consumers of autos was higher, by a ratio of ten to one, than the sum of annual wages in Detroit thus protected.[10] The net beneficiaries were United Auto Workers accustomed to receiving a share of the monopoly profit extracted from Americans buying their cars from the lonely and tariff-protected Big Three and a Half (GM, Ford, Chrysler, and American). The other beneficiaries were of course the stockholders of the Big Three and a Half, and, less obviously, a Toyota Motor Company in far Japan, enabled to capture still more of its very own monopoly profit by restricting its supply to the United States and thereby pushing the US price of the well-made Toyotas above the world price, without even a benefit accruing to the US Treasury that (by contrast with the quota) a tariff would have provided. Brilliant.

Similarly, the Multifiber Arrangement 1974–2004 tried to stop poor countries from supplying richer countries with textiles and clothing. The economist Douglas Irwin notes that in the United States, "the [annual] consumer cost of protection per [US textile and clothing] job saved, which measured the total loss to consumers divided by the number of jobs saved in the protected industry, was more than \$100,000 for industries in which the average worker earned perhaps \$12,000 annually."[11] That's 8.3 to 1.

A worse protection, still deemed sacred on the left, is the worldwide assault on young or unskilled seekers of any job at all, through job protections/favorings for the oldsters and the skilled. Job protections in slow-socialist régimes have created in Greece and South Africa and the slums of the United States a dangerously large class of unemployed youths.[12] A quarter of French people under twenty-five years of age and out of school are unemployed, and the rest are employed mainly on monthly temp contracts, because regular jobs held by old people in France are fiercely protected.[13] The employers in such a system are terrified to hire in the first place, because they cannot dismiss a worker who steals from the till or insults the customers or is in other ways unproductive. And even the honest and productive workers in France cling in terror to the wrong jobs, because they are unlikely to get the right ones if they quit. The protection-caused unemployment is higher still in Greece. It is appalling in South Africa.

In the United States the job protections have caused the ghettos to require, at any rate in the opinion of conservatives, armed occupation. The South and West Sides of Chicago should be hives of industrial activity, employing at low starter wages the unemployed youths now standing on street corners and joining gangs to enforce local monopolies of drug distribution. Interventions in the wage bargain in Chicago, such as the governmentally enforced minimum wage, and interventions in the location of economic activity, such as zoning, and interventions in income from business, such as taxes and licenses and regulations, and interventions in consumption, such as the War on Drugs itself, make such places economic deserts. No factories, no grocery stores, no non-coercive incomes. The word in common? High-handed "intervention" by our wise and incorruptible public masters. What would happen if, like Shenzhen in China, the South and West Sides were declared "enterprise zones"? Like Shenzhen, once a fishing village, now an enormous metropolis, they would prosper mightily.

15. And Stop Digging in Statism

The proverb is that if you find yourself in a hole, first stop digging.

We are speaking of a *humane* liberalism. Helping people in a crisis, surely, or raising them up from some grave disadvantage, such as social or economic or physical or mental disability, by giving help in the form of money to be spent in free markets, is a just role for the government. Still more just, because not coerced at all, is people donating effective help voluntarily on their own. Give the poor in Orleans parish the vouchers for private schools. Give money to the very poor of Chicago to rent a home privately. Rent a hundred hotel rooms for the homeless in Chicago during the terrible cold in February 2019. Turn over your book royalties from *Capital in the Twenty-First Century* to an effective charity.

Yet do not, I beg of you, *supply* schooling or housing or for that matter books about inequality directly from the government, because governmental ownership of the means of production, a full socialism, is usually a bad way to produce anything except, say, national defense (and even national defense is commonly done badly and corruptly, as in the many nations such as Egypt and Belarus using their guns to enslave their own citizens). Governmental provision makes the poor into serfs of the government, or of the government's good friends the teachers' union in the public schools and the bureaucrats in the public housing authority. Private provision gives people more choice, more opportunities of exit, and makes the supplies responsive to demands. The liberal 1.0 economist Ben Rogge noted that "the free market protects the integrity of the individual by providing him with a host of decentralized alternatives rather than with one centralized opportunity."[1]

The Swedes, whom Americans think are socialists, in 2009 gave up their government-owned and -operated monopoly of pharmacies, which any adult Swede can tell you were maddeningly arrogant and inefficient.

Mainly, let people create by themselves a growing economy, as they did spectacularly well from 1800 to the present, as liberalism inspirited the masses to devise betterments and to open new enterprises and to move to new jobs. The stunning Great Enrichment of a fully 3,000 percent increase since 1800 in real wages per person—which I have noted was especially important for the poorest—happened not because of the taxing and nudging and judging and protecting and regulating and subsidizing and prohibiting and unionizing and drafting and enslaving by politicians and organizers and bureaucrats and thugs armed with a monopoly of coercion. Mostly it happened despite them, by way of an increasingly free people. The government's rare good deeds in the story were the passing of liberal laws to make people free, as in the Civil Rights Acts of 1866 and of 1964—though passed in the brief interludes between governmental enslaving or re-enslaving or manhandling of people, in the Dred Scott decision, Plessy v. Ferguson, the Palmer Raids, Bull Connor's dogs, and the deportation of Dreamers. As Boudreaux puts it, commenting on the claim that the state is chiefly in the business of good deeds, "A state powerful enough to prevent you discriminating against, say, Catholics [in the private sector voluntarily] is powerful enough to force you to discriminate against Jews [in the public sector involuntarily]."[2]

The Enrichment and its associated liberation, that is, did not arise chiefly from government, beyond its modest role in the prevention of some portions of force and fraud and the few cases of genuine defense from foreign aggression, such as the largely unsuccessful War of 1812–1814 and the very successful Pacific War of 1941–1945. Yet strangely the economists since around 1848 have mainly made their scientific reputations by proposing this or that pro-governmental "imperfection in the market." The economists discerned over one hundred such imperfections. Natural monopoly. Spillovers. Ignorant consumers. And they have claimed again and again that a brilliant government of philosopher monarchs, advised by the very same economists, can provide simple solutions to the imperfections imagined on the blackboard. Anti-trust. The FDA. Industrial policy. Government seizure of railways and power companies.

In all this, however, the economists supplied no scientific evidence that the imperfections much damaged the economy as a whole in its mad career of raising income per head by liberal means 3,000 percent.[3] The most important fact about modern economic history, occurring at the very time the economists were bemoaning our "disgrace with fortune and men's eyes / . . . alone beweeping our outcast state" from the horrible imperfections in the market, was that the wretchedly distorted and imperfect markets were delivering a Great Enrichment to the poorest among us of thousands of percent. In Yiddish idiom: "We should have such imperfections!"

For instance, the governmental choosing of winners in the economy, by an "industrial policy," is "designed" to repair the shocking imperfections of foresight by private investors, so obvious to some professors of economics, without the bother of measuring whether the imperfection is actually large or whether the industrial policy actually works. Charles Schultze, chairman of the Council of Economic Advisors during Jimmy Carter's term in the White House, argued that "reality does not square with any of the four premises on which the advocates of industrial policy rest their case. America is not de-industrializing. Japan does not owe its industrial success to its industrial policy. Government is not able to devise a 'winning' industrial structure. Finally, it is not possible in the American political system to pick and choose among individual firms and regions in the substantive, efficiency-driven way envisaged by advocates of industrial policy."[4]

Therefore, industrial policy in fact almost never works for our common good, though it almost always works for the good of industrialists with lobbyists on K Street. Why, in sober common sense, would such choosing of winners work for most of us? Why would an official high up in the government, stipulating even that she is equipped with wonderful economic models and is thoroughly ethical, being an extremely bright if recent graduate of Harvard College, know better what would be a good idea to make and sell and buy than some ignorant hillbilly out in the market facing the prices that register the value ordinary people place on goods and services, and facing the actual opportunity cost in their production, and going bankrupt if he chooses badly? Why would it be a good idea to subsidize wind power in advance of a showing that extra spending on it in fact makes us better off, net of opportunity costs such as the high manufacturing and erection cost of the mills, or for that matter the mass slaughter of migrating birds? As the modern liberal economist Don Lavoie concluded from a detailed study in 1985 of such governmental planning and industrial policy, "Any attempt by a single agency to steer an economy constitutes a case of the blind leading the sighted."[5]

The hubris of industrial planning is an old story. An instance was the Europe-wide mercantilism, the "commercial system" that Adam Smith so despised (amusingly, Smith, like his father, ended his career as one of its functionaries). In Sweden the Göta Canal was built 1810–1832 by military conscripts, before Sweden turned liberal.[6] It was a singularly ill-advised project, immensely expensive in real costs, and reducing Swedish income on net, eventually used chiefly for a bit of pleasure boating. In the United States during the nineteenth century and beyond, the "internal improvements" financed by the government were mostly wretched ideas—such as canals in Pennsylvania and Indiana that were started during the 1830s, built like Sweden's on the eve of railways that made most of the canals socially and privately unprofitable, the longest being the Wabash and Erie, built at great cost 1832–1853.[7] And of course the internal improvements, such as the transcontinental railways heavily subsidized by federal land grants, were corrupted into favors for the few and rich.[8] The tariff in the United States, imposed by a federal government with no other source of income early in its history, quickly became a political football.[9] The Obama administration gave away a $535 million "loan" to subsidize US-made solar panels manufactured by Solyndra, promptly undersold by the Chinese. Then Trump protected the remainder.[10] Both big political parties do it. A humane true liberal party would not.

16. Poverty Out of Tyranny, Not "Capitalist" Inequality, Is the Real Problem

The economist Mark Perry noted in September of 2018 that "census data released today show continued gains for middle-class Americans and little evidence of rising income inequality."[1] But anyway, you should worry not at all about inequality if it is achieved by smart betterment. To tax away profits is to destroy their signaling role. It kills efficiency and, more importantly, betterment. The objection to such taxes is not about incentives to effort, as slow socialists assume when sneering at the profits from commercially tested betterment. It is about deciding where investment should be made, a price-and-profit signal in market economies that has proven to be much cheaper than the inefficiencies of central planning.[2]

And the inequality from clever betterments dissipates within a few years, through the entry of imitations. Meanwhile we get the betterments, forever. The imitation of Henry Ford's assembly line or Steve Jobs's smart phone spreads the benefits to us all, soon, in lower prices and higher quality and frenetic, ongoing improvements. Commercially tested betterment is therefore equalizing. Such a result of entry is not hypothetical. It has been the economic history of the world since the beginning, when not blocked—as until 1800 it routinely was blocked—by monopolies supported by the ur-monopoly of governmental coercion, and now again increasingly under Late High Liberalism. The Nobel (2018) economist William Nordhaus reckons that inventors in the United States since World War II have kept only 2 percent of the social value of the betterment they produce.[3] Look at your computer. Or Walmart. Two percent of the social gain arising from Walmart's early mastery of bar codes and big-scale purchasing—great betterments compared with the older and worse models of retailing—left a lot of money for the children of Sam and Bud Walton. But the rest of us were left with the 98 percent.

Local fortunes a century ago were built on local banking and local department stores. The banks in the United States (though not in Britain or Canada) were protected until very late in the twentieth century by state-level regulations preventing branch banking. By contrast the relatively unregulated department stores were promptly imitated, and at length bettered. And anyway from the beginning the profits of local department stores were eroded by rapidly falling transport costs, allowing people to shop elsewhere. Drive to Grand Rapids, or to the discount stores out on Route 80. Sears Roebuck and Montgomery Ward competed with the brick-and-mortar general store charging high prices, and with the local department stores, by shipping new mail orders on the completed railway network at low prices right to your mailbox. You could buy an entire house from Sears, sent on a railcar to your town to be assembled by local craftsmen. Amazon is doing the same again a century on (short of whole houses: but wait; you can now buy automobiles online, delivered from vending machines), using the government-monopoly-challenging parcel-post services such as United Parcel. United States Steel's share in national sales of all American steel companies attained its highest level, fully two-thirds, on the day it was founded in 1901. The share fell steadily thereafter, with Bethlehem and other companies entering.[4] Look at the thirty companies in the Dow Jones Industrial Average. Only five of the thirty date from before the 1970s. The twenty-five others have been replaced by such "industrials" as Visa and Verizon and Coca-Cola. In 2018 General Electric, in the index since 1896, was dropped in favor of Walgreen Boots, the pharmacy. "Industries" churn.

The sheer passage of human generations churns, too. How many rich Carnegies have you heard of? Andrew might have made his daughter and her four children and their children, or for that matter his cousins back in Scotland, fabulously wealthy, down to the fourth generation and beyond. But he didn't. Instead he built the library in Wakefield, Massachusetts, in which I dipped at age fifteen or so into the leftist classics. If you want to see how the dissipation of wealth through families works, look at the Wikipedia entry for "Vanderbilt Family," noting that old Cornelius (1794–1877), the richest American at the time, had fully thirteen children (pity Mrs. Sophia Johnson Vanderbilt, the mother of them all). His great-great-granddaughter, Gloria Vanderbilt (born 1924), therefore had to make her own fortune the old-fashioned way, by providing goods and services that people were willing to pay for. Her son Anderson Cooper of CNN does, too.

But you should indeed worry about inequality when it is achieved by using the government to get protection for favored groups. It is what a large government, well worth capturing in order to get the protection, is routinely used for, to the detriment of the bulk of its citizens. We humane liberals agree with the slow socialists about the evil of an inequality caused by such rent seeking, that is, by using the powers of the government to extract profitable favors for, say, big oil companies. But we modern liberals are then startled that our friends the slow socialists advocate . . . well . . . giving still more powers of coercion-backed extraction to the same government. Put the fox in charge of the henhouse, they cry. Surely Mr. Fox is a good and honest civil servant.

Guilds with governmental protection, such as the American Medical Association, and government regulations in building codes to favor plumbers, protect the well-off, who in turn fund the politicians enforcing the guilds and associated regulations. Neat, eh? Consider how many Huey and Earl and other Longs have dominated Louisiana politics since the 1920s. Look at Wikipedia for that one, too. Inherited political power allied to corruption is ancient. Political candidates in the late Roman Republic routinely bought votes, and anyway the rich of Rome had more power in the system of voting itself.[5] There is nothing new about politicians and businesspeople and billionaires buying Congress for special protection and gerrymandering the voting system. Mark Twain said, "It could probably be shown by facts and figures that there is no distinctly native American criminal class except Congress."[6] Better keep it under parole.

Understand that the greatest challenges facing humankind are *not* terrorism or inequality or crime or population growth or climate change or slowing productivity or recreational drugs or the breakdown of family values or whatever new pessimism our friends on the left or right will come up with next, about which they will write urgent editorials and terrifying books until the next "challenge" justifying more governmental coercion gets their attention. For Lord's sake, they say, we should *do* something! Do it with the government, they say, the only "we" in sight.

The greatest challenges have always been poverty since the caves and tyranny since agriculture, which have their cause and their effect through the governmental coercion of not allowing ordinary people to escape to have a go. The use of the word "liberal" is a language game, but not therefore "mere."[7] It has consequences, in allowing or not allowing people to have that go. If you eliminate poverty through liberal economic growth, as China and India are doing, and as did by the standards of the day the pioneers of liberalism in the Dutch Republic during the seventeenth century, you will get some equality of real comfort, the educating of engineers to control flooding (and latterly to protect from the ocean-rising effects of global warming), and the educating of us all for lives of flourishing. If you eliminate tyranny, replacing it with liberalism 2.0, you will get the rise of liberty for slaves and women and people with disabilities, and still more fruits of the Great Enrichment, as more and more people are liberated to seek out commercially tested betterments or to subsidize the local opera company. You will get stunning cultural enrichments, the end of terrorism, the fall of the remaining tyrants, and riches for us all.

How do I know? Because it happened in northwestern Europe gradually from the seventeenth century onward, accelerating after 1800. And despite the recent descent into populist tyranny by some countries, it is now happening at a headlong pace in large parts of the globe. The liberal parts of China enrich the people (at the same time the illiberal parts, now favored by Xi, impoverish them.) It can happen soon everywhere. World real income per head, roughly corrected for inflation and purchasing power parity, grew from 1990 to 2016 at about 2 percent per year. At such rates (and all the more at the now 7 percent rate of India or the once 10 and now 5 percent of China, in both of which an economic liberalism has been allowed to expand), income per person will double every thirty-six years. And worldwide it will double faster if one allows in the calculation for improving quality of goods and services, an allowance better than the usual indices of prices. In three generations at 2 percent even conventionally measured real income will quadruple, pulling the wretched of the earth out of their wretchedness.

By contrast, keep on with various versions of old-fashioned monarchy, or with slow or fast socialism, with its betterment-killing policies protecting the favored classes, especially the rich or the Party or the cousins, Bad King

John or Robin Hood—in its worst forms a military socialism or a tribal tyranny, and even in its best a stifling regulation of new cancer drugs—and you get the grinding routine of human tyranny and poverty, with their attendant crushing of the human spirit. The agenda of modern liberalism, ranged against tyranny and poverty, is achieving human flourishing in the way it has always been achieved. Let my people go. Let ordinary people have a go. Stop pushing people around.

I realize that you will find many of the items we modern liberals propose hard to swallow. You've been told by our progressive friends that we need to have tens of thousands of policies and programs and regulations or the sky will fall. And you've been told by our conservative friends that we need anyway to occupy and govern by the gun at immense cost all sorts of communities of poor people, among them the lesser breeds east and west of Suez, out of the eight hundred American military bases worldwide. You may view as shocking the contrary proposals to let people be wholly free to flourish in a liberal economy—right-wing madness, you will say, enriching the rich, as you imagine Charles Koch intends; or left-wing madness, leading to chaos, as you imagine George Soros intends. You will say from the left that liberalism has allowed monopoly to increase. (It has not. Illiberalism has, when the captured regulators of taxicabs and power companies could get away with it—although monopoly in fact has been dramatically reduced since 1800 by liberty of movement and by free trade, by the railway and the telephone and the internet.[8]) You will say from the right that liberalism has allowed terrorism to increase. (It has not. Illiberalism has—although in fact terrorism in the West has *declined* sharply in the past few decades.[9]) If you cannot think of any fact-based arguments against a humane true liberalism, you will assert anyway with a sneer that it is anyway impractical, out of date, old-fashioned, nineteenth-century, a Norwegian Blue pining for the fjords, a dead parrot. (It is not. The illiberal national socialism practiced by most governments nowadays is impractical and out of date, a thoroughly dead parrot, gone to his reward.)

But you owe it to the seriousness of your political ideas, my dear friends, to listen and consider. Clear your mind of cant. Lavoie noted "the impossibility of refuting a theory without first trying to see the world through its lenses."[10] Try out the lenses, too.

We are *not* doomed by the New Challenges. But we need to avoid shooting ourselves in the feet, as we did in 1914 and 1917 and 1933. Such shooting is a lively possibility, because we've done it before, by way of traditionalism and nationalism and socialism and traditional national socialism. If we dodge the political bullet, though, we can rejoice over the next fifty or a hundred years in the enrichment through humane true liberalism of the now-poor, a permanent liberation of the wretched, and a cultural explosion in arts and sciences and crafts and entertainments beyond compare.

Welcome to the liberal future. If we can keep it.

17. Humane Liberalism Is Ethical

This piece began in 2016 as an invited comment on the Reason *magazine website,* Reason.com, *about the essay* "The Case for 'Virtue Libertarianism' Over Libertinism," *by William Ruger and Jason Sorens.*

"Virtue libertarianism" is a good phrase and a good idea, put forward by the political economists William Ruger and Jason Sorens. I would call it "virtue liberalism," toward which I been slouching for some decades, as for example in the first volume, *The Bourgeois Virtues* (2006), of the trilogy the Bourgeois Era (2006, 2010, 2016). It's the difference between Chicago School libertarianism 1.0, fiercely opposed to any ethical reflection whatever; and Harvard-School social engineering 1.0, which is thoughtlessly attached to utilitarianism; and in opposition to both, the humane liberalism 2.0 that Adam Smith and I espouse.

As a former pure, Chicago School 1.0 economist I understand and admire and still use the so-called positive economics of supply and demand, with marginalism. As a Harvard BA and PhD, I can appreciate, too, the uses of cost/benefit analysis, with supply chains and production functions. But a humane liberal doesn't hesitate to face up to the ethical questions necessary to economics, and in a serious way. Some philosophers, I've noted, have called the result "bleeding-heart libertarianism." I took to calling it "motherly" or "Christian" (or Jewish or Hindu or Islamic or Buddhist) liberalism—or "sisterly true liberalism," or as I finally arrive here, a humane true and modern liberalism. It follows Smith's "allowing every man [and woman, dear Adam] to pursue his own interest in his own way, upon the liberal plan."

It is *humane*, acknowledging, as Smith and Mill did, a responsibility to the poor (that's the sisterly or humane side), but notes that making them into serfs of the government and its middle-class governors is not a good way of fulfilling the responsibility (that's the brotherly or tough-love side—but not necessarily *in*humane, as was, for example, the Trump-Sessions policy on immigrant children of Hispanics). At a conference in Barbados a while ago with many hundreds of self-described libertarians—think of it—I remarked to a man I had not formerly met, by way of expressing a sacred duty that we all acknowledged, "We must of course help the poor." He instantly shot back—it was like being punched in the stomach—"Only if they help me." I dunno. Scrub his toilets. Otherwise, get thee to the workhouse. "Are there no prisons?" asked Scrooge. The Barbados man's libertarianism was brotherly or fatherly. Remember Steve Chapman warning in libertarianism of "a selfish obsession with their own rights." Shape up, kid, or ship out.

But there is a motherly, or big-sisterly, or as I say "humane" version available, in which children are instructed at home and in college and on the job to be ethical humans in both the trading and the non-trading parts of their lives. We sisterly and humane liberals realize that we do the best job of helping the poor by making them un-poor—not by crippling them with drug wars ("Shape up, non-white kid, or go to prison"), or subordinating them at the welfare office, or making them clients of the politicians by giving them non-work government work, or making them get a government-issued license for hair braiding.

After all, the present *un*-poorness of most Americans and Europeans and now many others—their shocking prosperity by historical or international standards—has always come mainly not from redistribution or regulations or trade unions or other compulsions, but from a dynamic economy of people pretty much free to take this job and shove it. Classical liberalism partly freed Europe and its offshoots and imitators after 1800 from idiotic, poor-people-impoverishing supervision. Black Americans, for example, from World War I onward took their sharecropping jobs in a Klan-dominated South and shoved them, moving massively north to Chicago and New York. Consequently, with millions of such mutinies worldwide against being pushed around, the poorest of the poor worked for and benefited from the Great Enrichment.

In a modern, rich economy one can still have bad luck—Hurricane Katrina, for example, though the flimsy levees erected by the Army Corps of

Engineers were not exactly a matter of bad luck. You and I need to be taxed in such cases to help out. Gladly. But note that in Hurricane Katrina it was in fact private enterprise, such as Walmart and Home Depot, that helped people most.[1] The governmental agencies, from the New Orleans Police Department up to Brownie doing a heck of a job at FEMA, failed disgracefully. The New Orleans Police Department has a special medal worn by the police who in the crisis did *not* grossly violate their oaths of office and abandon the city.[2]

In such an economy as ours, which has attained by historical and international standards such shockingly high levels of real access to goods and services even for the relatively poor, a good deal of the relative misery of the poor comes from bad government policy, such as, I say again, the War on Drugs and its mass incarcerations wrecking the lives of the poorest of Blacks and Chicanos (both of whom in fact consume fewer drugs than their Anglo-white fellow citizens), or rent controls and building codes making very poor people unable to be housed. Homelessness is caused in part by governmental intervention in the housing market.[3]

And much of the rest of the misery comes from "bad choices," as people say. It's another reason, besides natural justice, that policy should not be enserfing, because the serfdom of too-long welfare leads to additional bad choices, a literal demoralization. As the British conservative philosopher Roger Scruton puts it, "Top-down government breeds irresponsible individuals, and confiscation of civil society by the government leads to a widespread refusal among the citizens to act for themselves."[4] It always has, inducing us to be passive. It's why the rich and ruling Romans provided bread and circuses to the poor of Rome and then Constantinople. When around 1800 such an enserfing hierarchy in northwestern Europe began to be relaxed slightly, ingenuity exploded. Government policy should let people be adult and responsible, by leaving them alone, so long as they are not using force or fraud to hurt other people. But then help out, too. Don't do help theater. Really help.

Such a humane liberalism is probably what most Americans really want, even on Election Day. Yet it's not much on offer. The progressive clerisy wants to interfere in economic and employment business, and the conservative clerisy wants to interfere in bedroom and foreign business. I believe they are merely confused, merely misled by false appeals to "help the poor" (when most non-military governmental expenditures, whether purchases or redistributions, go to middle-class people and their projects) or to "protect the nation" (when most military expenditures go to remote bases, and to another group of middle-class people and their projects). If the progressives and conservatives stopped to think it through, I am confident that they would speedily repent, and cease interfering in the lives of free adults who are not committing force or fraud. Surely. Humane liberalism combines free markets with free identity. It's the adult way, avoiding crushing people from above.

We modern liberals want to allow you to open a hairdressing salon without a professional license or a sewing-machine repair shop without a business license. In the United States nowadays some one thousand occupations are licensed by one or another government. That is, the occupations are monopolized, preventing the dis-favored people from offering cheaper or better goods and services to you. Effectively avoiding bad goods and services is usually best achieved, as I have said, by adult caution, and by competition in the market, and by the law of tort, and by shaming in a free press. Regulations constitute instead a pre-selection of plumbers and doctors favored by the government. The regulations are routinely justified by "safety." In practice they seldom keep safe the least advantaged, or much of anybody else except the existing license holders. They always monopolize. They always raise prices faced by the poorest. Consider long patents and longer copyright, and Jim Crow. Regulations have recently been getting worse, I've noted, drifting back toward practices of the medieval guilds. In the 1920s about 5 percent of the population worked at jobs requiring licenses. Now it's nearly a third. Jim Crow prevented Black barbers from cutting white people's hair.

Copyright in 1790 was 28 years, during the life of the author, 14 years after she died. Since 1998 and the Mickey Mouse Protection Act, it is after the death of a single author 70 years, and for a multi-authored work after the first date of copyright 120 years. The special problem of intellectual property is that it has no opportunity cost, and should in economic efficiency therefore be priced at zero. If you read *Hamlet* I am no less able to read it, too, considering that no one is still around to be dis-incentivized in writing the play by pricing it at zero. If you use a patent on a drug or a copyright on Mickey Mouse, I am no less able to use them, too, again assuming that at 70 or 120 years no one is around to be dis-incentivized to produce such good things. Ordinary property is on the contrary exclusive at every time scale—if one person uses it, another can't. Ordinary property therefore should be priced at its value in other uses. You can see why many modern liberal economists regard the present cry for protections of intellectual property as a government-sponsored scam to enrich the already rich, including the lawyers enriched by extending such "property." For shame!

In the bedroom, too, we modern liberals want you to be allowed to do what you harmlessly wish to do, and marry whomever you wish, or enter the bathroom of your gender choice. For a century from the 1880s to the 1980s in northern Europe and its offshoots such as the United States, the government at all levels exercised its police powers to interfere violently in consensual bedroom relations among adults. See the film *The Imitation Game*.[5] In France and Italy and Latin America, by contrast, homosexuality was never illegal. Sensible Latins.

Humane liberalism can be the basis for a new party, gathering up the ruined Republicans and the depressed Democrats. Call it the Liberal Democracy Party, taking the L-word back from our progressive friends. As the clear-minded curmudgeon of a century ago, the Baltimore journalist H. L. Mencken, said in 1926, "What democracy needs most of all is a party that will separate the good that is in it theoretically from the evils that beset it practically, and then try to erect that good into a workable system. What it needs beyond everything is a party of liberty."[6]

Maybe such a party could wean our fellow citizens from the conservative plan during the late nineteenth century of subordination of the working class, adopted later by New Liberals and Fabians in Britain and by Progressives in the United States, and then by New Deal Democrats and Clause Four Labourites. It is now embodied in the welfare state worldwide. As its inventor, the conservative Count Bismarck of Prussia and the German Empire, put it in a speech in 1889, "I will consider it a great advantage when we have 700,000 small pensioners [then nearly the entire poor male population over age sixty in the German Empire] drawing their annuities from the state, especially if they belong to those classes who otherwise do not have much to lose by an upheaval," for example, an upheaval against monarchy or in favor of the Social Democrats or against Bismarck's plans for a German-led peace in Europe.[7]

It's not going to be easy, such weaning, because the welfare state arose pretty much inevitably from mass voting—introduced in 1867 in Prussia (by Bismarck), in the same year in the United Kingdom (by Disraeli, another conservative), in 1848 in France, and decades earlier in the United States of America—as for example in the election of the populist Andrew Jackson in 1828. It led to the evils that beset democracy practically. The pattern High

Liberal, the American journalist Walter Lippmann, famously declared in 1914, in my view correctly, "To create a minimum standard of life below which no human being can fall is the most elementary duty of the democratic state."[8] But how to "create" it? By a humane liberalism that has in practice worked astonishingly well for the poor of the world, or by a regulatory socialism that has in practice repeatedly failed them?

Socialism, regulation, taxation, licensure, coercion, pushing people around are easy to understand, and are easy to sell with populist rhetoric to the less clued-in of a democratic electorate. Such systems of coercion are quicker than letting people make agreements with each other or letting them persuade each other. Coercion is the lawyer's as against the economist's proposal for governance. Pass a law today *requiring* such-and-such. That takes care of it, slam bang. Have a *program* favoring European-origin farmers in the southeast of the young United States, and violently remove the Cherokees, Choctaws, and others, leaving a demurring Supreme Court to protect the Native Americans, if it can. As Mencken on another occasion put it sardonically, "Democracy is the theory that the common people know what they want, and deserve to get it good and hard."[9] Or consult the French liberal Frédéric Bastiat in the turbulent year of 1848: "The government is the great fiction by which *everyone* endeavors to live at the expense of everyone else," as in Venezuela or Argentina or in revolutionary France.[10]

People have since the 1930s become used to the idea that every misfortune is the fault of the government for . . . well . . . not pushing people around enough. It's the standard rhetorical frame for a journalistic exposé of any misfortune. "Where on this unhappy occasion was our loving parent, the government?!" The Food and Drug Administration, with its effect later in suppressing the betterment of drugs, arose from Upton Sinclair's *The Jungle* (1906) and its exposé of tainted meat.[11] Watch what happens in the opioid epidemic—more proposals for more prohibitions enforced by the Drug Enforcement Agency, with more powers of coercion. (Well, maybe not this time: after all, the addicts in the present case are white and many of them middle class. Us.)

Virtue libertarianism? *Humane* liberalism? Yes. A flourishing society, and even its economic parts, needs ethics. That's what I learned from writing during the 2000s the three tomes of the Bourgeois Era. I slowly realized, against my economic training and my Chicago School microeconomics, that cash incentives are nice, but not enough. So-called neo-institutionalism in economics, by contrast, is a rehash of the incentive-mad policies of British Fabians or American Progressives, infantilizing adults. So too is "behavioral" economics, and its associated politics of governmental "nudging."[12] My friendly acquaintance the economist Robert Frank of Cornell tries to soften me up by telling me that the policy of nudging is "paternalistic libertarianism." Oh, Bob.

The ethical basis for a flourishing society, Ruger and Sorens say, and I agree, cannot be provided by an intrusive government. When governments like the East German Democratic Republic or government-like institutions such as the Catholic church in Ireland have attempted to teach ethics, they have failed ethically and practically. Progressive coercion in aid of a bright future, or conservative coercion in honor of a glorious past, have since 1789 blighted literally billions of lives. Loyalty to the Revolution and to king and country have had mainly hideous outcomes. Even nominally liberal societies such as our own American one or Britain's or post-apartheid South Africa's tend to rot when they leave ethical judgment to the government. It amounts to leaving ethics aside, because ethics is about free dispositions, not rules enforced by the government's coercion. Free will in ethics is one of the principles behind separation of church and state.

But when people hear the word "ethics" they think "preaching," and react as atheists do. Their reaction comes from a childish notion of ethical theory, such as "positive/normative" in the teaching of economics, or the Baltimore Catechism and the nuns to enforce it. (And, by the way, the New Atheists such as Richard Dawkins have also a childish notion of theology, much like their enemy Jerry Falwell had.) I would only ask my economist colleagues to become serious and grown-up about ethical theory and ethical practice. (And about theology, too; a modern liberal friend of mine told me that when he talked to Richard Dawkins, the fellow did not have a clue what "natural law" in the style of Aquinas meant. Why read Aquinas when Jerry Falwell is conveniently at hand?)

In the program of grown-up ethics, neither Kant nor Bentham nor Locke is a satisfactory guide. What works is the ancient, worldwide, and commonsensical theory of "virtue ethics." It is the sort Adam Smith advocated, namely, reflecting upon a handful of named and elemental virtues, each virtue, and the corresponding vice, backed by a library of books. (True, and against the practice of Professor Dawkins, you have to read the books. Irritating.) In Smith's case the virtues were four and a half—prudence, temperance, justice, and, with less approval, the fourth pagan and classical virtue, courage, and then the secular half of Christian love.

In St. Thomas Aquinas's case, and in that of the massive study of positive psychology, *Character Strengths and Virtues: A Handbook and Classification* (2004), edited by Christopher Peterson and Martin E. P. Seligman, the principal virtues are seven. The Elemental Seven in the West start with the classical "cardinal" or "pagan" four of courage, prudence, temperance, and justice. They then add the other three, the "theological" or "Christian" virtues of faith, hope, and love—that is, the virtues of having a project about the future, of having an identity about the past, and of imbuing the future and the past and the present with transcendence, such as Baseball or America or Science or God. The Western list is paralleled in every ethical tradition from Confucius to the *Mahabharata* and the coyote tales of Native Americans. Such virtues are "elemental" in the precise sense, thoroughly argued by Aquinas, that all the other virtues are made up from them, like molecules from physical elements. Honesty, for example, is justice and courage in speech, with a dash of temperance.

Stories open up an ethical kingdom, and a functioning economy. The (Sisterly Humane Real) Liberal Democracy Party would need to encourage, as Fred Smith of the Competitive Enterprise Institute urges, novels, poems, rock music, movies, country music that do more than attack yet again the wretched bourgeoisie—the class which in truth has enriched us all. Ideology matters. As the great Polish liberal economist Leszek Balcerowicz put it in 2017, "We should dedicate more attention to the influence of the *ideological* pressure groups whose members derive psychological benefits. . . . Contemporary attacks against economic freedom enjoy much support and legitimacy thanks to the statist orientation of mainstream economics, not to mention other social sciences."[13]

To put it another way, the ruling theory of humane liberalism should be, as the economist Bart Wilson and the economic Nobelist Vernon Smith put it, "humanomics," which is incentive economics plus human stories, both pursued with sophistication.[14] Humanomics doesn't give up on science. On the contrary, it yields the best scientific explanation of how we got rich, 1800 to the present, and how the whole world soon will, and it gives us, too, a reason to be good.

PART TWO

Humane Liberalism Enriches People

18. Liberty and Dignity Explain the Modern World

A little squib from a pamphlet with many other liberal authors edited by the estimable Tom G. Palmer, The Morality of Capitalism *(2011). The pamphlet has been translated into dozens of languages. Tom is a passionate and effective missionary for liberalism worldwide. His book* Realizing Freedom: Libertarian Theory, History, and Practice (2009) *is a bible of the movement.*

A change in how people honored markets and innovation caused the Industrial Revolution—and what is more significant a subsequent Great Enrichment, and then the modern world. The old conventional wisdom, by contrast, has no place for attitudes, and no place for liberal thought. The old materialist story says that the Industrial Revolution (at which it stops thinking) came from material causes, from investment or theft, from higher saving rates or from imperialism. You've heard it: "Europe is rich because of its empires"; "The United States was built on the backs of slaves"; "China is getting rich because of foreign trade."

But what if the Great Enrichment, 1800 to the present, was sparked instead by changes in the way people thought, and especially by how they thought about each other? Suppose steam engines and computers came from a new honor for innovators—not from piling brick on brick, or dead African on dead African?

Economists and historians are starting to recognize the big shift by around 1800 in how Westerners thought about commerce and innovation, and now the Chinese and Indians. People had to start accepting "creative destruction," the new idea that replaces the old. It's like music. A new band gets a new idea in rock music, and replaces the old if enough people freely adopt the new. If the old music is thought to be worse, it is "destroyed" by the creativity. In the same way, electric lights "destroyed" kerosene lamps, and computers "destroyed" typewriters. To our good.

The correct history goes like this: Until the Dutch (around 1600) or the English (around 1700) changed their thinking, you got honor in only two ways, by being a soldier or being a priest, in the castle or in the church. People who merely bought and sold things for a living, or innovated, were scorned as sinful cheaters, more or less worldwide, and especially in Europe. A jailer in the 1200s rejected a rich man's pleas for mercy: "Come, Master Arnaud Teisseire, you have wallowed in such opulence! . . . How could you be without sin?"[1]

In 1800 the average income per person per day all over the planet, I have noted, was, in present-day money, anything from $1 to $5. Call it an average of $3 a day. Sometimes $2. Imagine living in present-day Rio or Athens or Johannesburg on $2 or $3 a day. (Some people do, even now, but very few even now in most cities, the cities which nowadays contain half the world's population.) That's three-fourths of a cappuccino at Starbucks. It was and is appalling.

Then something changed, in Holland first and then in England. The revolutions and reformations of Europe, 1517 to 1789, gave voice to ordinary people as against the priests and aristocrats. Northwestern Europeans and in the long run many others came to admire bourgeois entrepreneurs like Ben Franklin and Andrew Carnegie and Nikola Tesla and Bill Gates. The middle class started to be viewed as good, and started to be allowed to do good, and to do well. People adopted "innovism"—a better word than the misleading "capitalism," to describe what happened 1700 or so to the present. People signed on to a Bourgeois Deal that has characterized now-wealthy places such as Britain and Sweden and Hong Kong ever since: "Let me innovate and make piles and piles of money in the short run, and in the long run I'll make *you* rich."

And that's what happened. Starting in the 1700s with Franklin's lightning rod and Watt's steam engine, and going mad in the 1800s, and still more mad in the 1900s and 2000s, the West, which for centuries had lagged behind China and Islam, became astoundingly innovative. Give the middle class— and the workers climbing up into it, and the workers themselves whether or not they climb—dignity and liberty for the first time in human history and here's what you get: the steam engine, the automatic textile loom, the assembly line, the symphony orchestra, the railway, the corporation, abolitionism, the steam printing press, cheap paper, wide literacy, the modern newspaper, cheap steel, cheap plate glass, the modern university, sewers, clean water, reinforced concrete, the women's movement, the electric light, the elevator, the automobile, petroleum, vacations in Yellowstone, plastics, a third of a million new English-language books a year, hybrid corn, penicillin, the airplane, clean urban air, civil rights, open-heart surgery, and the computer. The result was that, uniquely in history, the ordinary people, and especially the very poor, were made much, much better off. The Bourgeois Deal paid for it. The poorest 5 percent of Americans are now about as well off in air-conditioning and automobiles as the richest 5 percent of South Asians—though the South Asians are rising, too.

We're seeing the same shift play out in China and India, 40 percent of the world's population. The big economic story of our times is not the Great Recession of 2007–2009, unpleasant though it was. Now it's over. The big story is that the Chinese in 1978 and then the Indians in 1991 began to adopt liberal ideas in their economies, and came to welcome creative destruction. And it's far from over. Now their goods and services per person are quadrupling in every generation. In the numerous places that had long adopted bourgeois liberty and dignity, the average person makes and consumes over $100 a day, as against the $3 in the same dollars of recent purchasing power from which we all came. And the figure doesn't take full account of the radical improvement in the quality of many things, from electric lights to antibiotics to theories of economics. Young people in Japan and Norway and Italy are, conservatively measured (that is, without full corrections for quality), around thirty times better off in material circumstances than their great-great-great-great-great-grandparents. All the other leaps into the modern world—more democracy, the liberation of women, improved life expectancy, more education, more spiritual growth, more artistic explosion—depend on the Great Enrichment.

The Great Enrichment was so big, so unprecedented, that it's impossible to see it as coming out of routine causes, such as trade or exploitation or investment or imperialism. Economic science of an orthodox character is good at explaining routine. Yet all such routines had already occurred on a big scale in China and the Ottoman Empire, in Rome and South Asia. Slavery was common in the Middle East, trade was large in India, the investment in Chinese canals and Roman roads was immense. Yet no Great Enrichment happened.

Something must be deeply wrong, therefore, with explanations of the usual, material, economic sort. Depending on economic materialism to explain the modern world, whether left-wing historical materialism or right-wing orthodox economics, is mistaken.

Ideas of human dignity and liberty did the trick, making the inventions and then investments profitable for entrepreneurs and the nation. As the economic historian Joel Mokyr puts it, "economic change in all periods depends, more than most economists think, on what people believe."[2] It was ideas, "rhetoric," that caused our enrichment, and with it our modern riches and liberties.

19. China Shows What Economic Liberalism Can Do

A column from Reason *magazine, 2017.*

Let me tell you about my first trip to "Red" China in 2017, at Shanghai, and suggest a project to help our dear, dear statist friends get over their lamentable errors. Listen up, Senator Warren and Professor Stiglitz.

The Chinese character for "Shanghai" means "up [near the] ocean." But the original city is on the Huangpo River, a minor branch of the mighty Yangtze, about ten miles inland, and cannot nowadays directly dock the big ocean-going ships. No matter. Shanghai, about two-thirds up the east coast of China, has been since the 1800s the most open place in the country, forced open by Western governments establishing "concessions" in which Europeans lived and traded, out of reach of Chinese law.

The evening after I arrived, having settled into the modern hotel across from Fudan University, some of my students took me by Uber through the modern system of highways thronged with late-model cars to the Bund (rhymes with "fund"). It's the local, Persian-origin name for a promenade on a stretch of the river, on which the Europeans a century ago erected fifty or so buildings for banks, trading companies, and insurance, the very heart of pre-Communist capitalism in China. They are nice buildings, in 1920s Beaux Arts or Art Deco style, now illuminated at night. The reproduction of an old print I later bought at a poster store selling mainly old Communist Party items shows how the Bund looked in the 1920s, the river in front thronged with junks and the streets behind with rickshaws.

But what gobsmacked me as soon as we got out of the car was on the opposite side of the river, the Pudong district. Thirty years ago Pudong was farmland, wretchedly farmed because still collectivized. But then the local Communist Party officials decided to plat it and put in water and sewerage and some roads. The 1980s and especially the 1990s were the beginnings of local choice in commercially tested betterment under private enterprise—innovism—that has since raised Chinese real incomes by a factor of sixteen. A famous Hong Kong professor of my acquaintance had little trouble at the time persuading the officials *not* to erect in Pudong their own, government-financed version of the Bund. He persuaded them to let developers build on ninety-nine-year leases whatever they wanted, with private finance and profit-taking, doubtless with a little baksheesh on the side. The Communist Party officials were reading Milton Friedman. Literally.

The result has been literally hundreds of immense modern skyscrapers, dwarfing the proud European buildings of the Bund. The skyscrapers now stretch for miles back from the river, and are typically eighty stories high, festooned along the river with garish advertisements and corporate logos, like the loveliness of Times Square or Piccadilly, though gigantically larger. I was stunned by Pudong, and had to explain to the students what the American slang word "rube" means: a countryperson astonished that everything's up to date in Kansas City. In Shanghai I was the rube. When a colleague at the university arrived as a freshman in 1981 he said that there were two modern skyscrapers in the city, the Sheraton and the Hilton. Now there are two thousand—massive apartment blocks, office buildings, and dozens of hotels, few of which have any Western connection or financing. It's not the case that foreign investment financed the buildings. These were Chinese projects start to finish, and privately profitable.

Aside from the so-called French Concession, which looks like a little bit of Paris, Pudong and the rest of Shanghai are not beautiful, though the architectural standard is high. But the whole is immensely impressive, and filled with meaning.

What meaning would that be? This: Look at what can be built in two short generations if the government will but do its modest job competently, and for the rest leave people alone to profit themselves and to enrich the nation. Shanghai and in particular the Bund were the old center of 1920s economic modernity, and yet the ordinary Chinese at the time were the rickshaw drivers to the Europeans. Now in thirty years Shanghai and in particular Pudong have become the new center, and in a couple of generations the ordinary Chinese will be as well off as Europeans.

Our left-wing friends will object, "But the enrichment is not equal. The rich developers are disgraceful." Yet, John Rawls–style, even the poor—indeed, especially the poor—have been made startlingly better off. Wages are twice as high in Shanghai as in China's interior, inspiring the largest migration in human history, two hundred million people moving voluntarily, Robert Nozick–style, to the east coast to work in factories and to whiz around during the evening on electric scooters (for some reason without their headlights on). My Hong Kong professor friend, a teacher of the virtues of laissez-faire, says that he realized how courageous the migrants were in bettering their families when at midnight in a mainland city he saw the sparks of a welder high up on a skyscraper under construction, the man from Guizhou working, working through the night for the betterment of himself and his family. He was not a slave. He worked for wages. It was not a governmental enterprise, that usually reduces Chinese income, but a private owned building, that always raises it. It is not governmental compulsion by plan, but the liberal parts of China, which have brought its income per head to $30 a day per person from the Maoist $1 a day.

And in truth it is sinful of our gentle leftists to complain thus about inequality of outcome, or to suggest that it is the tyranny of the Communist Party that did the job, not the liberal part kindly permitted by the government. The growth of real wages at rates of 7 to 12 percent per year that came for three decades from private enterprise, and was only slowed by the persistence of state enterprise and crazy projects like high-speed rail, should in ethics overwhelm any envy concerning the baubles of the rich. After all, the complaint about end-state inequality, arising from the egalitarian thrust of European socialism after 1848, led to the disasters of world communism after 1917, as under Mao after 1949, or for that matter the experiments in national socialism down to the present. And the Middle Way of the welfare state is itself slowly breaking down. What made us rich was liberty, not helpful nudges and lovely industrial policies and wonderful protections enforced by the government's monopoly of coercion, on display in China in the hugely unprofitable governmental enterprises.

John Mueller of Ohio State wrote in 1999 a fine book called *Capitalism, Democracy, and Ralph's Pretty Good Grocery*. If you miss the little joke in the title, no wonder. It's taken from Garrison Keillor's somewhat obscure NPR radio show, *Prairie Home Companion*. In Keillor's imagined Lake Wobegon, Minnesota, Ralph's Pretty Good Grocery is in its advertising comically modest and Scandinavian ("If you can't find it at Ralph's, you probably don't need it"). Mueller reckons that commercially tested betterment and actual elections, as they imperfectly happen in places like Europe or its offshoots, and now India, and now (at least for the commercially tested parts, absent elections) in China, are pretty good. Commercially tested betterment, supported by an ideology of liberal innovism, is better than it is usually portrayed, and democracy is messier than it is usually portrayed. But for both, Mueller says, we would do well to leave well enough alone. The "failures" to reach perfection in, say, the behavior of Congress or the equality of the US distribution of income, Mueller reckons, are probably not large enough to matter all that much to the performance of the polity or the economy. They are good enough for Lake Wobegon. Venturing across Wobegon, with Senator Warren and Professor Stiglitz backseat driving, to buy instead at the Exact Perfection Store, staffed by lawyers and economic theorists—specialized in imagining failures in the polity or the economy without stopping to determine how important for the nation the failures in scientific truth are—leads to consequences we don't need.

Warren and Stiglitz and other sweet statists will say of Shanghai that The Government Did It. "Note," they will say, "all that platting and sewerage and road building." Their mistake is the Supply Chain Fallacy, in for example the historian Sven Beckert's fallacious claim that slavery was necessary for cotton and capitalism, or the economist Mariana Mazzucato's fallacious claim that if a scientist got a National Science Foundation Fellowship when she was a graduate student, then all her subsequent works can be attributed to the government.[1] As a prominent lawyer, professor, and politician put the Warren-Stiglitz-Beckert-Mazzucato claim some years ago, "You didn't build that." It's a legal way of thinking, not economic.

The economist points out that if in Pudong the private developers had not gotten sewerage or roads from the government, the developers would have built them without government help. Sometimes better. A Chicago architect friend of mine who has worked on such projects in both China and India tells me that self-building of roads and sewers is in fact what happens in India, whose local governments are corrupt and incompetent. Yet Indian real per capita income of poor people since 1991 has grown almost as fast as China's, and recently faster.

And, after all, Shanghai once had a *highly* interventionist government, certainly capable of doing the wonderful planning and correcting of market imperfections that our friends on the left dream of. But the Maoist government achieved nothing like the results that private development has produced in Pudong. If planning is such a fine thing, pre-1978 Communism would have been a paradise. Yet in fact when the Party adopted economic liberalism, and ceased killing growth by killing businesspeople, real income for the poorest started doubling every seven to ten years. India has the same story, after 1991, following forty-four wretched years of Gandhian socialism and egalitarianism resulting in poor-people-neglecting rates of growth—at which it would take seven decades, not one, to double.

Not all of what the Chinese government did after its tentative permitting of commercially tested betterment in 1978 has been a good idea. Fancy that: a government without a market test does unprofitable things, which reduce rather than raise income. Amazing. The Chinese government makes the same mistake as industrial policy does, with governmental "investments" in "infrastructure" projects that mainly glorify the politicians.

For example, as I mentioned, the Chinese system of high-speed trains, on which I have ridden, is a glorious governmental project, which now stretches through the entire immense country, all of the trains raised fifty feet on viaducts. Stunning. Glorious. But was it a good idea? China, still with an income per head despite its successes only one-fifth or one-fourth that of the United States, has more of such two-hundred-mph trains than the rest of the world combined. If the high-speed train half built between San Francisco and Los Angeles is idiotic, as are it and similar projects proposed by politicians who don't understand cost and benefit (actual headline: "Sen. Elizabeth Warren Backs High-Speed Rail Connecting Springfield, Worcester and Boston"), you are justified in worrying that government financing of such trains and heavy subsidies for their operation all over still-poor China is worse.[2] Like the TGV in France, the trains are nice for rich people, and are massively subsidized for their benefit. But such infrastructure (that magic word) reduces income for the rest of the nation.

What made China better off was not glorious infrastructure, and certainly not the wretchedly managed Chinese government enterprises, now busy under Xi buying up private firms, but its massive experiments in commercially tested betterment in private hands. The betterment was allowed by the Communist Party behaving itself moderately well since 1978 (for a change), at any rate in private economic matters, and at any rate by the wretched standard under Mao.

Here, then, is my program for our statist friends. (Will some true liberal billionaire such as Charles Koch please step forward to pay for the program?) Invite the most voluble of them, one by one, on an all-expenses-paid trip to the Bund in Shanghai. Stiglitz. Robert Reich. Bernie Sanders. Let the statist tourists look across to Pudong by night. Tell them how it happened. Turn back patiently their talk of inequality and the Supply Chain Fallacy. If they are not gobsmacked by what laissez-faire did in China, they are very, very hard to gobsmack. They won't believe their own lyin' eyes.

Well, let the remaining doubters go in peace. But publicize their stubbornness. Provide photographs. "Here is Professor Stiglitz staring at Pudong and claiming that it is a case of informational asymmetry." "Here is Senator Warren standing on the Bund marveling at what 81,640 pages of new regulations in the Federal Register yearly can accomplish."

But I predict that most of the subsidized tourists will convert on the spot to a humane and modern true liberalism.

20. Commercially Tested Betterment
Saves the Poor

A little essay from 2013 that appeared in Current History, *a British journal of popular history.*

Not, I should say at the outset, "capitalism." The word needs to be retired from historical and economic thinking, because it misleads people into believing that the modern world, in which the poor are ten to a hundred times better off than their ancestors, was initiated by the accumulation of *capital*. It wasn't. The idea of a blast furnace (a Chinese invention) or anesthesia (practiced in China for three thousand years), spectacles (this one European) or the computer (wholly Western) readily attracted investment. Ideas, not sheer investment, initiated economic change. It's like a mechanical watch. The gears are necessary, such as property rights and civil peace and, yes, investment. But the motive force is the spring, the ideas for betterment to be tested commercially. A society seeding a fourth of its grain, as in the European Middle Ages, had plenty of savings for the investment. But it didn't have the Great Enrichment because it didn't have the ideas flowing from a free people. Ideas, not savings, did it. Liberalism, not empire.

Declared Marx, adopting the investment obsession of the classical economists he was criticizing, "Accumulate, accumulate! That is Moses and the prophets." No. The Master got it wrong, as have most of the economists and their readers from the Blessed Adam Smith to the present. The great founder of sociology, Max Weber, for example, made the mistake. He imagined that the Protestant ethic encouraged hard work and high saving, instancing Benjamin Franklin. Weber didn't get the joke about Father Abraham and a penny saved (few have, actually). Franklin's special gift was *not* working hard—which hard work, after all, the peasant planting rice does daily. His gift was innovation, at a frenetic rate, for which he was honored and required no patents for—his stove, bifocals, battery, street lighting, postal sorting shelves, the lightning rod, the flexible catheter, the glass harmonica, a map of the Gulf Stream, and the theory of electricity.

What made us rich was not accumulation or exploitation, but Franklinian innovation—new ideas for blast furnaces, anesthesia, spectacles, computers, German universities, French reinforced concrete, Italian radios, British radar, American assembly lines. A new political liberty to have a go and a new social encouragement to take advantage of it, innovism, made us rich. In the century and a half before 1848 a great shift occurred, in what Tocqueville called "habits of the mind"—or more exactly, habits of the *lip*. People, especially American people, had long stopped sneering at market innovation and bourgeois virtues. Americans, Tocqueville observed, stood far from the traditional places of honor in the Basilica of St. Peter or the Palace of Versailles or the gory ground of the First Battle of Breitenfeld.

But wait. "*Bourgeois* virtues"? Yes. The phrase would not have startled a liberal up to 1848. Alessandro Manzoni's *I Promessi Sposi* (first version 1827; second 1842), the Italian *War and Peace,* devotes chapter 12 to explaining the dire consequences of interfering with the grain market, especially in a famine. Laissez-faire, laissez-passez. You could reprint the chapter for a lecture in Economics 101.

Yet *after* 1848 the Western clerisy of artists and intellectuals turned back to a hatred of commercially tested innovation and supply that had long characterized most societies. Confucians, for example, put the merchant, at least in theory, below the peasant and just above the night-soil man. And you know what Jesus of Nazareth said about camels, needles, and rich men. The hatred of commerce has persisted in some circles down to the present. Flaubert wrote, "I call bourgeois whoever thinks basely."[1] In 1935 the great liberal Dutch historian Johan Huizinga noted that anti-commercial remarks had become general among the clerisy of artists and intellectuals and other *bien pensant* folk.

"In the 19th century, 'bourgeois' became the most pejorative term of all, particularly in the mouths of socialists and artists, and later even of fascists."[2]

The bourgeois (which is merely the usual French and for a while the usual English word for the urban men of the middle class) were the innovators willing to subject their ideas to the democratic test of a market, and to supply Paris with grain and iron. The clerisy, on the other hand, especially since 1848, has cried, "Can't we do *better*?" No, only if we are free to imagine inconsistent structures—say, an innovative market in which diversely talented people participate, but with perfectly egalitarian incomes. The clerisy imagined in the nineteenth century nationalism, socialism, imperialism, and racism. Such theories resulted during the twentieth century in actually existing socialism and nationalism and national-socialist-racist imperialism, and the butcher bill for them all. In the late twentieth century the clerisy turned its hand to theorizing evil consumerism and environmental decay. Uh-oh. Watch out, dears, for fresh results in the twenty-first century.

From the novel *Madame Bovary* to the movie *Wall Street,* then, the fashion has been to indulge a hatred for the bourgeoisie. Yet, ironically, just when the hatred began, the commercially tested innovation and supply began to pay off spectacularly in northwestern Europe. Liberal innovism worked. And later the ordinary people in places like Japan and Botswana also experienced the Great Enrichment, a rise of incomes in real terms of thousands of percent over the misery of 1800. Unhappily, the acceleration in Western incomes in the nineteenth century came too late to short-circuit the socialist theories—except in the United States, about which the German economic historian Werner Sombart famously asked in 1906, "Why is there no socialism in the United States?" and answered, "All socialist utopias came to nothing on roast beef and apple pie."[3] The roast beef and apple pie soon became general, and by now, as the late Swedish professor of public health Hans Rosling showed in detail, are spreading to the poorest.

Yet the socialist utopia lives on. It keeps being tried, against the evidence. Youngsters in the United States, charmed by Bernie or Alexandria, say, "Let's try socialism," as though the dismal history of 1917 and 1933 and 1949 hadn't happened. And socialism lite hasn't worked so well, either, redistribution by trade union or by regulation or by expropriating the expropriators and other campaigns of the left. The Bismarckian tactic taken up by the right, of introducing the welfare state to steal the thunder of the socialists, has *not* been the way the poor have gotten better off. Imposing by act of

Congress a law of ten hours' pay for eight hours' work, say, would indeed raise the incomes of the portion of the working class that got it, at any rate in the first act, by 25 percent. Amazing. By a mere act of Congress, we can become enriched. It sounds like a grand idea, even if one time only, even if a gift of fey or elf. But 25 percent one time only, at the expense of still less productive workers thrown entirely out of work, the impoverishment that the left overlooks when it urges a higher minimum wage, is not of the same order of magnitude as the Great Enrichment, 1800 to the present—anywhere from 1,000 to 10,000 percent. The productivity of the economy in 1900 was very, very low, and in 1800 still lower. The only way that the bulk of the people, and the poorest among them, was going to be made better off was by making the economy much, much more productive. There's no outside Santa Claus, no feys or elves, to pay for higher and higher wages. As we oldsters learned in the 1950s from Walt Kelly's Pogo the Possum, "We has met the enemy [or in this case the friend], and he is us."

It happened. Radical creative destruction piled up ideas, such as the railways creatively destroying walking and stagecoaches, electricity creatively destroying lighting by kerosene and clothes-washing by hand, universities creatively destroying ignorance and prejudice. For the Great Enrichment—in the third act—one needed the Bourgeois Deal in the first, an innovistic ideology saying, "Let me, *une bourgeoise*, innovate with a test of profitability, and in the third act of the social drama I'll make you *all* rich." And she did.

The pro-bourgeois, anti-socialist United States exhibited the twentieth-century payoff. The liberal economist Tyler Cowen recently summarized the scientific evidence on the matter:

> We often forget how overwhelmingly positive the effects of economic growth have been. Economist Russ Roberts reports that he frequently polls journalists about how much economic growth there has been since the year 1900. According to Russ, the typical response is that the standard of living has gone up by around fifty percent. In reality, the U.S. standard of living has increased by a factor of five to seven, estimated conservatively, and probably much more. . . . In 1900, for instance, almost half of all U.S. households . . . had more than one occupant per room and almost one quarter . . . had over 3.5 persons per sleeping room. Slightly less than one quarter . . . of all

U.S. households had running water [mostly cold only], eighteen percent had refrigerators [that is, "iceboxes," literally], and twelve percent had gas or electric lighting [at low candlepower by modern standards]. Today, the figures for all of these stand at ninety-nine percent or higher. Back then, only five percent of households had telephones [with extremely expensive long distance rates], and none of them had radio or TV. The high school graduation rate was only about six percent, and most jobs were physically arduous and had high rates of disability or even death. In the mid-nineteenth century, a typical worker might have put in somewhere between 2,800 and 3,300 hours of work a year; the estimate is now closer to 1,400 to 2,000 a year.[4]

The spectacular cases in China and India over the last few decades, of beginning to catch up to such opulence, make much easier to credit the historical argument and its liberal causes, from the seventeenth-century Netherlands to the twentieth-century United States. A change in ideology—admiring the bourgeoisie instead of regulating or shooting it—has let China and India explode in sustenance for the poor. And the explosion is wider. The Great Recession of 2008 about which everyone yammers did not change the fact. World income per head is growing faster by an order of magnitude than at any time before 1800, or with few national exceptions before 1900 or 1950. Countries once miserably poor, such as Ireland and Norway, now have incomes per head for ordinary people a little below and a little above that of the glorious United States of America.

But what, it will be asked, about the ethical effect? For what shall it profit a man, if he shall gain the whole world, and lose his own soul? Certainly. Yet the economist and early practitioner of humanomics Albert Hirschman reminded us that "sweet commerce" is not the worst corruption of the human soul.[5] True, Benjamin Franklin was not a saint. He owned slaves, for example, surprisingly late, and he neglected and cheated on his wife and disinherited his son. But he did not achieve his wealth by ancient theft or modern coercion, as many aristocrats and some peasants in his time certainly did, and as the statist wishes us all to do now. He made deals. People often resent the dealers. But in the end they prefer them to thugs or thieves.

A colleague of Hirschman's at the Princeton Institute of Advanced Study, the political scientist Michael Walzer, was asked to respond to the question "Does the Free Market Corrode Moral Character?" He replied, "Of course it does." But then he noted that *any* social system in one way or another can corrode one or another of the virtues. That the bourgeois era has tempted fools to declare that greed is good "isn't itself an argument against the free market," Walzer writes. "Think about the ways that democratic politics also corrodes moral character. Competition for political power puts people under great pressure—to shout lies at public meetings, to make promises they can't keep."[6] Consider Trump and deep corrosion of the GOP. Or think about the ways socialism puts people under great pressure to commit the sins of envy or government-sponsored greed or environmental imprudence. Consider Stalin. Or think about the ways the alleged affective and altruistic relations of social reproduction in British colonial America before the alleged commercial revolution of the early nineteenth century put people under great pressure to obey their husbands in all things and to hang troublesome Quakers and Anabaptists. Consider the persecutors of Hester Prynne. That is to say, any social system, if it is not to dissolve into a war of all against all, needs ethics internalized by its participants, to leash its varied impulses to sin. "Capitalism" is no different.

What, you may ask then, is the future of this ill-named "capitalism"? Answer: world enrichment, in every sense—a rise of income from the $3 a day typical everywhere in 1800 to $130, as now in the United States, but also a spiritual enrichment, permitted by the education and leisure of $130 a day and beyond, with half as many hours in a working week and a quarter less working during a lifetime of education and retirement to earn it. And the spirit is not damaged by trying Monday through Friday to innovate and to supply in ways that make other people better off. Thank the Lord for the ideology of innovism, the Bourgeois Deal, the Great Enrichment, and the breakdown of hierarchy by the liberalism that caused them all.

21. Producing and Consuming a Lot Is Not by Itself Unethical

From The Bourgeois Virtues *(2006)*.

The clerisy of artists and journalists and college professors thinks that "capitalist" spending is just awful. In 1985 the historian Daniel Horowitz argued that the American clerisy have been since the 1920s in the grip of a "modern moralism" about spending. The traditional moralism of the nineteenth century looked with alarm from the middle class down onto the workers and immigrants drinking beer and obeying Irish priests and in other ways showing their "loss of virtue." Traditional moralists like the first US Commissioner of Labor, Carroll D. Wright, "had no basic reservations about the justice and efficacy of the economic system—their questions had to do with the values of workers and immigrants, not the value of capitalism." Horowitz notes that the later, modern moralist, post-1920, in the style of Veblen and Mencken and Sinclair Lewis, looks down from the clerisy onto the middle class itself. The middle class of course runs the economy. Therefore, "at the heart of most versions of modern moralism is a critique, sometimes radical and always adversarial, of the economy."[1] Horowitz is polite to his fellow members of the clerisy— Veblen, Stuart Chase, the Linds, Galbraith, Riesman, Marcuse, Lasch, and Daniel Bell—and does not say that their concerns were simply mistaken. Yet he does observe that "denouncing other people for their profligacy and lack of Culture is a way of reaffirming one's own commitment."[2]

The liberal Italian economist Sergio Ricossa (1927–2016) spoke in 1986 of a "seigneurial mindset" of the clerisy that considers market relationships as essentially debased and uncouth. As the historian of economics Alberto Mingardi explains:

> The seigneurial mindset informs what Ricossa calls "perfectionism" which is a set of doctrines that "preach a worldly kingdom of perfection, without the dominion of the economic side of life." What [a] "perfectionist"' from either the left or the right cannot stand is innovators multiplying goods and services available for all individuals, and people autonomously deciding whether they like them or not. . . . The seigneurial mindset finds consumers irrational. . . . "Imperfectionists," on the other hand, are happy to have the common people give it a go. They regard "perfection to be undesirable, even more than impossible, and the economic as only one among the sides of our life, not a part of demonology."[3]

Compare the modern liberal John Mueller's relaxed view of the imperfections of "capitalism" and democracy.

The seigneurial and perfectionist clerisy doesn't like the spending by hoi polloi, not one bit. It has been saying since Veblen that the many are in the grips of a tiny group of advertisers. So the spending on Coke and gas grills and automobiles is the result of hidden persuasion or, to use a favorite word of the clerisy, "manipulation." To an economist the peculiarly American attribution of gigantic power to thirty-second television spots is puzzling. If advertising had the powers attributed to it by the American clerisy, then unlimited fortunes could be had for the writing. Yet advertising is less than 2 percent of national product, much of it non-controversially informative—such as shop signs and websites or ads in trade magazines aimed at highly sophisticated buyers. When Vance Packard published his attack on advertising, *The Hidden Persuaders* (1957), he thought he would lose his friends on Madison Avenue. But most were delighted. A friend would say something like, "Vance, before your book I was having a hard time convincing my clients that advertising worked. Now they think it's magic."[4]

The American clerisy's hostility to advertising is puzzling also to a rhetorician. It's puzzling why a country so officially adoring of free speech would in its higher intellectual circles have such a distaste for *commercial* free speech. Perhaps the distaste is merely a branch of that great river delta of anti-rhetoric rhetoric in the West since Petrus Ramus and Frances Bacon five centuries ago. Yet the TV generation, and now the blog generation, is rhetorically sophisticated about commercial free speech, and therefore immunized. Children can spot the manipulation by age eight. By age eighteen it is routine in their humor—see *Saturday Night Live.*

Mass consumption is supposed to be motiveless, gormless, stupid. And anyway there's too damned much of it. The modern moralist looks down on consumers. Why do they buy so much *stuff*? The dolts. The common consumer does not own a *single* recording of seventeenth-century music by Musica Antiqua Köln. It has been *ages,* if ever, that she has read a nonfiction book about the Bourgeois Deal. Her house is jammed with tasteless rubbish. And so forth. One is reminded of the disdain around 1920 on the part of modernist litterateurs like D. H. Lawrence and Virginia Woolf for the nasty little commuters of London. An air of vulgarity hangs about Waterloo Station and the Mall of America.

But we make ourselves with consumption, as anthropologists have long observed. Mary Douglas and Baron Isherwood put it so: "Goods that minister to physical needs—food and drink—are no less carriers of meaning than ballet or poetry. Let us put an end to the widespread and misleading distinction between goods that sustain life and health and others that service the mind and heart—spiritual goods."[5] The classic demonstration is Douglas's article on the symbolic structure of the working-class meal in England, but in a sense all of anthropology is in this business.[6] Goods wander across the border between the sacred and the profane. The anthropologist Richard Chalfen shows it with home movies and snapshots.[7] Or as the anthropologist Marshall Sahlins puts it in the new preface to his classic of 1972, *Stone Age Economics,* "economic activity . . . [is] the expression, in a material register, of the values and relations of a particular form of life."[8]

The amount of American *stuff* nowadays is to be sure formidable. A standard photographic ploy is to get a family in Topeka, Kansas, and one in Lagos, Nigeria, to dump the entire contents of their houses out on the front sidewalk, and then pose for the camera *en famille* and *en stuff.* The contrast is remarkable. No wonder every town in America has a vibrant business in garage-sized storage lockers, where you can deposit your excess stuff.

One cause of the piles in the United States is what you might call a Consumer's Curse. Our houses, or storage lockers, are filled with our *mistaken* consumption, items that turned out not to be as delightful as we thought they were going to be. As the theologian David Klemm puts it, following Heidegger, "We understand things in their *potentiality* to be."[9] Men, think of your gadgets; women, your clothing. Even the relatively poor in the United States have closets full of such stuff.

But the full closets are not because we are stupid or sinful. Full closets arise because we produce astonishingly large amounts of stuff. Not being omniscient, we make mistakes in consuming from time to time about the delight-generating potential of a $250 electrostatic dust remover from the Sharper Image. (Look at that trade name for its "manipulative" power, by the way; and yet in 2008 it went bankrupt.) So occasionally we buy things that turn out to be not worth the price. When we mistake in the other direction we do not buy, and wait for the dust removers to come down in price. The occasions of optimism mount up, because there is no point in throwing away the stuff if you have the room—and Americans have the room, in the two-car garage if the attic is full, and at last the storage locker on the edge of town.

The Japanese have a similar Problem of Stuff, being also vastly more productive than their ancestors. But they have a different solution to excess consumption. The writer Steve Bailey tells how he furnished his house in Osaka when he was teaching there by collecting *gomi*, "oversized household junk," that the Japanese would leave on the street for collection every month. It was full furnishings: "refrigerators, gas rings, a stand-up mirror, a color television, a VCR, chairs, a bookshelf, a corner couch, and a beautiful table."[10] The shameless foreigners, the *gaijin*, competed with low-status Japanese junk men in raiding the *gomi* piles. The cause in Japan, Bailey explains, is the small size of the houses and the sacred taboo against getting or giving secondhand furniture.

As I said, the Americans and the Japanese have a great deal to pile up because they produce a great deal. Contrary to your grandmother's dictum— "Eat your spinach: think of the starving children in China"—consuming less in rich America or Japan would add little or nothing to the goods available in China. Countries are rich or poor, have a great deal to consume or very little, mainly because they work well or badly, not because some outsider is adding to or stealing from a God-given endowment. Goods do not come down from somewhere else, like manna. We make them. Of course.

Therefore, having a lot is not immoral. It is the good luck to be born in America or Japan or Denmark. The "luck" consists chiefly of a modern liberal ideology of innovism combined with reasonably honest courts and reasonably secure property rights and reasonably non-extractive governments and reasonably effective educational systems, and a reasonably long time for the reasonably good ideas, and especially the innovations, to do their work.

By all means let's spread the good luck around—by persuading people to a modern liberalism leading to the Great Enrichment, and a full life.

22. Trickle Up or Trickle Down Is Not How the Economy Works

The anti-Keynesian argument here is again from The Bourgeois Virtues, *with a version in White, ed. 2010. But I've been making the argument since 1970, as have many economists trained originally in Keynesianism but coming to doubt its relevance for anything but a short run of mass unemployment. The doubters are labeled "supply siders." I call them "economists with common sense."*

Yet every non-economist thinks that the great consumption at least "keeps the economy going." The critic of spending will acknowledge knowingly that "the economy" somehow benefits. The theologian Ellen Charry, to give one example among thousands, believes that advertising keeps the economy growing.[1] Non-economists imagine that God has so poorly designed the world that a lack of thrift tending to foolishness and avarice is, unhappily, necessary to keep the wheels of commerce turning, "creating jobs" or "keeping the money circulating." They imagine that people must buy, buy, buy or else "capitalism" will collapse and we all will be impoverished. They believe that advertising is necessary for the buy, buy, buy, though it corrupts. They believe that "capitalism" must be greedy, in the sense of prudence without the balancing virtues of love or justice or temperance, to keep on working.

It's the alleged Paradox of Thrift. Thriftiness—a Good Thing in Christianity and most certainly in Buddhism and the rest—seems able paradoxically to impoverish us. We will do poorly by doing good. And if we do well, we're probably damned by the sins of greed and gluttony necessary to do so.

Choose, ye sinners: God or Mammon. Dorothy Sayers, who was more than a writer of mysteries, though not an economist, complained in 1942 as a Christian about "the appalling squirrel cage . . . in which we have been madly turning for the last three centuries [note the erroneous supposition that luxury is new] . . . a society in which consumption has to be artificially stimulated in order to keep production going."[2]

It is economic nonsense. Many economists in the era of the Great Depression of the 1930s, and principally John Maynard Keynes, had reverted to such a non-economist's way of thinking, and we heard echoes of it in the reaction to the Great Recession of 2008, too. The theory is related to the claim that betterment has been exhausted, so-called "stagnationism," another fancy of the 1930s revived after 2008. It is a balloon theory of the economy, namely that people must keep puff-puffing or the balloon will collapse. It's one version of the old claim that expenditure on luxuries at least employs workpeople. Thus Alexander Pope, in a poem of 1731 subtitled "Of the Use of Riches": "Yet hence the poor are clothed, the hungry fed; / Health to himself, and to his infants bread / The laborer bears: what his [the rich man's] hard heart denies, / His charitable vanity supplies."[3] "Providence is justified in giving wealth to be squandered in this manner," Pope writes in the poem's Argument, "since it is dispersed to the poor and laborious part of mankind."

Since the 1940s most of us bourgeois economists have recovered our senses.[4] The old balloon theory has popped, and with it the paradox that sin is necessary to "keep production going," and the false paradox that vanity can in the end be charitable. It survives in Marxian critiques of the Adorno-Horkheimer type, but it is no longer believed by economists of the center, and certainly not by modern true liberals.

Nothing would befall the market economy in the long run, says the modern liberal economist, if we tempered our desires to a thrifty style of life, one beat-up Volvo and a little house with a vegetable garden, and a moderate amount of tofu and jug wine from the co-op. The balloon theory sounds plausible if you focus on an irrelevant mental experiment, namely, that tomorrow, suddenly, without warning, we would all begin to follow Jesus in what we buy. Such a conversion would doubtless be a shock to sales of Rolls-Royces and designer dresses at $15,000 a pop. But, the economist observes, people in a Christian economy would at length find other employment, or choose more leisure, which itself should be accounted as income.

That's the relevant mental experiment: the long run. In the new, luxury-less economy it would still be a fine thing to have lightbulbs and paved roads and other fruits of enterprise. More of these would still be better than less. "In equilibrium"—a phrase with resonance in bourgeois economics similar to "God willing" in Abrahamic religions—the economy would encourage specialization to satisfy human desires in much the same way as it does now. People would buy bibles in Koine Greek and spirit-enhancing trips to Yosemite instead of buying Harlequin romances and package tours to Disney World. But they would still value high-speed presses for the books and airplanes for the trips, getting more books and more trips for the opportunity cost.

Non-economists think that economics is about "keeping the money circulating." And so they are impressed by the claim by the owner of the local sports franchise that devoting tax dollars to a new stadium will "generate" local sales and "create" new jobs. To a non-economist the vocabulary of generating and creating jobs out of unthrifty behavior sounds tough and prudential and quantitative. It's not. It's stupid. No economist of sense would use such locutions. Indeed, you can pretty much depend on it that an alleged economist on TV is a phony if she talks of "generating" or "creating" jobs.

Even Adam Smith argued at one point that imagining the pleasure of wealth deceives us into labor. Admittedly the hope that our latest purchase will bring true happiness is a common enough imagining, by guys in Brookstone and by gals in the kitchen-equipment store. Smith notes that "what pleases these lovers of toys is not so much the utility, as the aptness of the machines which are fitted to promote it. All their pockets are stuffed with little conveniences."[5] We are in fact often deceived into laboring to get such "trinkets of frivolous utility." But the mistake is to think, as Smith says he does, that the deception is desirable: "And it is well that nature imposes upon us in this manner. It is this deception which rouses and keeps in continual motion the industry of mankind."[6] Smith is articulating the paradox of thrift in a jazzed-up version. Homer nods.

Such lack of thrift does indeed prompt us "to invent and improve all the sciences and arts" relevant to the particular item of luxury we lust for. What is correct about the argument is David Hume's "taking delight in praise" and the Iowa and Chicago economist Frank Knight's point that possession is not a "final interest." The social impulses, even dubious ones, do prompt us to invent and improve and to turn "rude forests of nature into agreeable and fertile plains"—an unmarked quotation, Smith's editor's note, from Rousseau's "les vastes forêts se changèrent en des campagnes riantes," though in Rousseau having a very different conclusion: "which had to be watered with men's sweat, and in which slavery and misery were soon to germinate and grow with the crops."[7] Smith devoted his life to refuting Rousseau's conclusion.

But as sheer industry, nothing is gained. It's the balloon theory again, the confusion of "continual motion" with *desirable* motion, directed just *this* way. The central error of Keynesianism is to say, "Don't just stand there: *do* something, *anything*." Pouring expenditure helter-skelter into an economy will not be directed in ways that are productive. Building bridges as an employment program will yield bridges to nowhere. It is not in itself good to be set to work raising the Great Wall of China, inventing and improving the science and art of great-wall making, when you could be getting on with your directed life, improving the science and art of making houses and automobiles, universities and museums.

Smith's mistake is what is known among older economists as the "Tang" fallacy, which is not about the Chinese dynasty but about the horrible powdered orange juice of that name, which was asserted in its advertising to be a spin-off of the American space program. The fallacy is to think that we would have missed out on priceless betterings such as Tang if we had left the money in the hands of ordinary people instead of throwing it away on moon shots. It is the central economic error, along with numerous lesser ones, of Mariana Mazzucato's praise for the "entrepreneurial state." "Job creation" through this or that unprofitable project—the Great Belt in Denmark adding a glorious bridge to a perfectly adequate tunnel connecting the main island with the Continent, or the tunnel under many kilometers of "The Heart of Holland" burying a high-speed railway—is not the optimal working of a market economy, but more like its opposite. After all, notably poor economies commonly have plenty of jobs. Unemployment was not the problem faced by the slaves in the silver mines of Attica or in the quarries of Syracuse. Our leaders, such as the Chinese Communist Party with its illiberal projects of high-speed rail and unprofitable state-owned enterprises, buy their power and prestige with our money. They "create jobs" that shouldn't have been, and that make us poorer, not richer.

The Dutch-English doctor and political rhymester Bernard Mandeville articulated the mistaken supposition in 1705: "Vast numbers thronged the fruitful hive; / Yet those vast numbers made them thrive. / Millions endeavoring to supply / Each other's lust and vanity. . . . / Thus every part was full of vice, / Yet the whole mass a paradise."[8] Mandeville's claim is that vice, vanity, folly, greed, and gluttony are the watch springs of economic growth. The force of sin creates, unintendedly, a rich and vital society.

Mandeville's insight into unintended consequences was important. But the particular consequence he imagined is nonsense. His economics was mistaken, though ever since it has been a comfort to the trickle-down, I've-got-mine school of political ethics. He was answered at the time by one George Blewhitt, the author of a pamphlet against the 1723 edition of Mandeville's book. Mandeville had argued that universal honesty would put locksmiths out of work and therefore would damage prosperity. Better for the hive to be dishonest. Blewhitt replied, "The change [to an honest way of life] must necessarily be supposed to be *gradual*; and then it will appear still plainer that there would arise a succession of new trades . . . in proportion as the trades in providing against roguery grew useless and wore off."[9] Spot on.

Adam Smith loathed Mandeville's embrace of vice. "Such is the system of Dr. Mandeville," wrote Smith in 1759 with palpable irritation, "which once made so much noise in the world, and which, though, perhaps, it never gave occasion to more vice than would have been without it, at least taught that vice, which arose from other causes, to appear with more effrontery, and to avow the corruption of its motives with a profligate audaciousness which had never been heard of before."[10] Trump, anyone? Smith did *not* say, ever, that greed is good. The men in the Adam Smith ties need to do a little reading of *The Nature and Causes of the Wealth of Nations* and especially of *The Theory of Moral Sentiments* on the train to Westport. The Christian and other opponents of the sin of avarice need to stop conceding the point to the men of Westport. There is no paradox of thrift, not in a properly Christian world, nor even in the fallen world we lamentably inhabit.

It's good news for ethical people. We don't need to accept avaricious production or vulgar consumerism or unloving work-obsession or glorious projects of political make-work on account of some wider social prudence they are supposed to serve, allegedly keeping us employed. "Keeping us employed." Have you ever in your *private, homely* activities, doing the laundry or planting the garden, seen your main problem as *finding jobs* at which to be employed? Isn't the main problem the opposite one, a scarcity of hours in which to bake the bread or fix the car or play with the kids or nurture friend-ships or sing praises unto the Lord thy God? If you agree, then you grasp the great economic principle that, as Adam Smith put it, "What is prudence in the conduct of every private family, can scarce be folly in that of a great kingdom."[11] And you will grasp why it is *not* economic prudence to "keep us all at work" by spending on luxuries and working, working, working.

23. The Liberal Idea, in Short, Made the Modern World

In 2016 I was interviewed for an article in The Indigo Era.

THE INDIGO ERA: Your recent book *Bourgeois Equality: How Ideas, Not Capital or Institutions, Enriched the World* (2016) focuses on the role of ideas, in particular, how we must focus on people, rather than technological innovations. Why do you place people at the center of your argument?

MCCLOSKEY: Not "rather than technological innovation." I think you're mixing up—as non-economists (and some misled economists) do—real, novel "innovation" with mere replacement of men by machines already long invented. On the contrary, I strongly emphasize technological innovation, which I call "commercially tested betterment," the result of the new ideology out of liberalism c. 1800, of "innovism." The contrast is with sheer accumulation, without betterment, brick on brick, or "good institutions" without betterment, such as the English common law—institutions which did not change much at the time and were often obstacles to innovation.

What misleads us about capital, such as buildings, or institutions, such as courts of law, is that they are easy to see. We are inclined to suppose therefore that they are what makes for riches. Build a castle; open a law court. Problem solved. But we need to inquire deeper, to ask what idea for a build-

First published as "Freedom and the Great Enrichment," *Global Perspectives*, vol. 1: *The Indigo Era* (September 2016).

ing inspired it, and what idea of ethics sustains the court of law. The ideas are the watch springs; the capital and institutions are the gears.

But, yes, people. It is people, after all, who devise the betterments, out of their imaginations. After 1800 their imaginations were fired by liberalism, that is, by a new if imperfect equality before the law and a new if imperfect equality of dignity in society. To get a great mass of commercially tested betterments, and the consequent Great Enrichment, northwestern Europe in the 1600s and 1700s and later needed to develop a mass of liberated people, inspired to innovate as never before. It did.

THE INDIGO ERA: You have written about how people in the poorest parts of the world will in time be as rich as those in the richest part of the world. How will this happen? What are the forces that will drive it?

McCLOSKEY: The forces that will drive the whole world to become rich are temperate self-interest and temperate governance. As Adam Smith put it in 1755, "Little else is requisite to carry a state to the highest degree of opulence from the lowest barbarism, but peace, easy taxes, and a tolerable administration of justice; all the rest being brought about by the natural course of things. All governments which thwart this natural course, which force things into another channel, or which endeavor to arrest the progress of society at a particular point, are unnatural, and to support themselves are obliged to be oppressive and tyrannical."[1] Surely there can be no *racial* reason—as we have come to understand after the scientific fall of eugenics—to go on supposing that sub-Saharan Africa or Latin America or the Middle East must forever be poorer than Europe or the Anglosphere.

THE INDIGO ERA: What do you mean by "ideas about betterment"? How will this shape the future global economy?

McCLOSKEY: In 1681 some French businessmen were asked by the French centralizer Colbert what the government could do for them. They replied, "*Laissez-nous faire,*" leave us to do it, which is to say, leave us alone to achieve Smith's "natural course of things." It was a new idea, developing into liberalism. By the late nineteenth century, though, the oxymoronic New Liberals very much did *not* want to leave people alone. They proposed to make citizens into children to be taken care of by the wise folk of the clerisy in government armed with a monopoly of coercion. What was actually happening in the economy meanwhile, when oppressive and tyrannical policies were not able to stop it, was the application of the new, true liberal idea, especially after 1800, to more and more countries, an ideology of innovism making ordinary people bold, and therefore fantastically creative. It caused a cascading multitude of ideas for machines and institutions.

Pessimism about growth has recently come back, but it will soon be seen to be false yet again, for something like the sixth time since 1800. The multitude of commercially testing betterers outside of Old Europe or the Old Anglosphere, as in Brazil, will bring the poorest among us to the highest degree of opulence.

THE INDIGO ERA: How will the "Great Enrichment" idea that has enriched our lives since the 1800s apply to the next two centuries?

MCCLOSKEY: In the next century, or more probably if we do not wreck it with nationalism and socialism the next fifty years, we will see South America, Africa, and the rest join in the Bourgeois Deal. I argue in my books that the new ideology of the Bourgeois Deal was "Let me earn profits from a commercially tested betterment—sign on to liberalism and its innovism—and I will make *you* rich." The enrichment will cause, and be caused by, a cultural explosion, casting into the shade the achievements of fifth-century Athenian drama and T'ang poetry and Renaissance painting.

THE INDIGO ERA: Do you think change in the world is accelerating? If so, do you believe that humanity will benefit from this increased pace of change, and why?

MCCLOSKEY: Yes, growth is definitely accelerating. Take world, real, inflation-corrected GDP per person, a pretty good measure of the goods and services available to humans. It has leapt up in the past few decades, and (with bumps from recessions) is growing at the fastest pace in world history. Having a decent little house and enough food and reasonable education for one's children—what Hans Rosling classified as the third of four levels—is a gigantic improvement over the miseries of 1800, or of 1900, or even of 1960.[2] I readily admit that GDP isn't everything. But to sneer at it, and to constrain growth carelessly in aid of redistribution or environmentalism or anticonsumerism, is to condemn the wretched of the earth to perpetual wretchedness. Latin America has suffered in this way since 1950 and the reign of the economic nationalism of the gravely misled economist Raúl Prebisch. The policy satisfies the egos of a proud clerisy of theorists advising governments, but it is unethical. The wretched urgently need thirty times higher real GDP per capita—which is what the Great Enrichment gave the formerly wretched of the now-rich places.

THE INDIGO ERA: Technology appears to be concentrating wealth, or at least entrepreneurial wealth, in the hands of fewer rather than more individuals. How will your Great Enrichment survive this trend?

McCLOSKEY: Concentration of wealth is not a trend, not in a way that matters, despite what you've heard. "Wealth" as defined in the newspapers is paper stocks and bonds, which are claims on physical assets such as factories or land or machines. But its distribution, which even on the measure in the newspaper was less equal in 1900 than it is now, and much less equal in 1800, is not the relevant story. *Human* capital has become in the past 150 years a much more important source of earnings. Earnings are the sum of returns on the total of physical *and human* capital. Human capital is of course much more equally distributed than ownership of factories or ships. We own ourselves, even if we are poor in stocks and bonds. Focusing on financial wealth is therefore misleading.

And out of the income the world consumes. Consumption in turn is much more equally distributed than income, not to speak of financial wealth. That you have sixty pairs of pants in your closet is lovely for you. But it is not a gigantic improvement over having three pairs, washable with newly invented detergents in newly invented washing machines for hire in a newly invented institution of free enterprise, the laundromat. (Rosling spoke of the Washing Line, the moderate per capita income of about $50 or $70 per head per day at which the women are freed from hand washing of clothes.)

And most importantly, what one might call *basic* consumption out of the total consumption—the modest housing, food, and education for a dignified human life—is much more equally distributed than total consumption or income or capital or financial wealth, even in now-rich countries, than it was in 1960, not to speak of in 1800. That is, the *important* equality has increased, not decreased, even recently.

In 1960 we needed to worry about the four billion people out of five billion on the planet who were at the miserable bottom. It would have been silly then to worry about how many bejeweled watches the vulgar rich had. By now the miserable bottom has fallen to one billion out of today's over seven billion.[3] The world is much more equal than it was, if measured in ethically relevant terms—basic consumption, rather than the irritating excesses of the top 1 percent. The bejeweled watches go on. But taking them from the rich would no more solve the problems of the bottom billion now than it would have in 1960. Foreign aid, or hanging the bankers from lampposts, or imposing confiscatory taxes on bejeweled-watch owners, won't do it. The statistics show that redistribution doesn't work permanently. Economic growth does.

To go on chattering about concentrated financial wealth when it's mainly not happening (and when it does in undesirable ways it has more to do with mistaken housing policy or big subsidies to free higher education than inheritance), and when it reverses because of entrepreneurial entry (Uber, for example), and when it is not the sort of inequality that actually matters—which is basic consumption for a dignified life—is to stir up in Trumpian or Corbynite fashion an insatiable envy and anger. The stirring up has had political results in the populism that we see now worldwide.

THE INDIGO ERA: The cultural factors which you argue are at the heart of the Great Enrichment would appear to benefit a limited number of countries at the expense of others. They have greater liberty and better education. How will the developing world, with less liberty, poor governance, and limited education, compete?

MCCLOSKEY: The crux in dealing with poverty is not exactly "cultural factors," but the parts called rhetoric and ideology. Most economists believe, erroneously, that culture is given and fixed in the short run and even in the long. But rhetoric, ideology, policies can change, quickly. If continuing to be badly governed—that is, if the rhetoric does not change—the developing world will not do well. If well governed by the modest standards articulated by Smith, it will grow rapidly, and get the education it needs. Innovism.

The cry for more education, by the way, is often a despairing excuse for not liberalizing the economy directly and quickly. I have seen it in South Africa. Blacks there do poorly, because they are excluded from employment by the labor law installed after 1994. It amounts to a progressive version of apartheid. The left then calls not for relaxation of the crippling labor laws that make it unprofitable, even dangerous, to hire poor people, but for more education, to make the poor worth hiring at the high minimum wage. The policy is cruelly back to front. If poor people had jobs they would soon enough see to the education of their children. Meanwhile they could get basic consumption by selling food on the street or working at a steady job in a factory. They did so in Singapore and Botswana and South Korea. They could in South Africa, too, if the progressives would relent. The worst form of government is to cripple the economy by bossing poor people around under orders from Washington or Pretoria.

Inability to "compete," though, is not the correct word to describe the problem. Trade is not a football game. The world is not zero-sum. France's prosperity does not damage Chad's. The correct word is "poverty." China and India grow at over 7 percent per year per capita. Brazil and South Africa are lucky to achieve 2 percent. Why? Because China and India have adopted a liberal theory of economic policy, an ideology of innovism that makes for growth—"liberal," at any rate, by the standard of their earlier, slow-growth régimes. Brazil and South Africa cling to illiberal theories, such as governmental capital accumulation, exports as growth, and coerced import substitution. Such lagging countries can change, quickly, if they will adopt real liberalism and innovism. How do I know? Because the successful countries since the Netherlands in the seventeenth century have. Every one.

THE INDIGO ERA: Are we wrong to place an importance on the role of institutions—like the law and government—[in] driving growth and providing a solid infrastructure for economic growth? If so, why?

McCLOSKEY: Yes, it is wrong to think of institutions as the key to prosperity. Good laws and honesty are fine things. But they are normally the result, not the cause, of growth. Chicago in 1880 had wretched enforcement of laws and a stunning level of corruption. Every law was for sale, along with every judge and every policeman. And yet Chicago was then the fastest growing city in the world, like Shanghai nowadays.

And "law and government" are in most cases oppressive and tyrannical, in the numerous countries lacking a Scandinavian standard of righteousness in governing. Neo-institutionalism—the orthodoxy nowadays at the World Bank, I have noted—fails as badly as did its earlier orthodoxy, the one that William Easterly calls "capital fundamentalism."[4] The World Bank's present-day formula of "add new legal institutions, and stir" works no better than did its old "add dams and roads, and stir."

We do not need at the outset a perfect government. Perfect government is unattainable, and anyway unnecessary for a free economy. We do not need more guardians. What we need, comprehensively, is liberty, allowing every person to pursue her own interest in her own fashion, constrained by a small government preventing some of the force and fraud but leaving most of the prevention to newspapers and courts of law and, especially, competition in the marketplace. To be sure, growth can't get going in the middle of a civil war. But beyond the establishment of peace, easy taxes, and a tolerable administration of justice, we do *not* need masses of police and civil servants guarding us. Or stealing from us.

THE INDIGO ERA: What are the most important factors that we need to consider for the economies of cities and countries to be strong, robust, and adaptable over the next century?

McCLOSKEY: As the theorist of vibrant cities, Jane Jacobs, said in all her work, what we do *not* need is arrogant architects such as Le Corbusier or high-handed commissioners such as Robert Moses "planning" our cities. "Germane correction," she wrote in 1984, "depends on fostering creativity in whatever forms it happens to appear in a given city at a given time. It is impossible to know in advance."[5] A motto to live by.

THE INDIGO ERA: Do you think that traditional economics is too quick to overlook the importance of culture and ideas? If so, why?

McCLOSKEY: Yes and no. Economists, astonishingly, consign culture to the background, because they do not want to bother to learn the humanistic disciplines needed to understand it. But they need urgently to learn the ideas, ideologies, rhetoric of a free society. The allegedly static background can in fact change extremely rapidly, and can have massive economic effects—thus for example communism as an idea in October 1917. Or, more cheerfully, liberalism as an idea in July 1776.

The economists identify such changeable ideas with the word "culture," which they then declare is unchangeable, without looking into the historical evidence. The economist's theory, considered coldly, is racist. Back in the 1960s we used to think that, say, India could never be rich, because after all most of the Indians were Hindus. The economist Oliver Williamson, for example, claims that norms change "on the order of centuries."[6] That would be convenient for Williamson's purpose in all his work of ignoring the norms. But it is historical nonsense. The norms often change quickly and dramatically, as for example when Romans became Christians, or north Germans became Protestants, or, after 1945, when the Germans in the British, French, and American sectors became democrats, more fiercely than many of the British, French, and Americans.

THE INDIGO ERA: You have emphasized the importance of liberty, and that "liberated people are ingenious." Could you expand on what this means for future generations of workers? What are the current constraints from which economies and people need to be liberated?

MCCLOSKEY: People need to be liberated chiefly from their watchmen— the bureaucrats, the police, the politicians. Who watches the very watchmen? Yet I am a *humane* true liberal, and acknowledge a responsibility to help the poor. But the chief way to help them is to allow them to work with self-respect for the paid benefit to others, as you and I do—that is, at the market rates that the watchmen are mainly in the business of preventing from operating. The watchmen interfere with natural liberties in order to favor the trade unionists, the Party members, and the urban bureaucrats, as against the peasants and street vendors and factory workers. Consider the fruit vendor Mohamed Bouazizi of Tunisia, who set himself on fire in despair because of persistent extortion by the police.

THE INDIGO ERA: You have also emphasized the importance of equality— in the sense that when people had equality before the law and equality of social dignity, it "made people bold to pursue betterments on their own account." Do you see a parallel in the twenty-first century with the rise in flexible working, self-employment, and entrepreneurs wanting to make their own decisions?

MCCLOSKEY: Self-employment often arises from restrictions on the terms on which people can be employed. Uber taxis are a good example, eroding the absurd monopoly of taxis city by city worldwide. In largely honest Amsterdam for many years the taxis were in the hands of the less than honest. In the United States, especially for instance in Florida until the granting in the 2018 election of voting rights, any "felon," now out of prison, often convicted of a little drug dealing, can't get paid work. He or she is forced into self-employment. I would rather reduce the vicious and corrupt regulations that create the incentive to self-employ in the first place. But given excessive custodianship, such self-employment—in the informal economy, for example— is the only way out. Mohamed Bouazizi again. Or Brazil.

THE INDIGO ERA: You have suggested that economists and historians have failed to explain the Great Enrichment, and you have suggested a move towards "humanomics." Could you expand on what humanomics might entail, and how the study of words and meaning might contribute toward a better global economy?

McCLOSKEY: The economy works to a surprising degree with sweet words—not commands, but attempts to change minds, persuasion, sweet talk. As the making of things and the delivery of services becomes, thankfully, more and more cheaply automated, humans will more and more be left to the business of sweet talk, deciding what to do and how. Sweet talk is already a *quarter* of labor income in rich countries, and rising. "The study of words and meaning" merely makes us wiser about persuasion. We'd better be, or else we are persuaded by the populist tyrants.

THE INDIGO ERA: What advice would you give to someone at school today about how they should set about shaping their future?

McCLOSKEY: Learn how to think. Restrain your reading of the conventional thinking in the *New York Times,* get out of the internet and start reading serious books. Read, however, on the correct assumption that half of what most people believe, for example in the *New York Times,* is mistaken. It is not "fake news," but precisely the sort of cant and prejudice that Trump himself evinced, if commonly progressive cant and prejudice instead of reactionary. Learn one subject, such as economics or literature or mathematics or philosophy, deeply and critically, in order to understand what "depth" and "criticism" really are. But then read widely, if necessarily somewhat superficially, in for example the best of the popularizers, such as by Matt Ridley or A. N. Wilson or John Horgan. Read the best novels—never the current best sellers, which are usually rubbish, but the old ones that have survived, such as Willa Cather or Jane Austen or Leo Tolstoy. Read history at the highest academic level you can stand. Read always with a pen in hand, and quarrel or agree with the author in the margins and endpapers. It will help keep you awake, which is the chief problem any reader faces, staying awake. Read, read, read, write, write, write, speak, speak, speak, and learn thereby to think for yourself.[7] Don't become a follower of any party line, as tempting as they are. Most of them are rubbish, too.

THE INDIGO ERA: You say you are an optimist. Is this, do you believe, an intellectual position or an attitude of mind?

McCLOSKEY: It's mostly an attitude of mind—one does not change gender, as I did in 1995, unless one is optimistic! But that it is a "mere" attitude does not make it mistaken as an intellectual position, too. As the great and optimistic historian and essayist T. B. Macaulay wrote in 1830, "On what principle is it that, when we see nothing but improvement behind us, we are to expect nothing but deterioration before us?"[8] On what principle, indeed, except an ever-fashionable pessimism, which over and over since 1800 has proven to be mistaken?

PART THREE

The New Worry About Inequality Is Mistaken

24. Forced Equality of Outcome Is Unjust and Inhumane

The Financial Times *and then the* New York Times *asked for brief columns on inequality. I give here a new and longer view of the subject. I am not an expert in the economics of inequality, as may be seen by an idiotic error I made at one point in the accounting of redistribution (it's fixed). Yet we all are required nowadays to have opinions about inequality, which people regularly mix up with injustice and poverty, even though the alleged inequality of "capitalism" is a small matter beside the equalizing power of the Great Enrichment. So I soldiered on. Brave Deirdre.*

The Liberal Lady Glencora Palliser (charmingly, née M'Cluskie) in Anthony Trollope's political novel *Phineas Finn* (1867–1868) declares, "Making men and women all equal. That I take to be the gist of our political theory," as against the Conservative delight in rank and privilege. But Joshua Monk, one of the novel's radicals in the Cobden-Bright-Mill mold, sees the ethical point more clearly, and replies to her, "Equality is an ugly word, and frightens," as indeed it had long frightened the political class in Britain, traumatized by wild French declarations for *égalité*, and by the example of American egalitarianism (well . . . American egalitarianism for male, straight, white, Anglo, middle-aged, high-income, non-immigrant, non-Jewish, mainline Protestants). The motive of the true liberal, Monk continues, should not be equality but "the wish of every honest man . . . to assist in lifting up those below him."[1] ("Honest" at the time also meant "honorable.") Such an ethical goal was to be achieved, Monk the humane true liberal would argue, not by direct programs of redistribution, nor by regulation, nor by trade unions, but by free trade and rights for women and tax-financed education—and in the event above all by the economic fruit of a liberal ideology of innovism.

And it came to pass. What I call the Great Enrichment is the chief scientific finding of economic history. The poorest people in the developed economies and billions in the poor countries have been the biggest beneficiaries of liberal economic growth. The rich became richer, true. But the poor have gas heating, cars, smallpox vaccinations, indoor plumbing, cheap travel, rights for women, low child mortality, adequate nutrition, taller bodies, doubled life expectancy, schooling for their kids, newspapers, a vote, a shot at university, and respect. Never had anything remotely similar happened, not in the glory of Greece or the grandeur of Rome, not in ancient Egypt or medieval China.

Yet you will have heard recently that our biggest problem is inequality, and that we must make men and women all equal. No, we should not—at least, not if we want to lift up the poor. Ethically speaking, the true liberal should care chiefly about whether the poorest among us are moving closer to having enough to live with dignity and to participate in a democracy. They are. Even in already rich countries, such as the United Kingdom and the United States, the real income of the poor has recently risen, not, as one hears daily, stagnated—if, that is, income is correctly measured to include better health care, better working conditions, more years of education, longer years of retirements, and, above all, the rising quality of goods and services—better autos and better medicine. Admittedly it is rising at a slower pace than in the 1950s. But that era of rising prosperity was a catch-up from the wretched setbacks of the Great Depression and the War.

It matters ethically, of course, how the rich obtained their wealth—whether from stealing or from choosing the right womb (as the billionaire investor Warren Buffett puts it), or from voluntary exchanges for the cheap cement or the cheap air travel the now-rich had the good sense to provide to the once-poor.[2] We should prosecute theft and raise property taxes and reintroduce inheritance taxes. But we should take care not to kill the golden geese giving us better plate glass and better tires and better medical devices.

What does *not* matter ethically are the routine historical ups and downs of the Gini coefficient, a measure of inequality, or the vulgar excesses of the

1 percent of the 1 percent, of a sort one could have seen on display three centuries ago in Versailles, or thirty centuries ago in Egypt. There are not enough really rich people to make expropriating them serve any purpose except stoking envy. If we seized *all* the assets of the eighty-five wealthiest people in the world to make a fund to give annually to the poorest half, it would raise their spending power by less than 10 cents a day.[3] The assets of the wealthiest eighty-five persons were reported in 2014 by Oxfam to total $1.7 trillion. (There is, by the way, something screwy about Oxfam's number here, because the world's interest-bearing assets are on the order of scores of trillions, and if including the assets of human capital, too, they are on the order of hundreds of trillions. But let's go with Oxfam's figure for the nonce.) If a fund of that size earned a robust 7 percent annual return, there would be $119 billion a year, which is only $326 million a day, to distribute among the poorest half, 3.6 billion people—or 9 cents per person.

All the foreign aid to Africa or South and Central America, to give another example of how redistribution does not accomplish a great deal, is dwarfed by the amount that nations in such areas would gain if the people of Europe or the United States abandoned tariffs and other protections for their already rich agriculture.[4] The way to help the poor, in short, is to let the Great Enrichment proceed by commercially tested betterment, as it has widely since 1800 and especially in the past forty years. Charity or expropriation is not efficacious, particularly considering that the charity in foreign aid or the expropriation by military coup has flowed into Swiss bank accounts, not into the subsistence of the poor. A high market price for the poor farmer, by contrast, goes to his children. Commerce works better than theft.

Gini coefficients do not matter much. The Great Enrichment does.

Anger about economic inequality in the United States dominated the presidential election of 2016, and keeps working for Trumpian-Republican or left-Democratic politicians. But while polemics about the issue have flourished across the political spectrum, clarity has not.

Look, for example, at the Illinois state constitution, adopted in 1970. It sought to "eliminate poverty and inequality."[5] Sounds good. Who wouldn't want to eliminate poverty? But "and inequality"? Eliminating poverty is obviously good, and is already happening on a global scale. The World Bank reports that the basics of a dignified life are more available to the poorest among us than at any time in history, by a wide margin. Shanghai, a place of misery not very long ago, now looks like the most modern parts of the United States, though having better roads and bridges. The real income of India is doubling every ten years. Sub-Saharan Africa is at last growing. Even in the already rich countries of the world the poor are getting better off, from better food and health care and housing.

What matters ethically is that the poor get opportunities to vote and to read and to have a roof over their heads, and to receive equal treatment by the police and the courts. Enforcing the Voting Rights Act matters. Restraining police coercion matters. But equalizing possession of Rolexes does not. The Princeton philosopher Harry Frankfurt put it this way: "Economic equality is not, as such, of particular moral importance."[6] We should allow the Great Enrichment to lift up the poor, in the style of Trollope's radical liberal, to a level Frankfurt labeled as "enough"— enough for people to function in a democratic society and to have full human lives. The Harvard philosopher John Rawls articulated what he called the Difference Principle: if the entrepreneurship of a rich person made the poorest better off, then the higher income of the rich entrepreneur was justified.[7] It makes a good deal of ethical sense. Equality does not.

Conspicuous displays of wealth, true, are vulgar and irritating. But they are not something that a non-envious principle of public policy needs to acknowledge. Difference, including economic difference, is not bad in itself. It is why we exchange goods with California and with China, or services with Oprah and Sir Elton John, and why the political railing against foreign trade is childish. It is why we converse, and why today is the great age of the novel and the memoir. It is why we celebrate diversity—or should.

My friend the economist Laurence Iannaccone, in a letter to me in 2018, made a set of points about *why* we, foolishly, think redistribution is so easy and desirable. Like me, he disagrees with "the assumption that wealth inequality derives from exploitation, and the notion that equal outcomes are 'natural.'" Redistributive schemes "all come more readily to those who've had less experience or exposure to the actual creation of wealth. . . . Manna [from heaven] is exactly how many of the left view wealth and income." Iannaccone notes a book of 2000 by Craig Gay (*With Liberty and Justice for Whom?: The Recent Evangelical Debate over Capitalism*), which showed that evangelical Christians on the left took wealth as given, manna, and "hence applied their Christian/ Biblical principles only to the problem of (static) distribution, whereas the evangelicals on the right emphasized incentives to the ongoing creation of wealth, innovation, etc."[8]

But if we are going to redistribute income, why not redistribute other things? It seems entailed. And yet:

> scarcely anyone supports redistribution of household production be-
> yond the limits of the family, or the redistribution of grade produc-
> tion beyond the limits of the individual student, or the redistribution
> of achievement or earnings in sports and entertainment. Everyone
> one sees the link between inputs and outputs in those "factories."
> And people *remain* resistant to redistribution in those contexts, even
> when you point out that household production, grades, and sport out-
> comes depend not just on effort but also on endowments of health,
> strength, IQ, social support, upbringing, discrimination, luck, and
> the like. Apparently, once you appreciate how a given production
> process really works, you're much less inclined to view the outcomes
> as unfair, even when those outcomes manifestly depend on more than
> mere effort.

Iannaccone adds to such ethical reflection an historical explanation of why redistribution of at least income continues to seem anyway desirable, namely, "how hard it's become for almost anyone to see the link between their *own* work/inputs and their income/outputs. For one thing, at any given moment, a remarkably large fraction of the population isn't working at all. . . . And even those men and women who work 'full time' during their 'prime' years tend to live off savings, retirement, and social security from their mid-60s onward." And, he continues, "an even more important consideration is [that] even those who are working . . . cannot really see the relationship between what they actually *do* and what they earn. The link was clear for 19th century farmers and . . . for almost everyone before the 19th century. But the path from inputs to output became vastly more complex in even the simplest 19th-century factory, much more so the knowledge- and service-based 'factories' of the 20th and 21st centuries. . . . Most of what you get these days looks like manna . . . [and even more] if it's your parent or spouse who's earning the income."

No wonder people in a modern economy lean toward favoring equality of result, as much as did their remote ancestors in hunter-gatherer bands. But they should reflect, recognizing the enriching power of a modern economy of specialization or of diversity, and draw back from a redistributive egalitarianism of envy.

A practical objection to focusing on economic equality is that we cannot achieve it, not in a big society, not in a just and sensible way. Dividing up a pizza among friends is easy and just, yes. We can really see the relationship between what we actually *do* and what we eat. But equality beyond the basics in consumption and in political rights can't be achieved in a specialized and dynamic economy. For one thing, cutting down the tall poppies entails coercion, of course. It's what the rhetoric of "distribution" implies. And for another, to achieve sensible results you need to know exactly which poppies to cut. Trusting a government of self-interested people to know how to redistribute goods and services ethically and sensibly is at best naïve. For most governments such trust would fail the laugh test. Nigeria. Saudi Arabia.

The cutting of course reduces the size of the crop of poppies—the right-wing evangelical's "incentives to the ongoing creation of wealth, innovation, etc." It's not exactly personal incentives so much as signaling. We need to allow for rewards that tell the economy to increase the activity earning them. If a brain surgeon and a taxi driver earn the same amount, we won't have enough brain surgeons. A surgeon-in-training will say, "Why bother going to medical school? I can drive an Uber instead. Less bother, same money." An all-wise central plan, to be sure, could force the right people into the correct jobs. But such a solution, like much of the case for a coerced equality, is violent and magical. The magic has been tried, in Stalin's Russia and Mao's China, with the violence on full display entailed in an economy without market prices and market wages sending their signals.

Humans retain a genetic disposition for equal shares arising from our deep ancestors spending hundreds of thousands of years in egalitarian societies of hunting and gathering. And anyway, as mammals we naturally share a socialism of sentiment, because we grew up in loving families, with Mom as the central planner. In a loving and traditional household, a policy of sharing works pretty well. The adults work hard to provide. But you don't give Dad more pizza just because he's the one who worked to pay for it, unless he's sweating at the coal face, not lolling in "the knowledge- and service-based 'factories' of the 20th and 21st centuries."

But sharing is not how most grown-ups get stuff in a liberal society. Free grown-ups get it by working to make goods and services for other people, typically in a modern economy very remote strangers, exchanging with them voluntarily. Grown-ups don't get them by slicing up manna dropping from Mother Nature into a zero-sum world. As Smith noted, "Nobody but a beggar chooses to depend chiefly upon the benevolence of his fellow-citizens. [A child or a severely handicapped person, Smith would have acknowledged, does not 'choose.'] Even a beggar does not depend upon it entirely. . . . With the money which one man gives him he purchases food."[9]

We could take by government coercion billions from billionaires like Bill Gates and give to the homeless, achieving more equality of income, if not of grades, IQ, beauty, or the luck of the draw. (Gates is in fact giving away his fortune, to his credit.) Short of wholesale expropriation, we can all join in supporting a safety net, though keeping the coercion involved in getting the taxes for it to a minimum. K–12 public education, or N–8, for example, should, the modern liberal affirms, be paid for by coerced taxes on all of us, though not directly provided by governmental schools. But most of the other things routinely listed as what our good government provides or pays for would better be provided and paid for privately.

It is easy to become muddled about that last, and to believe that because government at present supplies, say, roads, it must always do so. It is what I have called the Supply Chain Fallacy. Roads for example can be privately owned, as they commonly were in earlier centuries, and now easily with electronic monitoring. Hospitals could be liberated from monopolistic licensing, as could the competitors of doctors, such as nurse practitioners or foreign doctors. If medical care were provided through such markets, in the way food for the most part is, medical care would in the United States go for about half its present cost, judging from costs in other countries. And so forth. It's the path to a society of human dignity and prosperity.

And redistribution, of course, works only once. You can't expect the expropriated rich to show up for a second cutting. Expropriate me once, shame on you. Expropriate me twice, shame on me. In a free society the expropriated can move to Ireland or Switzerland or the Cayman Islands. And the millionaires can hardly re-earn their millions next year if the government has taken much of it. The rich invest and raise the productivity of the economy for us all (and, yes, for themselves; but the investment passes the Rawls test).

Which do we want, a small one-time (though envy- and anger-satisfying) extraction from the rich, or a free society of betterment lifting up the poor by gigantic amounts?

We had better focus directly on what we rationally want and can actually achieve, which is equality of social dignity and equality before the law, which lead in fact to substantial equality of result, and anyway to a radical lifting up of the poor.

25. Piketty Is Mistaken

The liberal think tank in London, the Institute of Economic Affairs, conducted an interview with me on the matter, published in the institute's newsletter for high schools.

IEA: *Capital in the Twenty-First Century,* by Thomas Piketty, is the book on every progressive's coffee table at the moment. The book has been dissected by a large number of economists. Does Piketty's argument about the growth of inequality stand up to careful scrutiny?

McCLOSKEY: No. Piketty is a serious economist. He's not a liar or a fool. But even serious, non-foolish economists can be wrong in their science. He is. For example, the only countries in which Piketty finds *actual, substantial* rise of inequality are the United Kingdom, the United States, and Canada. The three cases can be explained by government policies foolishly favoring the rich, such as making it crazy-difficult to build new housing in London, which drives up the price of existing housing—owned by the rich. "Capitalism" didn't cause the disaster of London housing. A half-socialism did.

For the countries that did not experience a rise of inequality, Piketty is warning against *the future*. But again his argument isn't correct. He says that commercially tested betterment *always* causes the rich to get richer and the poor to fall behind. So why not everywhere, every time since 1800 CE, or for that matter 1800 BCE? It didn't happen.

First published by the Institute of Economic Affairs, London, in 2016.

IEA: One of your criticisms of Piketty's work is that he does not take account of the role that human capital now plays in the economy. How will this affect future trends in inequality?

McCLOSKEY: Most income nowadays in a place like Britain comes not from the *physical* capital that Piketty measures, and the ownership of which he worries about. It comes instead from *human* capital—your skills and health and education. Why and how? Because innovism, commercially tested betterment, has made you the worker twenty to one hundred times better off than your ancestors in 1800. You can stay in school much longer or can get high-skill training if you are twenty times richer than your great-great-great-great-great-grandmum, who went to work milking cows at age eight. In 1800 the average person got her bread from laboring with her hands and back. Now you will get it from your better-educated brain. Once upon a time the bosses had all the capital, which was mostly invested land and factories and machines. Now most of the capital is human, owned by the worker. And the physical capital is also partly owned by workers, too, in pension funds and in personal houses. And public capital, such as roads, is not owned in an individual way by anyone, yet it profits. It is another big part of the country's capital, and Piketty also ignores it. Nor does he account for social capital, such as habits of the law-abiding. His accounting of "capital," in other words, is radically narrow. Equality of real comfort will go on rising, as it has in the past two centuries—indoor plumbing, color TV, better education, overseas holidays, longer life expectancy.

IEA: You have made your name as an economic historian. If we look back over the last two hundred years—and this is important because Piketty is basing his future predictions on past trends—what has been more important for promoting increased living standards for the poor: redistribution or economic growth?

McCLOSKEY: Economic growth by far, in the Great Enrichment. How great? As measured recently in real terms per person since 1800 by economic historians, it has been an amazing twenty to one hundred *times*. In other words (doing the junior-school math over-precisely), the Great Enrichment for the average person, including the very poor, was anything from *a 1,900 to a 9,900 percent* increase over the miserable base in 1800. Blimey.

IEA: And can we quantify the benefits of economic growth compared with redistribution on the living standards of the poor?

McCloskey: Yes, and the results are startling. Redistribution can only take one part of the pie and give it to another person. Think of a pizza divided between, and made by, Mr. Boss and Ms. Worker. If Mr. Boss starts with, say, 50 percent of the pie to eat, then taking it from him and giving *all* his share to Ms. Worker will increase her pizza portion by 100 percent. Good, if you don't at all mind the coercion applied to Mr. Boss, inaugurating a habit of redistributive coercion that commonly metastasizes until we are all compelled (look at every socialist régime in history). They came for Mr. Boss, and I did nothing, because I was not a boss. They came for the Jews, and I did nothing, because I was not a Jew. Then they came for me. And of course the distributive coercion against Mr. Boss can occur one time only, because you can't expect him to show up for the *making* of the *next* pizza if he lost all his earnings from the first one. He's no fool.

Still, 100 percent that one time is a fine thing for Ms. Worker. Hurrah. But compared with the 1,900 or 3,000 or 10,000 percent that came during the past two centuries from allowing commercially tested betterment to work, you can see that the 100 percent from even so extreme a redistribution is small. True, if there's a third person involved, Mr. Pauper, who originally gets only 10 percent of the pizza, he does very much better in percentage terms, if he gets all Mr. Boss's share. But it's still one time only, dwarfed by the Great Enrichment, which makes the pizza thirty or a hundred times bigger, and requires the redistributor to give the whole of taxes *only* to the poor—a policy with which the middle class will not agree. It never has.

The real hurrah is the Great Enrichment. Piketty and others who share his anger at rich people do not acknowledge that innovism inspiring commercially tested betterment has made *everybody* by historical standards extremely rich. Twenty or thirty times richer. He focuses on the often stupid consumption of yachts and diamonds by rich people, and neglects to observe that—compared with the world before liberalism and its economic ideology of innovism—the present standard of real comfort is dramatically more equal than it once was. A free economy turns out to be an equal one in things that matter. Let people cooperate and compete liberally, and the result is a substantive, and enormous, betterment of the poor.

IEA: Why, through most of human history, have most people been poor?

McCloskey: Mainly because commercially tested betterment was discouraged by the hierarchy, which meant that growth in population overwhelmed any betterment from, say, iron from China (tenth century BCE) or windmills from the Arab world (tenth century CE). It was all about "diminishing returns," as the economists put it. When the clergyman and great English economist Malthus was first explaining, back in 1798, why population growth kept us poor, diminishing returns to population growth *were* still keeping us poor, in an illiberal economy run by the landlords, guildsmen, swordsmen, and clergy.

By now another person on the planet makes the rest of us *better* off, not worse off, because she is supplied with much more human capital in her brain (the capital ignored by Piketty). She invents for us new devices and gives us opportunities to trade with her (By the way, the same holds for immigrants of any sort into, say, Britain. It can be shown in a diagram of marginal productivity of labor that the immigrants are unambiguously beneficial to the original British population. More opportunities for trade are better for people. Obviously.)

IEA: And what facilitated the improvement in living standards in the last two hundred years?

McCloskey: The commercially tested betterment, the Great Enrichment, was itself caused by another kind of equality, a new equality of legal rights and of social dignity and especially of social approval for opening a new chippy or inventing a drill press, all of which made every Tom, Dick, and Harriet into a betterer. In a word, innovism. Certain strange accidents in the history of northwestern Europe during the immediately preceding centuries, such as the Protestant Reformation after 1517 and the English Civil War during the 1640s, had made northwestern European people bold. The revolutions slowly made plausible the crazy new idea that we all should be equal in law and in dignity and in being allowed to have an economic go.

Along with liberal equality came another idea from the Levellers of the Civil War (they were in fact free traders), the Bourgeois Deal. In the first act, let a bourgeoise try out in the marketplace a supposed betterment such as window screens or alternating-current electricity or cardboard boxes or the little black dress. In a liberal society the inventive bourgeoise accepts, with a certain irritation, that in the second act there will be competitors imitating her success, driving down the price of screens, electricity, boxes, and dresses. (She accepts it unless she can stop it by applying to the government. Headline in the *New York Times* of August 6, 2018, with a similar story in the Chicago *Tribune* for October 31, 2018: "Uber and taxis join opposition to further entry." Surprise, surprise.). If you let her have a go in the first act, getting rich on her idea, by the third act the Bourgeois Deal claims that she will make *you all* rich. And she did, by the 1,900 percent conventionally measured and by upwards of 9,900 percent if including in the measure the much improving quality of plate glass or medical care or economic and historical analysis.

IEA: Given this, can works such as those by Piketty in fact seriously damage the position of the least-well-off by changing attitudes to make them more hostile to business, commerce, and wealth creation?

MCCLOSKEY: Yes, which is why I write my books. We grow up in socialist communities called "families," and are likely by age seventeen or so to think that the model can be applied to a "family" of 66 million or 330 million people. (I did). And then we never revisit the idea critically, or with reference to the historical evidence, ending at age seventy as bearded socialists eating cold beans out of the can and advocating re-nationalization of railways and admiring socialist Venezuela and hating innovative Israel. (I didn't.) The danger is that each new generation will not realize how good for the poor the Bourgeois Deal has been, and will forget how bad the earlier deals have been—the Bolshevik Deal, for example, in which the government takes over the railways and the electric companies and the newsagents and the newspapers and your employment, and everything else. Or the Bridle Deal, in which excessive regulations work against "unbridled" commercially tested betterment. I ask innocently, when has it been a good idea to "bridle" a person like a horse? Piketty's idea is to bridle most people so that some people will not become rich. It is a mistake.

The Bourgeois Deal has been by far the best way to help the poor, in Britain and India and Africa. And it results in real equality.

26. Europe Should Resist Egalitarian Policies

A Polish journal, Wprost *("Direct"), in 2015 conducted an interview with me on Piketty. For a few years everybody talked about the book, even though its theme was a diversion from our main task, which is not to envy the rich but to enrich the poor.*

WPROST: Thomas Piketty's *Capital in the Twenty-First Century* became a new Marxian bible for European intellectual elites, more and more concerned with inequality. Regardless of our views on economy and politics, should not we all be worried?

MCCLOSKEY: No. Piketty's own statistics show that inequality has in fact notably increased recently *only* in the United States, the United Kingdom, and Canada. Not, for example, in France. But he says it *will* increase, everywhere, always, as a tendency in any economy of commercially tested betterment. He's mistaken. Equality moves up and down in long waves. The key point is that it *never moves up or down very much*. For example, in the United States recently the share of labor in national income did fall. How much? From 63 percent to 58 percent. Five percentage points. Little cause for panic. And now the share is on its way up again.

If you look closely at the statistics, furthermore, you notice that one of the main sources of inequality is the low incomes of *young* people. When they are unemployed their incomes are of course zero. That *is* something to worry about, worldwide, and especially in Europe. But the problem has nothing to do with Evil Capitalists. It has to do with Evil Middle-Aged and Ordinary

People voting for populist governments to protect their own jobs with labor-market restrictions of just the sort the New Egalitarians think are good. They aren't.

WPROST: There is an ongoing discussion in the United States and Europe about special regulations to limit disparities between the high earners in the financial system and average workers. Do you see it as a small but healthy movement toward equality?

McCLOSKEY: I do think it's stupid for corporate "compensation committees" to give such high rewards to their good friends. It's bad publicity. It annoys people for no real gain in efficiency. It undermines the confidence people have in commercially tested betterment, liberal innovism. So I wouldn't mind some symbolic moves to shame it, such as were recently instituted in the United States. We can, for example, require corporations to report the ratio of CEO compensation to averages in the company. (True, there are statistical problems of accuracy with such reporting.) But the effect of super salaries of big bankers and CEOs on inequality is trivial nationally speaking—there are too few of them to affect the averages very much. And the crazy money they get in, say, the United States is taken not from the workers but from the *stockholders*—supposedly other moneyed capitalists!

The more important source of inequality is among workers themselves—that is, employees earning a salary—because there are a lot of them. If millions of people with high skills are earning high salaries, it matters for the national numbers. But no one argues that workers do not *earn* their incomes. Do we really want to restrict the earnings of people who are getting the earnings because their customers voluntarily pay them a lot? A somewhat silly case—but it makes the point—is the salary of football stars. Would you think it's a good idea to restrict the salaries of the Polish stars Robert Lewandowski or Zbigniew Boniek? The restriction would not reduce ticket prices. It would in fact merely increase the incomes of the rich owners of the teams, or the clubs run by rich people. When you pay a lot to see Lewandowski and Boniek play, and they get rich, are you being cheated? No. You do it voluntarily, and you delight in shouting, "Goal, goal, goal!"

WPROST: How about obligatory publication of wage differences between those in the corporation who earn the most, and those on the bottom of the ladder?

MCCLOSKEY: Yes, as I said, it seems to me harmless and a little helpful, shaming the fools on the compensation committees. But stockholders mainly do already get such information, and yet go on approving high compensation for their CEOs, by big majorities. They must think it is good for the value of their stocks. And the "problems with reporting" I mentioned include, for example, deciding what "average" salary to take—for an international company such as PKN Orlen should the average include its workers in the Czech Republic, or only those in Poland? It's worse for, say, Siemens.

WPROST: Piketty worries about capital: "Money tends to reproduce itself." He argues that rich can live off their fortunes better than any man can live off his or her work. Financial feudalism?

MCCLOSKEY: It has always been so that there are people who live off their lands or their bonds or their government sinecures. But it was much *worse* before the Great Enrichment. "Capitalism" has *improved* equality. You ask why.

First, because owning *land,* under real feudalism, was much more stable and generated a much, much bigger share of all incomes. Piketty confines his attention to the minor ups and downs of inequality in the "capitalist" era, and therefore does not acknowledge the point. The rents on land in Poland before 1800—and in truth up to 1900 and beyond—were *half* of Polish national income. *Half* was going to the truly rich big landlords, or to the less rich gentry, the *szlachta.* The same was true in old Japan, by the way, with the *samurai* in place of the *szlachta.* "Capitalist" Poland and Japan have had much more equal income, not less, than under feudalism. And I don't need to inform your older readers that communist Poland was not in fact a paradise of equality.

Second, commercially tested betterment, innovism, such as we have had since 1800 in Europe—with breaks for thrilling experiments suggested by the intelligentsia in nationalism and socialism—is also better for equality because "creative destruction" erodes the fortunes of the old rich.

Piketty downplays the main reason that we are so much better off than our ancestors. The reason is not the character of distribution, but the ingenuity encouraged by letting people run their farms or their factories the way they want, taking the risk of failure and the rewards of success. We all agree that creative destruction is good in science and art and journalism and football, yes? Why not also in the economy?!

And, third, Piketty is mistaken about "money reproducing itself." His technical argument is wrong. Think of it this way: if he were correct, *then all of national income would end up in the hands of rentiers*. Well, it hasn't. There's no logical limit to Piketty's "logic."

WPROST: In your book *The Bourgeois Virtues* (2006) you talk about liberal bourgeois values that enriched our humanity and gave us prosperity, but according to Piketty we are in danger. The gap between rich and poor and this bourgeois attitude can lead to catastrophic wars.

McCLOSKEY: Wars? It hasn't yet. Contrary to Leninist fairy tales about "capitalist" or "imperialist" wars fought for profits, the actual source of wars—after they stopped in Europe being about maintaining the glory of the upper classes or about killing Protestants and Catholics (think of the Great Deluge in Poland in the 1600s)—has been the unfortunate ideas I mentioned, dreamed up in the nineteenth century by the clerisy, namely, nationalism, socialism, and an anti-Semitism now reviving in Poland, as it shockingly did in Hungary's elections in 2018. Hitler's party was the Nationalsozialistische Deutsche Arbeiterpartei. Look at the words. The bourgeoisie wants peace and McDonald's, not blitzkrieg and Auschwitz. I ask, which do you Poles really want?

WPROST: You wrote that Piketty's book is an opportunity to "understand the latest of the leftish worries about capitalism," but aren't those traditional worries, almost two hundred years old, things that keep haunting our civilization and most of the time get resolved only by wars and revolutions?

McCLOSKEY: Yes, the leftish *and rightish* "worries" have been precisely the cause of wars and of revolutions and of counterproductive regulation, mostly disastrous. We "worried" about resource scarcity (which worry, by the way, is exceptionally bad economics) and so we (Germans) conquered Poland or we (Japanese) conquered Manchuria. We (Americans and Europeans) "worried" about monopolies, and so we came to favor gathering all enterprises under one giant monopoly called the government, or we introduced anti-trust regulators who were immediately captured by the industries they were supposed to regulate. We (Americans) "worried" about how very intemperate and European the workers were in their consumption of, say, beer, and so we introduced Prohibition, with known results. After not learning from that result, we (white Anglo-Americans again) worried that African-Americans and Hispanics were going to rape white women after taking drugs, and so we introduced the War on Drugs. And on and on. Nearly the only correct discovery of social science in the nineteenth century was "Let ordinary people run their economic lives the way they want and, as a result, everyone becomes vastly better off." The other social "discoveries"—racialist history, for example, or eugenics or tests of statistical significance—turned out to be mistaken, and commonly disastrous.

WPROST: Since the rich bourgeoisie is so influential, and in a way responsible for our civilization, should not they limit themselves—put a cap on their own affluence?

MCCLOSKEY: No, because entry of competitors into the market—creative destruction—keeps the rich bourgeoisie on a leash. True, they can influence politics. But that has always been true. We must work against rule by the rich, mainly by vigorously defending free speech and a free press, under serious attack nowadays in Poland. If we go the way of Putin's Russia, as the Law and Justice Party in Poland wants, we are doomed: the rich take over, and the powerful become through the government still more grotesquely rich, by suppressing competition.

Real monopoly is not native to commercially tested betterment. It is caused by the government, not prevented by it. Adam Smith wrote in 1776, "To found a great empire for the sole purpose of raising up a people of customers, may at first sight appear a project fit only for a nation of shopkeepers. It is, however, a project altogether unfit for a nation of shopkeepers; but extremely fit for a nation whose government is *influenced* by shopkeepers."[1]

On the other hand, I do approve of charity, such as John D. Rockefeller performed early and late in his long life, and am irritated as we all are by silly excesses in consumption by the super-rich. Here I agree with Piketty, who detests Liliane Bettencourt, the lazy heiress to the L'Óreal fortune. Her "charitable" foundation is endowed with *1.5 percent* of her enormous wealth. Contrast this with the Carnegie Foundation, which the American steelmaker endowed with 100 percent of his. The admirable "gospel of wealth," as Carnegie put it, is much less practiced in Europe than in the United States or Japan. Imitate the United States and Japan.

But understand: such charity cannot much change the distribution of income. The numbers tell. Most rich people in the United States give in the end a substantial part of their wealth to charities such as churches or universities. But the annual flow of their generosity, combined with the considerable generosity of much poorer people, especially when the poor are churchgoers, amounts to the very low single digits as a percentage of GDP. Two or three percent. Voluntary charity can't radically change the condition of the poor. Growth can and does, by literally thousands of percents.

Nor is involuntary charity, channeled through the government, the way forward. It turns out in the numbers that if we expropriated all the rich people, the ordinary people would be benefited only a little. By contrast, ordinary people like you and me are benefited immensely by creative destruction and the Bourgeois Deal: "Let me test my proposed betterment in free trade within and outside Poland, and let me keep the profits that accrue (until those irritating competitors get in to spoil the fun), and in the long run—and not so long, as you can see in Poland's recent history—I'll make *you all* rich, compared with what you got under the Aristocratic Deal or the Communist Deal or the Law and Justice Deal."

WPROST: In your publications you devoted quite some space discussing the source of richness. But does this really matter to the average, let's say, Pole, how his or her boss got his millions, because he/she would never live to see this kind of money?

MCCLOSKEY: Most of us are not going to be Bill Gates. But we need to let the Bill Gates types flourish, and the small entrepreneurs in your neighborhood, too, or else we will all be poor. The envy that causes us to cut down the tall poppies keeps us poor—if equal. I heard a folktale about it first in the Czech Republic, but I suppose it has a parallel in Poland. Jesus and St. Peter travel in disguise, asking peasant families for food and shelter for the night. After many refusals, at last a generous peasant couple provides. The next morning the travelers reveal their identities, and Jesus says, "To reward your charity, you may receive anything you want." The husband and wife consult in whispers for a moment, and the husband turns to Jesus, saying, "Our neighbor has a goat, which provides milk for his family. . . ." Jesus anticipates, "And so you want a goat for yourselves?" "No. We want you to kill the neighbor's goat." Envy is a sin, corrosive of community and of souls. And it is an economic disaster, making us all goat-less.

Viewing the commercially tested betterers—the entrepreneurs, the creative destroyers—as heroes *is* the right model. It inspires us. If our only heroes are kings and politicians and even football players, we do not give honor to the people who are in fact most improving our economies. And we have less interest in having a go ourselves as small entrepreneurs (who may occasionally become large, too).

WPROST: When you compare the US and the European bourgeoisie, you will see a big difference. It is a matter of new technology fortune in the United States and old money in Europe—inheritance. Does it make any difference for an economy and for equality?

McCLOSKEY: I don't think you're right about the contrast. There are both sorts in both places, and the differences that people imagine are big are in actual fact quite small. Take Sweden, for example, which I know from having lived there and having many friends there, some from Poland. People say that Sweden is "socialist." The older Poles know that this is silly, having experienced real, full socialism until 1989, and during that evil and impoverished time going over to Sweden for a month or so during holidays to make big money in a capitalist way. "Socialist" Sweden even nowadays is bourgeois and "capitalist," and not much less so than the United States. Sweden allows property and profits. It allocates most goods by unregulated prices. The Swedish government, though busybody by historical standards—as are most governments nowadays—does not own much of the means of production. Unlike the socialistic Americans, both Democrats and Republicans, who intervened to save General Motors and Chrysler during their post-2007 troubles, the Swedish government refused to bail out when it went bankrupt Saab Automobile (which was then sold in 2010 by that same General Motors). Nor did the Swedes object when the Chinese bought both bankrupt Saab and solvent Volvo. All "Swedish" cars are now Chinese.

   Occupational choice in Sweden is free, though encumbered as it is in the United States and Poland by cartels of doctors and electricians. Innovism is honored, though heavily regulated, as it is also in the United States and Poland. Corruption is low, much lower than it is in most states of the United States or in Poland, though with a correspondingly high level of intrusive "transparency" from government looking into private matters. Inheritance in Sweden is not the admired path to social status, as it also is not in the United States or Poland. Like most Americans, most Swedish people live in big towns, though decamping to red-painted shacks in the woods for their long summer vacations. Swedes are honest and bourgeois. And they are, conservatively measured, thirty times richer than their ancestors were in a country that in

1800 was almost as poor as Russia (which had recently been supplemented by sharing the last of Poland with Prussia).

WPROST: Polish bourgeoisie, or just Polish rich, most of them being first-generation millionaires, face all the same problems—envy, hate. They are asked to share and pay more to their workers. Very few Poles admire them for what they did. The Poles are rather concerned why they did not do more for them.

MCCLOSKEY: To rise into the top rank of rich countries, Poland needs to change its ideology toward innovism, the liberal admiration of progress through ingenuity. A change in ideology, first in Holland and then in Britain and especially in what became the United States, is what caused the Great Enrichment—increases in real comfort since 1800 by factors of ten or thirty or one hundred. First the clerisy (Voltaire and Smith, for example) and then ordinary people started to *admire* the bourgeoisie. The result was the success of the Bourgeois Deal. Remember killing the goat.

WPROST: When you look around, listen to intellectual debates in media or universities, you get a feeling that Piketty's ideas reflect the popular mood. Are we, as the Western civilization, turning toward socialism?

MCCLOSKEY: We're always turning toward socialism, and need to turn away. The Law and Justice Party is merely socialism in a fascist form. The problem is that people think of the government the way the tsar was thought about by Russians. The "good tsar" was supposed to be the father of the nation, and to arrange matters to work out well. The Chinese have a similar tradition.

People think that government "policy" (the very word in this meaning is a nineteenth-century coinage) is what makes people rich. Minimum-wage laws. Worker and foreign-trade "protection." It doesn't. Most governmental interventions make the average person worse off, not better—remember the middle-aged and ordinary people voting in effect to prevent young people from getting any jobs at all. We are collectively well off because of our own efforts and because we trade with other people left alone to make their own efforts—not because the tsar or the emperor or the government subsidized our activity (look at the disgraceful Common Agricultural Policy, with parallels in the United States: Polish farmers benefit, Africans get damaged).

When we are collectively poor it is because we have voted for bad policies, or because a band of robbers has taken over the government. Often both.

As the American sociologist William Graham Sumner (1840–1910) wrote lucidly in 1881, "If an industry does not pay, it is an industrial abomination. It is wasting and destroying. The larger it is the more mischief it does. The protected manufacturer is forced to allege, when he asks for protection, that his business would not pay without it. . . . He therefore asks the legislature to give him power to lay taxes on his fellow-citizens, to collect from them the capital which he intends to waste, and good wages for himself while he is carrying on that business besides."[2]

People *think* that taxes, subsidies, quotas, minimum wages, licensing, zoning, industrial policy, and all the other ways governments restrict the Bourgeois Deal will make you rich. Don't believe it. Don't be fooled.

27. Piketty Deserves Some Praise

I was asked in 2015 by the Erasmus Journal for Philosophy and Economics *to write a short review of Piketty. I got carried away and ended up with a fifty-page essay, which is here sliced into bite-sized pieces. The criticism of Piketty is an extended example of how to get into the details of the case for a liberal economy. It is an example of digging deep, to show that it can be done. We can't reply with bumper stickers: we need logic and evidence.*

Thomas Piketty wrote in 2013 a big book, 577 pages of text in the English translation, 76 pages of notes, 115 charts, tables, and graphs, that has excited the left, worldwide. "Just as we said!" the leftists cry. "The problem is capitalism and its inevitable tendency to inequality!" First published in French, the English edition was issued by Harvard University Press in 2014 to wide acclaim by columnists such as Paul Krugman, and a top position on the *New York Times* best-seller list. A German edition came out in late 2014, and Piketty—who must be exhausted by all this—worked overtime expositing his views to large German audiences. He plays poorly on TV, because he is lacking in humor. But he carries on, and the book sales pile up.

It has been a long time (how does "never" work for you?) since a technical treatise on economics has had such a market. An economist can only applaud. And an economic historian can only wax ecstatic. Piketty's great splash will undoubtedly bring many young, economically interested scholars to devote their lives to the study of the past. That's good, because economic history is one of the few branches of economics that is scientifically quantitative. In economic history, as in experimental economics and a few other fields, the economists actually confront the evidence—as they do not, for example, in most macroeconomics or industrial organization economics or international trade economics nowadays, which play with alternative worlds and inconclusive econometrics.

When you think about it, all evidence in any science must be in the past, and some of the most interesting and scientifically relevant is in the more or less remote past. As the British economic historian John H. Clapham said in 1922, rather in the style of so-called "Austrian" economists (though he was a "Marshallian" economist; both were free traders), "The economist is, willy-nilly, an historian. The world has moved on before his conclusions are ripe."[1] True, economic historians are commonly concerned with the past also for its own sake (I am, for example), and not only as a way of extrapolating into the future, which is Piketty's purpose. His book after all is about capital in the *twenty-first* century, which has barely gotten under way. But if you are going to be a scientific economist, or a scientific geologist or astronomer or evolutionary biologist, the past should be your present.

Piketty gives a fine example of how to do it. He does not get entangled as so many economists do in the sole empirical tool they are taught in graduate school, namely, multiple regression analysis on someone else's "data" (one of the problems is the very word *data*, meaning "things given"; real scientists should deal in *capta*, "things seized"). Therefore he does not commit one of the two sins of modern economics: the use of meaningless "tests" of statistical significance (he occasionally refers to "statistically insignificant" relations between, say, tax rates and growth rates, but I am hoping he doesn't suppose that a large coefficient imprecisely measured so far as sampling is concerned is "insignificant" merely because R. A. Fisher in 1925 said it was). Piketty constructs or uses statistics of aggregate capital and of inequality and then plots them out for inspection, which is what physicists, for example, also do in dealing with their experiments and observations.

Nor does he commit the other sin, which is to waste scientific time on existence theorems. Physicists, again, don't. If we economists are going to persist in physics envy, let's at least learn what physicists do. Piketty stays close to the facts, and does not wander into, for example, the pointless worlds of non-cooperative game theory, long demolished by experimental economics or by the historical evidence of massive human cooperation. He also does not have recourse to non-computable general equilibrium, which never was of use for quantitative economic science, being a branch of philosophy, and a futile one at that.

On both points, *bravissimo*.

His book furthermore is clearly and unpretentiously, if dourly, written, and I imagine is also in its original French. Piketty is to be commended for following the old rule, not so popular among *les français* nowadays, that "ce qui n'est pas clair n'est pas français," or "that which is not clear is not French." I can attest to its English version. True, the book is probably doomed to be one of those books more purchased than read. Readers of a certain age might remember Douglas Hofstadter's massive *Gödel, Escher, Bach: An Eternal Golden Braid* (1979), which sat admired but never read on many a coffee table in the 1980s, and younger readers Stephen Hawking's *A Brief History of Time* (1988). The Kindle company from Amazon keeps track of the last page of your highlighting in a downloaded book (you didn't know that, did you?). Using that fact, the mathematician Jordan Ellenberg reckons that the average reader of the 655 pages of text and footnotes of *Capital in the Twenty-First Century* stops somewhere a little past page 26, where the highlighting stops, about the end of the introduction. He proposes that the Kindle-measured percentage of a book apparently read, once called the Hawking Index (most readers of *A Brief History* stopped highlighting it at 6.6 percent of the book), be renamed the Piketty Index (2.4 percent).[2] To be fair to Piketty, a buyer of the hardback rather than the Kindle edition is probably a more serious reader, and would go further. Still, holding the attention of the average *New York Times* reader for a little over 26 pages of dense economic argument, after which the book takes an honored place on the coffee table, testifies to Piketty's rhetorical skill, which I do admire. The book is endlessly interesting, at any rate if you find intricate numerical arguments interesting.

It is an honestly and thoroughly, if somewhat tendentiously, researched book. Nothing I shall say—and I shall say some hard things, because they are true and important and exhibit in detail some of what is wrong with the anti-liberal case—is meant to impugn Piketty's integrity or his scientific effort. The book is the fruit of a big collaborative effort of the Paris School of Economics, which he founded, associated with some of the brightest lights in the techno-left of French economics. *Hélas*, I will show that Piketty is gravely mistaken in his science and in his social ethics. But so are many economists and calculators, some of them my dearest friends. Cast the first stone, ye who are wholly without a sin of mismeasuring your central concept or misunderstanding a key piece of economics or missing entirely the ethical point.

28. But Pessimism About Market Societies Is Not Scientifically Justified

More from the review of Piketty.

Reading Piketty's book is a good opportunity to understand the latest of the leftish worries about "capitalism," and to test its economic and philosophical strength. Piketty's worry about the rich getting richer is indeed "the latest" of a long line back to Malthus and Ricardo and Marx. Since the founding geniuses of Classical economics, a commercially tested betterment (a locution, I have noted repeatedly, to be preferred to "capitalism," with its erroneous implication, prominent in Piketty, that capital accumulation, not bettering, is what has made us better off) has enormously enriched large parts of a humanity now more than seven times larger in population than in 1800. It bids fair in the next fifty years or so to enrich everyone on the planet. Look at China and India (and stop saying, "But not *everyone* there has become rich"; they will, as the European history shows, at any rate by the ethically relevant standard of basic comforts denied to most people in England and France before 1800, or in China before its new beginning in 1978 and India before its own in 1991). The left in its worrying routinely forgets this most important secular event since the invention of agriculture—the Great Enrichment of the last two centuries—and goes on worrying and worrying, like the little dog worrying about his bone in the Travelers Insurance advertisement on TV, in a new version every half generation or so.

Here is a partial list of the worrying pessimisms, each of which had its day of fashion since the time, as the historian of economic thought Anthony Waterman put it, "Malthus' first [1798] *Essay* made land scarcity central. And so began a century-long mutation of 'political economy,' the optimistic science of wealth, to 'economics,' the pessimistic science of scarcity."[1]

Malthus worried that workers would proliferate, and Ricardo worried that the owners of land would engorge the national product. Marx worried, or celebrated, depending on how one views historical materialism, that owners of capital would at least make a brave attempt to engorge it. (The Classical economists are Piketty's masters, and his theory is self-described—before page 26—as the sum of Ricardo and Marx.) The last of the Classicals, John Stuart Mill, worried, or celebrated, depending on how one views the sick hurry of modern life, that the stationary state was around the corner.

Then the economists, many on the left but some on the right, in quick succession from 1880 to the present—at the same time that a liberal innovism was driving real wages up and up and up—commenced worrying about, to name a few of the grounds they discerned for pessimisms concerning "capitalism," greed, alienation, racial impurity, workers' lack of bargaining strength, women working, workers' bad taste in consumption, immigration of lesser breeds, monopoly, unemployment, finance vs. engineering, advertising, business cycles, increasing returns, externalities, under-consumption, monopolistic competition, separation of ownership from control, lack of planning, post-War stagnation, investment spillovers, unbalanced growth, dual labor markets, capital insufficiency, peasant irrationality, capital-market imperfections, public choice, missing markets, informational asymmetry, third-world exploitation, regulatory capture, free riding, low-level traps, middle-level traps, path dependency, lack of competitiveness, consumerism, consumption externalities, irrationality, hyperbolic discounting, "too big to fail," environmental degradation, underpaying of care work such as for elders, overpayment of CEOs, slower growth, and more.

One can line up the later items in the list, and some of the earlier ones revived à la Piketty or Krugman, with particular Nobel Memorial Prizes in Economic Science. I will not name here the men (all men, in sharp contrast to the method of Elinor Ostrom, Nobel 2009), but can reveal their formula: first, discover or rediscover a necessary condition for *perfect* competition or a *perfect* world (in Piketty's case, for example, a more perfect equality of income, supposing without serious ethical reflection that equality *is* perfection).

Then assert without evidence (here Piketty does a great deal better than the usual practice) but with suitable mathematical ornamentation (thus Jean Tirole, Nobel 2014) that the condition might be imperfectly realized or the world might not develop in a perfect way. Perfection here below, of course, is unlikely. No, impossible. Then conclude with a flourish (here, however, Piketty falls in with the usual low scientific standard) that "capitalism" is doomed unless experts intervene with a sweet use of the monopoly of coercion in government to implement anti-trust against malefactors of great wealth or subsidies to diminishing-returns industries or foreign aid to perfectly honest governments or money for obviously infant industries or the nudging of sadly childlike consumers or, Piketty says, a tax on inequality-causing capital worldwide.

A feature of this odd history of fault-finding and the proposed statist corrections is that seldom does the economic thinker feel it necessary to offer evidence that his (mostly, I said, "his") proposed government intervention will work as it is supposed to. And almost never does he feel it necessary to offer evidence that the imperfectly attained necessary condition for perfection before intervention is large enough to have reduced much the performance of the economy in aggregate. (I repeat: Piketty exceeds the usual standard here.)

The economic historian John Clapham made such a complaint in 1922 when the theorists were proposing on the basis of a diagram or two that government should subsidize allegedly increasing-returns industries. The economists didn't say how to attain the knowledge of which industries exhibited increasing returns, or how to accomplish the subsidy, or how much their nonquantitative advice would actually help an imperfect government to get closer to the perfect society. The silence was discouraging, Clapham wrote sharply, to "the student not of categories but of things." It still is now, near a century on. He chided the Cambridge economist A. C. Pigou: one looks into *The Economics of Welfare* to find that, in nearly a thousand pages, there is not even one illustration of what industries are in which boxes [that is, in which theoretical categories], though many an argument begins, 'when conditions of diminishing returns prevail' or 'when conditions of increasing returns prevail,' as if everyone knew when that was." He ventriloquized the reply of the theorist imagining without quantitative oomph "those empty economic boxes," a reply heard yet, with no improvement in its plausibility: "If those who know the facts cannot do the fitting, we [theorists finding grave faults in the economy] shall regret it. But our doctrine will retain its logical and, may we add, its pedagogic value. And then you know it goes so prettily into graphs and equations."[2]

A rare exception to the record of not checking out what national-level oomph an alleged imperfection might have was the book of 1966 by the Marxists Paul Baran and Paul Sweezy, *Monopoly Capital*, which tried (and honorably failed) to measure the extent of monopoly overall in the American economy.[3] For most of the other worries on the list—such as that externalities obviously require government intervention (as have declared in historical succession Pigou, Samuelson, and Stiglitz)—the economists have not felt it was worth their scientific time to show that the malfunctioning matters much in aggregate. Piketty at least tries (and honorably fails).

And speaking of "pedagogic value," the sheer number of the briefly fashionable but never measured "imperfections" has taught young economists—who naïvely suppose that their elders *must* have found some facts behind the pretty graphs and equations—to believe that commercially tested betterment has worked disgracefully badly, even though all the quantitative instruments agree it has worked since 1800 or 1848 spectacularly well.

By contrast, liberal economists such as Arnold Harberger and Gordon Tullock claiming that the economy works pretty well have done the factual inquiry, or have at least suggested how to do it.[4] The performance of Pigou, Samuelson, Stiglitz, and the rest on the left (admittedly in these three cases a pretty moderate "left") would be as though an astronomer proposed on some qualitative assumptions that the hydrogen in the sun would run out very, very soon, requiring urgent intervention by the Galactic Empire, but didn't bother to find out with serious observations and quantitative simulations roughly how soon the sad event was going to happen. Mostly in economic theory it has sufficed to show the mere direction of an "imperfection" on a blackboard (Paul Samuelson's "qualitative theorems" so disastrously recommended in his modestly entitled PhD dissertation *Foundations of Economic Analysis* in 1947) and then await the telephone call from the Swedish Academy quite early one October morning.

One begins to suspect that the typical leftist—most of the graver worries have come from the left, naturally enough, though perhaps not so very naturally considering the great payoff of "capitalism" for the working class—starts with a rooted conviction that commercially tested betterment is seriously defective. The conviction is acquired at age sixteen years, when the proto-leftist discovers poverty but has no intellectual tools to understand its source. I followed the pattern, and therefore became for a time a socialist. Then the lifelong "good social democrat," as he describes himself (and as I for a while described myself), when he has become a professional economist, in order to justify the now deep-rooted conviction, looks around for any *qualitative* indication that in some imagined world of categories rather than of things the conviction would be true, without bothering to seize relevant numbers from our own world (of which, I say yet again, our Piketty can*not* be accused). It is the utopianism of good-hearted leftward folk who say, "Surely this wretched society, in which some people are richer and more powerful than others, can be greatly improved. We can do *much*, much better!" The utopianism springs from the logic of stage theories, conceived in the eighteenth century as a tool with which to fight tradition, and deployed in *The Wealth of Nations*, among lesser books. Surely history is not finished. *Excelsior!*

True, the right can be accused of a certain utopianism as well, with its own adolescent air, when it asserts without evidence, as some of the older-model Austrian economists do, and as do some of the Chicago School who have lost their taste for engaging in serious testing of their truths, that we live already in the best of all possible worlds. Yet admitting that there is a good deal of blame to spread around in economics for proposing a science merely philosophical, and not seriously quantitative, the leftward refusal to quantify about the system as a whole seems to me more prevalent and more dangerous.

I have a beloved and extremely intelligent Marxian friend who says to me, "I *hate* markets!" I reply, "But Jack, you delight in searching for antiques *in markets*." "I don't care. I *hate* markets!" The followers of Marx in particular have worried in sequence that the typical European worker would be in such markets immiserized, for which they had little evidence, then that he would be alienated, for which they had little evidence, then that the worker in the typical third-world periphery would be exploited, for which they had little evidence. Recently the Marxians and the rest of the left have commenced worrying about the environment, on what the historian Eric Hobsbawm called with a certain distaste natural in an old Marxist "a much more middle-class basis."[5] Global climate change is a pressing problem, but viable solutions, such a carbon tax, are hardly Marxian. Broader worries on the left about the environment are often unsupported by evidence, and Marxist proposals for what to do about them are missing, save having us all return to Walden Pond and the life of 1845, or to commit mass suicide.

Long ago I had a nightmare. I am not much subject to them, and this one was vivid, an economist's nightmare, a Samuelsonian one. What if *every single* action had to be performed exactly optimally? Maximize Utility subject to Constraints. Max U s.t. C. Suppose, in other words, that you had to reach the *exact* peak of the hill of happiness subject to constraints with *every single* reaching for the coffee cup or *every single* step in the street. You would of course fail in the assignment repeatedly, frozen in fear of the slightest deviation from optimality. In the irrational way of nightmares, it was a chilling vision of what economists call rationality. A recognition of the impossibility of exact perfection lay behind the work of a few economists, such as Herbert Simon's satisficing, Ronald Coase's transaction costs, George Shackle's and Israel Kirzner's reaffirmation of the old Yogi Berra jest: it's hard to predict, especially about the future.

We young American economists and social engineers in the 1960s, innocent as babes, were sure we could attain predictable, mechanical perfection. "Fine-tuning" we called it. It failed, as perfection in human plans about humans must. Boudreaux remarks that "social engineering is one type of engineering at which no one—no matter his or her brilliance, education, skills, demeanor, or intentions—is remotely qualified to do. Among the greatest of all myths is the one that holds that society is much like a machine that can be improved if it is engineered by the right people."[6] The economy, like science or art, is more like an organism growing uncertainly toward the light than a steel machine repeating exactly today and tomorrow what it did yesterday.

The left believes passionately that the economy is easy and known and routine, and therefore suitable for mechanical compulsion. The right believes passionately the same about military compulsion. Yet the most detailed of military compulsions in history, those for the invasion of Normandy, went aft agley.[7] And planning and blundering through the Longest Day and its months-long aftermath was a snap by comparison with an economy. Perfection of a mechanical, repeatable, routine sort cannot in fact even be defined in an economy or a battle, because if such mechanical plans were definable ("buy stocks in January"; "always flank right") others would imitate them or at least anticipate them—and defeat them. If we were so smart, we would be rich.[8] Economists, and most generals, are not.

The political scientist John Mueller in 1999 argued that we should be seeking instead merely the "pretty good."[9] Mueller reckons that commercially tested betterment and liberal democracy as they actually, imperfectly are in places like Europe or its offshoots are pretty good. The "failures" to reach perfection in, say, the behavior of Congress or the equality of the UK distribution of income, Mueller reckons, are probably not large enough to matter all that much to the performance of the polity or the economy. As Raymond Aron, that rarest of things, a modern French liberal, noted, in Clive James's translation, "the liberal believes in the permanence of humanity's imperfection; he resigns himself to a régime in which the good will be the result of numberless actions, and never the result of conscious choice."[10] You could call it the invisible hand, noting that it is true also of other systems, such as language.

At least, then, Piketty is a serious quantitative scientist, unlike the other boys playing in the sandboxes of statistics of "significance" and theorems of "existence" and unmeasured imperfections in the economy and the setting of impossible tasks for an imperfect government (unhappily in this one last respect he joins the boys in their sandboxes). Indeed, Piketty declares on his page 27 (compare page 573), "It is important to note that . . . the main source of divergence [of the incomes of the rich compared with those of the poor] in my theory has nothing to do with any market imperfection [note that possible *governmental* imperfections are no concerns of Piketty]. Quite the contrary: the more perfect the capital market (in the economist's sense) the more likely [the divergence]." That is, like Ricardo and Marx and Keynes, he thinks he has discovered what the Marxians call a "contradiction" (page 571), an unhappy consequence of the very perfection of "capitalism."

Yet all the worries from Malthus to Piketty, from 1798 to the present, share an underlying pessimism, whether from imperfection in the capital market or from the behavioral inadequacies of the individual consumer or from the Laws of Motion of a Capitalist Economy. They share it in the face of the largest enrichment per person that humans have ever witnessed. During such a pretty good history, 1800 to the present, the economic pessimists on the left have nonetheless been subject to nightmares of terrible, terrible faults.

Admittedly, such pessimism sells. For reasons I have never understood, people like to hear that the world is going to hell. They become huffy and scornful when some idiotic optimist intrudes on their pleasure. Yet pessimism has consistently been a poor guide to the modern economic world. We are gigantically richer in body and spirit than we were two centuries ago. In the next half century—if we do not kill betterment by implementing left-wing schemes of planning and redistribution or right-wing schemes of imperialism and warfare, as we did on all counts from 1914 to 1989, following the belief of the clerisy that markets and democracy are terribly faulted—we can expect the entire world to match Sweden or France. Lagos and Rio will be as rich as New York and London.

Pretty good.

29. The Rich Do Not in a Liberal Society Get Rich at the Expense of the Rest

Another bite from the review of Piketty.

Piketty's central theme is the force of interest on inherited financial wealth causing, he claims, increasing inequality of the income earned from the wealth. He declares that "money tends to reproduce itself," a complaint about money and its interest rate repeatedly made in the West since Aristotle.[1] As the Philosopher said of some men, "The whole idea of their lives is that they ought either to increase their money without limit, or at any rate not to lose it. . . . The most hated sort [of increasing their money] . . . is usury, which makes a gain out of money itself."[2] Piketty's (and Aristotle's) theory is that the damned yield on capital usually exceeds the growth rate of the economy, and so the share of capital's returns in national income will steadily increase, simply because interest income—what only the presumably rich capitalists get and supposedly manage to cling to and supposedly live to reinvest—is growing faster than the income the whole society is getting Aristotle and his followers, such as Aquinas and Marx and Piketty, objected to such "unlimited" gain.

The argument is, you see, very old, and very simple. Piketty ornaments it a bit with some portentous accounting about capital-output ratios and the like, producing his central inequality about inequality: so long as $r > g$, where r is the return on capital and g is the growth rate of the economy, we are doomed to ever-increasing rewards to rich capitalists while the rest of us poor suckers fall relatively behind.

Such a merely verbal expression of Piketty's argument is conclusive, and does not need elaboration, so long as its factual assumptions are true. But they are not true: that, namely, only rich people have capital; human or social capital doesn't exist; the rich reinvest their return; they never lose it to sloth or someone else's creative destruction; inheritance is the main mechanism, not a creativity that raises g for the rest of us just when it results in an r, which itself is often shared by us all; and we care ethically only about the Gini coefficient, not about the condition of the working class.

Notice one aspect of that last: in Piketty's tale the rest of us fall only *relatively* behind the ravenous capitalists. The focus on *relative* wealth or income or consumption is a serious problem, among many in the book. Piketty's vision of a "Ricardian Apocalypse," as he calls it, leaves room for the rest of us to do very well indeed, most non-apocalyptically, as in fact since 1800 we have been doing. What is worrying Piketty is that the rich might possibly get richer, even though the poor get richer, too. His worry, in other words, is purely about difference, about the Gini coefficient, about a vague feeling of envy raised to a theoretical and ethical proposition.

Another serious problem with Piketty's mechanical reasoning is that r will almost *always* exceed g, as anyone can tell you who knows about the rough level of interest rates on invested capital and about the rate at which most economies have grown (excepting only China recently, where contrary to the prediction of Piketty, inequality by his accounting definitions has increased). If his simple logic is true, then the Ricardian Apocalypse looms, *always*. Let us therefore bring in the sweet and blameless and omni-competent government—or, even less plausibly, a world government, or the Galactic Empire—to implement "a progressive *global* tax on capital" (page 27) to tax the rich. It is our only hope.

Yet in fact his own *capta*, his own things ingeniously if not flawlessly seized by his research, as he candidly admits without allowing the admission to relieve his pessimism, suggest, as I have noted, that only in Canada, the United States, the United Kingdom, and perhaps other parts of the Anglosphere has the inequality of income increased much, and only recently. Strange: why does the increasing inequality only happen where people speak English? "In continental Europe and Japan, income inequality today remains far lower than it was at the beginning of the 20th century and in fact has not changed much since 1945" (page 321, and figure 9.6). Look, for example, at page 323, figure 9.7, the top decile's share of income, 1900–2010, for the United

States, the United Kingdom, Germany, France, and Sweden. Yet in *all* those countries $r > g$.

Indeed, it has been so, with very rare exceptions such as recent China, since the beginning of time. Yet after the redistributions of the welfare state were accomplished, by 1970, inequality of income did *not* much rise in Germany, France, and Sweden. In other words, Piketty's fears were not confirmed anywhere from 1910 to 1980, nor anywhere in the long run at any time before 1800, nor anywhere in Continental Europe and Japan since World War II, and only recently a little in the Anglosphere including the United States, the United Kingdom, and Canada (Canada, by the way, is never again mentioned).

It is a very great puzzle if money tends to reproduce itself, always, evermore, as a general law governed by the Ricardo-plus-Marx inequality in the rates of r and g as observed in world history. Yet inequality in fact goes up and down in waves, not very large in amplitude, for which we have evidence from many centuries ago to the present, which also doesn't figure in such a tale (Piketty barely mentions the work of the economic historians Peter Lindert and Jeffrey Williamson, who documented the fact, so inconvenient for his case). According to his logic, once a Piketty-wave starts—as it would at any time you care to mention if an economy satisfied the almost-always-satisfied condition of the interest rate exceeding the growth rate of income—it would never stop. Such an inexorable logic means we should have been overwhelmed by an inequality tsunami in 1800 CE or in 1000 CE or for that matter in 2000 BCE. At one point Piketty says just that: "$r > g$ will *again* become the norm in the twenty-first century, *as it had been throughout history until the eve of World War I*" (page 572, italics supplied; one wonders what he does with historically low interest rates right now, or the negative real interest rates during the inflation of the 1970s and 1980s). Why then did the share of the rich not rise anciently to 100 percent? At the least, how could the share be stable at, say, the 50 percent that in Medieval Europe typified its unproductive economies, with land and landlords dominant?

Sometimes Piketty describes his machinery as a "potentially explosive process" (page 444); at other times he admits that random shocks to a family fortune mean that "it is unlikely that inequality of wealth will grow indefinitely, . . . rather, the wealth distribution will converge toward a certain equilibrium" (page 451; he gives no account of the equilibrium). On the basis of the *Forbes* lists of the very rich, Piketty notes, for example, "several hundred new fortunes appear in [the $1 billion to $10 billion] range somewhere in the world almost every year" (page 441). Which is it, Professor Piketty? Apocalypse now, or (what is in fact observed, roughly, with minor ups and downs) a steady share of rich people constantly dropping out of riches or coming into them, in evolutionary fashion? His machinery seems to explain nothing alarming, and at the same time to predict something most alarming.

The journalist Matt Ridley has offered a persuasive reason for the (slight) rise in inequality recently in Britain. "Knock me down with a feather," Ridley writes,

> You mean to say that during three decades when the government encouraged asset bubbles in house prices; gave tax breaks to pensions; lightly taxed wealthy non-doms [that is, "non-domiciled," the rich citizens of other countries such as Russia and Saudi Arabia living in the United Kingdom]; poured money into farm subsidies [owned in the United States and especially in the United Kingdom by landlords mainly rich]; and severely restricted the supply of land for housing, pushing up the premium earned by planning permission for development, the wealthy owners of capital saw their relative wealth increase slightly? Well, I'll be damned. . . . [Seriously, now] a good part of any increase in wealth concentration since 1980 has been driven by government policy, which has systematically redirected earning opportunities to the rich rather than the poor.[3]

In the United States, with its pervasive welfare payments and tax breaks for our good friends the very rich, such as the treatment of "carried interest" that made Mitt Romney a lot richer, one can make a similar case that the government, which Piketty expects to solve the alleged problem, is the cause. It wasn't "capitalism" that caused the recent and restricted blip in the Anglosphere, and certainly not commercially tested betterment at the extraordinary rates of the past two centuries. It was Parliament and Congress.

The inconsequence of Piketty's argument, in truth, is to be expected from the frailties of its declared sources. Start by adopting a theory by a great economist, Ricardo, which has failed entirely as a prediction. Landlords did not engorge the national product, contrary to what Ricardo confidently predicted. Indeed, the share of land rents in national (and world) income fell heavily nearly from the moment Ricardo claimed it would steadily rise. The outcome resembles that from Malthus, whose prediction of population overwhelming the food supply was falsified nearly from the moment he claimed it was bound to happen.

All right. Then combine Ricardo's with another theory by a less great *economist,* Marx (yet the greatest *social scientist* of the nineteenth century, without compare, though mistaken on almost every substantive point, and especially in his predictions). Marx supposed that wages would fall and yet profits would also fall and yet technological betterments would also happen. Such an accounting, as the Marxian economist Joan Robinson frequently pointed out, is impossible. At least one, the wages or the profits, has to rise if technological betterment is happening, as it so plainly did. With a bigger pie, someone has to get more.

In the event, what rose were wages on raw labor and especially on a great accumulation of *human* capital, but capital owned by the laborers, not by the truly rich. The return to physical capital was higher than a riskless return on British or American government bonds, in order to compensate for the risk in holding capital (such as being made obsolete by betterment—think of your computer, obsolete in four years). But the return on physical capital, and on human capital, was anyway held down to its level of very roughly 5 to 10 percent by competition among the proliferating capitalists.

Imagine our immiserization if the income of workers, because they did *not* accumulate human capital, and their societies had *not* adopted the accumulation of ingenuities since 1800, had experienced the history of stagnation since 1800 that the per-unit return to capital has. It is not hard to imagine, because such miserable income of workers exists even now in places like Somalia and North Korea. Instead, since 1800 in the average rich country, the income of the workers per person increased by a factor of about thirty (2,900 percent, if you please) and in even in the world as a whole, including the still-poor countries, by a factor of ten (900 percent), while the rate of return to physical capital stagnated.

Piketty does not acknowledge that each wave of inventors, of entrepreneurs, and even of routine capitalists finds their rewards taken from them by entry, which is an economic concept he does not appear to grasp. The income from department stores in the late nineteenth century, such as Le Bon Marché, Marshall Field's, and Selfridges, was entrepreneurial. The model was then copied all over the rich world, and was the basis for little fortunes in Cedar Rapids, Iowa, and Benton Harbor, Michigan. Then in the late twentieth century the model was challenged by a wave of discounters, and they in turn by the internet. The original accumulation slowly or quickly dissipates. In other words, the profit going to the profiteers is more or less quickly undermined by outward-shifting supply, if governmental monopolies and protectionisms of the sort Ridley noted in recent British history do not intervene. Remember Nordhaus's calculation I mentioned that the inventors and entrepreneurs nowadays earn in profit only 2 percent of the social value of their inventions.[4] If you are Sam Walton the 2 percent gives you personally a great deal of money from introducing bar codes into the stocking of supermarket shelves. But 98 percent at the cost of 2 percent is nonetheless a pretty good deal for the rest of us. The gains from macadamized roads or vulcanized rubber, then modern universities, structural concrete, and the airplane, have enriched even the poorest among us.

Piketty, who does not believe in supply responses, focuses instead on the great evil of very rich people having seven Rolex watches by mere inheritance. He speaks often of Liliane Bettencourt, heiress to the L'Oréal fortune, the third-richest woman in the world, who "has never worked a day in her life, but saw her fortune grow exactly as fast as that of [the admittedly bettering] Bill Gates."[5] Ugh, says Piketty, which is his ethical philosophy in full.

Wage inequality in the rich countries experiencing an enlarging gap of rich vs. poor, few though the countries are (Piketty's finding, remember: Canada, United States, United Kingdom), is mainly, he admits, caused by "the emergence of extremely high remunerations at the summit of the wage hierarchy, particularly among top managers of large firms." The emergence, note, has nothing to do with his $r > g$.

The economists Geoffrey Brennan, Gordon Menzies, and Michael Munger make a similar argument in a paper written in advance of Piketty's book, that inheritance *inter vivos* of human capital is bound to exacerbate Gini-coefficient inequality because "for the first time in human history richer parents are having fewer children. . . . Even if the increased opulence continues, it will be concentrated in fewer and fewer hands."[6] The rich will send their one boy, intensively tutored in French and mathematics, to Sydney Grammar School and on to Harvard. The poor will dissipate what little they have among their supposedly numerous children.

Adam Smith's hoped-for "universal opulence which extends itself to the lowest ranks of the people" would give all access to excellent education— which is an ethically sensible object of social policy, and has the additional merit of being achievable.[7] Attempts to reduce Gini-coefficient inequality are not. If the poor are so rich (because the Great Enrichment has been unleashed) that they, too, have fewer children, which is the case worldwide, from Italy to Bangladesh, then the tendency to rising variance will be attenuated. The economist Tyler Cowen reminds me, further, that "low" birth rates also include zero children, which would make lines die out—as indeed they often did even in royal families, well-nourished. Non-existent children, such as those of Grand Duke of Florence Gian Gastone de' Medici in 1737, can't inherit, *inter vivos* or not. Instead their second and third cousins do, dissipating the wealth.

And the effect of inherited wealth on children is commonly to remove their ambition, as one can witness daily on Rodeo Drive or Upper Sloane Street. Laziness—or for that matter regression to the mean of ability—is a powerful equalizer. "There always comes a time," Piketty writes against his own argument, "when a prodigal child squanders the family fortune," which was the point of the centuries-long struggle in English law for and against entailed estates (page 451). Imagine if you'd had access to ten million dollars at age eighteen, before your character was fully formed. It would have been for you an ethical disaster, as it regularly is for the children of the very rich. We prosperous parents of the Great Enrichment can properly worry about our children's and especially our grandchildren's incentives to such efforts as a PhD in economics, or serious entrepreneurship, or indeed serious charity. However many diamond bracelets they have, most rich children—and maybe all our children in the riches that the Great Enrichment is extending to the lowest ranks of the people—will not suffer through a PhD in economics. Why bother? David Rockefeller did (University of Chicago, 1940, in economics), but his grandfather was unusually lucky in transmitting born-poor values to his son John Jr. and then to his five John-Jr.-begotten grandsons (though not to his one granddaughter in that line, Abby, who never worked a day in her life).

Because Piketty is obsessed with inheritance, moreover, he wants to downplay entrepreneurial profit, the innovism that has made the poor rich. It is again Aristotle's claim that money is sterile and that interest on money is therefore unnatural. Aristotle was on this matter mistaken, as anti-Semites have been for a thousand years. It is commonly the case, contrary to Piketty, and setting aside the cheapening of our goods produced by the investments of their wealth by the rich, that the people with more money got their more by being more ingeniously productive, for the benefit of us all—getting that

PhD, for example, or being excellent makers of automobiles or excellent writers of horror novels or excellent throwers of touchdown passes or excellent providers of cell phones, such as Carlos Slim of Mexico, at one point the richest man in the world (with a little boost, it may be, from corrupting the Mexican Congreso General).

That Frank Sinatra became richer than most of his fans was not an ethical scandal. The "Wilt Chamberlain" example devised by the philosopher Robert Nozick (Piketty mentions John Rawls, but not Nozick, Rawls's nemesis) says that if we pay voluntarily to get the benefit of clever CEOs or gifted athletes, there is no further ethical issue. The unusually high rewards to the Frank Sinatras and Jamie Dimons and Wilt Chamberlains come from the much wider markets of the age of globalization and mechanical reproduction, not from theft or inheritance.

It's not merely a matter of including depreciation in the accounting. The economist Eamonn Butler observes that "the idea [fundamental to Piketty's case] that capital is a permanent asset, which provides its lucky owners with a continuing stream of effortless benefits—like apples falling off a tree—is also mistaken. In fact, capital takes time, money and effort to preserve. It must be maintained and protected. And to keep its value in a changing and competitive world, it must be applied with constant diligence and focus."[8] So too labor's skills and location, and even, as every farmer knows, land. A changing economy requires constant diligence and focus by humans, which is more likely evoked by humans owning the capital, labor, and land than by remote central planners.

30. Piketty's Book Has Serious Technical Errors

More.

The technical flaws in Piketty's argument are many. When you dig, you find them. Let me list some more that I myself spotted. Other economists, I have heard, have spotted many more. Google "Piketty." I have not done the googling, because I do not wish merely to pile on. I respect what he tried to accomplish, and he therefore deserves from me an independent evaluation.

For example—this one is big, and is also true of Oxfam's calculation of the share of world wealth held by the top billionaires—Piketty's definition of wealth does not include human capital, owned by the workers. It has grown in rich countries to be the main source of income. It is combined with the immense accumulation since 1800 of capital in knowledge and social habits, owned by everyone with access to them. And Piketty ignores governmental capital, also very big, and not possessed exclusively by the dastardly rich.

Therefore his laboriously assembled charts of the (merely physical and merely private) capital/output ratio are erroneous. They have excluded the main forms of capital in the modern world. More to the point, by insisting on defining capital as something owned nearly always by rich people, Piketty mistakes the source of income, which is chiefly embodied human ingenuity, not accumulated machines or appropriated land.

He asserts mysteriously on page 46, for example, that there are "many reasons for excluding human capital from our definition of capital." But he offers only one: "human capital cannot be owned by any other person."[1] Yet human capital is owned precisely by the worker herself. Piketty does not explain why self-ownership à la Locke, without permitting alienation, is not ownership. If I own and operate improved land, but the law prevents its alienation (as some traditionalist or collectivist laws do), why is it not capital? Certainly, human capital is "capital." It accumulates through abstention from consumption, it depreciates, it earns a market-determined rate of return, it can be made obsolete by creative destruction. Capital.

Once upon a time, to be sure, Piketty's world, without much human capital or social capital or intellectual capital or even much governmental capital, was approximately our world, that of Ricardo and Marx, with workers owning only their hands and backs, and the bosses and landlords owning all the other means of production. But since 1848 the world has been transformed by what sits between the workers' ears. The only reason in the book to exclude human and social capital from "capital" appears to be to assure the conclusion Piketty wants to achieve, that inequality has increased, or will, or might, or is to be feared. In logic such a move is called begging the question. One of the headings in chapter 7 declares that "capital [is] always more unequally distributed than labor." No it isn't. If human capital is included—the ordinary factory worker's literacy, the nurse's educated skill, the professional manager's command of complex systems, the economist's understanding of supply responses—the workers themselves now in the correct accounting own most of the nation's capital, and Piketty's drama from 1848 falls to the ground.

The neglect of human capital on the Problems side of the book is doubly strange because on the Solutions side Piketty recommends education and other investment . . . in human capital. In his focus on raising by education the marginal product of workers unemployed by government programs—rather than helping them by correcting the governmental programs of interference in voluntary exchange that created the unemployment in the first place—he joins most of the left, especially those with university jobs supplying education. Thus in South Africa, I have noted, the left proposes to carry on with high minimum wages and oppressive regulations, solving the unemployment problem thus governmentally generated by improving through the same dubiously competent government the education and therefore the marginal products of unemployed South Africans.

No one, left or right or liberal, would want to complain about better education, especially if it fell from the sky at no opportunity cost. True, we bleeding-heart liberals would suggest achieving it by some other means than by pouring more money into a badly functioning nationalized industry providing elementary education, or into a higher-education system grossly favoring the rich over the poor—as it does strikingly in France, among other countries, by giving the rich student, better prepared, a tuition-free ride into the ruling class. In any case the sweet-sounding "we love education" ploy exempts the left from facing the obvious cause of unemployment in, say, South Africa, namely, a sclerotic system of labor-market and other regulations in aid of the Congress of South African Trade Unions, rigged against the wretchedly poor Black South African sitting jobless with a small income subsidy in a hut in the back country of KwaZulu-Natal.

I do not want to give the impression that Piketty's book is without good and interesting technical economics. He offers an interesting theory in chapter 14, for example, that the very high CEO salaries we have nowadays in the United Kingdom and especially the United States are a result of the fall in marginal tax rates from their extremely high levels during 1930–1970. In those halcyon days it was not so bright of the managers to pay themselves huge salaries, which after all the government would take away every year. Once this disincentive was removed, Piketty plausibly argues, the managers could take advantage of the clubby character of executive-remuneration committees to get dressed and go to town. And so Piketty recommends returning to 80 percent marginal income tax rates (page 513). But wait. Technically speaking, if on ethical grounds we don't like high CEO salaries, why not legislate against them directly, using some more targeted tool than a massive intrusion into the economy by way of taxes? Or why not shame the executive-remuneration committees? Piketty doesn't say.

A deeper technical problem in the book, however, is that Piketty, though an economist, does not understand supply responses. In keeping with his position as a man of the left, he has a vague and confused idea about how markets work, and especially about how supply responds to higher prices. He wants to offer pessimistic conclusions concerning "a market economy based on private property, if left to itself" (page 571). He had better, then, know what elementary economics, agreed to by all who have studied it enough to understand what it is saying, does in fact say about how a market economy based on private property behaves when left to itself. Roughly. Pretty well.

Startling evidence of Piketty's miseducation occurs as early in the English translation as page 6. He begins by seeming to concede to his neoclassical opponents (he is I repeat a proud Classical economist, Ricardo plus Marx; not much Mill). "To be sure, there exists in principle a quite simple economic mechanism that should restore equilibrium to the process [in this case the process of rising prices of oil or urban land leading to a Ricardian Apocalypse of landlords taking everything]: the mechanism of supply and demand. If the supply of any good is insufficient, and its price is too high, *then demand for that good should decrease, which would lead to a decline in its price.*"

The (English) words I italicize clearly mix up movement along a demand curve with movement of the entire curve, a first-term error at university. The correct analysis (we tell our first-year, first-term students at about week three) is that if the price is "too high" it is not the whole demand curve that "restores equilibrium" (though the high price in the short run does give people a reason to conserve on oil or urban land with smaller cars and smaller apartments, moving as they in fact do up along their otherwise stationary demand curves), but an eventually *outward-moving supply curve.* The supply curve moves out because entry in the medium and long run is induced by the smell of super-normal profits. New oil deposits are discovered, new refineries are built, new suburbs are settled, new high-rises saving urban land are constructed, as has in fact happened massively since, say, 1973, unless government has restricted oil exploitation (usually on environmental grounds) or the building of high-rises (usually on corrupt grounds).

Piketty goes on—remember: it does not occur to him that high prices cause after a while the whole *supply* curve to move out; he thinks the high price will cause the demand *curve* to move *in,* leading to "a decline in price" (of the scarce item, oil or urban land)—"such adjustments might be unpleasant or complicated." To show his contempt for the ordinary working of the price system, he imagines comically that "people should . . . take to traveling about by bicycle." The substitutions along a given demand curve, or one mysteriously moving in, without any supply response "might also take decades, during which landlords and oil well owners might well accumulate claims on the rest of the population" (now he has the demand curve moving *out,* for some reason faster than the supply curve moves out) "so extensive that they could they could easily [on grounds not argued] come to own everything that can be owned, including" in one more use of the comical alternative, "bicycles, once and for all."

Having butchered the elementary analysis of entry and of substitute supplies, which after all is the economic history of the world, he speaks of "the emir of Qatar" as a future owner of even those bicycles, once and for all. The phrase must have been written before the recent gigantic expansion of oil and gas exploitation in Canada and the United States when oil prices briefly spiked. In short, he concludes triumphantly (having seen through, rather in the style of a bright first-year student in week three of elementary economics, the obvious silliness found among those rich-friendly neoclassical economists), "The interplay of supply and demand in no way rules out the possibility of a large and lasting divergence in the distribution of wealth linked to extreme changes in certain relative prices, . . . Ricardo's scarcity principle." All on the bottom of page 6 and the top of page 7, a lot of economic error in one paragraph.

I was so startled by the passage that I went to the French original and called on my shamefully poor French to make sure it was not a mistranslation. A charitable reading might say at first that it was—very charitable indeed because after all the preparatory senselessness remains: "then demand [the whole demand curve?] for that good should decrease" ("alors la demande pour ce bien doit baisser"). Yet Piketty's English is much better than my French—he taught for a couple of years at MIT, and speaks educated English when interviewed. If he let stand the senselessness in the translation by Arthur Goldhammer (a mathematics PhD who has since 1979 translated seventy-five books from French—though admittedly this is his first translation of technical economics), especially in such an important passage, one has to assume that he thought it was fine economics, a penetrating, nay decisive, criticism of those silly native English- or German-speaking economists who think that supply curves move out in response to increased scarcity. (Yet she who has never left a little senselessness in her texts, and especially in translations out of her native language, is invited to cast the first stone.)

In the French version one finds, instead of the obviously erroneous English, "which should lead to a decline in its price," typical of the confused first-term student, the clause "qui permettra de calmer le jeu," that is, "which should permit some calming down," or more literally, "which would permit some calming of the play [of, in this case, supply and demand]." "Calmer le jeu," though, is in fact sometimes used in economic contexts in French to mean heading off a price bubble. And what "calming down" could mean in the passage other than an economics- and common-sense-denying *fall* in price without a supply response having taken place is hard to see.

The rest of the passage does not support the charitable reading. The rest is non-controversially translated, and spins out the conviction Piketty evidently has that supply responses do not figure in the story of supply and demand, which anyway is unpleasant and complicated—so much less so than, say, the government taking a radically larger share of world income in taxes, with its attendant inefficiencies, or the government encouraging the spurning of capitalist ownership in favor of "new forms of governance and shared ownership intermediate between public and private," with its attendant corruptions and lack of skin in the game (page 573).

Piketty, it would seem, has not read with understanding the theory of supply and demand that he disparages, such as Smith (one sneering remark on page 9), Say (ditto, mentioned in a footnote with Smith as optimistic), Bastiat (no mention), Walras (no mention; these last three writing in French), Menger (no mention), Marshall (no mention), Mises (no mention), Hayek (one footnote citation on another matter), and Friedman (pages 548–549, but only on monetarism, not the price system). He is in short not qualified to sneer at self-regulated markets (for example on page 572), because he has no idea how they work. It would be like someone, without understanding natural selection or the Galton-Watson process or modern genetics, scornfully attacking the theory of evolution (which by the way is identical to the theory the economists use of entry and exit in self-regulating markets—an early version of the supply response being what inspired Darwin).

In a way, it is not his fault. He was educated in France. French-style teaching of economics, against which the insensitively named Post-Autistic Economics movement by economics students in France was directed, is abstract and Cartesian, and never teaches the ordinary price theory that one might use to understand the oil market, 1973 to the present.[2] Because of supply responses, never considered in books by non-economists such as Paul Ehrlich's *The Population Bomb* (1968) or by economists who do not understand elementary economics, the real price of oil, for example, since 1980 has *fallen*.

The great liberal economist Peter Boettke speaks of the economist infected in the late nineteenth century by the aimless empiricism of the German historical school when he says that "the first generation [after 1848], while rejecting the analytic method of classical economics, was nonetheless trained in it. . . . The second generation, however, not trained in the classical method, lacked the mental tools necessary to interpret economic phenomena."[3] Yet he might as well be talking about the first generation of Samuelsonians, before 1948, contrasted with the second generation, and Piketty in the third. Samuelson himself learned actual economics as an undergraduate at the University of Chicago in the 1930s. In particular, writes Boettke, after 1848 among socialists and after 1948 among economic engineers, "the self-organizing principles of the market economy were no longer understood. . . . The generation of economists now entrusted with designing economic policy had lost an understanding of the basic properties of a market system."[4] It is an important one of Piketty's numerous technical errors.

More deeply yet, Piketty's "structural" thinking characterizes the left, and characterizes too the economic thinking of physical and biological scientists when they venture into economic issues. It is why the magazine *Scientific American* half a century ago loved input-output analysis (which was my own beloved also at the time, so I get it) and still publishes fixed-coefficient arguments by physical and biological scientists about the environment. The non-economic scientists declare, "We have such-and-such a structure in existence, which is to say the accounting magnitudes presently existing, for example the presently known reserves of oil." Then, ignoring that the search for new reserves is in fact an economic activity, or even ignoring the definition of what a "resource" might be, they calculate the result of rising "demand" (that is, quantity demanded, not distinguished from the whole demand curve), assuming no substitutions, no along-the-demand-curve reaction to price, no supply reaction to price, no second or third act, no seen and unseen, such as an entrepreneurial response to greater scarcity. In the mid-nineteenth century it was Marx's scientific procedure, too. Piketty follows it yet.

31. The Ethical Accounting of Inequality Is Mistaken

It is important in thinking about the issues Piketty so energetically raises to keep straight what exactly is unequal. Physical capital and the claims to it (bonds, stocks, deeds) are unequally owned, of course, although trade-union pension funds and the like do work the other way to some degree. The yield on such portions of the nation's capital stock is indeed the income of the rich, especially the rich by inheritance, whom Piketty worries most about. But, as I have noted, if capital is more comprehensively measured to include the increasingly important human capital such as engineering degrees and the increasingly important commonly owned capital such as superhighways and public parks and modern knowledge (think: the internet), the income yield on the capital is less unequally owned than are paper claims to physical capital.

Further, consumption in turn is much less unequally enjoyed than income. A rich person owning seven houses might be thought to be seven times better off than a poor person with barely one. But of course she's not, because she can consume only one house at a time, and can consume only one pair of shoes at a time, and so forth. The diamond bracelet sitting un-worn at the bottom of her ample jewelry box is a scandal, because she could have paid the annual school fees of a thousand families in Mozambique with what she foolishly spent on the bauble that was fashionable last season in Cannes. She ought to be ashamed to indulge in such expenditure. It is an important ethical issue, if not a public issue. But anyway the expenditure has not increased her actual, point-of-use consumption.

Further still, and crucially, the consumption of basic capabilities or necessities is very much more equally enjoyed nowadays than the rest of consumption, or income, or capital, or financial wealth, and has become more and more equal as the Great Enrichment spreads. Therefore economic growth, however unequally it is accumulated as wealth or earned as income, is already more egalitarian in its consumption, and by now is very equal indeed in such necessitous consumption. As the American economist John Bates Clark predicted in 1901, "The typical laborer will increase his wages from one dollar a day to two, from two to four and from four to eight [which was accurate in real terms of per-person income down to the present, though the calculation does not allow for the radically improved quality of goods and services since 1901]. Such gains will mean infinitely more to him than any possible increase of capital can mean to the rich. . . . This very change will bring with it a continual approach to equality of genuine comfort."[1]

In 2013 the economists Donald Boudreaux and Mark Perry noted that "according to the [Federal] Bureau of Economic Analysis, spending by households on many of modern life's 'basics'—food at home, automobiles, clothing and footwear, household furnishings and equipment, and housing and utilities—fell from 53 percent of disposable income in 1950 to 44 percent in 1970 to 32 percent today."[2] It is a point which the economic historian Robert Fogel had made in 2004 for a longer span.[3] The economist Steven Horwitz summarizes the facts on labor hours required to buy a color TV or an automobile, and notes that "these data do not capture . . . the change in quality . . . the 1973 television was at most 25 [inches] with poor resolution, probably no remote control, weak sound, and generally nothing like its 2013 descendant. . . . Getting 100,000 miles out of a car in the 1970s was cause for celebration. *Not* getting 100,000 miles out of a car today is cause to think you bought a lemon."[4]

Nor in the United States are the poor getting poorer. Horwitz observes that "looking at various data on consumption, from Census Bureau surveys of what the poor have in their homes to the labor time required to purchase a variety of consumer goods, makes clear that poor Americans are living better now than ever before. In fact, poor Americans today live better, by these measures, than did their middle-class counterparts in the 1970s."[5] In the summer of 1976 an associate professor of economics at the University of Chicago had no air conditioning in his apartment. Nowadays many quite poor Chicagoans have it.[6] The terrible heat wave in Chicago of July 1995 killed over seven hundred people, mainly low income.[7] Yet earlier heat waves, in 1936 and 1948, before air conditioning was at all common, killed many more.[8]

The political scientist and public intellectual Robert Reich argues that we must nonetheless be alarmed by inequality, Gini-coefficient style, rather than devoting all our energies to raising the absolute condition of the poor. "Widening inequality," he declares, "challenges the nation's core ideal of equal opportunity." "Widening inequality still hampers upward mobility. That's simply because the ladder is far longer now. The distance between its bottom and top rungs, and between every rung along the way, is far greater. Anyone ascending it at the same speed as before will necessarily make less progress upward."[9]

Reich is mistaken. Horwitz summarizes the results of a study by Julia Isaacs on individual mobility 1969–2005: "82 percent of children of the bottom 20 percent in 1969 had [real] incomes in 2000 that were higher than what their parents had in 1969. The median [real] income of those children of the poor of 1969 was double that of their parents."[10] There is no doubt that the children and grandchildren of the English coal miners of 1937, whom Orwell describes "traveling" underground, bent over double, a mile or more to get to the coal face, at which point they started to get paid, are much better off than their fathers or grandfathers.[11] There is no doubt that the children and grandchildren of the Dust Bowl refugees in California are. Steinbeck chronicled in *The Grapes of Wrath* their worst and terrible times. A few years later many of the Okies got jobs in the war industries, and many of their children later went to university. Some went on to become professors at Berkeley.

The usual way, especially on the left, of talking about poverty relies on the percentage distribution of income, staring fixedly for example at a *relative* "poverty line." As the progressive Australian economist Peter Saunders notes, however, such a definition of poverty "automatically shift[s] upwards whenever the real incomes (and hence the poverty line) are rising."[12] The poor are always with us, but merely by definition. It's the opposite of the Lake Wobegon effect—it's not that all the children are above average, but that there is always a bottom fifth or tenth or whatever in any distribution whatsoever. Of course.

The philosopher Harry Frankfurt noted long ago that "calculating the size of an equal share [of income in the style of poverty lines or Gini coefficients] is plainly much easier than determining how much a person needs in order to have enough"—"much easier" as in dividing GDP by population and reporting with irritation that some people earn, or anyway get, more.[13] It's the simplified ethics of the schoolyard, or dividing the pizza: "That's unfair." But I have already quoted Frankfurt's wise remark on the irrelevance of inequality in ethics: "economic equality is not, as such, of particular moral importance." It doesn't matter ethically whether the poor have the same number of diamond bracelets and Porsche automobiles and professional sports teams as do owners of successful hedge funds. It does indeed matter, I have also said, whether they have the same opportunities to vote or to learn to read or to have a roof over their heads.

We had better focus directly on what we want to achieve, which is equal sustenance and dignity, eliminating poverty, or what the economist Amartya Sen and the philosopher Martha Nussbaum call insuring adequate capabilities. The size of the Gini coefficient or the share of the bottom 10 percent is irrelevant to the noble and ethically relevant purpose of lifting up the poor to a condition of dignity, Frankfurt's "enough."

Much of the research on the economics of inequality stumbles on this simple ethical point, focusing on measures of relative inequality such as the Gini coefficient or the share of the top 1 percent rather than on measures of the absolute welfare of the poor. Speaking of the legal philosopher Ronald Dworkin's egalitarianism, Frankfurt observed that Dworkin in fact, and ethically, "cares principally about the [absolute] value of people's lives, but he mistakenly represents himself as caring principally about the relative magnitudes of their economic assets."[14] Piketty himself is mainly indignant at the rich. He gets around to caring much about the poor finally in the last phrase in the last sentence of the book. On rare occasions he mentions the issue in the body of the book.[15] Mostly it's indignation about Liliane Bettencourt.

Dworkin and Piketty and much of the left, in other words, miss the ethical point, which is the liberal one of lifting up the poor. By redistribution? By equality in diamond bracelets? No: by the dramatic increase in the size of the pie, which has historically brought the poor to 90 or 95 percent of "enough," as against the small amounts attainable by redistribution without enlarging the pie. Yet the left works overtime, out of the best of motives—and Piketty has worked very hard indeed—to justify its ethically irrelevant focus on Gini coefficients and especially on the disgraceful consumption of the very rich.

The economic historian Robert Margo noted in 1993 that before the US Civil Rights Act of 1964, "blacks could not aspire to high-paying white collar jobs" because of discrimination. Yet African-Americans had prepared themselves, by their own efforts, up from slavery, to perform in such jobs if given a chance. "Middle-class blacks owe their success in large part to themselves," and to the increasingly educated and productive society they lived in. "What if the black labor force, poised on the eve of the Civil Rights Movement, was just as illiterate, impoverished, rural, and Southern as when Lincoln freed the slaves? . . . Would we have as large a black middle class as we do today? Plainly not."[16]

For the poor in the countries that have allowed the ethical change of modern liberalism to happen, Frankfurt's "enough" has largely come to pass. "Largely," I say, and much more than alternative systems have allowed. I do not say "completely," or "as much as every honest person would wish." But the contrast between the condition of the working class in the proudly "capitalist" United States and in the avowedly social-democratic countries such as the Netherlands or Sweden is not in fact very large, despite what you have heard from journalists and politicians who have not looked into the actual statistics, or have not lived in more than one country, and think that half of the American population consists of poor urban African-Americans. The social safety nets are in practice rather similar among rich countries.

But the safety nets, with or without holes, have not been the main lift for the poor in the United States, the Netherlands, Japan, Sweden, or the others. The main lift has been the Great Enrichment. Boudreaux noted that the clothing of a literal billionaire who participated in an economic seminar about Gini coefficients didn't look much different from that of an "impoverished" graduate student giving the very paper. "In many of the basic elements of life, nearly every American is as well off as Mr. Bucks [his pseudonym for the billionaire]. If wealth differences between billionaires and ordinary Americans are barely visible in the most routine aspects of daily life, then to suffer distress over a Gini coefficient is to unwisely elevate ethereal abstraction over palpable reality."[17] Mr. Bucks undoubtedly had more houses and more Rolls-Royces than the graduate student. One may ask, though, the cheeky but always relevant question: So what?

32. Inequality Is Not Unethical If It Happens in a Free Society

And so beyond technical matters in economics, the fundamental *ethical* problem in Piketty's book is that he has not reflected on why inequality by itself would be bad. The absolute condition of the poor has been raised overwhelmingly more by the Great Enrichment than by redistribution. The economic historians Ian Gazeley and Andrew Newell documented in 2010 "the reduction, almost to elimination, of absolute poverty among working households in Britain between 1904 and 1937." "The elimination of grinding poverty among working families," they show, "was almost complete by the late thirties, well before the Welfare State." Their chart 2 exhibits income distributions in 1886 prices at 1886, 1906, 1938, and 1960, showing the disappearance of the classic expression of misery for British workers, "round about a pound a week."[1]

To be sure, it's irritating that a super-rich woman buys a $40,000 watch. The purchase is ethically objectionable. She really should be ashamed. She should be giving to effective charities any income in excess of an ample level of comfort—two cars, say, not twenty, two houses, not seven, one yacht, not five. Andrew Carnegie enunciated in 1889 the principle that "the man who dies thus rich dies disgraced."[2] Carnegie gave away his entire fortune (well, he gave it at death, after enjoying a castle in his native Scotland and a few other baubles). But that many rich people act in a disgraceful fashion does not automatically imply that the government should intervene to stop it. People act disgracefully in all sorts of ways. If our rulers were assigned the task in a fallen world of keeping us all wholly ethical, the government would bring all our lives under its fatherly tutelage, a nightmare achieved approximately before 1989 in East Germany and now in North Korea, or in China with Xi Jinping giving it a modern technological face.

Piketty argues that growth depends on capital accumulation—not, as it actually does, on a new ideology and the bettering ideas that such an ideology of innovism encourages, and an ethics supporting the ideology. Piketty, like many American High Liberals, European Marxians, and conservatives everywhere, is annoyed precisely by the ethical pretension of the modern CEOs. The bosses, he writes on page 318, justify their economic success by placing "primary emphasis on their personal merit and moral qualities, which they described [in surveys] using terms such as rigor, patience, work, effort, and so on (but also tolerance, kindness, etc.)."[3] As Boudreaux puts it, "Piketty prefers what he takes to be the more honest justifications for super-wealth offered by the elites of the novels of [the conservatives] Austen and Balzac, namely, that such wealth is required to live a comfortable lifestyle, period. No self-praise and psychologically comforting rationalizations by those early-19th-century squires and their ladies!"[4] Piketty therefore sneers on page 529 from a conservative-progressive height that "the heroes and heroines in the novels of Austen and Balzac would never have seen the need to compare their personal qualities to those of their servant"). To which Boudreaux replies, "Yes, well, bourgeois virtues were not in the early 19th century as widely celebrated and admired as they later came to be celebrated and admired. We should be pleased that today's [very] high-salaried workers brag about their bourgeois habits and virtues, and that workers—finally!—understand that having such virtues and acting on them is dignified."

The theory of great wealth espoused by the peasants and proletariat and their *soi-disant* champions among the leftish clerisy is non-desert by luck or theft, the wretches. The theory of great wealth espoused by the aristocracy and their champions among the rightish clerisy is desert by inheritance, itself to be justified by ancient luck or theft, an inheritance we *aristoi* of course should collect without psychologically comforting rationalizations. The theory of great wealth espoused by the bourgeoisie and by its friends the liberal economists, on the contrary, is desert by virtue in supplying ethically, without coercion, what people are willing to buy.

The bourgeois virtues are doubtless exaggerated, especially by the bourgeoisie, and sometimes even by its friends. But the results of the virtue bragging have not been so bad for the rest of us. Think of the later plays of Ibsen, the pioneering dramatist of bourgeois life. The bank manager, Helmer, in *A Doll House* (1878) describes a clerk caught in forgery as "morally lost," having a "moral breakdown."[5] Helmer's speech throughout the play is saturated with an ethical rhetoric we are accustomed to calling "Victorian." But Helmer's wife, Nora, it turns out, whose rhetoric is also ethically saturated, has committed literally the same crime as the clerk. She committed her forgery, though, in order to save her husband's life, not as the clerk did for immoral profit. By the end of the play she leaves Helmer, a shocking move among the Norwegian bourgeoisie of 1878, because she suddenly realizes that if he knew of her crime he would not have exercised the love ethics of protecting her from the consequences of a forgery committed for love. An ethical bourgeoisie—which is what all of Ibsen's plays after 1876 explore, as later did the plays of Arthur Miller—has complicated duties. The bourgeoisie goes on talking and talking about virtue, and sometimes achieves it. Placing primary emphasis on bourgeois virtue, in any case, is not itself a sin.

The original and sustaining causes of the modern world, I would argue contrary to Piketty's lofty sneers at bourgeois virtues, were indeed ethical, not material, and were located especially in a liberal ideology by bourgeois and non-bourgeois alike supporting such virtues. The cause was the widening adoption of two mere ideas, the new and liberal economic idea of liberty for ordinary people and the new and democratic social idea of dignity for such people. The single word for them is "equality" of respect and before the law. The two linked ethical ideas, deemed preposterous before the eighteenth century, led after 1800 to a paroxysm of betterment.

The word "equality," understand, is not to be taken, in the style of some in the French Enlightenment, as equality of material outcome. The French definition is the one both the left and the right unreflectively assume nowadays in their disputes: "You didn't build that without social help, so there's no justification for unequal incomes." "You poor folk just aren't virtuous enough, so there's no justification for equalizing subsidies." The more fundamental definition of equality, the Scottish one, is the egalitarian opinion people have of each other, whether street porter or moral philosopher.[6] The Glasgow professor of moral philosophy Adam Smith, a pioneering egalitarian in this sense, championed the Scottish idea.[7]

Forcing in an illiberal way the French style of equality of outcome, cutting down as I've said the tall poppies, envying the silly baubles of the rich, imagining that sharing income is as efficacious for the good of the poor as are equal shares in the proverbial pizza, treating poor people as sad children to be nudged or judged by the experts of the clerisy, we have found, has often had a high cost in damaging liberty and slowing betterment. Not always, but often.

It would be a good thing, of course, if a free and rich society following Smithian liberalism produced a French and Pikettyan equality. But wait. In fact—old news, this, though surprising to some, and to Piketty—it largely has, by the only ethically relevant standard, that of basic human rights and basic comforts in antibiotics and housing and education, compliments of the liberal and Scottish plan. Introducing the Scottish plan, as in Hong Kong and Norway and France itself, has regularly led to an astounding betterment and to a real equality of outcome—with the poor acquiring automobiles and hot and cold water at the tap that were denied in earlier times even to the rich, and acquiring political rights and social dignity that were denied in earlier times to everyone except the old rich.

Even in the already advanced countries in recent decades there has been no complete stagnation of real incomes for ordinary people. You will have heard that "wages are flat" or that "the middle class is shrinking." But you also know that you should not believe everything you read in the papers. Quality improvement, as the director of the Consumer Price Index acknowledged to me personally on two occasions, makes the price index we use to calculate real income misleading, as much as 2 percentage points in real betterment per year. Medical benefits and pensions, and governmental transfers such as Medicare and Social Security, have increased, too. And the middle class has moved up, not down.

This is not to say that no one even in rich countries such as the United States is unskilled, addicted, badly parented, discriminated against, or simply horribly unlucky. George Packer's recent *The Unwinding: An Inner History of the New America* (2013) and Barbara Ehrenreich's earlier *Nickel and Dimed: On (Not) Getting By in America* (2001) carry on a long and distinguished tradition of telling the bourgeoisie about the poor, back to James Agee and Walker Evans, *Let Us Now Praise Famous Men* (1941), George Orwell, *The Road to Wigan Pier* (1937), Jack London, *The People of the Abyss* (1903), Jacob Riis, *How the Other Half Lives: Studies Among the Tenements of New York* (1890), and the fount, Friedrich Engels, *The Condition of the Working Class in England* (1845).

They are not making it up. Anyone who reads such books is wrenched out of a comfortable ignorance about the other half. In fictional form one is similarly wrenched by Steinbeck's *The Grapes of Wrath* (1939) or Farrell's *Studs Lonigan* (1932–1935) or Wright's *Native Son* (1940), or in Europe, among many observers of the Two Nations, Zola's *Germinal* (1885). Such books made many of us into socialists. The wrenching is salutary. It is said that Winston Churchill, scion of the aristocracy, believed that most English poor people lived in rose-covered cottages. He couldn't imagine back-to-backs in Salford, with the outhouse at the end of the row. Wake up, Winston. But waking up does not imply despairing, or introducing policies that do not in fact help the poor—or proposing the overthrow of the System, if the System in fact is enriching the poor over the long run, or at any rate is enriching the poor better than those other systems that have been tried from time to time.

The economist Eamonn Butler notes that the System

> is a highly moral system too. The human relationships in capitalism are not forced but voluntary. People invest, create, supply, buy and sell things as they choose. No government ordains their actions: the decisions are theirs. Indeed, the only role for the power wielded by the state is to ensure that individuals are not forced—or robbed, or defrauded, or otherwise violated. [I have pointed out that there are many non-governmental ways such desiderata are achieved, too.] Capitalism is not based on commands, but on the rule of law in which general rules (such as honest dealing, honoring contracts and shunning violence) apply to everyone—including the government authorities.[8]

By contrast, the policies of the left, and many of the right, are, as they used to say in the Party, "objectively" anti-poor. Consider the parallels with racism. When a Trumpista is accused of racism, he replies, out of a psychological theory, that he is not personally prejudiced against Blacks or Jews. That may be. After all, Trump's daughter, whom he clearly loves, converted to Judaism, and he put his Jewish son-in-law in charge of Mideast policy. But Trump's appeal to his base was "objectively" racist, and anti-Semitic, in that it encouraged the perpetuation of what the left calls "structural" racism, that is, institutions such as restrictive covenants and redlining and racist motorcycle gangs and ancient anti-Semitic conspiracy theories. The result was startling increases in anti-Semitic crimes in the United States during Trump's presidency. Regardless of Trump's psychological state, the result of his political tactics was the perpetuation of racism. You don't get a get-out-of-racism-free card by looking into your heart and finding that you are innocent of racial hatred. And the same is true of the policies alleged to relieve poverty that in fact perpetuate it. Our friends on the left, and some on the right, look into their hearts and find that they want the poor to prosper. But then they vote to sustain structures of poverty, such as the minimum wage or occupational licensing or trade protectionism.

Righteous if ill-informed and inexpensive indignation inspired by survivor's guilt about alleged victims of something called "capitalism," and envious anger at the silly consumption by the rich, do not yield betterment for the poor. Remarks such as "there are still poor people" or "some people have more power than others," though claiming the ethical high ground for the speaker, are not deep or clever. Repeating them, or nodding wisely at their repetition, or buying Piketty's book to display on your coffee table, does not make you an objectively good person. As James Baldwin said about *Uncle Tom's Cabin* ("a very bad novel," he noted), "We receive a very definite thrill of virtue from the fact that we are reading such a book at all," encouraging the fatuous sentiment expressed to him once by "an American liberal": "As long as such books are being published, everything will be all right."[9] No it won't.

You become a good person, and make things all right, not by reading or writing poverty porn but by actually helping the poor. Open a profitable business. Arrange mortgages that poor people can buy. Invent a new battery. Vote for better schools. Adopt a Pakistani orphan. Volunteer to feed people at Grace Church on Saturday mornings. Argue for a minimum income and against a minimum wage. The promoting of policies that in their structural effects reduce opportunities for employment, or the making of indignant declarations to your husband after finishing this week's Sunday *New York Times Magazine,* does not make you virtuous, because the action does not help the poor.

The economy and society of the United States are not in fact unwinding, and people are in fact getting by a little better than they did before, and cumulatively a whole lot better. The children of the sharecropping families in Hale County, Alabama, whom Agee and Evans objectified, to the lasting resentment of the older members of the families, are doing pretty well, holding decent jobs, many of their children going to college.[10] That even over the long run there remain some poor people does not mean the system is not work-ing for the poor, so long as their condition is continuing to improve, as it is, contrary to the newspaper stories and the pessimistic books, and so long as the percentage of the desperately poor is heading toward zero, as it is.[11] That people still sometimes die in hospitals does not mean that medicine should be replaced by witch doctors, so long as death rates are falling. Economically speaking, in Mao's China or Chavez's Venezuela the witch doctors were put in charge. Let's not let Bernie and Alexandria cast their spells of magic and free lunches.

And poverty is indeed falling, even recently, even in already rich coun-tries. If income is correctly measured to include better working conditions, more years of education, better health care, longer retirement years, larger poverty-program subsidies, and above all the rising quality of the larger num-ber of goods and services (smartphones, hip replacements, air conditioning), the real income of the poor has risen, if at a slower pace than in the 1950s—which followed, I have noted, the calamitous time-outs of the Great Depres-sion and the War.[12] The economist Angus Deaton notes that "once the rebuilding is done [as it was in, say, 1970], new growth relies on inventing new ways of doing things and putting them into practice, and this turning over of virgin soil is harder than re-plowing an old furrow."[13] Nor are the world's poor paying for the growth. The economists Xavier Sala-i-Martin and Maxim Pinkovskiy report—on the basis of detailed study of the individ-ual distribution of income, as against the clumsier procedure of comparing distributions nation by nation (though it in fact gives similar results)—that "world poverty is falling. Between 1970 and 2006, the global poverty rate [de-fined in absolute, not relative, terms] has been cut by nearly three quarters. The percentage of the world population living on less than $1 a day (in PPP-adjusted 2000 dollars) went from 26.8 percent in 1970 to 5.4 percent in 2006."[14]

33. Redistribution Doesn't Work

The most fundamental ethical and economic problem in Piketty's book, then, is that the main event of the past two centuries was not the "second moment," in statistical jargon, the spread in distribution of income, on which he focuses. The main event was its "first moment," the Great Enrichment of the average individual on the planet by a factor of ten and in now rich countries, once very poor, by a factor of thirty or more.

The greatly enriched world cannot be explained by the accumulation of capital—as to the contrary economists had argued from Adam Smith through Karl Marx to Thomas Piketty, and as the very name "capitalism" implies. Bricks, BAs, and bank balances—the capital accumulations—were of course necessary, but so was a labor force and the existence of liquid water. Oxygen is necessary for a fire. But it would be unenlightening to explain the Chicago Fire of October 8–10, 1871, by the mere presence of oxygen in the earth's atmosphere. Better: a long dry spell, the city's wooden buildings, a strong wind from the southwest (there's the oxygen), and, if you are determined to be prejudiced against Irish immigrants, Mrs. O'Leary's cow. The modern world can't be explained by routine brick piling, such as the Indian Ocean trade, English banking, the British savings rate, the Atlantic slave trade, the enclosure movement, the exploitation of workers in cotton mills, or the original accumulation of capital in European cities, whether of physical or of human capital.[1] Such routines are too common in world history and too feeble in quantitative oomph to explain the ten- or thirty- or hundred-fold enrichment per person unique to the past two centuries.

It was ideas, not bricks. The ideas were the springs, released for the first time by a new liberty and dignity, the ideology, I have by now repeatedly noted, known to Europeans as "liberalism," causing "innovism." The modern world was *not* caused by "capitalism," which is ancient and ubiquitous— quite unlike liberalism, which was in 1776 revolutionary. The Great Enrichment, 1800 to the present, the most surprising secular event in history, is explained instead by bettering ideas, sprung from liberalism, which allowed the ordinary people for the first time to have a go.

Consider in light of the Great Enrichment one of Piketty's and the left's favorite suggestions for policy: taxing the rich to help the poor. It seems in the first act a fine idea. Let's remake society, the generous adolescent proposes, as one big family of 330 million people. Surely the remaking will solve the problem of poverty, lifting up the poor by big amounts, such as the 20 or 30 percent of income stolen at present by the bosses. In an ancient society of slaves, the slave-owning child had no such guilt, because the poor were very different from you and me. But once the naturalness of hierarchy was questioned, as it was by liberalism in the late eighteenth century in northwestern Europe, and in the nineteenth century more generally, it seems obvious to the generous adolescent to adopt socialism. The Swedish political motto from the 1920s on, *folkhemmet,* was "the national home." It came from home-thought.

But a nation is not a home. In the Great Society—in the sense advanced by Smith and Hayek, meaning a big society as contrasted with a little band or family—the source of income is not the hunter's kill or the father's pay packet but the myriad and often hidden specialized exchanges with strangers we make every day. Equality of "distribution" pizza-style is not natural to such a society, of 9 million in Sweden and certainly not one of 330 million in the United States. Unless people are paid by results, the Great Society will perform badly, as in the German Democratic Republic. It was true even in a small early Christian sect in Thessaloniki in northern Greece in the late first century. St. Paul said of it, "If any would not work, neither should he eat" (2 Thess. 3:10). Such rules are the only way in anything but a loving, small group to get a large pie made.

And in important ways even French-style equality is improved by an ethic of commercially tested betterment. Most importantly, it achieves the vastly larger pie that enriches the poor. But further: free entry erodes monopolies and other governmental institutions such as guilds that in traditional societies keep one tribe rich and the other poor.[2] And a market in labor erodes unfair pay gaps among equally productive workers in, say, cotton textiles, regardless of gender or race, paid by the piece. Crucially it erodes the gap between on the one hand a professor who teaches with the same scant equipment that Socrates used—a place to draw diagrams (a stretch of sand in Athens, Greece, or a whiteboard in Athens, Georgia) and a crowd of students—and on the other an airline pilot working with the finest fruits of a technological civilization. The pilot produces tens of thousands of times more value of travel services per hour than a Greek steersman in 400 BCE. The professor produces, if she is exceptionally lucky or skilled, half the insight per student-hour as did Socrates. But equality of physical productivity doesn't matter in a society if it is a free, trading, and mobile one. Entry and exit to occupations are what matter. Some professor could in the long run have become an airline pilot, and some pilot a professor, which is enough to give even workers like the professor who have not increased in productivity in the past twenty-five hundred years an equal share of the finest fruits. That's an equality of justice, even French style.

What people earn is not merely an arbitrary tax imposed on the rest of us. Such an arbitrary tax is what an inequality within the little socialism of a household would be, Cinderella getting less to eat than her ugly sisters out of mere spite. Earnings, however, support an astonishingly complicated, if largely unplanned and spontaneous, division of labor, whose next move is determined by the differentials—the profit in trade or in occupation. If medical doctors make ten times more than cleaners, I have already said, the rest of the society, which pays voluntarily for the doctors and cleaners, is saying, "If cleaners could become doctors, viewing the matter in the long run, shift more of them into doctoring." The Pakistani cleaner's daughter goes on to become a doctor at St. Bartholomew's. If we reduce the Great Society to a family by taxing the rich to the limit, we destroy the signaling. People wander between cleaning and doctoring without such signals about the value people put on the next hour of the services. Neither doctoring nor cleaning gets done well. The Great Society becomes the unspecialized society of a massive household, the single directed factory of Lenin's imaginings. The 330 million people become miserably equal, and lose the gigantic gain from specialization. Back to $2 a day.

Redistribution, although it assuages bourgeois guilt, and if voluntary may help them into heaven, has not been the chief sustenance of the poor. The social arithmetic shows why. If all profits in the American economy were forthwith handed over to the workers, the workers (including some amazingly highly paid "workers," such as sports and singing stars, and big-company CEOs) would get 20 percent or so more of national income, right now. That is, 20/80, or a 25 percent increase. But one time only. The expropriation is not a 25 percent gain every year forever. It's merely this one time, because you can't expropriate the same people year after year and expect them to come forward with the same sums ready to be expropriated again and again. Landlords, yes (which is why economists view taxes on land as a good idea). Free workers or free entrepreneurs able to move out from under the tax, no.

Most redistribution in practice goes to the middle class, because the middle class votes. Thus farm subsidies. But if the 20 percent seized from the rich was directed at the bottom 20 percent, earning perhaps 5 percent of GDP, their gain would be a very significant 300 percent, a factor of four. But then their income reverts to the previous level—or at best (if the profits can simply be taken over by the government without damage to their level, miraculously, and then distributed to the rest of us by saintly bureaucrats without sticky fingers or favored friends) continues with whatever rate of growth the economy was experiencing. All this supposes, unnaturally and contrary to the evidence of communist experiments from New Harmony, Indiana, to Stalinist Russia, that the expropriation of the income of capital will not reduce the rate of growth of the pie.

Or, to speak of expropriation by regulation, as I have said before, the imposing of a ten-hour pay for eight hours of work by act of Congress would, again, raise the share of national income accruing to the portion of the working class that got it, one time, by 25 percent. It would do so in the first act, under the same, unnatural supposition that the pie was not thereby reduced—when the managers and entrepreneurs desert the now unprofitable activity of deciding what is to be done. The redistribution sounds like a good idea, unless you reflect that at such rates the bosses would be less willing to employ people in the first place. And those who did not get it (agricultural workers, for example) would find their real incomes reduced, not raised. Wages are not a social custom which can be raised by contagion from one sector to another. Wages respond to two things only, the productivity of workers and their mobility.

Here's another idea for income transfers, then: If we took away the alarmingly high share of US income earned by the top 1 percent, which was in 2010 about 22 percent of national income, and gave it to the rest of us, we as The Rest would be 22/78, because 78 is the income share of the bottom 99, or a little over 28 percent better off.[3] One time. Then reverting to normal. No great shakes, and dwarfed by the Great Enrichment from letting the market work. (I repeat that the very poor would be proportionately much more bettered if by a political miracle the income expropriated went to them, and not to the middle class or to the sticky fingers of the political bosses and their friends.)

Or put it still another way. Suppose the profits were allowed to be earned by the people directing the economy, by the owner of the little convenience store in your neighborhood as much as by the malefactors of great wealth. But suppose the profit earners, out of a gospel of wealth, and following Catholic social teaching, decided that they themselves should live modestly and then give all their surplus to the poor. The economist David Colander declares that "a world in which all rich individuals . . . [believed] that it is the duty of all to give away the majority of their wealth before they die . . . would be quite different from . . . our world."[4] But wait. The entire 22 percent would raise the incomes of the rest—many of them university professors getting Guggenheim fellowships or the sweetly left-wing folk getting Macarthur "genius" awards—but by a magnitude nothing like the size of the fruits of modern economic growth.

The point is that 20 and 22 and 25 percent are not of the same order of magnitude as the Great Enrichment of 3,000 percent, which in turn had nothing in historical fact to do with such redistributions or charitable contributions. True, as the German historian Jürgen Kocka points out to me, the workers' struggle, by furthering the dignity of individuals, may well have contributed to the widespread dignity behind modern ingenuity. Yes, although it would go the other way, too, undermining their dignity by defining them as victims. But the arithmetic remains that the one-time redistributions are two orders of magnitude smaller in helping the poor than the Enrichment from greater productivity since 1800. If we want to make the non-bosses or the poor better off by a significant amount, then 3,000 percent beats a range from 20 to 25 percent every time. Chairman Mao's emphasis on class warfare spoiled what gains his Chinese Revolution had achieved. When his heirs shifted in 1978 to "socialist modernization" they (half consciously) adopted commercially tested betterment, innovism, and achieved in thirty years a rise of Chinese per-person real income by a factor of 20—not a mere 20 percent but

2,000 percent.[5] Deng Xiaoping's anti-equalizing motto was, "Let some people get rich first." It's the Bourgeois Deal.

Unlike China growing (for a long while) at 10 percent per year and India (now) at 7 percent, the other BRIICS of Brazil, Russia, Indonesia, and South Africa have stuck with anti-"neo"-liberal ideas such as Argentinean self-sufficiency and 1960s British unionism and 1990s German labor laws and a misunderstanding of South Korea's "export-led" growth. Indeed, the literature of the "middle-income trap," which speaks in particular of Brazil and South Africa, depends on a mercantilist idea that growth depends on exports, which are alleged to have a harder time growing when wages rise.[6] (By a miracle, places like France and Denmark and the Netherlands somehow escaped the trap.) The countries with market-denying laws, such as slowing entry by new business and onerously regulating old business, drag along at less than 2 percent growth per year per person—at which a mere doubling takes a third of a century and a quadrupling takes twice as long. Slow growth yields envy, as the economist Benjamin Friedman has argued, and envy yields populism, which in turn yields slow growth.[7] That's the real "middle-income trap," an ideological not an economic one. Getting out of it requires accepting, as Holland did in the sixteenth century and Britain in the eighteenth, and as China and India did in the late twentieth, the Bourgeois Deal.

Our common purpose on the left and on the right, and on the liberal position sitting above the left-right axis, is to help the poor. The advocacy by the learned cadres of the left for equalizing restrictions and redistributions and regulations that can be shown to harm the very poor, then, can be viewed at best as thoughtless. Perhaps, considering what economic historians now know about the Great Enrichment—but which the left clerisy, and many of the right, stoutly refuse to learn—it can even be considered unethical. The left clerisy such as Tony Judt or Paul Krugman or Thomas Piketty, who are quite sure that they themselves are taking the ethical high road against the wicked selfishness of Tories or Republicans, might on such evidence be considered dubiously ethical. They are obsessed with first-act changes that cannot much help the poor, and often can be shown to damage them grievously. And they are obsessed with an angry envy at the consumption of the uncharitable rich, of whom they personally often enough are examples. One might ask what you do with your royalties by way of helping the poor, Professor Piketty. Professor Krugman?

The left explains the inability of workers themselves to grasp the hard-left dogma that all employment is exploitation by saying that the workers are in the grip of false consciousness.[8] If the Bourgeois Deal is sound, though, the falsity in consciousness is attributable not to the sadly misled workers but rather to the leftish clerisy themselves. The politics is reversed. Workers of the world unite: demand commercially tested betterment under a régime of private property and profit making. Still better, become bourgeois, as large groups of workers in rich countries do believe they have become, approaching 100 percent in the United States, measured by self-identification as "middle class."

It would then seem at least odd to call "false" a consciousness that has raised the income of poor workers in real terms by a factor of thirty. If workers have been fooled by accepting the Deal, then for such a way of being fooled let us give two and a half cheers—the deduction of half a cheer is because it's not dignified to be "fooled" by anything. Let us have two and a half cheers for the new dominance since 1800 of a liberal and bourgeois ideology and the spreading acceptance of the Bourgeois Deal. Innovism rules.

On the next-to-last page of his book Piketty writes, "It is possible, and even indispensable, to have an approach that is at once economic and political, social and cultural, and concerned with wages and wealth."[9] One can only agree. But he has not achieved it. His gestures to cultural matters consist of a few naïvely used references to novels he has read superficially.[10] His ethics is a narrow ethics of envy. His politics assumes that governments can accomplish anything they propose. And his economics is flawed from start to finish.

Capital in the Twenty-First Century is a brave book. But it is gravely mistaken. And so too, spreading from his book, is the recent cant about inequality. Enrichment, not equality, should be our ethical goal.

PART FOUR

And the Other Illiberal Ideas Are Mistaken, Too

34. The Clerisy Had Three Big Ideas, 1755–1848, One Good and Two Terrible

Based on a column in Reason, *2017.*

Between the Great Lisbon Earthquake and the revolutionary year of 1848 the European clerisy had three big political ideas. One was very, very good. The other two were very, very bad. We're still paying, and praying.

The good one, flowing from the pens of people like Voltaire, Tom Paine, Mary Wollstonecraft, and above all the Blessed Adam Smith, is what Smith described in 1776 as the shocking idea of "allowing every man [or woman, dear] to pursue his own interest in his own way, upon the liberal plan of equality, liberty, and justice."

Admittedly, true liberalism took a long time to get to a pretty good approximation of its ideal. "All men are created equal" was penned by a man who kept in slavery for a long time his five surviving children by Sally Hemings, and Sally herself, still more startlingly, appears to have been a half-sister of Jefferson's wife, out of his wife's father. Even his co-author in the *Declaration*, Ben Franklin, had once owned slaves. In 1774 Nathaniel Niles declared, "For shame, let us either cease to enslave our fellow-men, or else let us cease to complain of those who would enslave us."[1] The next year Samuel Johnson had good reason to launch a sneer from London: "How is it that we hear the loudest yelps for liberty among the drivers of negroes?"[2]

But the liberal yelps re-echoed, and had force, if only from the repeated embarrassment over two centuries of not allowing slaves, apprentices, women, immigrants, anarchists, socialists, communists, Okies, Nisei, Blacks, Jews, Chicanos, gays, Vietnam protesters, criminal suspects, people with disabilities, gender crossers, ex-cons, drug users, refugees, and citizens of Puerto Rico and the District of Columbia their own equality, liberty, and justice. In 1776 John Adams, who was no democrat, worried about opening the Pandora's box of, as the historian Alan Taylor puts it, "promising equal rights in an unequal society": "There will be no end of it. New claims will arise. Women will demand a vote. Lads from 12 to 21 will think their rights not enough attended to, and every man who has not a farthing will demand an equal voice."[3] He was right. The box could not be closed.

The fruits of the new liberalism, when it could make its way against the two bad new ideas, or the old one of traditional hierarchy, were stunning. Liberalism, uniquely in history, made masses of ordinary people bold—bold to try betterments in a commercial test. The boldness of commoners aplenty pursuing their own interests and passions resulted in the Great Enrichment. And now, despite the best efforts of governments and international agencies to bungle the job, it's spreading to the world, from Hong Kong to Botswana, China to India.

The two *bad* ideas of 1755–1848 were nationalism and socialism. A concoction of both ingredients was introduced in 1922 and is still for sale in Europe, and now among a substantial portion of Trump's supporters, he himself approving at least of the fraught "nationalist" part, and anyway believing in authoritarianism in the economy.

Nationalism when first theorized in the early nineteenth century was entwined with the Romantic movement, though of course in England it was already hundreds of years old, as it was in Spain, inspiring reactive nationalisms in France and Scotland and Portugal and the New World, and eventually Ireland. In Italy in the form of *campanilismo* and the pride of cities it was older still. Italians will reply when asked where they are from, even if speaking to foreigners, "Florence" or "Rome" or at the widest "Sicily." Not "Italy."

An important evil of nationalism—aside even from its intrinsic collective coercion, in line only with an "ancient" liberty, and its tendency to define minorities such as Jews and Muslims or Mexicans as "not us"—is that it inspires war. The eight hundred US military bases around the world keep the peace by waging endless war on others, bombing civilians to protect Americans from non-threats. We of the Anglosphere in July 2016 "celebrated," if that is quite the word, the centenary of the beginning of the Battle of the

Somme, a fruit of nationalism which by its conclusion four and a half months later had cost the Allies and the Central Powers combined over a million casualties, most of them dismembered by artillery. Thank you for your service. The battlefield has monuments to the British dead (not the German, because the British eventually "won" the War; neither side won the Battle) with appalling numbers of names inscribed.

The other bad idea of the era was socialism, which can be also linked to Romanticism, and to a secularized Christianity, with its charity defined by the Sermon on the Mount and its apocalyptic view of history. Socialism is all of a piece with nationalism, substituting coercion for agreement, ranging from central planning in the USSR to building permits in Chicago. The joke is that a communist is a socialist in a hurry and a socialist is a regulator in a hurry and a regulator is a corrupt politician in a hurry.

What is bad about socialism, the same collective coercion aside, is that it leads to poverty. Even in its purest form, in a family, it can discourage betterment by encouraging free riding. The not-so-sweet forms of socialism at a larger scale, paired with nationalism, are of course a lot worse. Thus North Korea, Cuba, and other workers' paradises. The other joke is that under capitalism man exploits man. Under socialism it's the other way around.

What to do? Revive liberalism. In the United States, take back the word from our friends on the left. They can keep "progressive," at any rate if they don't mind being associated with Progressivism circa 1910 and its racism and its enthusiasms for forced sterilization and its plan, still in force, to use the minimum wage to drive immigrants and Blacks and women out of the labor force. And we should persuade our friends on the US right to stop using the L-word to attack people who do not belong to the country club. (In Latin America, by contrast, the so-called liberals are conservatives, and run the country club.)

Read Adam Smith, slowly, both his books, and try to return our spirits to that dawn of 1776 in which the radical idea was not nationalism or socialism or national socialism, but "the obvious and simple system of natural liberty," allowing all men and women to pursue their interests in their own ways.[4]

It was a strange but very, very good idea.

35. The Economic Sky Is Not Falling

In 2016 for the British journal of opinion Prospect.

For reasons I still don't understand, people simply *love* to be told that the sky is falling. Yet it seldom does. (Actually, never.) For example, a gaggle of Tory/ Liberal economists, such as Lawrence Summers, Andrew McFee, Edmund Phelps, Jeffrey Sachs, Laurence Kotlikoff, Tyler Cowen, Edward E. Gordon, and Robert J. Gordon have argued recently that Europe and the United States, on the frontier of betterment, are facing a slowdown of new ideas, and a skill shortage. Technological unemployment and "uncompetitveness" and sadly slow growth, it is said, will be the result.

Maybe. Yet in the past couple of centuries numerous other learned economists have predicted similar slowdowns, none of which happened. The Keynesian economists in the late 1930s and the 1940s were confident in their prediction, along the same lines as the current pessimists, of a world of "stagnationism." The prediction was instantly falsified by the continuing Great Enrichment, and the fastest rates of world economic growth in history.

Similarly, in the first three-quarters of the nineteenth century the Classical economists, Marx among them, expected landlords, or in Marx's case capitalists, to engorge the national product. On Malthusian grounds they expected earnings per person to stay at the $2 or $3 a day in today's prices typical of human life since the caves. It didn't happen.

First published by *Prospect* magazine, March 2016.

And contrary to recent alarms, even in the already rich countries the real income for the poor people continues to grow. Thirty years ago hip-joint replacement was experimental. Now it's routine. Tires and autos were unreliable. Now they never wear out. Once, nothing could be done about clinical depression. Now something can. Further, in terms of real comforts—a roof, heating, ample clothing, decent food, adequate education, effective medicine, long life—the income is more and more *equally* spread. *Pace* Piketty.

And worldwide the poorest among us are getting rapidly richer. It is no longer 1960, dears, when the poor countries looked hopeless, trapped in an Asian Dilemma.

The Italian economists Patrizio Pagano and Massimo Sbracia argue that the failures of stagnationisms to actually emerge—though proposed after every major recession, they note—was not so much because of the (anyway inevitable) bad prediction of wholly new technology as because of not grasping the further rewards of already existing technology, such as nowadays computers.[1] The economic historian Joel Mokyr, a deep student of the history of technology, recently offered some persuasive assurances on the matter of slowdown, directed specifically at the sky-is-falling convictions of his colleague at Northwestern University, the gloomy Robert Gordon.[2] Mokyr argues that by now the already existing sciences and technologies about biology and computers and the study of materials promise gigantic enrichment.[3]

Thomas Babbington Macaulay asked in 1830, "On what principle is it that, when we see nothing but betterment behind us, we are to expect nothing but deterioration before us?" He continued: "If we were to prophesy that in the year 1930 a population of fifty million, better fed, clad, and lodged than the English of our time, will cover these islands, that Sussex and Huntingdonshire will be wealthier than the wealthiest parts of the West Riding of Yorkshire now are, that machines constructed on principles yet undiscovered will be in every house, many people would think us insane."[4]

Whiggish and bourgeois and progress-minded and vulgarly pro-betterment though Macaulay was, he was in his prediction exactly right, even as to the UK population in 1930. If one includes in 1930 the recently separated Republic of Ireland, he was off by less than 2 percent.

And even the pessimistic, anti-Whiggish economists such as Robert Gordon—"gloomsters," the headline writers call them—would not deny that we have before us fifty or a hundred years in which now middling and poor countries such as South Africa and Brazil and Haiti and Bangladesh will catch up to what is already in the rich countries a stunningly successful level of average real income.

The Nobelist Edmund Phelps, one of the pessimists, believes that many rich countries lack dynamism.[5] Some of Robert Gordon's proposed "headwinds" are of that character. Such fears have not been fulfilled, which suggests that Gordon's statist proposals to shelter us from the headwinds are not good ideas. But let's suppose Europe and its offshoots do stagnate. Still, China and India, making up four in ten of world population, have since 1980 become radically more free-market than they once were, and therefore are quickly catching up. Despite recent slowdowns in China (not in India) they will continue growing, if they continue liberalizing.

To appreciate what will happen over the next fifty or hundred years if such growth continues, as there is every reason to think it will, it's a good idea to learn the "Rule of 72." The rule is that something (such as income) growing at 1 percent per year takes seventy-two years to double. (Rest assured that the fact is not obvious without calculation. It just happens to be true. You can confirm it by taking out your calculator and multiplying 1.01 by itself seventy-two times. Or you can trust me.) It follows that if the something grows twice as fast, at 2 percent instead of 1 percent, the something will double, of course, in *half* the time, thirty-six years. A runner going twice as fast will arrive at the mile mark in half the time. Similarly, something growing at 3 percent a year will double in a third of the time as the 1 percent, or seventy-two divided by three, or twenty-four years.

Apply then your newly won brilliance in arithmetic to our economic prospects. Even at the modest 4 percent per year per person that the World Bank implausibly reckons China will experience out to 2030, the result by then will be a populace almost twice as rich. The specialists on China's economy Dwight Perkins and Thomas Rawski reckoned in 2008 on a 6 to 8 percent annual growth out to 2025, by which time the average Chinese person will have a 1960s-US standard of living.[6] China and India during their socialist experiments of the 1950s through the 1970s were so badly managed that there was a massive amount of ground to be made up merely by letting people open shops and factories where and when they wanted to, without approval from the authorities. As Perkins pointed out in 1995, "When China stopped suppressing such activities, . . . shops, restaurants and many other service units popped up everywhere . . . [because] Chinese . . . had not forgotten how to trade or run a small business."[7] Or large business. No genetic argument can be put forward that implies that Chinese or Indians or Africans or Latin Americans should do worse than Europeans permanently.

We have in fact seen between 1990 and 2016, even with the Great Recession, a real (constant 2011 dollars at purchasing power parity) growth rate worldwide of 2 percent per year per person, which is for example the average rate over two centuries in the United States.[8] It will result in a doubling of the material welfare of the world's average person within a long generation ($72/2 = 36$ years), or two short ones, with economies of scale in world invention kicking up the rate. In two such long generations, seventy-two years, it would mean a quadrupling, which would raise the average real income in the world at the end of this century to the levels attained in 2016 in the United States, a country that for well over a century has sustained the world's highest per-person income of any place larger than Norway. Pretty good. And it will be pretty good for solving many if not all of the problems in the soul and in the society and in the environment. A certain Spartan/Puritan line in Western thinking supposes that enrichment always corrupts. It hasn't.

All the economists who have looked into the evidence agree that the average real income per person in the world is rising fast, with every prospect of continuing tomorrow, and for the coming century or more. The result will be a gigantic increase in the number of scientists, designers, writers, musicians, engineers, entrepreneurs, and ordinary businesspeople devising betterments spilling over to the now-rich countries allegedly lacking in dynamism or facing headwinds. Unless one believes in mercantilist/business-school fashion that a country must "compete" to prosper from world betterment, even the leaky boats of the Phelpsian/Gordonesque "undynamic countries" will rise.

In short, no economic limit to fast world or US or European growth of per-person income is close at hand, no threat to "jobs," no cause for pessimism—not in your lifetime, or those of your great-grandchildren. Then, in the year 2100, with everyone on the planet enormously rich by historical standards, and hundreds of times more scientists and entrepreneurs working day and night on improvements in solar power and methane burning, we can reconsider the limits to growth, and the falling sky.

36. The West Is Not Declining

This piece, written in 1990 and updated some here, has the same theme as the previous piece, written twenty-six years later—which shows either that I never evolve, or that the rhetoric of zero-sum failure and decline does not.

Start with a riddle, by guessing the time and place. You will be graded on your answer.

A nation speaking the language of Shakespeare wins a world war and takes command of the balance of power. It builds the largest economic machine in history, and is acclaimed on all sides as having the most energetic businesspeople, the most ingenious engineers, the smartest scientists, and the wisest politicians. Then everything goes to hell. An upstart challenges its economy, beating it at its own game. The former paragon, a decade or two after the hosannas, comes to be scorned, at any rate at home, as having the laziest businesspeople, the stupidest engineers, the dullest scientists, and the most foolish politicians. It becomes in the opinion of the world (or at any rate in the opinion of home-front journalists and politicians and most professors) a New Spain or a New Holland, a byword for a failed empire.

Time's up.

If you guessed "America, 1917–present," give yourself half credit, fifty points. Sorry, that's not a passing grade. True, the story fits American history

First published as Deirdre Nansen McCloskey, "Competitiveness and the Antieconomics of Decline," in *Second Thoughts: Myths and Morals of U.S. Economic History*, edited by Deirdre Nansen McCloskey, pp. 167–173, 1993. Reproduced with permission of Oxford University Press and with permission of the Licensor through PLSclear. © 1993 by Oxford University Press, Inc.

as commonly told from entry into the War to End All Wars down to Trump, but it also fits more places. If you guessed "Britain, 1815–1956," you again earn the fifty points, and ten points extra for recognizing that there is a world outside the United States. The story fits British history as commonly told, from Waterloo to the Suez crisis. But the answer warrants only a bare pass.

The better answer is "Both, down to details of the words people used at the time to describe what was happening." British opinion leaders in the 1890s and 1900s read books with titles like *Made in Germany* (1896) or *The American Invasion* (1902).[1] Where have you seen those? You've seen them since the 1980s in airport bookstores from Kennedy to Honolulu, with America in place of Britain as the patsy. By 2019 it had become plain that the Trump administration had taken on such notions with gusto. The book of 1896 might as well be reprinted in 1989 with "Japan" or in 2019 with "China" in place of "Germany." Make "observations, Gentle Reader, in your own surroundings," wrote a Briton terrified by German imports. "You will find that the material of some of your own clothes was probably woven in Germany. . . . The toys, and the dolls, and the fairy books which your children maltreat in the nursery are made in Germany. . . . Roam the house over, and the fateful mark will greet you at every turn."[2] Make observations nowadays in your garage, your living room, your den. You will see Toyota, Sony, and Yamaha, and by 2019 hammers and computers from China, all around.

That answer, however, is too clever by half. Give yourself a B−, and try to be a little wiser next time. Sure, warning that "The End Is Near" gives one a reputation for tough wisdom, and sells newspapers. A *New Yorker* cartoon showed a couple passing a bearded prophet holding up a sign declaring, "The End Is Near," and the man says to the woman, "Say, isn't that Paul Krugman?" The US version of the story is made better by a supposedly horrible example, such as Britain, the only European country many Americans think they know, and therefore think they know how to improve. The British analogy haunts the American clerisy. On the upside, each country in succession became the world's banker. On the downside, both fought a nasty colonial war, against Boers and Vietnamese. Both in the end became debtor nations, with long-lasting deficits in trade. (The terrible deficit is the same that you have with your grocery store—a nightmare that I am sure keeps you and Peter Navarro up at night.)

Both stories, however, are quite wrong, which is the correct answer for an A+ and an invitation to graduate school. As much as the American clerisy delights in telling the stories around the fern bar, urging us to buckle up our football pads for *The Zero-Sum Solution: Building a World-Class American Economy* (Lester Thurow 1985) or to finally get down to *The Work of Nations: Preparing Ourselves for 21st-Century Capitalism* (Robert Reich 1991)—and latterly Donald Trump's and Peter Navarro's less literate lunacy, the Grocery Store Nightmare—the failure story is wrong about America. It was just as wrong about Britain a century ago. The story of *The Rise and Fall of the Great Powers* (Paul Kennedy 1987) is a fairy tale with no moral.

The correct story is that both countries were and are amazing economic successes. Angus Maddison (1926–2010) was a Scot living in France and working in Holland. He was a bear of a man fluent in seven languages and in statistical thinking, the leading authority on the history of world trade and income. In 1989 he published a little-noticed pamphlet entitled *The World Economy in the Twentieth Century,* under the auspices of the Organization for Economic Cooperation and Development, the research institute in Paris for the rich and democratic countries. Using the best statistics on income available then (in his honor they have been improved since, with roughly the same results), Maddison found that Americans are still richer than anyone else, after a decade of "failure." In 1987 Americans earned $13,550 per head (in 1990 prices), about 40 percent higher than incomes of, say, the Japanese or the (West) Germans. By now in present-day prices it is over $45,000, and remains higher than the incomes of the Japanese or the unified Germans, as always.

Britain, too, in 1987 was—and still is—rich by international standards. After a century of "failures" the average Briton earned a trifle less than the average Swede and a trifle more than the average Belgian. The British average was over three times that of Mexico and fourteen times that of India. If you don't believe it, step outside your hotel in Mumbai—though in a couple of generations the Indians will be catching up.

America, therefore, has not "failed." And neither has Britain. The American story as it is told thrillingly, tragically in the lecture rooms repeats the British story, eerily. But it is a matter of false rhetoric from the start. British observers in the early nineteenth century, like Americans in the Jazz Age, were startled at the ease with which the country had assumed industrial leadership. Britain was the first, yet right from the start of its "dominance," a few of its clerisy were nervously wary of the strangeness of a small island bestriding the world. In 1839, early in British success, one James Deacon Hume warned a committee of Parliament that the existing protectionist tariffs on imports of wheat would encourage other countries to move away from agriculture and toward industry themselves, breaking Britain's "domination" of world manufacturing: "We place ourselves at the risk of being surpassed by the manufactures in other countries. . . . I can hardly doubt that [when that day arrives] the prosperity of this country will recede much faster than it has gone forward."[3]

Nonsense. It's the "competitiveness" rhetoric, and it has always been nonsense. In the 1840s or the 1990s or nowadays, Britain is made better off, not worse, by the industrialization of the rest of the world, in the same way that you would be made better off by moving to a neighborhood of more skilled and healthy people. British growth continued from 1840 to the present, making Britons richer and richer.

Likewise, Americans are made better off when Japan or China "defeats us" at car making or TV assembling, because "we" (really, individuals making decisions about what to do, and not the collectivist "we" of nationalist fantasies) then go do something we are comparatively good at—banking, say, or growing soybeans—and let the Japanese and then the Koreans and then the Chinese do the consumer electronics.

Richer and richer. No falling sky. No tragedy. According to Maddison, Britain in 1989 was about three and a half times richer per person than it was a century ago; America about five times richer. Now more so. It is true that Britain and America have over the period grown more slowly than some other countries, such as Sweden and Japan, because Britain and America started richer, though then still poor by their recent standard. The story of growth over the past century has been a story of convergence to British and American standards of excellence. Germans in 1900 earned about half of what Britons earned; now they earn about the same.

It is not a "race" that Britain "lost." The falling British share of world markets was no index of "failure," any more than a father would view his falling share of the poundage in the house relative to his growing children a "failure." It was an index of maturity. It was also true for America. It is good, not bad, that other nations are achieving American standards of competence in running supermarkets and making food-processing equipment.

Three cheers for foreign "competition."

37. Failure Rhetoric Is Dangerous

A continuation.

The story of "failure" has consequences, which is why it needs to be challenged. It confuses prestige of a sporting character, being tops in what the soccer-inventing British call the "league tables of economic growth," even if the absolute number registers only tiny differences in wealth. More ominously than the sporting metaphors, it speaks of free exchange in metaphors of war. In 1902, at the height of xenophobic hysteria in Britain about "competitiveness" against Germany and the United States, the British economist Edwin Cannan declared, "The first business of the teacher of economic theory is to tear to pieces and trample upon [hold on there, Edwin] the misleading military metaphors which have been applied . . . to the peaceful exchange of commodities. We hear much . . . in these days of 'England's commercial supremacy' and of other nations 'challenging' it, and how it is our duty to 're-pel the attack' and so on. The economist asks 'what is commercial supremacy?' and there is no answer."[1]

We have heard much by now of America's commercial supremacy and how it is our duty to repel the attack. It is economically idiotic and politically dangerous talk. In 1884–1914 it led to a world war, and then the horrors of mid-twentieth-century Europe. We should cool it, recognizing for instance

First published as Deirdre Nansen McCloskey, "Competitiveness and the Antieconomics of Decline," in *Second Thoughts: Myths and Morals of U.S. Economic History,* edited by Deirdre Nansen McCloskey, pp. 167–173, 1993. Reproduced with permission of Oxford University Press and with permission of the Licensor through PLSclear. © 1993 by Oxford University Press, Inc.

that most jobs are lost to greater and good technology, and those in Massachusetts and Illinois are lost to Texas and California, not to China and Korea; or that richer neighbors will pay more to us in goods and services for our goods and services. David Landes (1924–2013), at Harvard a professor of history, and later, by virtue of a friendship with Robert Fogel, also of economics (David never cracked a book on elementary economics), brought the mistaken story of Britain's decline to academic respectability. In his eloquent and learned and deeply erroneous book, *The Unbound Prometheus: Technological Change and Industrial Development in Western Europe from 1750 to the Present,* Landes summarized a century of journalistic and historical lament for lost supremacy and lost empire. He used the metaphor of leadership in a "race," speaking in chapter titles of "Closing the Gap" and "Short Breath and Second Wind," with a military version in "Some Reasons Why," taken from a poem about a cavalry charge.[2]

The main question, according to Landes, is "Why did industrial leadership pass in the closing decades of the 19th century from Britain to Germany?"[3] Briefly, his answer is "Thus the Britain of the late 19th century basked complacently in the sunset of economic hegemony. . . . Now it was the turn of the third generation, the children of affluence, tired of the tedium of trade and flushed with the bucolic aspirations of the country gentleman. . . . They worked at play and played at work."[4]

Fine writing, but it merely restates the nonsense about competitiveness—nonsense on both grounds, political and economic. The European story is commonly told this way by diplomats and their historians in terms of footraces and cavalry charges among ironmasters and stockbrokers. The balance of political power in Europe since Peter the Great is supposed to have depended on industrial leadership. Waterloo and the Somme are supposed to have been decided on the assembly line and the trading floor. The supposed link between a lead in war and a lead in the economy became before World War I a commonplace of political talk, and has never since left the historical literature. To think otherwise, said Landes, without offering actual arguments, is naïve.

The early twenty-first-century version of Landes's worldly-wise nonsense comes out in praise for illiberal leaders, such as Russia's Putin or China's Xi or Turkey's Erdogan or Hungary's Orbán, with eastern European imitators, or in a less violent key (though he too jails his political opponents and censors the press) Lee Hsien Loong of Singapore, and especially his father,

Lee Kuan Yew. After all, write the economic illiterates, the tyrants "win." "Maybe tyranny combined with economic liberty," they continue, "is the New Model." Illiterates are always looking for a New Model, because then they don't need to understand the old ones. It frees them from having to crack a book on economics.

But, no. For one thing, tyranny regularly and on average has destroyed economies, not improved them, and democracy has since 1776 regularly liberalized economies and enriched ordinary people. Step forward to be examined, Robert Mugabe of Zimbabwe, whose sad example stayed the hand of the large Communist wing of the African Nation Congress in South Africa. Stories of Mussolini's or Hitler's or Stalin's economic successes have been shown repeatedly to be false. Betting on a man on a white horse to make his people well off economically enriches only the bookies taking the bet, at favorable odds.

People regularly confuse "success" in rigged elections or in aggressive foreign policy with the enriching of ordinary people in their ordinary economic pursuits. Consider Hitler's dream of *Lebensraum*, colonizing the East by murdering Jews and Slavs. How did that work out? The confusion keeps the man on the white horse in the saddle, because it's nice to think of the greater glory of Mother Russia even if you are living with your granddaughter in a depressed mining town in a single room without a bath or stove on a pension of $400 a month. You can always use the Good Tsar rationale, that Putin can't know the terrible corruption of his local administrators. If he did, he would surely come to the rescue. It has ever been the relationship of tsar and peasant over the heads of the boyars, such as Good King Richard over the bad sheriffs and barons favoring Bad King John, or the English sovereign against rural landlords allegedly creating deserted villages by enclosure.

The left regularly, and with unhappy side effects, muddies the water by attacking the very idea of a calculated national income, which summarizes the economic well-being of ordinary people by their own lights, that is, by how much they are willing to pay for goods and services. It is the liberal criterion. The left yearns for a collectivist criterion instead. The right has similar yearning, for the collective glory of The Nation, similarly achieved by coercion and its threat.

Better, however, to leave off such rough-trade fantasies of collectivism and listen, really listen, to what people say in markets. Oh, yes, I know: it is said that markets have terrible "imperfections," over a hundred lovingly modeled in economics books since 1848, though none shown to be important enough to justify bringing in the perfect wisdom of governmental compulsion.[5] Yet during the reign of the numerous imperfections (monopoly, bad information, behavioral errors), the poorest of the poor found their material welfare rise astoundingly. Let, then, the market speak in GDP per person on the obvious and simple liberal plan, and you get modern educated and enriched people by the billions.

And in any case GDP rises only when the tyrants relent, for whatever part of the economy they do *not* presume to lay down by edict. The birth of liberalism enriched places like the United States before the Civil War, or indeed the Russian Empire in the 1890s and 1900s, letting people make money supplying railways with rails, say. But Japan with its Tokugawa tyranny until 1868 stagnated, and China with its Manchu and then Maoist tyranny until 1978. The tyrants deny the market test, and so embark on projects that regularly reduce Russian or Chinese or Argentinian GDP per person. Private parties make mistakes, too, of course. But they do not have the monopoly of coercion to fall back on. They go out of business instead of being able to force the collective farms to buy wretched tractors until the cows come home, or don't. Politics does not make people better off economically. Strict economy does.

The alleged link between the economy and politics is anyway nonsense. After all, a large enough alliance of straggling, winded followers, to use Landes's racing metaphor, could have fielded more divisions in 1914. The Russian Empire did. The case of Soviet Russia in 1941 or North Vietnam in 1968 suggests that military power does not necessarily follow from economic power. In 1861–1865 the Union sacrificed more men than the entire United States has done in any other war, in order to put down a rebellion by a less populous section, nearly 40 percent of its population enslaved, which the North out-produced at the beginning in firearms by thirty to one, in locomotives twenty-four to one, and in pig iron thirteen to one. In World War I the shovel and barbed wire, hardly the most advanced fruits of industry, locked the Western Front. Strategic bombing, using the most advanced techniques and the most elaborate factories, largely failed in World War II, wholly failed in Korea, and was therefore tried again with great fanfare, to fail spectacularly again, in Vietnam. It worked finally against trivial military and economic powers in Iraq and Serbia. Or did it? How did that work out? The Serbians still hate the other Europeans, as responsible for NATO bombing, and Syria . . . well.

The equation of military power with economic power is good newspaper copy, but poor history and worse economics. The economic nonsense in the metaphor of leadership and competitiveness is that it assumes silently that first place among the many nations is vastly to be preferred to second or twelfth. Leadership in sports talk is number-one-ship. In the motto of the UCLA coach Henry Russell "Red" Sanders (it is not as people believe the coinage of Green Bay's Vince Lombardi), "Winning isn't everything . . . it's the only thing." Not in the economy. The metaphors of disease, defeat, and decline are too fixated on Number One to be the apt ones for an economic tale. The Red Sanders motto governs games. Only one team wins the Pac-12 championship. The fixation on Number One, though, forgets that in economic affairs being Number Two, or even Number Twelve, can be very good indeed. The prize for second in the race of economic growth was not poverty. The prize was great enrichment. In other words, since 1750, Britain has grown very well indeed, thank you very much, with pauses for total war or experiments in Clause Four socialism. The United States has doubled real income per head every thirty-six years or so for two centuries. By contrast, the diseases of which the pessimists speak so colorfully are romantically fatal; the sporting or military defeats are horribly complete; the declines from former greatness irrevocably huge.

From a wider, longer view the story of failure in a race is even more strikingly inapt. Before the British, the Dutch were the "failure." The Dutch Republic has been "declining" practically since its birth. With what result? Disaster? Poverty? A "collapse" of the economy? No. The Netherlands has ended up small and weak, a tiny linguistic island in a corner of Europe, stripped of its empire, no longer a strutting power in world politics—yet fabulously rich, with among the highest per capita incomes in the world (now as in the eighteenth century), a domestic product per head quadrupling since 1900, astoundingly successful by any standard. The Jordaan ("garden") neighborhood in Amsterdam was in the mid-nineteenth century a working-class quarter with miserably small houses and apartments; a large family would be packed into a 161-square-foot room, as was also the case in the Lower East Side in New York. Now the houses and apartments in Old and New Amsterdam have been put together to make bigger dwellings for a couple of yuppies.[6] Sometimes one bachelor.

The better story is one of normal growth—though in longer focus the two centuries of the Great Enrichment have been strikingly not "normal" for humans. Maturity was reached earlier by Britain and America and the Netherlands than by Japan and Germany and Sweden. Everyone concedes that in shipbuilding, insurance, bicycles, and retailing Britain did very well indeed from 1870 to 1914. But even the British "failures" of the late nineteenth century were small by international standards, even in industries such as steel and chemicals in which Britain is supposed to have done especially badly.[7]

Whether it did well or not, however, Britain's growth did not depend importantly on keeping right up with Number One. Britain in 1890 could have been expected to grow slower than the new industrial nations. The British part of the world got there first, and was therefore overtaken in rate of growth by others for a time. If we are going to keep up this tiresome metaphor of a footrace, someone who already passed the finish line is going to be moving slower than someone who is still running. Belgium was another early industrial country and had a similar experience of relative "decline," seldom noted. So more recently has the United States. So what?

On the whole, with minor variations accounted for by minor national differences in attention to detail, the rich nations converge. Natural resources are a trivial element in modern economies. Technology, on the other hand, has become increasingly international. It's as though technology were the new land, except not located in one country but in every country—as it is. If people are left alone to adopt the most profitable technology, then they end up with about the same incomes, whether they live in Hong Kong or Dresden. There is a good deal of foolish econometric work entertaining the possibility that nations might *not* converge. What's foolish about it is that there is no genetic or biological or geographical reason for a permanent great divergence. Short run, sure. In fifty years, no.

The main British story since the late nineteenth century is what Americans can expect in the century to come. British income has tripled while others achieved British standards of living. A 228 percent increase of production between 1900 and 1987, at a rate continuing to the present, is more important than a 10 percent "failure," sometimes and at some exchange rates, to imitate, say, German obsessive habits of attention to duty. Looked at from Ethiopia or even from Argentina, Britain is of course one of the rich nations.

The tragedy of the past century is not the relatively minor jostling among the leaders in the lead pack of industrial nations. It is the appalling distance between the leaders at the front and the followers at the rear. And if one must use the image of the race course, then the whole field, followers as well as leaders, advanced notably—usually by factors of three or more since 1900 in real output per head. The main story is the general advance. The tripling and more of income per head relieved much misery and has given lives with scope to billions of people otherwise submerged. Think of your great-grandparents. Think of the parents of the present Chinese.

In other words, the trouble with the pessimistic choice of story in the literature of British and American "failures" is that it describes such a happy outcome of growth as a tragedy. Such talk is at best tasteless in a world of real tragedies—Argentina, for example, once rich, but for decades subsidizing much and producing little under a persistent ideology of Peronism; or India before 1991, trapped in poverty after much expert socialist advice (though now, having taken "capitalist" advice, the wonder of the world). At worst the pessimism is immoral, a nasty self-involvement, a line of nationalist guff accompanied by a military hand playing "Land of Hope and Glory" or "The Marine Hymn." The economists and historians appear to have mixed up the question of why Britain's income per head was in the 1990s six times that of the Philippines and thirteen times that of India—many hundreds of percentage points of difference that powerful forces in sociology, politics, and culture must of course contribute to explaining, at any rate for the short run, before the inevitable convergence implied by picking up the hundred-dollar bill of international technology—with the more delicate and much less important questions of why British income in 1987 was 3 percent less than that of the French or 5 percent more than that of the Belgian.

Telling a story of America following Britain into "decline" is dangerous nonsense. It is merely a relative decline, caused by the wholly desirable enrichment of the rest of the world. It is dangerous because it leads us to blaming foreigners, for which see Trump's administration, for our real failings, in high-school education, say, or in the maintenance of bridges.

So cheer up. We Yanks are not going the way of Britain, if that means what the pessimists mean. In the more accurate and optimistic story it means continuing to succeed economically, as Britain has. If such success means cricket on Saturdays and drinkable if warm beer, then hip hip hurray.

38. The Word "Capitalism" Is a Scientific Mistake

Another column from Reason.

My ninety-five-year-old mother just read her daughter's *Bourgeois Equality: How Ideas, Not Capital or Institutions, Enriched the World* (2016). More exactly, Mom listened to the audio book, brilliantly read by Marguerite Gavin, in a mere thirty hours. Highly recommended.

Mom loved it. A woman of taste, you see. Surely her delight had nothing to do with my authorship. After all, mothers are well known to be wholly objective in their assessment of their children's accomplishments. Mom would be expected anyway by her intellectual habits to like the book, which is liberal. She watches a lot of business news and is enthusiastic for a free economy, especially Apple, Walmart, and T.J. Maxx—though, again like her daughter, she's willing to lean some toward the bleeding-heart version of a liberal economy.

Maybe a little more than her daughter. Some years ago she and I went to a celebration of the second Roosevelt at the Auditorium Theatre in Chicago, and adjourned to my apartment nearby for a heated discussion about the character of FDR's economic policy. I said the policy was lousy, as economists such as Robert Higgs and John Wallis and historians such as Ellis Hawley have long shown. She was indignant. For Mom, born in 1922, that man in the White House was the soothing voice of the fireside chats, the man who saved America from fascism. "By trying it out," I retorted, and our heated discussion continued. (You can see where I get my interest in ideas, and my tendency to heated if in the end courteous discussion about the ideas.) Right now she's listening to Amity Shlaes's *The Forgotten Man* (2007). I'm hoping Amity can wean her from the amiably leftist view of the New Deal. When Mom gets new information, she changes her mind. (What do you do?)

On one point of terminology, though, it's hard to change minds. Like so many people, economists and non-economists alike, Mom wanted to hear *Bourgeois Equality* as saying that capital, as in the very word "capitalism," is the key to our riches. Yet repeatedly in the book, and in its title, I deny it.

What's going on? "Capitalism" is what the Dutch call a *geuzennaam*, literally a "beggar name," assigned by one's sneering enemies, such as "Quaker" or "Tory" or "Whig," but then adopted proudly by the victims themselves. *Forbes: Capitalist Tool*, for example. The word "capitalism" is of course a Marxist coinage. Marx himself didn't use it, but let's not get pedantic: his followers such as Sombart certainly did, and the Master himself did freely use "capitalist" for the bosses who invested surplus value on top of their original accumulation of capital.

Like most economists and others before and after, Marx claimed that the accumulation of capital was the watch spring of modernity. The Marxian sociologist Immanuel Wallerstein, for example, wrote in 1983 that "the word capitalism is derived from capital. It would be legitimate therefore to presume that capital is a key element in capitalism."[1] No it wouldn't. That we insist on ruminating on something called "capital" does not imply that its accumulation was in fact unique to modernity, or causal.

And it was not. Romans and Chinese and all humans back to the caves have always accumulated capital, abstaining from consumption to get it. Think of the peasant putting seed back into the ground, or making paddy fields, or for that matter stone tools laboriously knapped and then polished for the beauty of it. What drove our enrichment were new ideas for investing the abstention, not the subsequent, actual investments in the ideas, necessary though the investments were. Necessary things, like gears in a watch, are not always the motive force, which is in the case of a watch the spring. Touching bases after a home run is necessary for it to count, but the home run was the cause of the score. It would obviously be unhelpful to call touching second base on the way home "the cause." In the Great Enrichment the ideas were the cause. The watch springs.

I agree with Hernando de Soto, who proposes that poor people in the *favelas* in Latin America get legal title to the land on which they squat, which they can then sell in order to educate their children or acquire a grubstake to enter the economy as entrepreneurs, or at least as now geographically or educationally mobile workers.[2] He is focusing on how to let very poor people get into the economy and benefit from economic growth. Like me, he thinks the poor people have plenty of good ideas for legal economic activity that would raise them and their children up, just as people have raised themselves up since 1800. A fruit stand. A cobbler shop. Then their grandchildren can become lawyers or computer programmers in a future economy in Peru or Brazil.

The poor need, he points out, just a little capital. Sure. Yet he would agree with me that merely piling capital up, with no profitable ideas—by the government taxing the farmers, say, and then adopting a five-year plan, or engaging in industrial planning to spend it on unproductive projects—is not what the poor need. Capital is necessary (as are air and labor and land and sunshine and peace). But ideas for enrichment, such as the fruit stand or containerization, are more than necessary. They are in most cases sufficient, because capital in the face of very, very good ideas is easily acquired. Capital is not the constraint. Ideas, with the legal permission to apply them, are. The arrogance of Latin American governments has been to suppose that poor people are bereft of ideas, and only university graduates or populist politicians have ideas. Some in Latin America have seen that such arrogance allied with populism is not the ticket, though voters keep falling back into the old habits. In the United States, too.

So powerful is the conviction in economics since Smith that capital accumulation is causal that in 1956 even the Austrian economist the great Ludwig von Mises got it wrong.[3] He wrote, "Saving, capital accumulation, is the agency that has transformed step-by-step the awkward search for food on the part of savage cave dwellers into the modern ways of industry." But it was not the "agency" if that means "the spring in the watch." He was correct only in the sense that accumulation was necessary. "The pacemakers of this evolution were the ideas that created the institutional framework within which capital accumulation was rendered safe by the principle of private ownership of the means of production." True, there needed to be the minimally liberal idea of protections for property. But these have been extremely widespread in human societies, from the caves on down. "Every step forward on the way toward prosperity is the effect of saving." Nonsense. Saving is necessary, yes, but so are an infinity of other things necessary. It then seemed to occur to him what the actual spring was, because he mentioned it, only to dismiss it: "The most ingenious technological inventions would be practically useless if the capital goods required for their utilization had not been accumulated by saving." It's one more iteration of the necessity as sufficiency. Try substituting "liquid water" for "capital accumulation" and "capital goods," and "getting liquid water" for "saving." Then proceed to a liquid water theory of economic growth.

I recently got into a little email debate on the matter with my friend the economist Mark Skousen, after my maiden trip in 2017 to his Freedom Fest, which happens every August in Las Vegas. The following year he and I had a debate on the matter at the conference itself. (You should go to Freedom Fest next year, especially if like me you have never seen the stunning vulgarity of Las Vegas ["the meadows"—even its name is phony], and if like me and my mother you delight in getting into serious discussions about liberalism. Freedom Fest is a hoot.)

Mark objected to my anti-"capitalism." "You must have capital to advance the economy," he wrote to me. "Entrepreneurs have plenty of great ideas and budding technology to change the world [no, dear Mark: they did not much before 1800], but unless they get financing [which they did when the ideas were really good: railways, Edison, the internet], they will remain unfulfilled."

That's right, but as Mark admitted the financing is merely a necessary condition, not sufficient. He commits Mises's mistake to mix them up. The explosion of human ingenuity after 1800, by contrast, *was* sufficient. The ideas were so good that financing was seldom (how does "never" work for you?) much of a problem. Consider the steam engine, though its application was delayed by Watt's patent. Consider reinforced concrete, unpatentable. Anyway, necessary conditions are endless, mostly not pertinent, such as "having liquid water at the usual temperatures" or "the existence of a labor force" or "the absence of an active civil war." And the finding of economic history is that the pertinent necessary conditions were shared by a great many societies, for millennia. Yet such societies did not have anything approaching the Great Enrichment that came to northwestern Europe after 1800.

Consider 1492 China, which had long peace, excellent property rights, enforcement of law, absence of crushing within-China tariffs (still another contrast to Europe), and plenty of capital, building massive projects with ease, putting even Roman capital projects into the shade. Yet China did not have the massive explosion of ingenuity tested commercially that, finally, especially after 1800, enriched northwestern Europe, which was in 1492 an appalling, quarrelsome backwater.

Why, then? Answer: not capital or institutions or science or coal, but Adam Smith's "liberal plan of equality, liberty, and justice," a liberalism 1.0 and then 2.0 first seen in northwestern Europe. Liberating ordinary people turned out to inspirit them to extraordinary ideas, which redirected the capital, and the liquid water, and the labor force. Skousen claimed that "the scarcity of investment capital has kept us from advancing as fast we could." No it hasn't. The historical and economic evidence tells against such a notion, popular at the World Bank during the long reign of capital fundamentalism. Pour capital into Ghana, yet it fails. Don't give Red China a red cent, yet it succeeds. The liberating ingenuity in human minds is what mattered, as in the Chinese economy after 1978 and the Indian after 1991. Give people liberty and you give them life.

If the capital fundamentalism of the Wall Street theorists were correct, then their enemies the socialists would be correct, too. The socialists assume that the key to capitalism is capital, and therefore that the big problem is its allocation. So do the Wall Street theorists. Both believe that ideas or entrepreneurship or management are *easy*. Ideas, they say, are a dime a dozen. That's why the Wall Street theorists dote on the TV program *Shark Tank,* in which ideas are easily shot down by investors, and it's why the socialists think that the government can easily arrange the allocation of investment, from Washington. Both are sure that the future is easy to lay down. Liberals aren't.

So, no. Mom and Mark, Smith and Marx, and even Mises, are mistaken. "Capitalism" is a scientific mistake compressed into a single word, a dramatically misleading coinage by our enemies, and still used by the sadly misled among our friends.

They are friends who have not slowly read *Bourgeois Equality,* or for that matter *The Bourgeois Virtues* (2006) or *Bourgeois Dignity* (2010). Or listened to that last in thirty hours. Get to it, guys.

39. Marxism Is Not the Way Forward

I wrote a paper for the "conservative" (how we throw such terms around, the better to stop listening!) American Enterprise Institute. Other people in the volume that resulted (Strain and Veuger, eds., 2016) got to write on figures in political philosophy they on the whole approved of. Though I was once, briefly, a sort of Marxian, and still regard Marx as amazing, I do not approve of his economics and his history and his politics, and especially not that of his followers.

Karl Marx has had since 1848 the tightest grip on the social imaginary of the clerisy, out of all the men we are discussing here.[1] He famously declared that he was not a Marxist. But his followers are influenced by Marx still, in departments of history and English, in studies of culture and of economic development. The followers, many of them among my dearest friends, are not always declared Marxists, or even, to assign a name to a less rigorous position, "Marxian"—people cheerfully influenced by Marx, though not so cheerful about Stalin or Mao. And beyond the various ranks of official believers, are the implicit followers during the age of materialism, 1890 to 1980, "marxoids" one might say—without intending to sneer too much, and including most social thinkers, not all of them on the left.

In the early and mid-twentieth century in progressive and a good deal of conservative writing on history, for example, the prevailing rhetoric wished

First published as "Economic Liberty as Anti-Flourishing: Marx and Especially His Followers," from *Economic Freedom and Human Flourishing: Perspectives from Political Philosophy*, edited by Michael R. Strain and Stan A. Veuger (Washington, DC: AEI Press, 2016). https://www.aei.org /publication/economic-freedom-and-human-flourishing-perspectives-from-political-philosophy/. Reproduced with permission of AEI Press. © 2016 by AEI Press.

always to see motives of class and economics hidden behind *every* professed sentiment. You can see it in Charles Beard's *An Economic Interpretation of the Constitution* (1913) or Georges Lefebvre's *Quatre-vingt-neuf* (*Four Score and Nine;* translated as *The Coming of the French Revolution*, 1939) or Christopher Hill's *The English Revolution 1640* (1940). It was a reaction to the nationalist tradition in the Romantic writing of history. "Aha, you alleged 'patriot,' you 'liberal,'" declared the hard-nosed anti-Romantics under the spell of Marx the inverted Romantic. "You can't fool us. We see your disgusting economic interest behind your so-called 'ideas.'" Even an anti-Marxian such as the British historian Hugh Trevor-Roper, ennobled by Margaret Thatcher and famous for his opposition to materialist explanations of the English Civil War (what Hill had called a revolution), wished in his first book, in 1940 on Charles I's Archbishop Laud, to slip in at the outset a quantitative estimate of, say, 90 percent for profane prudence—as against the faith or courage celebrated by Romantics such as Jules Michelet or Thomas Carlyle or John Lothrop Motley or Thomas Babington Macaulay. Trevor-Roper conceded on page 3 that "political ambition is only one among" the instincts sublimated in religion under Charles I. Yet, he continued, "in politics it is naturally by far the most potent."[2] Well, sometimes. You don't know on page 3.

The American appeals-court judge Learned Hand said in 1944, "The spirit of liberty is the spirit which is not too sure that it is right; the spirit of liberty is the spirit which seeks to understand the minds of other men and women."[3] Admitting that there's enough blame for voluntary lack of understanding of the minds of other men and women to fill the usual political spectrum, and to blame even some of the liberals sitting above the spectrum, the followers of Marx have since 1848 seldom adhered to such liberal principles as Hand's. It's been even less so now—although I am lovingly acquainted with exceptions (listen up George, Jack, Steve, and David).[4]

Some years ago I mildly remarked to a gathering of my beloved departments of history and of English at the University of Illinois at Chicago that the speaker who had just concluded his presentation, a fashionable Marxian imported from New York, just might not have got the economic history exactly right. The speaker responded in a sentence, "Oh, I see that you are a neoliberal," *and then sat down.* That was it, and none of my colleagues, mostly themselves Marxians or marxoids or cautious fellow-travelers, would speak up to insist that he respond more fully to their colleague, who after all had some slight claim to knowing a little about economics and history. I was startled by his exhibition of proud ignorance, and saddened by the implicit agreement in the room that one is *not* to listen, really listen, to their friends' questions and objections, and certainly not to those of enemies of one's party.[5]

The result of a century of name-calling-as-argument, from "Bernsteinian revisionism" and "economism" to "bourgeois" and "neoliberal," and of not listening, really listening, has had the scientific result one might expect. In a cartoon cover of the *National Review* by Thomas Reis in August 2014, a super-cool little Karl Marx, with a Starbucks coffee in his hand and an MP3 player in his ear and a jaunty little hat on his head, sports a T-shirt inscribed, "Still Wrong."[6] Right.

Yet I enrage my friends on the right by stating the obvious, that Marx was the greatest social scientist of the nineteenth century, without compare. But then I enrage my friends on the left by adding, which is my point here, that he was nonetheless mistaken on almost every point of economics and of history. Which is why I haven't got any friends.

In their persistence in scientific error, the followers of Marx are more interesting than the man himself, who after all tried hard to use his amazing intellect to see to the bottom of what was at the time known of economics and of history. *Capital* was subtitled *A Critique of Political Economy*, and, quite unlike his later followers, Marx went to great trouble to understand the scientific economics of his time that he was critiquing. In 1867 it was to be expected that he would get many points wrong, considering the state then of economics and of history. Most points, actually.

For example, his foundational labor theory of value was wrong, as every serious student of the matter has agreed for the past century and a half. Smith himself had introduced the notion, and it was still believed by such splendid figures as David Ricardo and John Stuart Mill, Mill being a contemporary of Marx. Neither Mill nor Marx had the benefit of the Neoclassical Revolution in the history of economic thought, during the 1870s. The Revolution brought, in the works of Walras, Jevons, and Menger, the correct view, confirmed thereafter in ten thousand scientific studies, that value is determined by how much people want things, considering the income available. Value does not depend on how much effort the sellers put into the things. You can get an A for effort but fail the final exam. The wage, it was soon realized, is determined not by bargaining strength but by the market value of what the last worker produces, considering that labor can move, or be moved. Performance matters.

Why, then, is Marxism, or at any rate the materialist interpretation of history and an economics innocent of any analysis beyond *Capital* in 1867, so persistent? Why haven't the Marxists, Marxians, and marxoids listened to their friends' questions and objections? The list of honorable exceptions, leftists who have engaged with economics since 1867 in a serious and scholarly fashion, would include very few names—Michel Foucault (2008) and Ted A. Burczak (2006, 2018), to name two—but not, alas, such eminent figures as David Harvey, Immanuel Wallerstein, and Frederic Jameson.

Why? For one thing, the elements of Marxism are fairly easy to master, but sufficiently mysterious—some would say confused and contradictory—to attract young people, especially young men. St. Augustine, who had been a professor of rhetoric, wrote of the difficulties in the Bible that "I do not doubt that this situation was provided by God . . . to conquer disdain in our minds, to which those things which are easily discovered seem frequently to be worthless."[7] *Capital* and especially the posthumous volumes II (1885) and III (1894) are read seriously only by the young and devout.

For another, an identity as a leftist is acquired early and seems then to be hard to shed—although of course it is a notable truth of twentieth-century biography that very many thoughtful people have gone away from the left, from socialism or regulation to conservatism or liberalism, and none the other way. Not one. Leszek Kołakowski, for example, was once in Poland an ardent young Communist, as Robert Nozick was once a socialist. I myself am a case in point of the usual story of movement from socialism to liberalism.

The mechanism of acquiring a left-wing identity starts when a sensitive adolescent in a non-slave society first notices that some people are much poorer than her family. She is likely to conclude, not at that age being a worker herself, that the best remedy is to open worker-Daddy's wallet. It is not an efficacious plan, and depends on coercion, and regularly corrupts its recipients, or is stolen on the way to the poor. But it is why the left wings of the Democratic and Labour parties toy perennially with a bankrupt socialism. Look at the Democratic primaries in 2019–2020.

The historian Eric Hobsbawm (1917–2012), for instance, describes in his engaging autobiography of 2002 how he wanted to become a Communist at age fourteen, and became one at sixteen—though, come to think of it, who would *not* in Germany in 1931 want to become something like a Communist?[8] Not anyone with a heart. (By 2002, true, one might inquire about the brain.) Hobsbawm pauses in his book from time to time to explain why, in the face of Stalin's crimes and the suppression of the Hungarian uprising and the rest, he only ceased being a dues-paying if unorthodox member of the Communist Party of Great Britain a few months before it dissolved itself, in 1991. His explanation, a strange one in such an intelligent man, was that he didn't want to give satisfaction to McCarthyites (whose British version had, to be sure, blocked him from many well-deserved academic appointments). He was faithful to the end, as people often are once their identities are formed, becoming uninterested in contrary facts that might be acquired in adulthood. It is rather like the atheism at age fourteen that bright boys and some bright girls espouse, never to be reconsidered, which then spills out of the mouths of fifty-year-old people who have meanwhile not cracked a serious book on theology. Likewise, I have noted, most of the Marxists and many of the Marxians and marxoids have not cracked a serious book on economics published after 1867.

Marxism is like atheism in another way, too (of course, it *is* atheism, as one may study in the reaction of the Chinese Communist Party to the Falun Gong). It appeals to a macho, anti-ethical positivism. Positivism was a minority view until the 1890s even among the clerisy, but came into wide favor in the ethics-denying generation stunned by the Great War. But as the ethical philosopher Bernard Williams said about the temptations facing the Amoralist, "He must resist, if consistent [in claiming that ethics is bosh], . . . [a] tendency to think of himself as being in character really rather splendid—in particular, as being by comparison with the craven multitude notably courageous," standing alone against the soft and bourgeois conventions of ethics.[9] Or as the conservative political philosopher J. Budziszewski puts it, describing his youthful and nihilistic self before he became a conservative Episcopalian, "Like Nietzsche, I imagined myself one of the few who could believe such things—who could walk the rocky heights where the air is thin and cold."[10] Courageously tough.

On a British television show in 1994, Hobsbawm was asked by the liberal Michael Ignatieff whether "the murder of 15, 20 million people [in the USSR under Stalin, a low estimate] might have been justified" in light of its contribution to founding a communist society.[11] Hobsbawm *without hesitation* replied, "Yes." Hard-minded. Or party-line-ish. Or thuggish. Oh, Eric.

A Marxian will object to all this that she espouses historical materialism not because of her identity formed at age fourteen as a leftist ("a *good* social democrat," she will say in a revealing phrase, the conservatives or liberals being of course *bad* people, and anti-poor), but because Marx was substantially, scientifically, correct, giving a correct analysis of the past and present and future.

Yet she is mistaken, scientifically. The American humorist Josh Billings long ago said that it's better to know less than to know so much that ain't so. To take a recent example of the persistence of such a marxoid just-so story, Daron Acemoglu's and James Robinson's *Why Nations Fail* (2012) has much in it with which to agree: Europe's advance was highly contingent; political and economic liberty are linked; economic growth can't get going in the midst of a civil war. But Acemoglu and Robinson expressly and even a little proudly rely on a startlingly out-of-date and marxoid account of the Industrial Revolution. "Our argument about the causes," they assert, "is highly influenced by" a list of "scholars in turn . . . inspired by earlier Marxist interpretations" of the 1920s through the 1960s, such as R. H. Tawney, Maurice Dobb, and Christopher Hill.[12] The *locus classicus* of such interpretations, and the introduction of the very phrase "the industrial revolution" into English, had been *Lectures on the Industrial Revolution of the Eighteenth Century in England* (1884), delivered by a university lecturer and ardent social reformer, Arnold Toynbee (1852–1883), in 1882, the year before his death at age thirty-one. Toynbee in turn depended on the story of triumph and tragedy put forward in *The Communist Manifesto*.

For example, Toynbee (and then Tawney and Hobsbawm and Acemoglu and Robinson) declared that "as a matter of fact, in the early days of competition the capitalists used all their power to oppress the laborers, and drove down wages to starvation point. This kind of competition has to be checked. . . . In England both remedies [combination and legislation] are in operation, the former through Trades Unions, the latter through factory legislation."[13] None of this is factually correct, though all of it fills the popular view of industrialization. There were no "early days of competition"— competition was common in any society of trade, as its enemies such as the medieval guildsmen sharply realized. Competition comes from entry, which is ancient, though of course irritating to those already rich from devising new stone tools or new electronic computers. Competition, which sets one capitalist against another for our benefit, such as Uber and Lyft competing against taxi monopolies, needs to be encouraged, not checked. Supply and demand, not "power," is what determines wages, as one can see in the ups and downs of real wages in response to population downs and ups, for example in the age of Malthus before 1798. The workers in the Industrial Revolution did not find their wages reduced, and did not starve. England's last starvation time was in the 1590s. Workers in the Industrial Revolution had moved eagerly to cities, not pushed by enclosures, even though Manchester and Lille and Boston were still even in Toynbee's time death traps of waterborne disease. Real wages in Toynbee's year of 1882 were in fact sharply rising, and had not ever fallen during industrialization—this long before the full legalization of Trades Unions. Children were being taken out of English factories long before the factory legislation began seriously to bite, and anyway children had always worked in agricultural societies. Capital accumulation was not the heart of the Great Enrichment.

The just-so story is mistaken in every detail, as economic historians have established scientifically in the past century or so. In other words, Acemoglu and Robinson are accepting a mistaken leftist tale in economic history proposed in 1848 or 1867 or 1882 by brilliant amateurs, before the professionalization of history, a story then rehearsed by Fabians at the hopeful height of the socialist idea after 1917, and then elaborated by a generation of (admittedly first-rate) Marxian historians, before thoroughgoing socialism had been tried and had failed, and before much of the scientific work had been done about the actual history—before it was realized, for instance, that other industrial revolutions occurred in, say, Islamic Spain or Song China, as the historical sociologist Jack Goldstone observed in 2002: "Examined closely, many premodern and non-Western economies show spurts or efflorescences of economic growth, including sustained increases in both population and living standards, in urbanization, and in underlying technological change."[14]

It is time, in short, to get beyond *The Communist Manifesto* as a work of history or economics.

40. Some on the Left Listen

An interview by two professors of English literature, Will Stockton (Clemson) and D. Gilson (Texas Tech), whom I will call, without prejudice, the Leftist. I'll call myself the Liberal. The piece was intended to be published somewhere, but wasn't.

THE LIBERAL: I am always glad to respond to queries from my friends on the left. I was myself once a Joan Baez–style socialist, so I know how it feels, and honor the generous impulse.

We liberals tend to think of people on the left as merely misled, and therefore improvable by instruction—if they will but listen. People on the left, on the other hand, think of people on what they believe is the right, in which they cast real liberals, too, as non-people, as *evil,* as "pro-business," as against the poor. An extreme case is the Duke University historian Nancy MacLean's unscholarly assault on James Buchanan, a great liberal economist. Therefore the left is *not* ready to listen to the instruction so helpfully proffered by the liberals.

Almost no one among students of literature who considers herself deeply interested in the economy, and since she was sixteen left-leaning, bothers to read with the serious and open-minded attention she gives to a Harvey or a Wallerstein or a Jameson anything by a Buchanan or a Friedman or a Mill or a Smith. (Foucault, I have noted, was an interesting exception.) Please, dears.

I've also noticed that the left assumes that it is dead *easy* to refute what they call the neoliberals. Yet the left does not understand most of the arguments made by the liberals, neo- or archeo-. I don't mean the left disagrees

243

with the arguments, offering reasoned objections. I mean it doesn't understand them. Not at all.

This is easy to show. For example, go to the bottom of page 6 of the English translation of Thomas Piketty's *Capital in the Twenty-First Century* to see a butchering of the elementary analysis of entry at the smell of profits. This from an *economist* on the left. The writings of Robert Reich, Tony Judt, and Naomi Klein can provide other instances, more and more egregious.

For example, the left supposes that the liberals/libertarians/ "conservatives" rely on what it calls trickle-down economics, even though the enrichment of the poor from trade-tested betterment since 1800 has been more like a fire hose than a trickle, and has had nothing to do with trickling down from the making of Rolexes or the building of mansions. The left supposes, too, that the "invisible hand" is a mere dogma, even though trade-tested betterment is the result of cooperation and competition in markets, observable every time you find a loaf of bread miraculously available for you in the grocery store. The invisible hand has repeatedly been shown to be radically bettering compared with the alternatives, such as East Germany. And anyway such hands are routine in human society, as in language or manners, mainly *not* governed by a law-or-advice-giving French Academy or Judith Martin.

I have faced the easy-refutability assumption ever since I stopped being a marxoid myself and started to grasp the argument and evidence that people like Robert Nozick or Milton Friedman or Israel Kirzner put forward. When I deploy very ordinary nineteenth-century liberal arguments, my leftish interlocutors are regularly *astonished*. Commonly, they have never heard them articulated. They are gobsmacked that anyone would seriously claim, for example, that supply and demand curves pretty much govern prices of milk and autos and houses in actual economies from Venezuela to Virginia.

THE LEFTIST: I'd like to begin by asking you to respond to the term "neoliberalism," at least as it refers to a general set of political and economic ideas and policies. In the words of David Harvey, "neoliberalism," as variously put into practice by state leaders like Ronald Reagan in the United States and Margret Thatcher in Britain, as well as Deng Xiaoping in China, "proposes that human well-being can best be advanced by liberating individual entrepreneurial freedoms and skills within an institutional framework characterized by strong private property rights, free markets, and free trade."[1] Neoliberal politicians and economists promote the deregulation of industry, labor, and financial markets. They promote the privatization of formerly state provisions like education and prisons.

THE LIBERAL: I know David Harvey a little—he hosted me for a talk I gave in the early 1990s (as Donald!) at Johns Hopkins, and a couple of years ago we reconnected briefly at a speech he gave in Chicago. (He seemed then a little uneasy about my gender change, which is understandable.) Though he has never grasped elementary economics, or done the homework necessary to grasp it, I admire his vigor and intelligence in argument, and in particular his courageous battle long ago against the IRS. That sweetly statist institution audited him in the Nixon era numerous times, as punishment for his eloquent opposition to the Vietnam War. Good for David.

I entirely agree with his definition of (neo)liberalism. So understood, it's the same as the old, classical liberalism of Adam Smith and J. S. Mill. By contrast, the century-long weirdness in the definition of "liberal" in the Anglosphere—as slow socialism—came from Britain late in the nineteenth century and from the United States in the early twentieth century. "Neoliberalism," properly defined nowadays, brings us back to the Blessed Adam Smith's definition in 1776, as "allowing every man [and woman, dear] to pursue his own interest in his own way, upon the liberal plan of equality, liberty, and justice."

I take it we all approve of such a plan. I take it that no one here is *against* equality, liberty, and justice. So from now on I am going to call what you call neoliberalism just "liberalism." In my book *Bourgeois Dignity* (2010) I claimed that liberalism caused the modern world, an argument much expanded and justified in *Bourgeois Equality* (2016), the third volume of the trilogy. I wish I had had the wit to add the word "liberal" to the subtitle of the 2016 book, *How [Liberal] Ideas, Not Capital or Institutions, Enriched the World.* It's too late now, but if I someday get a new edition I'll add "liberal."

Put it this way. As a liberal I want you to be permitted to do things, such as setting up as a lawyer free of regulation or buying a car from Japan or Korea free of tariffs or sending your children to any K–12 school you or a poor neighbor wants (with, however, IRS-imposed taxes, which for this purpose I enthusiastically support, on relatively high-income people like you and me and David Harvey to *finance* the poor person's choice—with vouchers, for example, such as "socialist" Sweden has introduced since the 1990s).

By contrast, in his opposition to neoliberalism, David, as a socialist, slow or fast, wants you when trying to do such things to be in fact violently coerced, limited, restricted, leashed by a law backed by police. He wants you to have access only to an expensive lawyer or to have to pay more for an auto to favor US jobs or to get free education only through an ideologically interested state and a state-capturing bureaucracy and its trade unions, all of them backed by the threat or the actuality of governmental coercion—such as by the IRS. If you practice as a lawyer in Illinois without a license (to be acquired only by four plus three years of education, and passing a state-set examination; all this unlike such terrible lawyers as Abraham Lincoln, without so much as an elementary school degree, reading law in Steven Logan's office), you are fined and then jailed. If you try to arrange a trade between Mr. Ishishi in Japan who makes and sells autos and Mr. Smith in New York who is willing to pay for one, and if you refuse to pay the tariff to the US government to spend on wars such as Vietnam or Iraq II, you are audited and fined and then jailed. And so forth. Many statist educational or health systems worldwide *prohibit* private side deals for further education or health. You'll forgive me, I hope, when I say that it all reminds me of the prohibitions of queers 1880–1990; that, too, was backed by governmental coercion, against which, like the war on Blacks using cheapened cocaine in the 1990s, the left on the whole did not complain.

The *definition* of neo- and nineteenth-century and down-to-the-present-European "liberalism" is laissez-faire, laissez-passer. By all means, let us have courts to adjudicate some property rights and have some police to go after some parts of force and fraud and have a Coast Guard to prevent some evil countries like Canada from invading Maine and have a nuclear deterrent to prevent thugs like Putin from getting their way all the time. Use independent courts and adversarial procedures to handle non-agreed agreements, such as bank fraud and food poisoning and gross negligence. Do not use state pre-regulations, which are most usually taken over by special interests being "regulated," such as doctors with prescription powers and the big drug companies. Enforce the First Amendment and the Voting Rights Act.

Get the rest of governmental coercion out of our lives, and depend mainly instead on voluntary agreements. Retain governmental coercion only for the few good functions of government I have mentioned—not, as it happens, the most common example that comes to people's lips in opposition: roads. Roads should be privatized, as they were in the hundreds of turnpikes in Britain and North America in the eighteenth and nineteenth centuries, and still are in country roads in Sweden. We should remove from our lives, and send to work on mutually agreeable making and selling, all the coercion-enabled people like Big Bill Thompson or the denizens of Tammany Hall or the inquisitors at the National Industrial Recovery Administration or the accountants in the modern IRS collecting massive sums to spend on warfare and corruption and the regulation of lawyers and subsidies to cotton farmers under "programs" favoring the richest among us.

Laissez-faire has been tried out extensively since the eighteenth century. No one claims it has been pure. But its impurity is not decisive, considering the actual performance of the state mercantilism it replaced or the state socialism that reactionaries of right or left want to replace it with. Laissez-faire is always under attack. Interfering in other people's business is attractive to authoritarians. (Ask yourself, now: Are you one? If so, why?) Hong Kong after 1947 has been close to pure laissez-faire. Leaving adults alone, I suppose you agree, has its own intrinsic merit. And a consequence has been that average income in Hong Kong—in 1947 equal to the pathetic level of the mainland—is now within hailing distance of that of the United States. The poorest people in Hong Kong are now rich by international standards. Social-democratic countries include, if you look seriously and quantitatively at the programs, the United States. No poor person is refused entry to an emergency room in the United States, But in countries with single-payer the emergency rooms are often hard to get to. The claim is that social democracy helps the poor, despite the small share of governmental expenditure and regulation that in fact does so. The claim persuades the modern slow socialists to favor coercion over agreements, comprehensively.

The size of the safety net in presumably "neoliberal" economies like the United States and the United Kingdom is about the same as in presumably social-democratic economies like France or Sweden. We are all social democrats now. Tories in Britain support the National Health Service. The big change in all the now-rich countries was from 1910 to 1970. Nowadays the differences among them, compared to the great magnitude of historical change attributable to commercially tested betterment, are not much. And the commercial enrichment pays for the National Health Service.

Yes, I know that you believe that Reagan and Thatcher were monsters who hated the poor, and impoverished them. But look at the numbers. Real incomes per head of the poorest among us have risen sharply since, for example, the much-admired 1950s. In 1956 a refrigerator cost 116 hours of work to buy. That's why in the 1950s many poor American households didn't have one, and none in the United Kingdom. Now a refrigerator costs 15 hours of work, and uses less electricity.

The big modern examples of improvements through economic liberalism are China and India. But the biggest example of the economic good of liberalism is historical, the Bourgeois Revaluation, as I call it, supported by a liberal ideology birthed in the eighteenth century, which despite all the attacks by statists, especially in the twentieth century under socialism and fascism, led to the modern world.

Liberalism did not need to be perfectly laissez-faire to do its work. Moving in a liberal direction, as India did after 1991, sufficed to raise growth rates per person from 1 percent a year to 7 percent per year. At 7 percent per year, Indian real income has doubled every ten years. In a couple of generations the Indians, if they keep being a little liberal, will have income equal to that of Americans.

THE LEFTIST: Do you think this political-economic description of neoliberalism is fair or accurate? Would you describe political and economic policy over the last fifty-odd years as neoliberal, or is there another term that better suits?

THE LIBERAL: I think David's definition is just fine, so long as factual claims about consequences are not slipped into it. We know factual consequences only by inquiring into facts, not by the very definition of words. But the term that better suits, I affirm, is plain "liberal," which is to say someone who believes in the obvious and simple plan of equality, liberty, and justice, as against the conservative pride of rank and tradition, or the various schemes by socialists and fascists since 1848 to glorify the state and to leash tightly the individual and to substitute collective governmental coercion for individual mutual agreement, for the glory of the Nation or of the Revolution.

THE LEFTIST: To follow Harvey's understanding of neoliberalism a bit further, we might understand the "neo-" prefix as a reference to the resurgence of classical liberalism along more comfortably statist lines.

THE LIBERAL: Yes. It's a useful distinction. Got it. But there's nothing much "neo" about it. David didn't like the retreat from socialism, such as has happened in Sweden and in his native Britain. But, yes, the so-called liberals did adopt "more comfortably statist lines." Shame on you, Hillary.

THE LEFTIST: The neoliberals also shrink the social safety net, cutting welfare, unemployment, and other programs that aid the poor.

THE LIBERAL: No, they don't, on several counts. For one thing, "programs that [are 'designed to'] aid the poor" are not the same as "programs that [actually] aid the poor." I do wish progressives would note the difference, at any rate as a possibility to be looked into. I am a Christian liberal, and acknowledge a responsibility to help the wretched of the earth. "For the needy shall not always be forgotten" (Ps. 9:18). I tithe to my Episcopal church, which runs charities that work. I recently housed in my own home two homeless people for four and a half years. But I want to *actually* help the poor, not merely make myself *feel* charitable and Progressive over my second cappuccino perusing the editorial pages of the *New York Times*. Using governmental coercion to force other people to help the poor is attractive if you don't think too much about governmental coercion, or have never been a victim of it, or have never thought through how clumsy the government's help is, or have never personally helped any poor people.

For instance, the minimum wage is said nowadays to be "designed" to help the poor. In actuality it drives the very poorest among us out of getting any job at all. Thus ex-cons, or Black young men, or Chicano high-school dropouts. A hundred years ago when the minimum was designed and imposed by literal Progressives, first in Australia and then state by state in the United States, it was designed explicitly, confessedly, without shame, on openly eugenic grounds to drive immigrants, Blacks, Chicanos, people with disabilities, and women entirely out of paid labor, leaving the white, skilled, able-bodied, middle-aged, American-born men in possession of all the jobs. Look it up. It was white nationalism before Trump revived it.

Modern progressives don't know the history, and think as they read and sip and turn the page that raising the minimum wage helps the poor. It doesn't. It injures the poorest, in aid of, for example, union members. Until recently I belonged happily to a union, the recently formed union of faculty at UIC. I walked the picket line, chanting the labor songs of my youth. And as a kid I belonged briefly to the National Maritime Union. But unions, good for dignity and better management, and the regulations like the minimum wage and occupational licensing, are not why we are rich. We are rich compared with our ancestors because of commercially tested betterments such as electric lights and penicillin and universities and autos.

THE LEFTIST: Let me shift to yet another description of neoliberalism: as an economic discourse that encroaches on previously non-economic aspects of life. For instance, Wendy Brown argues that under neoliberalism, "all conduct is economic conduct; all spheres of existence are framed and measured by economic terms and metrics, even when those spheres are not directly monetized. In neoliberal reason and in domains governed by it, we are only and everywhere *Homo economicus.*"[2]

THE LIBERAL: I dealt with that claim in a review of Michael Sandel's book *What Money Can't Buy.*[3] Briefly, no. Brown's claim would be like claiming that Christianity is stupid because of the stupidity of Jerry Falwell (who has gone to his reward; one wonders exactly where). Your "only and everywhere *Homo economicus*" is, I readily concede, characteristic of the more boyish (note the gender) of my colleagues in economics. It would not describe, say, Albert Hirschman, Robert Fogel, Nancy Folbre, or even my former colleague Milton Friedman. I suggest that you actually do the reading, as Foucault did. It's not wise to weaken your argument by choosing straw men to attack. In theological terms, go after Dietrich Bonhoeffer or Sarah Coakley, not Jerry Falwell.

THE LEFTIST: You have defended at length the virtues of the bourgeoisie. But what do you say to the claim that there are spheres of human existence that need to be lived apart from economic calculation? Or, to put the question more strongly, what do you say to those many humanities scholars, like Brown, who worry about the impoverishment of politics and ethics caused by the reduction of humans to *Homo economicus?*

THE LIBERAL: I say yes, of course, many, many spheres of human existence need to be lived apart from economic calculation. I have said so at length in three fat tomes, most especially on the particular point in the first one, *The Bourgeois Virtues*. I worry that economists and many others, in love with what I call there Prudence Only, such as "realists" in international relations, impoverish our thinking—for example about love.

41. But They Have Not Noticed the Actual Results of Liberalism

More of the dialogue with the left. Not, we hoped, deaf.

THE LEFTIST: The overall result [of neoliberalism] has been rising wealth inequality; a stagnating, if not shrinking, middle class; an entrenched school-to-prison pipeline.

THE LIBERAL: Now we have drifted into talking about alleged consequences, and have left definition behind. It's important, as you will agree, to keep the definitions of words separate from alleged facts about the world. Otherwise we are, in the correct meaning of the phrase, "begging the question," that is, inserting factual conclusions and practical theorems into the very definitions and axioms we start with. *X* implies *X*.

All of the consequences you allege are mistaken, not-*X*, if they are supposed to be connected to liberalism. Some of them did happen, sadly, such as the school-to-prison pipeline for poor Blacks and Chicanos. It's outrageous. But the pipeline happened not because of new freedoms of enterprise, but because of anti-liberal policies such as, to take one prominent example among many, the War on Drugs. But over-regulation by local governments played a part, too. It has made some poor inner-city neighborhoods into places in which gangs with bullets, not grocery stores with price leaders, compete. Chicago from January to September of 2016 exceeded the number of murders in all twelve months of 2015, largely in half a dozen of its fifty neighborhoods. Therefore in such places no entrepreneur wants to open a business to sell fresh vegetables in grocery stores or to employ people in manufacturing. And the city's regulations on zoning stop it anyway.

Naturally the Republicans, the worst of whom are mostly statist protectionists and social fascists, not Christian liberals, approved of the War on Drugs and the steeper prison sentences introduced in the 1990s. But consider that nearly all *Democratic* politicians bought into the War on Drugs, too.

For shame. True liberals like Milton Friedman and Nick Gillespie and me, by contrast, have for fifty years been opposing with every ounce of our energies the War on Drugs and the military draft and occupational licensure and longer prison terms and other interferences in equality, liberty, and justice. We believe in the liberal plan. You do, too, yes?

I have leftish friends telling me, to take another instance, that they oppose Uber and Lyft. Wow. They don't seem to realize that by doing so they are carrying water for the multimillionaires who own the taxi medallions. They do not realize that a taxi monopoly gives benefits in the exact magnitude of the hundreds of thousands of dollars to buy a second-hand license only to the holders of the state-restricted license to enter, and that such a monopoly cannot give benefits to a mere driver *qua* driver, whose skills are commonplace, and are *not* made artificially scarce by the coercively enforced law (or by non-law coercion from black-cab drivers in London, protecting their now-obsolete monopoly of The Knowledge). Nor do they realize that the new competitors to the old taxis will seek riders in minority neighborhoods (as old taxis notoriously will not). The seeking is good money, and many of the Uber and Lyft drivers come from such neighborhoods. A poor man who has at least a car—as many of the poor do in the United States—can at least earn a living.

My leftish friends earnestly think they are in favor of the poor. Without intending to, however, they regularly and grievously damage them. They are objectively anti-poor. For shame, for shame. Now that you have listened to the instruction I have kindly provided, you will stop being anti-poor, yes? Galileo in Bertolt Brecht's play puts it this way: "I say to you: he who does not know the truth is merely an idiot. But he who knows it and calls it a lie, is a criminal. Get out of my house!"[1]

The middle class has not "stagnated." Worldwide, for example, it has exploded. Ask the Chinese or the Indians. (I often query my progressive friends as to why they seem to care only about *US* people. I don't get it. Aren't we post-eighteenth-century liberals supposed to care also about foreign souls?) And even in old-rich countries like France and the United States, the middle-class people have gotten better off, even in the past thirty years. I heard Joe Stiglitz on NPR in August 2016 saying that the real wage hasn't increased in the United States over the past 40 years. Come on, Joe: look at the real data on non-wage benefits and correctly deflated prices of cell phones and air-conditioning. In 2006 he praised the economic policies of Hugo Chávez as aiming "to bring education and health benefits to the poor, and to strive for economic policies that not only bring higher growth but also en- sure that the fruits of the growth are more widely shared."[2] Wrong again, dear. Joe in my experience is a sweet fellow. But he's a theorist only, and be- lieves you can prove great social truths standing at a blackboard. He is will- ing to grasp at so-called facts in a way that a mere bench scientist like me finds startling. Joe, get out of my house.

People at all income levels in the United States and the European Union need much less work than they did forty years ago to get a refrigerator or in- ternet connection, made possible by private cooperation and competition. They could get more food and fiber from Chile or Chad at a similarly low price if the government got out of protecting rich Californian or German farmers. Let's do it.

The statistics you hear about stagnant wages and rising inequality do not track the fate of individuals or families of the "middle class." They look instead at who is in the middle at the moment, regardless of their life course. If you do track them, you find that the infamous "hollowing out" of the middle class is mainly caused by many in the middle rising into substantial riches.

Preventing poor people from rising into the middle class, in turn, is caused not by a vibrant, laissez-faire economy but by such progressive- approved items as closed-shop unionism. I like to point out in my lectures that I am normally the only person in the room who could become an electri- cian in Michigan, because my grandfather Fritz, my uncle Joe, and my cousin Phil were already in the union. That's the only way you get an apprentice- ship. Guess how the Michigan electricians view candidates for apprenticeships from the wretched of the earth.

Nor has inequality increased. Yes, I understand. You are *indignant* that I would say such a stupid, crazy thing, considering how often you hear that it *has* increased. But you know that you can't believe every claim you read in the newspaper, even if the claim is popular. Clear your mind of cant. Note the practice of repeating errors until they sound true by, say, the Trumpistas, with intent to deceive, or for that matter, with no intent to deceive, by the benevolent *New York Times*.

If you will take your copy of Piketty off the coffee table and read it, you will find that his data show that in only three of the many countries he studied has inequality increased substantially in the past few decades, namely, the United States, the United Kingdom, and Canada. Aha, you will exclaim— in just the lands of Reagan and Thatcher! (Set Canada aside—"as usual," a Canadian would ruefully note.) No, you are mistaken. The *cause* of the US-UK inequality (which by the way has recently declined) has been the very prosperity of the two countries compared with Old Europe. And the United States and especially the United Kingdom have implemented inegalitarian subsidies to home ownership urged by both Republicans and progressives, reinforcing the long-extant and illiberal constraints on urban building— zoning and building codes in the United States, planning permission in the United Kingdom.

Who as a result has benefited most from restrictions on building in, say, London? The beneficiaries have been the Dukes of Norfolk and Westminster, who own the land made more scarce by booming London. When I said this to a large audience of Labourites at a BBC program broadcast from the National Theatre in London, I was amused that the audience booed. That's intelligent. Stop the private building of housing in London through swingeing restrictions on the building of houses, then complain that housing in London is expensive, and demand more public housing.

THE LEFTIST: The neoliberal, unlike the classical liberal, believes that the government often can help to ameliorate problems like poverty, inadequate health care and housing, and limited education opportunities.

THE LIBERAL: My advice is to examine skeptically what you call a "problem." The government can't solve all of them. Sometimes it rains. The supposition to the contrary is the Enlightenment faith that people can do anything they rationally propose to do. Tom Paine (who by the way was an ardent free-trader) said in 1776, "We have it in our power to begin the world over again."[3] Well, sometimes. (And yet he also meant by his remark, in liberal fashion, that any one of us should be allowed to start an ironworks or a distillery free of governmental supervision.)

The liberal of the Smithian and Millian and Isaiah Berlinian sort observes that many problems are caused by state action undertaken . . . to solve problems. I do not want to fall into a version of the Supply Chain Fallacy. It was prominently displayed in a 2013 book by Mariana Mazzucato, *The Entrepreneurial State: Debunking Public vs. Private Sector Myths,* which asserted that if *any* government action helped birth a technology to *any* degree at *any* time, then *most* of the technology is to be attributed to the wisdom of government. So let me confine my counter-examples to *big* causes, not merely some minor cause in the supply chain.

Poverty was massively caused, for example, by "protective" interventions by the state into labor markets, because the main effect of the protection is to keep the poor from competing with the middle class or the upper working class. That was its original purpose in Progressivism, I have noted, and was admirably well-achieved. For example, legislation in the 1920s in some states "protecting" women from working overtime automatically excluded them from supervisory jobs, because the little boss needs to come early and leave late. I don't suppose I need to mention Jim Crow and (inspired by Jim Crow) apartheid, among the numerous examples of state-enforced poverty. And on and on.

Inadequate health care was massively caused by state intervention into the market for doctors and drugs and nurses and hospitals. It's a long and complicated story, but note that until the early twentieth century a druggist could treat your disease (admittedly, until antibiotics, his treatment was not very effective, but the same was true of doctors, at a higher price). Entry to doctoring was relatively free. The doctors therefore earned until the 1930s about as much as lawyers and professors. But from the 1950s on they earned *three times* as much. Midwives could once in the United States deliver children—the monopolization of birthing by obstetricians started early in the nineteenth century, with their "instruments." Until the very late nineteenth century, and the coming of hospital hygiene, the lying-in hospitals where the doctors liked to work were death traps. Employment-based medical insurance came about to evade wage controls in World War II, and is peculiar to the United States and Germany. The government forbids us to import radically cheaper drugs from Canada. And so forth. Therefore local and federal protections of monopolies in US health care have easily doubled its cost.

Inadequate housing was one of the earliest "problems" to be addressed by the government, in the form of slum clearance. The theory was that bad housing *caused* disease, poverty, and, especially, sexual abuse. (The Victorians were very interested in sex.) And so the government introduced zoning, building codes, and planning permission, and knocked down slums to make nice housing for the rich, such as Sandberg Village in Chicago, and high-rise concentration camps for the poor, such as the Robert Taylor Homes in Chicago. Homelessness is more of a problem now than once, because regulations have made cheap housing expensive.

I do wish my progressive friends would take to heart the old joke about the three most unbelievable sentences in English: "The check is in the mail"; "Of course I'll respect you in the morning"; and "I'm from the government, and I'm here to help you." When the police approach a Black youth in Chicago, he does not suppose they are about to help him. The experience of white, middle-class people with the police, I don't need to tell you, is different.

THE LEFTIST: The help simply comes in the form of public-private partnerships like the Affordable Care Act (as opposed to a more progressive single-payer system).

THE LIBERAL: You'll forgive me if in my cynical economist's way I think of the numerous "public-private partnerships," including Obamacare, as resulting in the privates getting rich, the bureaucrats getting powerful, and the poor among the public getting the shaft. In Benton Harbor, Michigan, which when I was little in the 1940s was lily white but then became largely Black, there used to be a public park on the city's shore on Lake Michigan that Blacks used. The park was taken in 2013 by eminent domain in order for a public-private partnership to build a golf course and vacation resort—not, you may safely assume, for local Blacks. Similarly, in *Kelo v. City of New London* (2005), the Supreme Court decided in favor of a public-private partnership in which the homes of poor and middle-class people were demolished for a "comprehensive redevelopment plan."[4] The plan never happened. For more than a decade now the acres in New London have sat empty.

Better the liberal plan, I say, under which park goers and home owners would have to be approached by developers carrying bushels of cash. When you progressives say "public-private partnership," we liberals hear "public-private conspiracy."

42. And Are Unwilling to Imagine Liberal Alternatives

A conclusion to the interview.

THE LEFTIST: It therefore seems to me that both neoliberals (think Barack Obama and Hillary Clinton) and critics of neoliberalism would argue that your "Separation of State and Economy" bumper sticker is deceptive.

THE LIBERAL: Yes, if by this you mean (which the next phrase shows you don't) that some nasty and self-interested people in the economy reach into the state and influence it for their own benefit. (Like you, I do not purpose to "deceive," by the way. I tell the truth as I see it, as you do. No tricks. Listen, really listen.)

I warmly commend Adam Smith to your readers. He wrote only two books (which means that he would not have succeeded in modern academic life). If the readers are serious about challenging their ideas, they should take down both books and slowly read. Your point was put this way by Smith: "To found a great empire for the sole purpose of raising up a people of customers, may at first sight appear a project fit only for a nation of shopkeepers. It is, however, a project altogether unfit for a nation of shopkeepers, but extremely fit for a nation whose government is influenced by shopkeepers."[1] Spot on, as you will agree. We liberals join with you, and Charles Koch, in opposing crony capitalism.

THE LEFTIST: Even a "laissez-faire" marketplace requires state support. The state defines and then protects property rights through the police and court systems.

THE LIBERAL: This trope of argument tires me out , I confess. I hear it all the time from progressives of the Sanders sort and from US "liberals" of the Clinton sort. They appear to think that any real liberal argument can be refuted with thirty seconds of thought. No, eight seconds. Observe here that a true argument, that we need *some* government (which no true liberal denies—we are not radical anarchists, though admittedly we look upon them with sisterly affection), is recruited to make a much more questionable argument, namely, that we need a government taking by compulsion 35 percent or more of GDP for its projects, a government furthermore that unjustly regulates a good deal of the rest of the GDP.

The cowboy humorist Will Rogers used to criticize the guv'ment, back in the 1920s when its take at local, state, and federal levels combined was 10 or 15 percent. Now it's 35, and much higher in most other rich countries. Will Rogers's statue stands in the Capitol, and is commonly the backdrop for TV interviews of congresspeople. I wish the congresspeople would turn around and start listening to old Will.

A quite small part of the 35 to 55 percent appropriated by governments in rich countries goes to the poor. And the defining and protection of property at all levels would cost perhaps 5 percent of GDP, adding in even the protection against dangerous foreigners, such as Trump's image of Honduran refugees. The regulations largely enrich the rich, for example Trump's real estate company, by eminent domain— which is a state-sponsored, and gross, violation of property rights. Some protection. As an economic historian put it, reacting in 1971 to the claim by an economic theorist that feudal lords had offered "protection" to peasants, "The possibility that the main, if not the only, danger against which the peasant very frequently was in need of protection was the very lord is not mentioned."[2] Or the very government, attending on a modern lord.

And by the way, the definition and protection of property rights is in fact largely done by private agreement. Yes, the state is the definer and protector "of last resort," as it is usually put. But if we are not to leap headlong into the Supply Chain Fallacy, we need to ask *how much* the last resort matters. Business contracts, for example, are "enforced" (note the "forced," which is here a metaphor; yet by the hand of the government it is literal) *not* by governmental coercion but by the worry that if I violate a contract, my fellow businesspeople will hear the news and shun me. How do you think handshake contracts are enforced among the Hasidic diamond merchants who wander on 47th Street with a half a million dollars' worth in their coat pocket? By going to the police? By appealing to a *goyisher* judge?

THE LEFTIST: How do you answer the claim that the separation of economy and state that you call for is impossible?

THE LIBERAL: I answer it by noting that, in the way that liberals have always had in mind, the separation is of course "possible." It's happened. My answer is like the joke: Do you believe in infant baptism?" "*Believe* in it?! I've *seen* it!"

I've seen it for example in the United States in the nineteenth century—though I admit that the period, wedged between sclerotic feudalism and sclerotic regulation, was brief. The period's laissez-faire caused commercially tested betterment, which didn't give the ideologues and vested interests time to catch up by imposing top-down laws. I met a very successful young entrepreneur, a recent graduate of St. Cloud State University in Minnesota, who was using cutting-edge technology in retailing. He told me that he could trick the regulators by continuing to innovate ahead of their regulations. As the proverb has it, it's easier to apologize to the government for having done X than to get permission from the government beforehand to do X. Later the leaders of a new payment company in Brazil told me the same thing. American and Brazilian consumers are thus enriched.

A line to the contrary from the left replies indignantly that governmentally enabled internal improvements such as canals and ports were fundamental to the success of the economy. It is the theme of Arthur Schlesinger Jr.'s old book, *The Age of Jackson* (1945), or indeed a number of other books after the War in which academic New Dealers defended a moderate version of slow socialism, such as Richard Hofstadter in his early work and (as I have mentioned) a brilliant early book by my father, Robert G. McCloskey.[3] The New Deal line has the difficulty of the Supply Chain Fallacy. True, in the United States the canals of the 1830s in Indiana, for example, were backed by government bonds, which were sold mainly to the British. But in Britain itself the earlier canals, for example in the 1790s, were entirely private. And the internal "improvement" of the Indiana canals turned out to be a disastrous investment—because presently the railways came. The state defaulted, and for a long time Americans visiting London were treated with less than sweet hospitality.

THE LEFTIST: You yourself allow that the state may also provide for K–12 education, presumably because you understand that education and economic growth go hand in hand.

THE LIBERAL: And so did Adam Smith, who devotes many chapters of *The Wealth of Nations* to the matter. Scotland had the advantage over England that a fierce Calvinism required all the boys and even the girls to be able to read. I certainly recommend (so did Smith) that you and I be taxed, as I said, to *finance* the education of the poor. I approve of it not chiefly because of economic growth (what kind of vulgarian do you suppose I am?!), but because of the human scope that literacy provides.

Yet *financing* by voucher is not the same as governmental *provision*, from schools staffed by public employees under the orders of the government. There is no good reason that the means of producing education should be thus socialized, or at any rate no more reason than that the means of producing milk or giving rides in taxis should be. Scottish universities in Smith's time were much superior to Oxford and Cambridge, in both educating and researching. Scottish students paid the professors directly. (Smith was a famously good teacher, and did well by it financially.) In England, by contrast, the ancient endowments paid for the fellows to loll about drinking ancient port. Remind you of anything in US academic life?

THE LEFTIST: [Neoliberalism has caused] a transformation of public higher education into "outcome"-obsessed job-training centers.

THE LIBERAL: About higher education we agree that the triumph of the Administrative University has been deplorable. Yet I say again that it's not caused by laissez-faire but by the opposite, the impulse to central planning, the rationalist side of the French Enlightenment—the view that we can easily lay down the future with endless administrative rules in the *Federal Register* of eighty thousand new pages every year, or in universities' bulky faculty handbooks. Dirigisme again. The turn in universities to imposed "practicalities" on the students (as though an education in accounting was always more practical than one in reading good English literature or in making good mathematical proofs) is worldwide, as is the proliferation of university administrators to encourage the practicalities, each equipped with a large salary, a secretary, and several assistants. Being worldwide, it can hardly be blamed on Reagan and Thatcher (though, incidentally, Thatcher was no liberal in educational policy—she centralized K–12 education, for example, and meddled in the universities; on the other hand, she democratized the very definition in the United Kingdom of a "university").

THE LEFTIST: You attributed the rise of the Administrative University to the "central-planning impulse." Can you say more about this connection? I hazard to claim that most academics would argue exactly the opposite, citing decreased public support for higher education alongside rising tuitions and the proliferation of associate deans.

THE LIBERAL: By "central-planning impulse" I mean the conviction people have, on both left and right, that things can easily be planned, and need to be. One argument you hear is that in olden days the economy was simple, and so could regulate itself, but a complex modern economy needs to be planned. The truth is the opposite. The more complex and specialized and spontaneously bettering an economy is, the *less* it can be planned, the less a central planner however wise and good can know about the trillions of preferences and plans for consumption and production and betterment. A household or your personal life might possibly be plannable, though anyone who believes it with much confidence has not lived very long. But a big, modern economy has vastly too much going on to plan.

In a big, modern university it would be much better if the bosses hung up their suits and returned to teaching, or went home to watch TV, and left us alone to do the work. Rely on the professionalism of professors. Fire the associate deans, every one, and spend the money on more professors and graduate students, not on paper and planning. Encourage the existing faculty to hire new people better than themselves. Insist that the faculty read the work of people they propose to hire or fire or promote. Stop asking for letters of recommendation.[4] And so forth.

I tried between 1980 and 1999 in various small ways to improve the University of Iowa, which back in the 1930s and 1940s was among the most innovative universities in the world (see, for example, the Writers' Workshop). No go. The administrators wanted mediocrity, and with some difficulty, chiefly by crushing faculty initiatives, they got it. At Notre Dame a depressing case is the Department of Economics, which once was interesting and original, to the point of being one of the few economics departments in the

United States with Marxists. But the administration then killed it.[5] At my own UIC, my dean, the public intellectual and Milton scholar Stanley Fish, tried to make the place into a Chicago version of UCLA or CCNY or NYU. His bosses hated him and his ambition, and killed it. And so forth.

It's worldwide, and has nothing to do with reduced governmental funding for universities. In systems such as the one in the Netherlands, with massive funding for faculty and for mainly upper-middle-class students, the tendency is the same: hire more deans and deanlets, add more mediocrities running the place, demand more planning, write more reports, such as the disgraceful one on American graduate education by William Bowen and Neil Rudenstine.[6]

THE LEFTIST: Robert Nozick once attributed the widespread opposition to capitalism among intellectuals—particularly "wordsmith" intellectuals—to an educational system that rewards students for academic achievement. Junior wordsmiths learn to associate reward with education itself and, at the same time, to think of themselves as among the most valuable members of society. But markets do not operate this way. Do you agree with Nozick's diagnosis?

THE LIBERAL: Maybe, but I think there's a more plausible explanation, as I've said before. It is that we are born into a family, which is an experience of a little socialist community, and especially so if our family is not operating a farm or a small business. After our socialized families, if we live in a world enriched by commercially tested betterment, many of us go to university, and if we come from rich families the experience is paid for by someone else. Then if we are clever and slightly crazy we go to graduate school in economics or in English. It would be like starting in a monastery at birth and not leaving it until age thirty or so. You would come to think that income falls like manna and is "distributed" by Mom, or the graduate dean, or the abbot. You would come to think that allocation of resources is of course to be centralized. You would regard the Market as something outside and alien.

I expect that literary people who get immediately into the market, as was usual before World War II (and before the rise of *academic* poets and novelists), or indeed anyone who has to work seriously while in college, will be less automatically socialist than their colleagues. Think of Samuel Johnson. "No man but a blockhead," he declared, "ever wrote except for money."[7] "There are few ways," he said on another occasion, "in which a man can be more innocently employed than in getting money." His interlocutor at the time, the Scottish printer Strahan, who also lived by trade, remarked, "The more one thinks of this, the juster it will appear."[8]

THE LEFTIST: Finally, do you find the dominance of leftist ideologies among the humanities professoriate to be an educational problem—a lack of intellectual diversity, if you will? If so, how would you correct it?

THE LIBERAL: Oh, yes, it is a problem. I was one of three "conservatives" in my beloved Department of History at UIC, and the lone one in my equally beloved Department of English. I so love them both. But they were startlingly un-diverse intellectually, and especially politically. Yet it will swing back, as it has in the past, and I live in hope that my colleagues will come to realize that a real liberalism leads to riches and liberty for the working class. Meanwhile, as I am sure you agree, and as my dean Stanley Fish used to say, Do your job, and gladly learn and gladly teach.

43. A Post-Modern Liberal Feminism Is Possible and Desirable

My contribution to a panel on the market and feminism, organized by the economist S. "Charu" Charusheela at the New York meetings of the American Economic Association in early 1999, focused on a paper by the literary critic Gayatri Chakravorty Spivak. Afterward we went to lunch with the Nobel economist Amartya Sen—with Gayatri, Charu, and yours truly decked out in spectacular saris.

I've been most things in my life: a positivist social engineer, a Fabian socialist, a man. Now I'm a free-market feminist, a quantitative post-modernist, and a woman. I'm not ashamed of these changes of mind. It is claimed that when Keynes encountered a complaint that he had changed his mind on some economic question, he shot back, "When my information changes, I change my mind. What do you do?"[1]

My main point here is that it's possible to be post-modernist and pro-market and feminist all at once. It's not only possible; it's desirable and natural. The three ideas, I claim, hang together. Together they do good work in the world. Gayatri Spivak and I agree largely about the post-modernist and feminist ends. It's about the middle bit, the economics and the economic history, that we disagree. I say that a modern liberal innovism fits post-modernism and feminism better than does Marxism. She says the opposite.

This work was first published in *Rethinking Marxism*, Winter 2000, available online at: https://www.tandfonline.com/doi/abs/10.1080/08935690009359022.

My post-modernism is that of a former modernist. It comes out of an unease I began to feel around 1975 with modern economic method, modern architecture, modern painting, modern academic music, modern social engineering. Post-modernism is about how we know. It says that we do not know in a modernist way, a simpleton's version of Science applied to a dogmatist's version of Reality, the method my former colleagues in economics at the University of Chicago 1968–1980 used to believe. The Nobel economist George Stigler of Chicago was an especially simple and dogmatic exemplar. But so were my anti–Chicago School teachers back at Harvard. Around 1960 we all were positivists and behaviorists and modernists. Look at the Danish furniture of the time, or 1960s architecture in the International Style.

My particular form of post-modernism is the oldest, as all humanists know, the "rhetorical." It dates from 467 BC, when the new (free-guy) democracy of Syracuse needed a disciplined theory of how we persuade in order to reflect on their politics after the tyrants had been overthrown. It is very similar to recent po-mo forms, such as deconstruction. In fact the masters of deconstruction such as Paul de Man and Jacques Derrida were rhetoricians first, if only from their *lycée* Greek. I myself combine rhetoric with the American pragmatism of James, Dewey, and latterly Richard Rorty, which gives me a non-grounded philosophical grounding to do rhetoric, in somewhat the same way that Hegel gives Gayatri a grounding to do deconstruction.[2]

I don't think that merely philosophical groundings matter very much for what we do. Gayatri and I agree that texts, like allegedly positivist facts, are made, not born. We agree that you need to pay close attention to the work that "mere" words do. Thus post-modernism.

Yet most post-modernists are socialists. They are vigilant about the failures of markets and not at all vigilant about the failures of governments messing about in markets. My point is that such an unhappy political fact is an accident of history, not inevitable. There's nothing in post-modernism entailing socialism. Rather the contrary, something I wish that conservative opponents of the little they understand of post-modernism and deconstruction and other scary French ideas would recognize. Classical Marxism is a notably positivist project, and recent versions of socialism lite, from Sweden in the 1960s to environmentalism today, nonetheless still believe old Comte, *savoir pour pouvoir,* know in order to control. Marx and Engels called their project *scientific* socialism (though "scientific" was being used not quite in the modern English sense).

I'm not saying that only the left participates in an antique positivism. Our middle-of-the-road economic friend Max U, the Samuelsonian seeking man (*Homo petens*), marches in that old parade, too. It's all of a piece, the scientism of circa 1960, left or right or middle, and it is precisely not the project of post-modernism.

What I mean also by "rather the contrary" is that a market society is alert, flexible, innovative, bubbling up, democratic, unintended, creative. It is the opposite of centrally planned, and is in fact the intersection of the little, shifting plans by individuals. The approach of the sociologist Howard S. Becker is to be contrasted with the approach of Pierre Bourdieu or any other social theory that focuses on nasty striving, such as pre-Gramsci Marxian thought or the economist's illiberal theory of games. Becker writes (rather similarly to another Becker, the economist Gary, whom Foucault, I repeat, studied seriously):

> The metaphor of "world"—which does not seem to be at all true of the [Bourdieuian] metaphor of "field"—contains people, all sorts of people, who are in the middle of doing something which requires them to pay attention to each other, to take account consciously of the existence of others and to shape what they do in the light of what others do. In such a world, people . . . develop their lines of activity gradually, seeing how others respond to what they do and adjusting what they do next in a way that meshes with what others have done and will probably do next. . . . The resulting collective activity is something that perhaps no one wanted, but is the best everyone could get out of this situation and therefore what they all, in effect, agreed to.[3]

It is the vision of liberal economics since Adam Smith. Becker and Smith are suggesting that notwithstanding the attempts of modernist experts to lay down the future, in a free society you can't tell what's next.

I am aware that the left will object to my cheerful description of "late capitalism." Marxians believe that the last stage of capitalism is a socialism without the revolution, and every reader of the *New York Times* believes that giant multinationals run the world. I think both views are mistaken.

As the liberal feminist and cultural critic Virginia Postrel writes in her important book *The Future and Its Enemies* (1998), the modernist project of prediction and control is "stasist."[4] ("Stasist" from *stasis*, Greek for equilibrium, not "statist," though it is that, too.) Free and enriching societies are on the contrary "dynamist." A 1960s glass box building goes with stasis, cyberspace art with dynamism, not the other way around. Most academic Marxians live in a glass box. My post-modern friend Jack Amariglio and his *Rethinking Marxism* crowd have been trying to find the exit, and they sometimes pick up stones to make one.[5]

To pair post-modernism with Marxism has always seemed to me odd. I'm suggesting that the market, not socialism in any of its forms (all involve a Society taking charge of details in the economy, that being the point of the word "socialism"), is the most natural pairing with post-modernism. Understand, I speak here of tone and spirit. We are agreeing that entailment, logical connection, is not at stake. I am not claiming that a liberal and bourgeois economy is logically either necessary or sufficient for post-modernism. I *am* ready to claim, with Tyler Cowen's *In Praise of Commercial Culture* (1998), that a bourgeois market economy has in fact been a good forum for developments in art and thought, such as post-modernism. "Forum," you know, means in Latin "marketplace."

And I want to suggest, further, that feminism is a natural third term: post-modern market feminism. Yes, I know. Many of you believe that the market has been a great enslaver of women. Understand: I am disagreeing with you, on economic and historical grounds, and suggesting that we sit together quietly and discuss the evidence pro or con. The market I claim has been the great liberator of women (and of slaves and of poor people and of religious minorities and of sexual minorities).

The economic logic is that markets provide women with an option of exit otherwise denied to a daughter or wife or widowed mother. We agree that power in the household is the heart of the matter. And I very much agree with Gayatri's point that gender power interacts with class power and economic power and racial power (and religious power and ideological power and intellectual power and the pushings around of any power allied with the state), making it unscientific to take them one by one.[6] It is my point, too. In societies in which women are forbidden by law (as in Afghanistan) or by custom (as in India, in some castes) to work outside the home, a woman has less choice.

Less than what? Here the critics of liberal innovism sneer indignantly at the jobs available, joining in their sneering the aggrieved husbands. Free to sleep under the bridges. Free to take jobs with Nike. After all, they say, a wretchedly paying job making athletic shoes for the American market is hardly un-alienated work. Hire me and you exploit me, they add.

But ask the woman, the liberal democratic economist suggests, if she would rather that the shoe company not make her the offer. Ask her if Nike doesn't pay more than taking in washing. Look at the length of the queue that forms when Nike opens a new plant in Indonesia. And ask her if she'd rather not have any market opportunities at all, and be left at home instead entirely to the devices of her father or husband or mother-in-law.

But I'm not very impressed by such logical arguments by themselves. It's part of the modernist project in economics to claim that great social truths can be proven standing at a blackboard. Thus did Ricardo and Pigou and Samuelson and Stiglitz claim. I'm an economic historian, which in economics is a vulgar, low-caste occupation. I think you have to see how markets and commercially tested betterment and bourgeois values have in practice interacted with other systems such as politics or popular culture to see if they have on the whole been emancipatory for women.

The news could have been bad. In some parts, it is. You could possibly argue—as I would not, considering that prostitution is an old profession and male lechery an old habit—that on the whole a market valuation of humans has commercialized female sexuality, with disastrous effects in self-esteem among young women in rich countries, showing itself for example in voluntary starvation. Even commercially tested betterment could have been partly bad news. In 1848 it looked like a good bet to a lot of people that it was going to be. The half century after 1848 proved a lot of people's bets to be mistaken. Real wages in Britain from 1855 to 1913 doubled, women's, too.[7] Women were twice subaltern, but women's wages kept pace in the rise, if always lower. And the twentieth century, despite a wretched thirty years 1914–1945, has dramatically improved on the doubling—against the expectations of John Stuart Mill and other orthodox economists much influenced by Malthus, such as Marx.

It will surprise no one that in the OECD (i.e., presently rich) countries for which Angus Maddison was able to assemble data, the unweighted average (i.e., one country = one observation) real GDP per capita expressed in 1980 dollars rose from $1,800 in 1900 to $10,000 in 1987.[8] That's a factor of 5.6 times more shoes, education, bread, books (and, yes, land mines and jet fighters, though the bads among the goods are a tiny portion of the whole, and the customers for them are governments, not individuals). Eighteen hundred dollars against ten thousand dollars is the difference between barely surviving and doing pretty well. It has freed women from an enslavement to kitchen and yard. A majority of college students in the OECD nowadays are women.

The most important event in *women's* history, then, is modern prosperity. The detailed stories of women's lives show the liberation. The young women of Massachusetts who staffed the early American cotton industry in competition with the British metropolis did not regard themselves as disadvantaged by the offer. The revolution since 1800 and especially since 1900 has taken place mainly in the production of goods. Professors teach pretty much as they did in Plato's Academy, but cups and shoes and rice and building materials cost a tiny fraction in labor power of what they cost in 1848. Housework, one part of national income not included in most conventional statistics, has been transformed. The movement of food preparation into the market has liberated many hours of female labor. In 1900 a typical American household of the middle class would spend forty-four hours per week in food preparation.[9] Forty-four hours: baking bread, canning, making pies from scratch. Child care is now moving further into the market, but unlike factory-made food has not been transformed in technique. It still takes a pair of adult eyes and a pair of hands to watch a small child, or two or three of them, which is Elizabeth Wayland Barber's explanation for why women invented cloth, a business that could be combined easily with child-minding.[10]

A woman may now choose not to work outside the home (in perhaps a terrible job, and then starting the Second Shift when she gets home to her shack; or the quite different way Gayatri and I "work"). But anyway that her sisters choose market work has radically changed the balance of power within the family. Such is the policy of the pioneering feminist economist Barbara Bergmann—become imitation men as fast as you can, she says; get out there in the market and sell, sell, sell. She sees the market as the road to women's liberation.

To speak positively, to put forward propositions as bravely as Gayatri has from her side, let me give a post-modern market feminist view of the economy. How can one be a feminist and a free-marketeer? Aren't all those guys hostile to women's liberation?

Yes, but. Wall Street economics, admittedly, is not hospitable to women. This is because Wall Street economics misunderstands, in a man's way, how economies operate. I regard the Prudence Only view as inaccurate and dangerous. It just won't do to sneer from the boardroom (or more exactly the male-only clubroom) that Prudence rules.

But for an audience of socialist feminists I want to stress that the people on the picket lines sneer the same way. Prudence rules in the theories of both Interest Marxism and Interest Capitalism. Again, my former colleague Stigler was a good example. The left and right agree: Gabriel Kolko was a Marxian historian who showed brilliantly that the Interstate Commerce Commission was seized by the Prudent interests of the railways; we in Economics at Chicago in the 1970s thought his stuff was pretty neat.[11] But one should not be confused about how the economy operates just because some Republican twits are confused. That some theories about the economy are mistaken should not make it impossible for us to see the evidence.

Love is missing. It's missing in all social theorizing from Bentham on. Such theorizing is ridiculous, as many women will readily understand. It's not tough and realistic to exclude considerations of love (and courage and temperance and justice) from our social theorizing in favor of models from Prudence Only. A feminist theory of the economy is one that takes account of what motivates people, tending to what I and a few other economists have been calling "humanomics." It means there will be all sorts of different people, from cloistered nun to bond salesman, and variations within these, with all sorts of different reasons for coming to market.

I know it is not excitingly edgy. I am not standing before you in a corset and waving a whip and telling you that markets are sexy. I can offer no immodest insight into market society. But I think that feminism's unique contribution to social thinking is the acknowledgment and celebration of difference. Theories of Man are for men. For motives that I am beginning to forget, men like their social theories simpleminded. They just *love* saying that Man is such-and-such, and Woman so-and-so. And so they posit a single-minded Agent, without love.

There are many ways of being a woman. In one interview Gayatri said that she dislikes high feminism where "highly privileged women see their face in the mirror and define 'Woman'—capital W—in terms of the reflection that they see there; sometimes they look at their face, sometimes they look at their genitals, and in terms of that they adjudicate about women as such. I have very little patience with that."[12] At this I stood up and cheered.

A feminist theory of desire and economy notes that humans are various, and suggests we listen to their stories. It is in sharp contrast with the toys that pass for social theorizing in these latter days: that humans are *entirely* Prudential; or *all* Love; or *pure* Courage (these in order would be economistic [whether Marxian or neoclassical], religious, and conservative theories). We can do better, we Marxians and non-Marxians alike, in being post-modern and feminist and, yes, admirers of markets, together.

44. Imperialism Was Not How the West Was Enriched

A conclusion to the Spivak colloquy.

Gayatri Spivak and I emphatically agree that history is a tale we tell. This does not mean we do not believe in examining archives or getting relevant dates right. I am not sure that our position is post-modern as much as merely sensible. Any thoughtful historian knows she is *telling* a story, *selecting*, studying, as Lord Acton put it, "problems," not "periods."[1] She understands she is not just copying down What Happened from the archive. What Happened isn't in the archive. A pile of paper with marks on the sheets is. Stories do not lie about on the sidewalk waiting to be told. Stories are not out in the world like pebbles. They are manufactured in people's heads and told on their lips, constrained by what the sheets and pebbles might give evidence of in solving explanatory problems.

But Gayatri and I disagree on the story that should be told about the three centuries past and the century to come. I think she overlooks the gigantic enrichment that has come from allowing liberal innovism to operate. Because she overlooks it she can tell a story of immiserization, contrary to fact. The same can be said of the student of Chinese history, Kenneth Pomeranz, in his fine book with Steven Topik, *The World That Trade Created*. Pomeranz and Topik tell many interesting and accurate stories about the bad

This work was first published in *Rethinking Marxism,* Winter 2000, available online at: https://www.tandfonline.com/doi/abs/10.1080/08935690009359022.

effects of creative destruction. But they never once acknowledge the gigantic improvements coming from it for ordinary people. Not once. It is a bad habit on the left. The left blames "capitalism" for the losses of some few people from progress, progress that would take place under any political system if the system allowed betterment at all. And betterment is what saved us.

We quantitative post-modernists, though, are very patient with mistakes that come from not being quantitative. I think the numbers justify a narrative of Progress. I believe that the whole world in the next century will get as rich as present-day suburban America, if we let liberal innovism operate. (It does *not* mean "let the country-club Republicans have everything they want." It means enforcing human rights, in particular the human right to dispose of one's labor, even if female.) I therefore do not believe, for example, in the Malthusian emplotment of the environmentalists. Malthusianism, as I have suggested, has been a poor guide to modern economic history. (It was an excellent guide to ancient and medieval economic history. The point is that the character of the history changed sharply circa 1800, just about the time that Malthus formulated his theory.)

My vision is commercially tested betterment, liberal innovism. I see no reason why Bengalis or Ecuadorians should have any fundamental problem doing things well. In the long run there can be no racial or cultural or gender reason why the average woman in a country now poor should not be able to participate in, say, an optics industry up to German standards or a computer-programming industry up to Indian standards or a retail trade industry up to US standards. A country that does all things well (for example, coming up to Bengali standards in poetry) achieves the well-doing standard of living.

How does it happen? Profit. If there is a better, American way of organizing grocery stores or shopping malls, retailers in Britain and Denmark will be tempted to adopt it—as they did, quite profitably until the entry of the imitators, as usual, drove down the supernormal return. Growth is not mysterious. Here I sharply disagree with my economist colleagues of the New Growth Theory or of Path Dependence. Growth is simple, though only at the microeconomic level of discovery, not at the level of the magical aggregates my colleagues like to think about. How simple? Do things the way the best doers are doing them presently. The more things you do well the richer you will be. Train up your young people to do them this way. And discover new good ways of doing things. It is simple in gross, but unpredictable in detail. It is enriching, and creative. It is feminist humanomics.

There is nothing except war and "protection" and organized theft—all of which are specialties of overweening governments, the liberal notes—that can stop it from happening. Japan protects its agriculture and its retail trade, and keeps women in subordinate roles, and so has fallen short of an American standard of riches. One can hope that Japanese consumers and Japanese women will not put up with such "protective" nonsense forever.

I am less patient with the other part of Gayatri's story, the colonial part. I think she has been misled by Samir Amin. It seems strange to go on blaming imperialism for the woes of a Third World whose growth rate has *accelerated* steadily in the past fifty years. India, the most confidently anti-imperialist and anti-capitalist former colony, had once the lowest growth rate in Asia. The slow growth, I would say, was not because it was once Victoria's jewel but because it followed for decades after independence the policies of the political theorist of the London School of Economics, Harold Laski, of keeping the market out.

Come to think of it, Laski-Nehru-Gandhi socialism *was* a result of a kind of imperialism: intellectual. You could only recently buy American breakfast cereal in India. The former colonies that have embraced innovism— Hong Kong is of course the leading if admittedly weird example—have done extremely well. You can buy anything in Hong Kong. And now, much more than before, you can do so in India. Even parts of Africa seem to be emerging from their self-inflicted wounds of socialism and thuggery since independence.

In parallel with all this, the phrase "the international division of labor" plays in Gayatri's writing a spooky role. She thinks that poor countries are permanently indentured to the rich. I think on the contrary that her worry shows a lack of historical perspective. The American South was once a primary producer for the mills of Lancashire. For that matter Lancashire was once a primary producer for the cheese markets of medieval London. The notion that such relations are "structural" (a magical word among Marxians that allows one to bypass history) is false. One indicator: the all-Asia average of manufactured exports (as again primary commodities) as a share of total exports changed from a mere 8 percent in 1953 to 64 percent in 1986.[2] The same statistic for Latin America went from 4 percent to 24 percent. It isn't "structure." It's growth.

Contrary to Amin and Gayatri and some others, the impact of imperialism *on the imperial powers* was trivial. I admit to being mystified by the contrary claim of post-imperialist critics. Gayatri and other post-colonialist critics seem to take the very sensible point of the subaltern school of historians, that the colonial experience was identity-making for the colonized, especially for the highly educated among them, but then turn it into an all-purpose influence *on the colonizers*, educated or not. I know, I know: the Other, the Orient, and so forth. But aren't most of the Others in the imaginations of Germans and Americans *inside* Germany and America? Don't women and Jews and immigrants and African-Americans provide a sufficiently rich palette of Not Us that most identities could be colored with it alone? Isn't it possible that even when a quarter of the world's population sat in the Empire, most British people got their identities from their British life, not from their mainly tangential participation in the Empire? The opposite case, that colonization was a central experience for Europeans, results I think in a lot of implausible history.

I think it is implausible, for example—to torture Gayatri with a small and not very important example—that "the constitution of the sexed object in terms of the discourse of castration was, in fact, something that came into being through the imposition of imperialism."[3] Something is wrong. After all, it is Freud's Vienna circa 1900 we are talking about here, the capital (and dubiously even that) of the one European power that did *not* have expansive imperial ambitions outside Europe. The sort of imperialism that the Austro-Hungarian empire exercised looks pretty good from the point of view of the Balkan Problem 1914–1999. That peculiar "empire" was a (clumsy) common market, and it kept from carrying out their desires some people very eager to slit the throats of their non-Christian or non-Serbian neighbors. It is strange to cast Freud as a part of the Raj, but typical of the impulse to make overseas imperialism the central event in European history. It wasn't.

The more important example is what I as an economist and economic historian think is the bizarre overemphasis on the experience of imperialism in the seventeenth and eighteenth centuries. The cultural importance of imperialism per se, as against exploration per se, is easy to exaggerate, but I am no critic of such matters and will fall silent, noting merely that *The Tempest* is not the only play that Shakespeare wrote. About the economics and economic history, I can testify. One can plausibly claim that some part of the wealth of the province of Holland resulted from stealing from the Javanese. But mostly its modern explosion after 1848 came from internal sources: good education, well-enforced laws, a calling to trade, a good location. The point is that countries are rich mainly because of internal matters, not because of stealing from their colonies. That Spain and Portugal are exceptions rather proves the rule. They wasted their silver extracted from Native Americans on European wars. Once the mines of the New World ran out, they became the poorest countries in Western Europe. It happened because they had not adopted, as the northwestern Europeans in the same centuries did, a new admiration for the bourgeoisie.

There's a reason, in other words, that the periphery is called that. It's peripheral to the economies of the core. The claim that Poland was crucial to the prosperity of Holland circa 1650, or the United States and Ireland crucial to the prosperity of Britain circa 1800, or South Asia and Latin America crucial to the prosperity of Europe circa 1950, is mistaken. Nor does the reasoning play well in the present. It is a cliché of economic history that the rich countries mainly trade with and invest in each other. However intrusive European economic activity was from the point of view of the periphery, from the point of view of the Europeans, the periphery was economic trivia. I revert to my quantities. Again using Maddison as a guide, external financing as a share of GDP in fifteen developing countries 1950–1986 was about 2 percent. How much was the total investment effort of these countries? About 16 percent.[4] Seven-eighths of real investment in poor countries was undertaken by the countries themselves.

The fault, dear Brutus, is not in our stars / Or in our empires or our imperial masters / But in ourselves, that we are underlings, / or overlings.

45. Liberalism Is Good for Queers

The late, brilliant Kevin Barnhurst asked me to pen an introduction to his 2007 edited collection of queer media studies, Media/Queered: Visibility and Its Discontents, *which I update here.*

The three long essays in this book, by Katherine Sender, Vincent Doyle, and Amit Kama, illustrate what I regard as an exciting possibility for a new turn in queer studies. But it's one that will not please everyone, least of all these authors. Most queer academics think of themselves as progressives, or socialists, anything but advocates for free markets. Having been there myself—a long time ago, and in another gender, I was a folk-singing version of a not very scholarly Trotskyist—I can understand the progressive point of view. I can remember its attractions. As one peruses the pages of *The Nation* or Noam Chomsky's latest, it *feels* like one is doing good. Imagine that: you can do good just by reading, and nodding your head.

And I know the charm of political opinions left or right as an identity. We acquire our political identities at the romantic age of young adulthood. Like gender, settled in one's personal theories at age two or so, most people don't trouble to rethink later their political opinions acquired at age twenty or so. Saul Bellow said of his early Trotskyism, "Like everyone else who invests in doctrines at a young age, I couldn't give them up."[1] People come as young people to *hate* the bourgeoisie or to *love* capitalism or to *detest* free markets or to *believe passionately* in the welfare and regulatory government. It becomes part of a cherished identity, a faith. I appeal to you to rethink your faith.

Fair warning, then: I want to make the *true, modern, humane liberal* case in queer media studies. Consider the evidence here assembled. In all three essays, I claim, Sender, Doyle, and Kama do show—often reluctantly, or inadvertently—the power of the market for good. That is, they show the power of the market for advancing the project of human liberty, and in particular queer liberty.

The focus is on the media, and it should be noted right away that the media examined do not depend on government handouts, or even a sweetly faux-socialistic co-op of journalists. They are *commercial* outlets, profit-making, as is especially clear in the essays by Sender and Doyle. And they are mass media, with a sovereign listener supplied with a TV clicker, or at least an on-off switch. From a perch in Israel, Kama observes that a mediated discourse coming over various kinds of airwaves allows in practice more dignity and more genuine human contact than does much of person-to-person communication. Status, gender identity, an un-deconstructed hierarchy of differences squat like toads on many a person-to-person conversation. Imagine you are dropped into a conversation about the "gay lifestyle" in the Oval Office with Trump. Add a few TV cameras. As much as you can in private diss his opinions with eloquence, in a public one-on-one, you will be rendered speechless, and he will start his schoolyard bullying. The ethos of the President, the ignorant assurance, the skill at partisan shouting, all the other inequalities of the tête-à-tête, mano-a-mano, win. We should stop being sentimental about person-to-person interactions, downgrading the media. Listen up, Socrates.

Academics often think of personal conversation between two honestly engaged individuals as the ideal: un-coerced, un-commercialized human communication. I love it, too, this ideal speech situation of Habermas, and have practiced it clumsily over my life with a few people I love. Lloyd, Derek, Joanne, Arjo, Steve, John, Ralph, step forward. But without love, notice, a so-called personal conversation never sheds the burden of ethos, the who-you-are that oppresses every chat you have with your boss or every competitive sports-talk session you have with your male buddies. More room exists for queer talk and queer behavior and queer theorizing in a rich, *commercial* society in the media than in a conversation between two people.

Some worry that the commerce of media empires will stifle free speech. But as long as we are allowed to make up new media, like new printing presses in the sixteenth century or new mail services in the seventeenth century—witness the internet, the explosion of blogs and arm's-length conversations over email with strangers—I doubt it. Now that we're on the subject, by the way, there's nothing bad about *paying* someone else to make your arguments, as did Colonel McCormick, who ran the Chicago *Tribune* as a mouthpiece for reaction during the 1930s and 1940s. That he didn't let New Dealers write in his newspaper was not "censorship," as is sometimes loosely claimed. Arguing with people is not against the Constitution, nor is paying for the argument, so long as you don't rely on the government—that is, as long as you don't call in the cops. What the First Amendment says is that the *government* shall make no *law* abridging liberty of speech. It's not about being unable to get an audience of half a million readers for your side of the argument because you don't own a big-city newspaper. You can say to yourself or your hubby, "Oh, that's a lot of nonsense. The *Tribune is* wrong again, and if it goes on saying that I'm going to stop buying the bloody newspaper." It's an argument in a free market society. It is in fact pretty much what happened to the Chicago *Tribune*, which nowadays is a moderate left-Republican paper.

Having a media problem, in other words, is not the same thing as being disenfranchised or censored, not unless the government is involved. There's no ideal speech community of easy access to serve as the utopia relative to the actual, messy market for Google or newspapers or whatever. The transgender community, for example, faced a media problem in our battle against Michael Bailey, who was forced to step down as chair of psychology at Northwestern University after publishing *The Man Who Would Be Queen* (2003). "Most gay men are feminine," Bailey writes, "or at least they are feminine in certain ways."[2] The professor's gaydar can spot those Certain Ways from across the street—on the basis, for example, of the lisping pronunciation a man gives the sound of *S*, Rock Hudson to the contrary. And from a long city block away Bailey can spot the *real* gender crossers—those are the pretty ones, the ones whom the professor finds sexually "attractive" enough to want to sleep with. According to his primitive theory they're just an extreme form of gay men. He can distinguish them from former men who are *not* attractive to him, a type that, contrary to what they will say (because they are all liars), experience "sexual arousal at the idea of" themselves as women.[3]

Bailey is attacking the by-now accepted scientific view that whom you love and who you identify yourself to be are not the same issue. *Au contraire,* says the professor. It's not that formerly male gender crossers have an identity of womanhood, felt or desired, the way you feel or desire that you want to be a lawyer, say, or a resident of Florida. Nor do the more feminine-looking (because earlier changed), pretty ones have such an identity. No "identity" about it. Both are driven by sex, because that's what *men* are interested in. Sex, sex, sex, says Bailey.

No one should be surprised that Bailey's ideas have been seized on by the religious right. John Derbyshire, a homophobe who contributes frequently to *National Review* in print and online, wrote a nice piece about the book, drawing the moral "male homosexuality, in particular, seems to possess some quality of being intrinsically subversive when let loose in long-established institutions, especially male dominated ones."[4] For God's sake, let's not let the queers *loose.*

It's a gay issue too. The gay press didn't catch on. My Episcopal pastor at the time, who is gay, allowed himself to be interviewed for Bailey's "research" because the gay press had not exposed the professor. Kama's structural analysis of the careerism of the gay presses is relevant to this particular controversy. Members of the gay press think, "Oh well, Bailey is about those trannies, who are anyway embarrassing in the Gay Pride parade. Let's not make too much of *them.*"

But I have no complaints about the capitalist media here. *Reason* magazine, a profit-making institution, and the voice of modern liberalism in the United States, allowed me to rant against Bailey for seven pages. The internet campaign against Bailey—run by Lynn Conway, an emerita professor of electrical engineering at the University of Michigan and a member of the National Academy of Engineering (she was fired by IBM for transitioning from male to female in 1967, and then went on to invent crucial pieces of modern computation)—has been effective, though the science page of the *New York Times* exhibited its usual journalistic standards by printing a calumny against me and Conway without talking to us.[5] (News from queers must not be fit to print.) My only complaint—and it should be yours—is that Bailey was supported by the National Academy of Sciences, a government agency, by its Joseph Henry Press, which was turned under the Bush administration to the uses of homophobes. *That's* censorship, the encouragement of hate speech and then hate action by government-financed entities.

What I'm saying is that the market is not the enemy of queers. The restaurants and bars from which the drag queens exploded in political action in the 1960s in San Francisco and then in New York were after all profit-making entities. The enemies were the government's cops, not the "capitalist" owners of the coffee shops. Governments use conservative institutions, anti-queer institutions, anti-free institutions, institutions that keep citizens sitting where they can be taxed and won't cause trouble. Government, dears, is not your friend.

There's a lot of talk on the left about coercion in the marketplace. But all three of these essays show market institutions working for queer rights. Imagine if the government ran all the newspapers and all the television stations and all of the internet and all the public forums. It's not too hard to imagine: China or Iran or Putin's Russia or Erdogan's Turkey provide examples. It's been tried. It doesn't work for queers.

I have a highly sophisticated Polish friend who is straight but in other respects is among the coolest and clued-in people I know. She has worked since before communism fell as a distinguished professor of management in Sweden. The issue of homosexuality in Poland came up. She said, "Oh, I don't think we have many homosexuals in Poland." "Dearest," I said, "what are you talking about? Poland like everywhere else has 5 or so percent of the population gay, and one-quarter of 1 percent of born males or females transgendered." She was stunned by the news. She had grown up in a non-market environment, where all the news, all the publications, everything came straight from the Polish Communist Party, or from the Polish Catholic Church.

I want to shake your age-twenty political convictions a little. If you think that being progressive about matters of gender identity and of sexual preference fits just perfectly with being *against* the market, consider in your heart, I beg of you, that you may be mistaken. The Polish Communist Party, the Catholic Church, the House of Representatives, the Trump administration, or whatever non-market institutions with a governmental backing you have in mind are not good places for queers. The way forward is not more government. The way forward is a liberal society, achieved by changing people's minds. With media.

46. The Minimum Wage Was Designed to Damage Poor People and Women

The secret history of the Progressives' favorite economic regulation is given here in a revised piece from Reason *magazine.*

What to do with George, your dear progressive friend who stoutly defends the minimum wage? One idea is to point out how the minimum wage excludes low-productivity workers from jobs. (To the smart-aleck economist's supposition that "monopsony" is widespread, and so the minimum wage *raises* employment, *Café Hayek*'s Boudreaux has challenged George and his progressive economist friends to pick up the unlimited profits implied by the supposition. No takers yet.) As the economist Thomas Sowell says, and you could say to George, "Reducing the number of jobs available by pricing inexperienced young workers out of the market solves no problem for these workers. The only clear beneficiaries would be those who acquire such arbitrary powers over their fellow human beings, and are thus able to feel both important and noble, while in fact leaving havoc in their wake."[1] Most people, and even many economists, reject such common sense, the economists by doing mistaken statistical exercises, the non-economists by mixing up "the entry-level wage offered voluntarily" with "the *legal* minimum wage enforced by the government."

Another idea is to try to explain the difference between a minimum *wage*, which interferes in voluntary deals, and a minimum *income*, such as Milton Friedman, James Tobin, Paul Samuelson, Philippe Van Parijs, Deirdre McCloskey, and other economists of varied politics have proposed. If you don't like the income that poor people have, then tax yourself to give them money. Don't make it impossible for them to get employment at all by making it illegal to offer them the amount their labor is in fact worth to a business. In my experience this argument, though water tight, is very hard to get across to people who are not accustomed, as most economists are, to seeing as distinct a wage from work and an income from whatever source, including non-wage sources.

A third and perhaps more effective idea is to tell George where the minimum wage came from historically. After all, George uses freely the false historical argument that the Industrial Revolution was caused by exploiting workers, and he thinks that we got rich subsequently by struggling against the exploitation. As the old spoof history of England, *1066 and All That* (1931), put it, "Many very remarkable discoveries and inventions were made [in the early nineteenth century]. Most remarkable among these was the discovery (made by all the rich men in England at once) that women and children could work for 25 hours a day . . . without many of them dying or becoming excessively deformed. This was known as the Industrial Revelation."[2] George clearly believes that history is relevant to the assessment of a present result. If he is a historian himself he will defend his present enthusiasm for bigger government, as I have noted, by claiming that internal improvements from the Age of Jackson on were crucial to American economic growth. That's mistaken, too.

All right. The minimum wage arose in the early twentieth century in the United States as a Progressive policy *designed to damage low-wage workers*. Designed. And unlike many other laws "designed" to achieve a result, the minimum wage achieved what it was trying to achieve, damaging the low-wage workers to the point of unemployability. Splendid.

The first minimum wage was instituted in Victoria, Australia, in 1894, but it quickly spread to other places. The minimum wage, writes the Princeton economist Thomas Leonard in *Illiberal Reformers,* a book on the American history of all this, was "the holy grail of American progressive labor reform, and a Who's Who of progressive economists and their reform allies championed it."[3] The inability to command a wage 50 percent above the going unskilled rate would keep out the riffraff. "Removing the inferior from work benefited society by protecting American wages and Anglo-Saxon racial purity."[4] "Of all ways of dealing with these unfortunate parasites," wrote the British socialist Sidney Webb in 1912 in the University of Chicago's *Journal of Political Economy,* "the most ruinous to the community is to allow them to unrestrainedly compete as wage earners."[5]

What was to become of them when the minimum wage excluded them from employment? Henry Rogers Seager, a Progressive economist at Columbia, gave in 1913 the usual reply: "If we are to maintain a race that is to be made of up of capable, efficient and independent individuals and family groups we must courageously cut off lines of heredity that have been proved to be undesirable by isolation or sterilization."[6] "Cut off." One cannot but admire Professor Seager's high courage in damaging poor people. By 1919, fifteen American states had enacted minimum wages, focused especially on women. In the United Kingdom a minimum wage, supported by Sidney and Beatrice Webb, was instituted in 1907. American economists were in the lead—influenced, Leonard shows in his book, by the German Historical School against "English" laissez-faire economics. A distressingly high percentage of the restrictionists were elected from the leading universities to the presidency of the American Economic Association.

E. L. Godkin of *The Nation* had articulated the true liberal complaint that the minimum wage is a bad interference in what workers are worth, and that if the resulting annual income (remember the difference) is judged to be undignified, then we well-to-do taxpayers should make it up to a minimum *income.*[7] The present-day readers of *The Nation,* among them George, would not agree. In 1923, the Supreme Court's decision in *Adkins v. Children's Hospital* briefly challenged the doctrine that it's a good and proper purpose of public policy to prevent the allegedly inferior (women, Blacks, immigrants from eastern and southern Europe, the third "generation of imbeciles") from having any job at all. But in 1938 a non-packed Court reversed itself and acceded to the federal minimum wage for men and women.

"Race suicide" theory, adopted with rare exceptions by most social scientists before National Socialism shamed it, held that the inferior races with low wage "standards" would drive down wages of "Saxons," thus reducing their fertility—unlike the wretched Blacks and immigrants, who would always have large families. Leonard notes that the low-wage folk, including women, were simultaneously objects of pity and objects of fear, a "strange and unstable compound of compassion and contempt." He summarizes the argument about a "race to the bottom," that "the decent capitalist . . . who wanted his workers to have a living wage . . . could not compete with unscrupulous rivals, who hired low-standard women, children, immigrants, blacks, and the feeble-minded."[8]

The race-to-the-bottom argument is still heard from amiable and well-meaning people on the left, such as (I have noted) the former secretary of labor Robert Reich and the Harvard professor Michael Sandel. But not only on the left. That economic growth started in northwestern Europe has often been spun into a theory of the racial superiority of the Saxons, despite the crushing evidence that highly non-Saxon folk, such as the Chinese and the Indians, if they adopt free-market policies, can do it too. The Euro-centric theory is still heard in conservative circles, a notion that European superiority started deep in history, back in the Germanic forest.

The minimum wage was the simple one among numerous race-purity laws against the outcome of markets. American Progressivism was part of a worldwide rejection of a laissez-faire that had been briefly regnant among the clerisy of artists, intellectuals, journalists, professionals, and bureaucrats in the mid-nineteenth century. "By the late 19th century," notes the historian Jürgen Kocka, "capitalism was no longer thought to be a carrier of progress."[9] The ethical case against "capitalism" was summarized by Reverend H. H. Williams of Oxford, writing on "Ethics" in the eleventh edition of the *Encyclopædia Britannica* in 1910: "The failure of 'laissez-faire' individualism in politics to produce that common prosperity and happiness which its advocates hoped for caused men to question the egoistic basis upon which its ethical counterpart was constructed."[10]

Even in 1910 Reverend Williams's mistake was factual. Commercially tested betterment had by then begun to yield common prosperity and happiness. Yet the clerisy, such as Williams, had long turned against the bourgeoisie and its doctrine of spontaneous order. According to the Progressives, laissez-faire was too slow in its evolutionary effects—and amorally so, rewarding innovism, which the Progressives such as Thorstein Veblen regarded as a wholly irrelevant guide to social efficiency. The Progressives wanted to speed up social evolution, and to moralize it, and to engineer it, as in Prohibition. They wanted in short to "interfere on behalf of the really fittest" (as argued by the Progressive writer Herbert Croly—who later turned against social engineering, too late). One of the numerous problems with such engineering lies in the phrase "really fittest": How do you know? A defect now may turn out to be an advantage later. In Darwin's science you know what works only after the event.

The Progressives in the United States favored inequalities and hierar-chies in all directions, such as race, class, gender, IQ, expertise, wages. No one who reads the Progressives can doubt their illiberality. Read any dozen pages of Leonard's book and a true liberal will weep. "It is well known," Leonard notes, "that modern liberalism [editor's note: so-called liberalism] permanently demoted economic liberties." Then for good measure, in aid of a eugenic program, the Progressives "assaulted political and civil liberties, too."[11] The right to open a shop was hedged by zoning and building codes, because after all economic rights are trivial. And then the right to make a wage bargain or to keep one's income or to keep one's property was similarly re-stricted in furtherance of the general will. No problem. Eminent domain and civil forfeiture, hurrah.

The results of the minimum wage were terrible, especially on Blacks. As Sowell puts it,

> Back in 1948, when inflation had rendered meaningless the minimum wage established a decade earlier, the unemployment rate among 16-17-year-old black males was under 10 percent. But after the min-imum wage was raised repeatedly to keep up with inflation, the un-employment rate for black males that age was never under 30 percent for more than 20 consecutive years, from 1971 through 1994. In many of those years, the unemployment rate for black youngsters that age exceeded 40 percent and, for a couple of years, it exceeded 50 percent. The damage is even greater than these statistics might suggest. Most low-wage jobs are entry-level jobs that young people move up out of, after acquiring work experience and a track record that makes them eligible for better jobs. But you can't move up the ladder if you don't get on the ladder.[12]

Beware. George, get woke.

47. Technological Unemployment Is Not Scary

From Reason, *August 2017. It was nice to see it translated into French on the blog of Jasmin Guénette at* Huffington Post, *in October 2017, because the French are even more spooked by technological unemployment. Always have been.*

As a sophisticated person you know that technological change is what mainly makes the jobs in manufacturing drift away from Youngstown, Ohio. You know that most of the drift goes to other American cities, such as Houston or Chattanooga. You know that Appalachian jobs in coal mining are not coming back, because new techniques of gas extraction and new gas fields have permanently cheapened natural gas. You know that foreign competition, which the Trump administration blamed, is not mainly what's happening. And even if it was happening you know it would be good, not bad, for most Americans. Stuff, not jobs, are what we have economies for. If we can get more stuff by technological change or by trading with China and Mexico, good.

But still many sophisticated people fret. The more simpleminded fret is Trumpism about foreign trade. Trump repeated the ancient notion that free exchange between you in Chicago and Tatsuro in Toyota City is somehow a warlike aggression by Tatsuro, from which you, or at any rate the workers of Youngstown, need "protection." America, Trump declared, needs to "compete," as though trade were war. It's not. Trade, whether foreign or domestic, is mutually advantageous dealing between two people.

The pattern of trade is in fact determined not by what economists call "absolute" advantage, like having a lot of nuclear weapons to compete with in war, or a lot of .300 hitters to compete with in baseball, or a lot of machines to compete in warlike exporting. It is determined by what is said to be one of the few non-obvious truths in economics, "comparative" advantage. Well, not *too* non-obvious. It says merely that we get more in a family or company or world if we cooperate. That, surprisingly, is all there is to it.[1] Not so hard. We export airplanes and the Bangladeshis export knitwear because what we Americans sacrifice to acquire the knitwear from Bangladesh is smaller if we provide the airplanes, compared (there's the "comparative") with what Bangladeshis would sacrifice to make the airplanes themselves. We both cooperate, and things work out well. Pretty obvious, eh?

When you get worried by some business-school type wailing about how we need to arm ourselves to compete in the deadly war for exports, take down your battered old Econ 101 text and slowly re-read the chapter on foreign trade. You'll never again believe the business-school types, or their siblings among historians and journalists and Trump advisors who didn't trouble to read the chapter in the first place.

But, you sophisticates go on to say, isn't "technological unemployment" the big problem? Artificial intelligence is on the march. Non-economists of a quantitative bent, famous physicists and the like, ask what we are going to do when *all* the jobs go away. Masses of people will stand around on street corners, they imagine, when driverless trucks take over the jobs of the 3.5 million truck drivers in the United States.

Even some worthy though gloomster economists believe it. Robert Gordon of Northwestern does, for example, in the policy chapters of his recent book *The Rise and Fall of American Growth* (2016). The brilliant Tyler Cowen does, too, with scary talk in his own recent book, *Average Is Over* (2013). Tyler gives a chart of labor's income as a share of the total, showing an alarming fall since 1990, and declares that "if there is one picture that sums up the dilemma of our contemporary economy, it is that one." The size of the scary fall? From 63 to 58 percent.[2] Five percentage points. The great if misled John Maynard Keynes (1883–1946) believed we would lose jobs because of technology. Even the still greater David Ricardo (1772–1823), who straightened out us economists on comparative advantage, believed it. All brilliant, and even great. And wrong.

The fear that otherwise sensible folk have about technological unemployment can be expressed in one word: robots. It means in Czech "required work" but has become scarier and scarier each year, in association with HAL the rebel computer in *2001: A Space Odyssey* and the metaphysically implausible fear about the singularity and other nightmares of *Astounding Science Fiction*.

Yet robots are *good*. Workers move from wretched assembly-line jobs at Ford near Detroit or at Volvo near Gothenburg to better jobs standing in a white coat monitoring the robots, at the higher wages made possible by the higher tech. Or, mainly, they move to jobs outside the auto industry, the real rewards of which are now higher because people can buy the radically cheaper stuff made by the robots.

And if their new jobs are *not* higher paying it may be because the United Auto Workers of America or the IF Metall union of Sweden was able to extract monopoly profits from the company and therefore from consumers. Not good. Robert Reich, a reliable source of sweetly leftish errors of facts and ethics, declares that "the decline in unionization [of private companies] directly correlates with the decline of the portion of income going to the middle class."[3] For one thing, it doesn't. The fabled "hollowing out of the middle class" happened mainly because people rose, not fell. But in any case paying selected workers on the car assembly line more than they can earn elsewhere, at the expense of other, sometimes poorer, workers buying cars first- or secondhand, is hardly an ethical formula for raising up the working class, or for that matter the middle class.

Walter Reuther, president of the United Auto Workers long ago, replied to a young Ford manager enthusiastic about robots on the assembly line, "How are you going to get them to buy Fords?"[4] Reuther's, and Reich's, argument, though well-intentioned, is fallacious, in that it favors protecting jobs rather than gaining output. Employees of the car companies are a trivial share of the car-buying public. You can't create prosperity merely by buying from your own employer, hoisting yourself up by your bootstraps. A Chinese city famous for its distilled liquor tried to raise its profits by requiring its workers to drink large amounts of its own product. You can see that it was not going to work out, and eventually the Communist Party official ordering it saw the problem, too. The left's trickle-up economics is as illogical as the right's trickle-down version. Neither focuses on what increases real income, which is bettered production, not more jobs. It's not trickling from Keynesian expenditure that enriches us, up or down, but the fire hose of commercially tested betterment in technology.

Look at the history. Compared with horses, our cars and trucks are "robots." Yet the advent of cars and trucks did not produce mass unemployment from insufficient demand for the services of horse traders or livery stable workers. In 1800 about four out of five Americans lived on farms. Now one in fifty or a hundred do. But the betterment of mechanical harvesting and hybrid corn did not dis-employ the 78 percent once on farms. Fundamentally, all tools—a blast furnace and a spinning jenny, or for that matter an Acheulean hand ax or a Mycenaean chariot wheel—are "robots," that is, contrivances that make labor more productive.

Reich recently listed the usual technological lineup of villains allegedly driving down American wages: "Automation, followed by computers, software, robotics, computer-controlled machine tools and widespread digitization, further eroded jobs and wages."[5] No they didn't. They raised real wages, correctly measured, according to the common sense that a human supplied with a better tool can produce more. If Rosie the Riveter gets better tongs to insert the rivets, she gets higher wages, because employers have to compete for the now more-productive worker, and she can give her children more to eat. If everyone gets better tools they move out of old jobs and produce more for everybody in their new jobs with the new tools. Time to get more earthmoving equipment, not more shovels.

After all, the point of an economy is production for consumption, not protection of existing jobs using antique tools—horses, shovels, candles, hand-controlled drill presses. Any contrivance substitutes for raw labor, as does the cactus spine that the Galapagos finches use to dig grubs out of tree bark. The finches use "robots." In one of the South African languages, Afrikaans, the word "robot" means what it means elsewhere. But it is also the normal Afrikaans word for "traffic light." The robot substitutes for the labor of a policeman with white gloves on a pedestal. And in the third act the substitutions are good for workers as a whole, not bad.

If the nightmare of technological unemployment were true it would already have happened, repeatedly and massively. Unemployment would not be 5 percent, or in a bad year 10 percent. It would be far into the double digits—50 percent, say, if blacksmiths unemployed by cars or TV repairmen unemployed by printed circuits never got another job. In 1910 one out of twenty of the American workforce was on the railways. My father's father was, and a great-grandfather on my mother's side. Then the motor truck came. In the late 1940s, there were 350,000 manual telephone operators working for AT&T alone. In the 1950s elevator operators by the hundreds of thousands lost their jobs to passengers pushing buttons and listening to sweetly recorded messages announcing the floors. Typists have vanished from offices—the lawyers or their assistants write the briefs directly. And on and on, if you attend to history.

"Enough already with the history," the gloomsters reply, irritated. "The future threat from technological unemployment is unique. History doesn't matter." All right, consider the future. Here's a present and stable fact highly relevant to the future, which I'll bet you don't know. (I didn't until 2015.) *Each month* in the United States, which is a place with about 160 million civilian jobs, *1.7 million* of them vanish. Each month through a perfectly normal creative destruction, necessary for economic progress in any society, over 1 percent of the jobs go the way of the blacksmiths and parlor maids of 1910. It's not that people quit. That's a separate statistic. It's that the jobs are no longer available. The employers who "provide" or "create" the jobs (the one is the Democratic expression, the other the Republican, but neither makes economic sense) move or go out of business. Or they get merged or downsized, or the employers decide anyway that the extra salesperson on the floor of the big-box store isn't really necessary in view of the costs of employment, such as the minimum wage or compulsory paid vacations.

What you hear about on the evening news is the monthly *net* increase or decrease in jobs, 200,000 in a good month. It is the hirings *net* of letting people, and jobs, go. But the gross figure of over 1 percent per month is the relevant one for worries about technological unemployment. It's 14 percent a year all told. In a few years at such rates, if dis-employment meant permanent unemployment, a third or a half of the labor force would be standing on street corners, marching toward 100 percent. You can confirm it by looking around: in 2000, for example, there were well over one hundred thousand people employed in video stores. Consider Blockbuster. Or in another field, Tower Records. What are their employees doing now? Standing on street corners?

Of course people are hurt. Change can hurt. But what to do?

We could "save their jobs" by cutting off all change. You would do next year exactly what you do this year. Capital as well as labor would be employed perpetually the same way. But then, having stopped creative destruction, we would perpetually have the same income. That's nice if you're doing well now. It's not so nice if you're at the bottom, or young.

I am a modern Christian, or humane, liberal, and fervently wish to help the poor. If the beneficent churning from creative destruction, which does help them, were tiny, then helping by taxes or charity would suffice. I would gladly pay, even out of compelled taxes, to compensate workers in Youngstown for the equity loss on their homes, say, at any rate if they would undertake to move to Houston or Chattanooga. But I just showed you that the churning is *not* tiny. We can't help with subsidies to 1.7 million people a month, constantly changing in identity to add up to 14 percent of the labor force yearly. We can't, that is, short of fantasies of the Big Rock Candy Mountain, with "cigarette trees and lemonade springs" and abundance for all, right now, free, without disturbing anyone's pattern of employment of capital or labor.

Nor is job retraining a good idea if it is to be directed not by the worker herself but by wise heads in Washington or Columbus. The wise heads don't know the future, and they end up training machinists for jobs that won't exist. Workers themselves know best how to retrain, within the limits of an inevitable uncertainty that no one can remove, and know when to move out, such as the hundreds of thousands who moved to North Dakota during the brief oil boom there. The workers, to put it mildly, have skin in the game. We need to make the labor force as flexible as the capital force. For that we need liberty, not government programs.

Massive subsidies, such as the French state gave to former shipbuilding workers in Le Havre, allowing them to stay there and play boules and drink aperitifs at a low level of income, are massively unfair to other people who accept the Bourgeois Deal of a liberal economy: "Take a chance, let me make profits, and I'll make *you* rich." It's the formula for a bettering economy, in which we all get boules and aperitifs.

The case is similar to the philosophical, and practical, arguments for free trade in goods and services. (Indeed, economists have long pointed out that liberty of movement of labor has the same economic effects as liberty of movement of goods. It is one argument among many in favor of moving back to the liberal liberty of movement that enriched us all in the nineteenth century. If you like free trade, you'll love free migration.) Utilitarians have long argued, by the so-called "Hicks-Kaldor compensation criterion," first articulated by utilitarian economists in the early 1940s, that the gainers from free trade could always *theoretically* compensate the losers. You can show it in a diagram, if you assume that all else is well in the economy.[6] So free trade is a net gain.

The reply from the left has always been that the compensation should therefore actually go through. Compensate the losers, the Harley-Davidson workers in Milwaukee, say, thrown out of a job by the city's shifting comparative advantage in assembly, or by tariffs on steel suggested by a secretary of commerce who was once a hired flack for the steel industry. Otherwise, if we stay merely at theoretical compensation and do not pay it, we are faced with the necessity of making ethical comparisons between those who win and those who lose, a comparison dubious at best. Make the gainers compensate the losers in money. Ethical problem solved.

Boudreaux, one of the most profound and eloquent defenders of liberalism in our foreign trade, and elsewhere, shows why we can't in justice compensate workers (or landlords or capitalists or the Harley-Davidson motorcycle company). Boudreaux replies to the utilitarians with a *reductio*:

> *If* it were true that trade is unambiguously beneficial only if the "winners" [actually] compensate the "losers," then it would also be true that, say, women entering the workforce is unambiguously beneficial only if the "winners" compensate the "losers," and that the opening of a new restaurant in town is unambiguously beneficial only if the "winners" compensate the "losers." . . . An essential role of competition, including trade, is to *impose* losses on less-efficient producers in order to incite them either to become more efficient or to switch to other lines of production. And so if the "winners" from trade *were* actually to compensate the "losers," one of the market's most vital signals (namely, losses) and one of its most vital incentives (namely, the desire to avoid losses) would become so muted and weak as to be utterly ineffective.[7]

Another present-day liberal, the economist and mathematician Stephen Landsburg, makes the same ethical point: "Suppose, after years of buying shampoo at your local pharmacy, you discover you can order the same shampoo for less money on the Web. Do you have an obligation to compensate your pharmacist? If you move to a cheaper apartment, should you compensate your landlord? When you eat at McDonald's, should you compensate the owners of the diner next door? Public policy should not be designed to advance moral instincts that we all reject every day of our lives."[8]

Or as Mill put the point in *On Liberty*, "Society admits no right, either legal or moral, in the disappointed competitors, to immunity from this kind of suffering; and feels called on to interfere, only when means of success have been employed which it is contrary to the general interest to permit—namely, fraud or treachery, and force."[9] As Boudreaux put a similar point, "What no person is free to do is to oblige *others* to subsidize his or her choices. I, for example, should be free to work as a poet but not empowered to force you either directly to buy my poetry or to obstruct your freedom to spend your money on mystery novels, movies, and other items that compete with my poetry."[10]

In the real world, unhappily, if the poor are to be raised up, there is no magic alternative to such competition. An ill-advised and undercapitalized pet store, into which the owner pours his soul, goes under. In the same neighborhood a little independent office for immediate health care opens half a block from a branch of the largest hospital chain in Chicago, and also seems doomed to fail the test of voluntary trade. The testing of business ideas in voluntary trade is obviously necessary for betterment of the poor (as it is, too, by often nonmonetary tests for betterment in art and sport and science and scholarship). But such failures are deeply sad if you have the slightest sympathy for human projects, or for humans. But at least the pet store, the clinic, the Edsel, Woolworth's, Polaroid, and Pan American Airways face the same democratic test by trade: Do customers keep coming forward voluntarily? As a result does real income for the poorest rise?

We could all by state compulsion backed by the monopoly of coercion remain in the same jobs as our ancestors, perpetually "protected," though at a permanent $3 a day. Or, with taxes taken by additional state compulsion, we could subsidize new activities without regard to a test by voluntary trade, "creating jobs" as the anti-economic rhetoric has it. Aside even from their immediate effect of making national income lower than it could have been, forever, such ever-popular plans—never mind the objectionable character of the compulsion they require to get the wherewithal to enforce the protection or pay the subsidy—almost never work in the long run for the welfare of the poor, or the rest of us. In view of the way a government of imperfect people in practice behaves, job "protection" and job "creation" almost always fail to achieve their gentle, generous purposes. The protections and the creations get diverted to favorites. Laws requiring minority or female businesses to be hired for supplying the government, for example, tend to yield phony businesses run in fact by male whites. In a society of lords or clan members or Communist Party officials, or even the rule of well-to-do white voters not restricted by inconvenient voting times and picture IDs, the unequal and involuntary rewards generated by sidestepping the commercial test are seized by the privileged. The privileged are good at that.

And the Bourgeois Deal without compensation for the disturbances of progress has a still deeper philosophical justification. As argued by the economists John Harsanyi, James Buchanan, and Gordon Tullock, and by the philosopher John Rawls, the politically relevant question is which society you would rather enter at birth, without knowing where in it you would end up.[11] Choose: One in which all jobs are protected, bureaucrats decide who gets the limited amount of special subsidies, journalists direct attention to the losers instead of to the winners, and the economy slides into stagnation and youth unemployment? Or one in which labor laws are flexible, workers decide their own futures, journalists know some economics, and the economy lifts up the poorest among us? It is a choice between a poor but stable economy and a rich but risky one. At some tradeoff—the one that seems to exist in the actual world—most people would choose riches. And a stable share of $3 a day is in fact riskier than a risky share of $100 a day.

Technological unemployment is not a serious problem. Poverty is.

48. Youth Unemployment *Is* Scary, and Comes from Regulation

The central duty of an academic economist is to give the news that such and such a policy beloved of politicians and journalists is bad, when it is.

Thus Trumpism in foreign trade. You have a deficit in your balance of payments with your local coffee shop. The shop gives you a cappuccino. You give them money. A balance of payments deficit. Does it appall you? I thought not, just as we economists have been saying all these years since 1776. Notice that if government statisticians did not collect the numbers on the balance of payments, you would not feel them. It's not true of high inflation or mass unemployment or rising real income. In fact, many economists regard the collecting of the national balance of payments as a silly nuisance, serving merely to encourage bad economics, such as protectionism—better called favoritism combined with defective accounting. The great economist Arnold Harberger (1924–) is fond of pointing out that the salaries of all the academic economists worldwide could be covered many times over by the economic gain from their repeated showing that protectionism is bad. We are told that embargoes on Iran and North Korea will hurt such evil people. Tariffs are self-imposed embargoes, hurting . . . uh . . . Americans. Whoops.

So it is my duty to tell you, whether you like it or not, that protecting jobs with regulations and minimums and other imposed conditions is bad, and especially bad for our children and grandchildren when they enter, or try to enter, the labor force. Nowadays it has become a crisis of democracy.

You know the proverbial expression "the canary in the coal mine." A caged little bird was taken into the mines as an early signal of bad air, such as a buildup of carbon monoxide. If the bird died, the miners fled.

You also know that it's crucial to socialize young men in the puberty rite of responsible jobs. Elephants and lions sidestep the task violently, expelling young males as chronic disturbers of the peace or revolutionaries. We do it violently, too, occupying with police the West Side of Chicago. The young men are the only criminals or revolutionaries on the scene, their leaders being of course older. But as the longshoreman and sage Eric Hoffer argued in his 1951 book *The True Believer: Thoughts on the Nature of Mass Movements,* the youths are the cadres, the followers, the storm troopers.[1] No cadres, no revolutions. For good or ill.

That's the threat from youth unemployment. But the main reason in ethics that we should worry about it is that a life without the dignity and the social benefit of employment is a sorry life, whether the youth is a laborer or a university professor. They are all of them our children and grandchildren, and it would be appalling not to heed the warning. The high rate of youth unemployment in many places nowadays, and its increase over recent decades, signals bad economic air. Let's flee the mine.

One-quarter of French young people age sixteen to twenty-five, male or female, not in educational programs, are unemployed. The United Nations' International Labour Organization (ILO) declared in 2016 that "global youth unemployment is again on the rise." The ILO's report finds that "the number of unemployed youth globally will rise by half a million in 2016 to reach 71 million."[2] It is seventy-one million revolutionary cadres and damaged lives, a mere 1 percent of the world's population, true, but a highly volatile part, and anyway seventy-one million lives blighted. The report says the status of young people "neither employed, nor in education or training (NEET) . . . carries risks of skills deterioration, underemployment and discouragement. Survey evidence for some 28 countries around the globe shows that roughly 25 per cent of the youth population aged between 15 and 29 years old are categorized as NEET."[3] "In South Africa, more than half of all active youth are expected to remain unemployed in 2016, representing the highest youth unemployment rate in the [sub-Saharan] region." "Southern European countries are those which report the highest NEET rates [for 25–29 year olds], peaking at 41 per cent in Greece. However, relatively high NEET rates for youth aged 25–29 are also found in the United Kingdom (17 per cent), United States (19.8 per cent), Poland (21.6 per cent) and France (22.5 per cent)." Among twenty-five OECD countries, the five with the highest unemployment rates of twenty- to twenty-nine-year-olds, at roughly 25 to 35 percent, are in descending order Greece, Turkey, Italy, Spain, and Mexico. The five with the lowest, roughly 10 to 15 percent, are in descending order Denmark, Austria, Germany, the Netherlands, and Sweden. For a somewhat larger group of thirty-seven countries in 2016 mostly in the OECD (that is, well-off countries by international standards), the rates of people searching for work and not finding it for fifteen- to twenty-four-year-olds ranged from Japan's 5.2 percent and Iceland's 6.5 percent to South Africa's 53.3 percent and Greece's 47.4 percent. Spain's is 44.5 percent, Italy's 37.8 percent, Portugal's 27.9 percent, France's 24.6 percent.[4]

Undeniably the actual and potential businesses in such places do not want to hire young men. One explanation commonly put forward by the right is that the schools have failed to make the young men worth hiring. Strange: do they become more educated when they get older? A version of the education explanation, given credence for instance by low rates of youth unemployment in Germany at present, is an absence of apprenticeships and other training for the trades. Yet earlier systems, which did not educate or apprentice the young men, did not result in disproportionate unemployment. Also strange.

The ILO attributes the problem to insufficient aggregate demand. Certainly some sort of demand is the problem, but the great variation across countries suggests that the problem is microeconomic, not macroeconomic, a problem of how markets are allowed to work in detail, not how much aggregate demand suffices or does not. The Great Recession of 2008 for example, cannot go on and on explaining why young people stand on street corners seven times more frequently in Greece than in Iceland.

A few years ago in a hotel in Thessaloniki, northern Greece, I and a few other modern liberals spent the day giving public talks in favor of unencumbered markets. We expected three hundred or so people to show up, but a thousand did, overwhelmingly young. We had to split the sessions between the top-floor ballroom and a basement room, and run tag teams of speakers through both venues. The young people were looking for answers for their plight. It was heartbreaking. Being unemployed anyway, the young men and women of Thessaloniki could just as easily attend the next week's similarly introductory meeting of the Communist Party or the neo-fascist Golden Dawn, and doubtless did. In May 2018 at a public meeting, a gang of nationalists beat up the seventy-five-year-old mayor of Thessaloniki, a critic of Golden Dawn. The cadres were forming.

Why, then, do businesspeople not want to hire young people? If one has a job-slot theory of employment, the answer might be a mismatch of skills. One hears a good deal these days about how automation or artificial intelligence will cause mass unemployment. Yet one would suppose that young, flexible workers, who unlike their elders already are a little computer savvy, and at least a thousand of whom in Thessaloniki understand English, would be just the ticket. But they are not, at any rate not in France and Greece and South Africa.

And the job-slot theory anyway is mistaken. The economy adjusts, if the polity permits it, to the mix of skills available. Jobs in a market economy are not slots, given and done. If so, we would all be thirteenth-century peasants. The jobs that are worth doing at the going wage adjust to the demands of customers and the skills of the available workers and the technological betterments on offer and the relative prices of various techniques. If self-driving vehicles surprise us in the next decade, the projections of job slots for bus and truck drivers will of course be wrong.

Another theory of employment is the wages-fund theory. According to it, the bosses have a pile of capital expendable on wages. Bargaining power determines how much the workers get. The theory is zero sum. Join the Party or join the struggle on the picket line to extract more of the fruits of labor for the laborers. Something like the wages-fund theory lies behind the notion that bosses can be squeezed and squeezed with more and more interventions in the wage bargain, more paid vacation time, better working conditions, more job security, without consequences in lower employment or lower GDP. It is the theory behind the claim by some economists and by many more politicians that, say, a higher minimum wage will *not* result in lower employment. The experiment was performed in many US cities and states in 2018. Watch Seattle.

The correct theory of employment is the one devised by the neoclassical economists of the late nineteenth century, such as the Austrian Carl Menger and the Englishman Alfred Marshall and the Swede Knut Wicksell and the American John B. Clark. It was brought to modern form by John R. Hicks in *The Theory of Wages* (1932). The theory says that a voluntary deal to hire someone depends on the someone making enough (for the employer) to be worth the additional hire at a wage the worker, in turn, is willing under the circumstances to accept. It's what you do when you decide whether you hire anyone, as for example a nanny or a plumber in your home. Is the worker worth the hire? And the worker decides whether the wage is competitive with other wages. Obvious. The going wage for nannies or plumbers is determined by economy-wide supply of and demand for such labor, unless the polity or a monopoly supported by the polity intervenes. The theory is the merest common sense, though fiercely denied in favor of slots or wage funds, even by some misled economists. Only a few, actually.

What of it? This: if the law or unions or whatever intervenes in the wage bargain, the quantity supplied of labor can exceed the quantity demanded. The excess is called unemployment. The case is the same as, say, rent control, with supply and demand reversed. And it is the same as the wage controls in the United States during World War II that eventuated in the bizarre US system (also in Germany) of attaching health insurance to one's present employment.

Why then youth unemployment? In a nutshell, job security for oldsters. Take for example the German labor law prevailing in the 1990s, since relaxed in Germany, that was adopted by South Africa at the coming (thank God) of democracy. In South Africa it is nearly impossible to dismiss a worker once she is hired. The first day I visited South Africa, in 2004, I left a not very valuable satchel in the restaurant where we had just eaten. Three minutes after driving away from the restaurant I said to my host, "Oh, I left a satchel at the place. It's not got anything valuable in it, and is itself cheap, but can we turn around?" To my astonishment he replied, "It's fruitless. It's already been stolen." He explained that because of the labor law, restaurant workers routinely seize with impunity anything the customers leave, and keep it. Likewise, if the workers steal money from the till, or don't show up for work, they cannot be dismissed in South Africa unless convicted in a court of law. Would you hire anyone, much less a young, untried person, under such conditions? The common sense of the Hicksian theory of wages says no. The result is 53 percent youth unemployment, and high unemployment of Black South Africans of any age.

The minimum wage, too, is high in South Africa. The Congress of South African Trade Unions insists on it. COSATU, largely communist, had an honorable role in the struggle against apartheid and is viewed with indulgence by politicians. The result of the high minimum wage is that low-wage workers are disallowed from competing with trade unionists. The poor sit at home, pacified by a small income subsidy to somebody in the family. Low-skilled people, such as young people, don't have a chance.

In France the extravagant job protections for people who already have jobs means that oldsters cling desperately to the wrong job and youngsters haven't got a shot at steady employment. On the West Side of Chicago, the War on Drugs combined with the minimum wage combined with protective regulations on businesses combined with licensing requirements for occupations combined with zoning that prevents the opening of businesses large and small combined with building codes in favor of union plumbers and electricians combined with business taxes make for no jobs for young people at all, and frozen jobs for old people.

In other words, high youth unemployment is a signal, a strong one, a canary in the coal mine. It indicates that the polity has intervened too vigorously in the wage bargain and the associated conditions of employment.

The West Side of Chicago should be a hive of commercial activity. A century ago, before the interventions took hold, it was. Time to air out the coal mine.

49. Do Worry About the Environment, but Prudently

I was invited in November of 2001 to talk to a little conference in Chicago about the Earth Charter. The participants were shocked that anyone disagreed *with the charter.*

The Earth Charter, on the model of the United Nations Charter on Human Rights, is circulating in Green circles. You can find it with a Google search. Some of what's in the Charter is good and true. But the rest, I'm sorry to say, is bad and false:

"The gap between rich and poor is widening."

True only in that nations have stayed poor by rejecting commercially tested betterment, such as North Korea now, and India during its decades of rule by London School of Economics socialists. It is false for, say, South Korea, Thailand, the Czech Republic, and for India in the years of liberalization after 1991.

"An unprecedented rise in human population has overburdened ecological and social systems."

The Malthusian fear, first articulated two centuries ago, has proven to be false. World population increased between 1800 and 2001 by a factor of six (and a factor of over seven by 2019: "unprecedented" indeed). Yet all serious demographers—consult Hans Rosling, for example—have noted that economic growth has in fact *slowed* population growth, chiefly because it makes child vaccination and family planning affordable. All demographers expect world population to level off and start falling in the next few decades. Small families and clean air are, as the economists put it, "normal" goods, increasing as income does.

Instead of resulting in impoverishment, the increase in population has been accompanied by enrichment, world income per head increasing by a factor of ten, and much higher in many countries. The result has been that people have demanded cleaner air, as a normal good. In January 2002, for example, reports started appearing that the Chinese resolved to control smoke emissions in their worst cities. They did, some. And in many ways we Westerners have a better environment than in 1800, being now rich. In the 1940s particulate matter in cities from coal smoke was as bad in Chicago and London as it is now in Beijing or Shanghai. And the worst biological damage to the environment has happened under non-market régimes, such as the old Soviet Union.

"We must realize that when basic needs have been met, human development is primarily about being more, not having more."

Granted, and true essentially of the numerous rich in places like the United States. But tell it to the poor in the United States, who still need to have more. And basic needs have not so far been met for the bottom billion of the world. They will never be met if Green ideas are implemented. Basic needs can be met only through economic growth—as China and India, for example, have realized.

"We urgently need a shared vision of basic values to provide an ethical foundation for the emerging world community."

Yes, we do need the basic values of love, courage, temperance, justice, prudence, faith, and hope. These flourish in market societies. It was Quaker businesspeople, many of them former slave traders, who questioned and then abolished slavery. Environmentalism itself is a result of prosperity from innovism.

"[We need to] ensure that communities at all levels . . . provide everyone an opportunity to realize his or her full potential."

Which entails commercially tested betterment, that is, liberalism, a community of laws, the free pursuit of full potential.

"Recognize that the liberty of action of each generation is qualified by the needs of future generations."

A good capital market for trading private property best achieves serious concern for the future. No owner of a productive forest wants to see it ravaged in the future, because then the *present* cash value of her property is ravaged. The ravaging occurs when, say, the Amazonian forest is not owned privately.

"Transmit to future generations values, traditions, and institutions that support the long-term."

Which is best achieved by teaching children the value of free exchange, private property, and respect for new souls. Liberalism.

"Integrate into formal education and life-long learning the knowledge, values, and skills needed for a sustainable way of life."

Which is to say, continue the propagation of an environmentalist religion in the public school, K–12, and extend it to colleges. Perhaps we should set up loudspeakers on every corner to broadcast the charter. (← Sarcasm.)

"Adopt at all levels sustainable development plans and regulations that make environmental conservation and rehabilitation integral to all development initiatives."

We are invited to repeat the errors of socialism—that "planning" has been on the whole a good idea, and has helped the poor and the environment. Neither is true. Planning supposes in a rationalistic style that we know *right now* enough to lay down the future. We don't.

"Place the burden of proof on those who argue that a proposed activity will not cause significant harm, and make the responsible parties liable for environmental harm."

In our state of ignorance such a burden would bring all economic progress to a halt, dashing the hopes of the world's poor to enjoy a higher standard of living. Yet a higher standard of living makes environmental improvements attractive and attainable.

"Prevent pollution of any part of the environment and allow no build-up of radioactive, toxic, or other hazardous substances."

No buildup? Even if safely contained? The standard is here, as often in the document, imprudent in its non-economizing extremes.

"Act with restraint and efficiency when using energy, and rely increasingly on renewable energy sources such as solar and wind."

"Efficiency" is an economic concept, here misused. Pursuit of the lowest *energy* efficiency by itself will reduce other efficiencies. It would be like pursuing above all other efficiencies an efficiency in using, say, school buildings, cramming in children and teachers by the thousands, three shifts to the day, seven days a week, all year, to get the most "efficient" use of buildings. We properly wish to be efficient in the overall use of all inputs taken together that have opportunity cost. It is foolish to key on one. Anyway, often enough the renewable resources result in more pollution, not less. It has happened, for example, with "energy-saving" uses of corn for ethanol fuel. And solar panels and windmills are not themselves pollution-free in their production or use. Zero pollution is impossible.

"Internalize the full environmental and social costs of goods and services in the selling price, and enable consumers to identify products that meet the highest social and environmental standards."

Another economic concept misunderstood. The best way to internalize is to make private property, so that people have an interest in (say) stopping the overharvesting of Amazonia.

"Promote the equitable distribution of wealth within nations and among nations."

If the idea is (and it is) to redistribute present wealth, it will not work, because redistribution is not sustainable, either practically or politically. The most equitable distribution is via economic growth, which enormously enriches the poor.

"Ensure that all trade supports . . . progressive labor standards."

That is, prevent poor workers in Bangladesh from having a job making knit goods to trade. They get enough to send their children to school by offering their knit goods to the poor of the United States cheaper than Americans can make them. If one imposes the "standards" of the labor market of Chicago on Dhaka, no one in Dhaka will have a job. It is the old tension on the left between protectionism and internationalism. The "progressive labor standards" are in effect a tariff on non-US goods. They would be a total embargo, such as we impose on fascist régimes, but in this case imposed on ourselves.

"Promote the active participation of women in all aspects of economic, political, civil, social, and cultural life as full and equal partners, decision makers, leaders, and beneficiaries."

The great liberatrix of women has been the market, in which a woman is not her father's or her husband's or her son's chattel to be passed from one to the other, but a mill girl or market woman with her own income and dignity. Cultures like ancient Greece or traditional China or traditional Islam, which have prevented women from participating in economic life outside the home, have not been good for women. In northwestern Europe, women could work outside the home. Which best liberates women?

You can see that I hope the charter fails in most of its proposals. But I am not hopeful. A document written by biologists and other environmental enthusiasts entirely innocent of economics is of course going to contain a good deal of economic nonsense. One that fails to recognize how bad the project of social engineering has been for human liberty is of course going to contain a good deal of political nonsense. One that does not care about poor people is going to hurt poor people.

Yet since when has nonsense, or inadvertent damaging of poor people, been a bar to the success of a passionately proposed and ill-considered manifesto, left, right, or center, Red, Blue, or Green? Thus in the 2018 campaign for president, the Green New Deal. Are you quite sure that the old New Deal was a good one in every one of its policies? If so, think again.

50. Illiberalism, in Short, Is Fact Free, and Mostly Unethical

A response to the discussion of John Tomasi's book Free-Market Fairness (2012) *on the Bleeding Heart Libertarians blog, week of June 11, 2012. I mention some of the other assigned discussants. My response on the blog got an astonishing number of replies, to which I duly replied. Some people liked it ("the best blog post ever," said one man, a person with evident good taste). Others, such as a High Liberal professor of law at the University of Chicago, hated it.*

To a discussion by political philosophers, a mere fact-woman like me, an economic historian trained in the 1960s as a transportation economist, has really only one thing to contribute. It is, to modify Cromwell's imprecation to the Scottish Presbyters, "Think it possible that you may be [factually] mistaken."

I realize that Kant laid it down that what humans are factually like, or what their history factually was, is forbidden to play a part in ethical reflection. We are supposed to be looking for principles that any Rational Creature would adhere to, whether a six-headed being in outer space or the man on the Clapham omnibus. As an economist I can see the charm in assuming a character Max U, or Rational Robert, and then proceeding. And I know that most psychologists find it charming to believe that ethical thinking starts with their own recent experiments. The experiments are a lot simpler than reflecting also on art and literature and philosophy since the Rig Veda and the Epic of Gilgamesh. (Some exceptions in psychology to such scorning of human wisdom are, in the younger generation, Jonathan Haidt, and, in my generation, Mike Csikszentmihalyi, and, in an earlier generation, Jerome Bruner.)

But the modern cleverness, after Hobbes and then Kant and Bentham and now with the fierce modernists of freakonomics and behavioral economics and the hedonic measurement of happiness, seems less relevant to human experience—which is after all why we would want an ethical theory in the first place—than the writings on virtue since the beginning of writing. We can't, and shouldn't, stop being humans, who were once children, and will die, and who reason and love and hope in human ways. As the philosopher Will Wilkinson puts it in our discussion, "If hammered into reflective equilibrium with the help of clever thought experiments and modeling assumptions" of the political philosophers since Hobbes, we nonetheless, *and even* (Will observes) *in the very rules of our reflections,* "are also going to be, to a very large extent, creatures [that is, present-day humans] of our environment."[1] Kant's decision to omit anthropology (which he in fact taught every Saturday in term) was a human and rhetorical choice, not written in the starry heavens above.

So: I'm from economics and history, and I'm here to help you. In the factual background, assumed in the elegant contributions here by Elizabeth Anderson and Samuel Freeman, there's a very particular story (less so in the contribution by Richard Arneson and not at all in Wilkinson).[2] It has been embodied since the late nineteenth century in what John Tomasi, Jason Brennan, and their friends, I have noted, call High Liberalism. The High Liberal political philosophers such as Anderson and Freeman and Dworkin and Nussbaum rely, against Kant, on a factual story which they take to be so very obvious as to not require defense. You can hear versions of it every night on MSNBC (you can hear other misleading master narratives on Fox News, so understand that I am not recommending *those*). I claim that the High Liberal master narrative is quite mistaken, as anthropology or economics or history.

The High Liberal story is, in a few brief mottos to stand for a rich intellectual tradition since the 1880s: Modern life is complicated, and so we need government to regulate. Since markets fail very frequently, the government should step in to fix them. Government can do the regulation well, and will not be regularly incompetent or regularly corrupted. Without a big government we cannot do certain noble things (the interstates, NASA, poor relief). Antitrust works. The big danger is not big government armed with guns but big business armed with business plans. Businesses are malevolent, and will poison customers and exploit workers if government regulation and union contracts do not intervene. Unions got us the forty-hour week. Poor people are better off chiefly because of big government and unions. That we are social implies that we should be socialists. That we are Christians implies that we should be socialists. That we are anything implies we should be socialists. Liberalism has failed. The United States was never laissez-faire. Internal improvements were a good idea, and were governmental from the start. Profit is not a good guide. Consumers are usually misled. Advertising is bad. Globalization has hurt poor people. The Great Recession was the Last Crisis of Capitalism.

Thus Anderson: "Externalities, asymmetrical information, and other collective action problems are . . . pervasive in economic life. Countless ways of conducting business reap gains for some while imposing unjust costs on others. Create a cartel. Stuff rat feces in sausages." She does not say why a restaurant would want to stuff rat feces in sausages, poisoning its customers. And so too Freeman: "It is a truism to say that in order to achieve the benefits of an efficient market economy (increasing productivity, greater economic output, increasing productive capital, etc.), the basic *rules* of property, contract, and exchange must be structured [by government] to realize efficient market relations." He does not say how such a minimal role for government ends up spending a third to a half of GDP.

To all this, in the words of the little boy protesting in his high chair in the classic *New Yorker* cartoon, I say it's spinach, and I say to hell with it. The master narrative of High Liberalism is factually mistaken. Externalities do not imply that a government can do better. Publicity in fact does better than inspectors in restraining the alleged desire of businesspeople to poison their customers with rat feces. Efficiency is not the chief merit of a market economy—bettering is, a matter of innovation over time. Rules arose in merchant courts and in Quaker fixed prices long before governments started enforcing them. Alienable property is a habit of humans (and indeed of animals and plants, down to butterflies in patches of sunlight) and is as ancient as archaeology can discern, not necessarily and inevitably governmental. Exchange, too.

I know that such replies will be met with indignation. But think it possible you may be mistaken, and that merely because an historical or economic premise is embedded in front-page stories in the *New York Times* does not make it sound as social science. It seems to me that a political philosophy based on fairy tales about what humans are like, or about what happened in history, is going to be less than useless. It is going to be mischievous.

How do I know that my narrative is better than yours? The experiments of the twentieth century told me so. It would have been hard to know the wisdom of Friedrich Hayek or Milton Friedman or Matt Ridley or Deirdre McCloskey or John Tomasi in August of 1914, before the experiments in very big government were well begun. But anyone who after the twentieth century still thinks that thoroughgoing socialism, nationalism, imperialism, mobilization, central planning, rationalization, regulation, passports, immigration restrictions, occupational licensing, zoning, building codes, minimum wages, eugenics, prohibition, price controls, protectionism, subsidies, infrastructure spending, deficit spending, industrial policy, tax policy, tariffs, labor unions, official business cartels, marketing orders, import-export banks, government spending, intrusive policing, adventurism in foreign policy, faith in entangling religion and politics, or most of the other thoroughgoing nineteenth-century proposals for governmental action are still neat, harmless ideas for improving our lives is not paying attention.

Let me list a few score of findings from actual historico-economic inquiry over the past few decades. They are not merely my opinions (though they have become those, too), but findings from hundreds of serious scientific inquiries into the past by economists and economic historians. I readily admit that there are others, perhaps more, that argue in many cases the opposite. They are, I believe, mistaken; but that is not the point here. The point of listing the findings is to get people to consider that they *may* be mistaken, not that they certainly *are*, if only to improve the scientific quality of their own work by challenging its unexamined factuality. Mere indignant assertion or counter-assertion is not going to help us get such matters straight. As Wittgenstein said, "Certainty is *as it were* a tone of voice in which one declares how things are, but one does not infer from the tone of voice that one is justified."[3] We need to inquire soberly into the facts.

In the nineteenth and twentieth centuries ordinary Europeans were hurt, not helped, by their colonial empires. Economic growth in Russia was slowed, not accelerated, by Soviet central planning. American Progressive regulation and its European anticipations protected monopolies of transportation like railways and protected monopolies of retailing like High Street shops and protected monopolies of professional services like medicine, not the consumers. "Protective" legislation in the United States and "family-wage" legislation in Europe subordinated women. Government-armed psychiatrists in northern Europe and its offshoots jailed homosexuals, and in Russia jailed democrats. Much of the New Deal prevented rather than aided America's recovery from the Great Depression.

Unions raised wages for plumbers and auto workers but reduced real wages for the non-unionized. Minimum wages protected union jobs but made the poor unemployable. Building codes sometimes kept buildings from falling or burning down but always gave steady work to well-connected carpenters and electricians and made housing more expensive for the poor. Zoning and planning permission has protected rich landlords rather than helping the poor. Rent control makes the poor and the mentally ill unhouseable, because no one will build inexpensive housing when it is forced by law to be expensive. The sane people and the already rich get the rent-controlled apartments and the fancy townhouses in once-poor neighborhoods.

Regulation of electricity hurt householders by raising electricity costs, as did the trammeling of nuclear power, which is much less dangerous than carbon energy. Enrichment improved the environment. The Securities and Exchange Commission did not help small investors. Federal deposit insurance made banks careless with depositors' money. Federal control of the money supply resulted in the Great Inflation of the 1970s and 1980s. The conservation movement in the western United States enriched ranchers, who used federal lands for grazing, and enriched lumber companies, which used federal lands for clear cutting. American and other attempts at prohibiting trade in recreational drugs resulted in technological change in drug formulating and higher drug consumption and the destruction of inner cities and the incarceration of millions of young men, especially Blacks. Governments have regularly outlawed needle exchanges and condom advertising, and denied the existence of AIDS.

Germany's economic *Lebensraum* was obtained in the end by the private arts of peace, not by the public arts of war. The lasting East Asia Co-Prosperity Sphere was built by Japanese men in business suits, not in dive bombers. Protectionism in foreign trade has regularly damaged a great many poor people and helped a few rich people. Protectionism in domestic trade, as in the US farm program and the EU's agricultural policy, has done the same. Europe recovered after its two twentieth-century civil wars mainly through its own efforts of labor and investment, not mainly through government-to-government charity such as Herbert Hoover's Commission or George Marshall's Plan. Government-to-government foreign aid to the Third World has enriched tyrants, not helped the poor.

The importation of socialism into the Third World, even in the relatively non-violent form of Congress Party Fabian-Gandhism, stifled growth, enriched large industrialists, and kept the people poor. Malthusian theories hatched in the West were put into practice by India and especially China, resulting in missing girls and sterilized women. Birth rates have fallen, or are falling, to replacement rates in poor countries, not because of governmental coercion but because of female autonomy, birth control, infant vaccination, and enrichment. The capitalist-sponsored Green Revolution of dwarf hybrids was opposed by green politicians the world around, but has made places like India self-sufficient in grains. Government power in many parts of sub-Saharan Africa has been used to tax the majority of farmers in aid of presidents' cousins and a minority of urban bureaucrats. Government power in many parts of Latin America has prevented land reform and sponsored disappearances. Later it merely impoverished the countries by diverting investment to idiotic governmental projects. Government ownership of oil in Nigeria and Mexico and Iraq and Venezuela was used to support the party in power, benefiting the people not at all. Arab men have been kept poor, not bettered, by using government power to deny education and driver's licenses to Arab women, and to kill journalists. The seizure of governments by the clergy has corrupted religions and ruined economies. The seizure of governments by the military has corrupted armies and ruined economies.

Industrial policy has propped up failing industries from Japan to France, such as small-scale retailing, instead of choosing winners who actually win. Regulation of dismissal has led to high unemployment, once in Germany and Denmark, and especially still in Spain and South Africa. In the 1960s, the public-housing high-rises in the West inspired by Le Corbusier condemned the poor in Rome and Paris and Chicago to holding pens. In the 1970s, the full-scale socialism of the East ruined the environment. In the 2000s, the "millennial collectivists," Red, Green, or Communitarian, oppose a globalization that helps the poor but threatens trade-union officials, crony capitalists, and the careers of people in Western non-governmental organizations.

Yes, I know, you will lean toward rejecting all these factual findings because they are "right wing" or "libertarian." I ask you merely to stop imagining alternative facts that suit your politics. I ask you to listen, really listen, and to consider.

Notes

Preface

1. Smith 1776 (1976), IV.ix.3, p. 664.
2. The notion of "*modern* liberalism" I got from the brilliant young Chilean public intellectual, Axel Kaiser. Leland Yeager (2011) speaks wisely of the capture by US statists of the word "liberal."
3. See, for example, McCloskey 2012a (the review of a book by Michael Sandel) and McCloskey 2018a (on Patrick Deneen).
4. What is crucial, Rorty wrote, is "our ability to engage in continuous conversation, testing one another, discovering our hidden presuppositions, changing our minds because we have listened to the voices of our fellows. Lunatics also change their minds, but their minds change with the tides of the moon and not because they have listened, really listened, to their friends' questions and objections" (Rorty 1983, p. 562). I carry this motto around in my purse. I apologize for not always coming up to her standard.
5. The late, great Hans Rosling records the error in response to his questionnaire, even among alleged experts (Rosling, Rosling, and Rönnlund 2018).
6. Caplan 2007, p. 133. This is the first case of scores in which I have pillaged the liberal news from my friend Donald Boudreaux's blog, *Café Hayek,* imparting thereby to my book a false impression of breadth of reference.

1. Modern Liberals Recommend Both Golden Rules, That Is, Adam Smith's Equality of Opportunity

1. The analysis of the virtues here is greatly elaborated in McCloskey 2006a, arguing against the pronounced tendency in European thought since the seventeenth century to treat ethics (from Greek *ethos,* character) as being exclusively about the middle, other-regarding level.
2. Kibbe 2014.

3. On the US/UK definition as against the Continental definition, see Schlesinger 1962.
4. Palmer 2009, p, 13.
5. Klein 2017a.
6. Kling 2018.
7. Smith 1776 (1976), IV.ix.3, p. 664.
8. The phrase is of course from the plowman-poet Robert Burns shortly after Smith had died. But Smith had shown in all his writings decades earlier that he was just such an egalitarian.
9. Bernstein 2017.
10. Klein 2017c. David Boaz uses a similar locution at Boaz 2015, p. 145.
11. Peart and Levy 2008a.
12. Hayek 1960 (2011), for example pp. 84–85.

2. Liberalism Had a Hard Coming

1. Rumbold 1685 (1961). It is irritating that Jefferson, a few days before his death, at which, unlike Washington, he did *not* liberate his slaves, used without acknowledgment Rumbold's metaphor of the saddle.
2. Wilson 1791 (1967), vol. 1, p. 161, namely, article 1, section 8, clause 10. I am grateful to Steven J. Schwartzberg for the quotation.
3. Hughes 1994, p. 191.
4. Glare, ed., 1982, pp. 1023, 1025.
5. Weber 1922, p. 29.
6. Flaubert 1867 (2014), p. 5883.
7. Hale 1990.
8. Quoted in Kaplan 1974, p. 250.
9. Dicey 1919, "Introduction to the Second ed.," part C, p. liii.

3. Modern Liberals Are Not Conservatives, Nor Statists

1. Hayek 1960 (2011), p. 523.
2. Leoni 2008.
3. Boudreaux 2017a.
4. Hayek 1960 (2011), p. 522.
5. Smith 2002.
6. Boudreaux 2018d.
7. Schmidtz 2011, pp. 784–785.
8. Melville 1856.

9. Spencer 1891 (1981), p. 14. Donald Boudreaux's blog, *Café Hayek* (14 November 2017), directed me to the passage, as it has directed me and others to all manner of liberal ideas, for years.

10. Mencken 1922, p. 292. Again from Boudreaux. I'll now stop admitting my indebtedness.

11. Epstein 2009, pp. xii–xiii.

12. Boaz 2015, p. 1.

13. Boudreaux 2017a.

14. Brennan 2016; Caplan 2007.

15. Klein 2017b.

16. Prestona and de Waal 2002.

17. Smith 1790 (1976), III.3.4, p. 137.

18. Brennan and Tomasi 2012. By "neo-classical" they do not mean Samuelsonian economics of the orthodox sort, but classical liberal, that is, Millian.

4. Liberals Are Democrats, and Markets Are Democratic

1. Follett 1920; see also 1942, esp. chap. 1.

2. Davies 2018.

3. Lange and Taylor 1938, pp. 57–58.

4. Mises 1951; Boettke 2000.

5. Smith 1762–1766 (1978), p. 352.

6. Tomasi 2012.

7. Whitman 1855 (1980), lines 346–349 and 1327.

8. As did Jack D. Sparks, a childhood friend of my mother's in St. Joseph, Michigan.

9. Bob Kearns invented an intermittent-windshield-wiper system for automobiles, and his idea was promptly stolen by Ford, which Kearns successfully sued; see Seabrook 1993.

10. Food trucks have blossomed across the United States in recent years, though my Chicago has onerous government restrictions on them; see Thiel 2017.

11. McCloskey 2018d.

5. Liberals Detest Coercion

1. Higgs 2012 (2015), p. 285.

2. Barzel 2002, pp. 3, 268, and throughout.

3. *Oxford English Dictionary* entry for "police."

4. McCloskey and Klamer 1995.

5. Pollock's *Number 16* sold for that amount at a Christie's auction on November 12, 2013.
6. Bauer 1957, pp. 113–114.
7. De Rugy 2018.
8. Hayek 1960 (2011), p. 531.
9. Quintilian 1929, 95 CE, 12.1.1 ("Vir bonus dicendi peritus").
10. Aristotle, *Rhetoric,* 1355b8, Kennedy trans. In Kennedy 1963, p. 19.
11. See Booth 1974.
12. Smith 1762–1766 (1978), A.vi.56, p. 352.
13. Taylor 2016, pp. 1–2, 324.
14. Wood 2009.
15. Steinfeld and Engerman 1997.

6. Liberalism Had Good Outcomes, 1776 to the Present

1. Tucker 2017. See also Tucker's brilliant interview with Dave Rubin: www .youtube.com/watch?v=WZlSn5GSV2U.
2. For the factual evidence for these remarks, and for much else, consult McCloskey 2006a, 2010, 2016a.
3. Goldstone 2002.
4. *Economist* 2013. And especially Rosling, Rosling, and Rönnlund 2018, throughout.
5. Reinhart and Rogoff 2011; on the worldwide recovery from the Great Recession of 2008, see McCloskey 2016a, pp. 53–54.
6. Maddison 2010.
7. Boudreaux 2016.
8. Again, for detailed argument and evidence about such numbers see McCloskey 2006a, 2010, 2016a.
9. Schumpeter 1942 (1950), p. 68.

7. Yet After 1848 Liberalism Was Weakened

1. Thus Skidelsky 2018, p. 16, among numberless assertions of such an equivalence in the Anglosphere.
2. Hayden 2013, p. 60.
3. Mill 1859, p. 1.
4. Dicey 1919, "Introduction to the Second ed.," part C, p. liii.
5. Constant 1819 (1872).
6. Leonard 2016, pp. 11ff.

7. Nelson 1991.

8. Spencer 1853 (1981), pp. 267–268.

9. Roosevelt 1941.

10. Long 1934.

11. Boaz 2015, p. 34; Schumpeter 1954, p. 394.

12. See Castillo 2013.

13. See Catanese 2013.

8. The "New Liberalism" Was Illiberal

1. Mazzucato 2013; the idea is old, even in the United States. "You gotta go down and join the union," as I sang in my socialist youth.

2. O'Siadhail 2018, p. 129.

3. Schlesinger 1945; Robert G. McCloskey 1951.

4. Field 2011.

5. Sen 1985; Sen 1999; Nussbaum and Sen 1993.

6. Smith 1776, I.viii.36, p. 96.

7. In 2018 I discovered that Tom Palmer had reasoned before 2009 in the same way I am here to the same conclusion (Palmer 2009, pp. 32, 35–36).

8. Quoted in Lyons 1937.

9. Rousseau 1762.

10. Palmer 2009, pp. 30–31.

11. Quoted in Palmer 2009, p. 31.

12. The motorist won an appeal on constitutional grounds in the federal district court. The state of New Hampshire, in its pursuit of "live free or die," then appealed to the US Supreme Court, which accepted the case and voted 6–3 in the motorist's favor (*Wooley v. Maynard*, 430 U.S. 705 [1977]).

13. Yeager 1976, p. 560.

14. Kant 1781.

15. For "somewhat dull" see P. J. O'Rourke's description of a strip club in communist Poland, run, he writes, as though by the US Post Office (O'Rourke 1988).

16. For example, Deneen again (McCloskey 2018a).

9. The Result of the New Illiberalism Was Very Big Governments

1. Higgs 2008; Tanzi and Schuknecht 2000, p. 6.

2. McCloskey 2018d.

3. Tirole 2017, pp. 155–156.

4. Brennan and Buchanan 1980 (2000), p. 11
5. Tolstoy's letter to a friend, having just witnessed in Paris an execution by guillotine. Quoted in Wilson 1988, p. 146. Wilson remarks that such sentiments "were to be crucial elements in [Tolstoy's] mental furniture." Tolstoy became, slowly, a Christian anarchist.
6. Rothbard 1982 (1998), p. 174.
7. Spencer 1853 (1981), pp. 294–295.
8. Posner and Weyl 2018.
9. Mill 1859, pp. 10–11.

10. Honest and Competent Governments Are Rare

1. Locke 1689 (1983), p. 47.
2. Transparency International 2017.
3. *Economist* 1992.
4. Warden 2007; Meisner and Sweeney 2017.
5. Brooks 2018.
6. The occasion was the annual Fórum da Liberdade arranged by Instituto de Estudos Empresariais at which spoke the judge Antonio Di Pietro. The professor mentioned below was Adriano Gianturco.
7. On broadcasting, for example, see Hazlett 2017.
8. Madison 1788.
9. Pearson 2015.
10. Hirschman 1970.
11. Buchanan 1991 (2001), p. 254.
12. Bain 2018.
13. Das 2001.
14. Macaulay 1830 (1881), p. 183. The word "capitalist" at the time meant any investor.
15. Lenin 1917 (1964).
16. See Shils 2007.
17. Ingersoll 1897, p. 112.
18. Trilling 1948b, p. 27.

11. Deirdre Became a Modern Liberal Slowly, Slowly

1. An example of adopting the theory uncritically is Tirole 2017.
2. Smith 1790 (1976), VI.ii.2.17, pp. 233–234.
3. McCloskey 2018d, again.

4. Safi 2017.
5. Reid 2017.

12. The Arguments Against Becoming a Liberal Are Weak

1. Hamburg 2015.
2. Walker and Nardinelli 2016.
3. On the FDA see Briggeman 2015 and Bhidé 2017, p. 28, and on development of drugs for early-stage cancer see Budish, Roin, and Williams 2015. On the meaninglessness of tests of statistical significance see Ziliak and Mc-Closkey 2008 and the statement of the American Statistical Association in Wasserstein and Lazar 2016, pp. 131–133. On corruption of the procedures at the FDA, see Piller and You 2018.
4. Locke 1689 (1983), p. 37.
5. Trilling 1948a, p. xlii. The late James Seaton (1996, p. 35) alerted me to Trilling's worry.
6. Boaz 2015, pp. 258ff.
7. Paine 1776 (1922), p. 1.
8. Thoreau 1849 (1996), p. 1.
9. Quoted in Mingardi 2017, p. 29.
10. Pettegree 2014, pp. 11, 368.
11. Boudreaux 2017b.
12. Chapman 2019.
13. Peart and Levy 2008b; Persky 1990.
14. Deneen 2018, pp. 30–32.

13. We Can and Should Liberalize

1. Posner 2018.
2. Boudreaux 2017c.
3. Smith 1790 (1976), VI.ii.2.17, p. 234.
4. Leighton and López 2011.
5. Tullock 1975; I am following here the exposition in Leighton and López 2011, pp. 104–106.
6. US Government Accountability Office 2005; cited in Leighton and López 2011.
7. North, Wallis, and Weingast 2009.
8. *Dilbert, Chicago Tribune,* August 9, 2018.
9. Leighton and López 2011, p. 106, referring to Winston 1993.

10. North, Wallis, and Weingast 2009, pp. 192–193.

11. Buchanan 1990 (2001), p. 307.

12. North, Wallis, and Weingast 2009, pp. 190–194.

13. Higgs 2001, p. 469.

14. Quoted in Schultz 2015, p. 77.

15. Radford 1945; Berndt and Berndt 1964, pp. 302–305.

16. Higgs 1987.

17. Bell 2018.

14. For Example, Stop "Protection"

1. The only, and rare, exception occurs when a country has price-setting power in its foreign markets, as Britain did in the 1840s; see McCloskey 1980.

2. Dvorkin 2017; see also Caliendo, Dvorkin, and Parro 2015.

3. Quoted in Mingardi 2017, p. 25.

4. Stossel 2015.

5. Will 2018.

6. Rahn 2018a.

7. Diamond 2019, from the Bureau of Labor Statistics annual layoffs and discharges rates, which ranged from 14.0 to 14.8 percent during the years 2013–2017.

8. Lebergott 1966, table 2.

9. Malkin 2017.

10. According to Crandall 1984, p. 16, in 1983 "the cost per job saved . . . was nearly $160,000 per year" in 1983 dollars.

11. Irwin 2017, p. 591.

12. Thus chapter 48 of this book.

13. Organisation for Economic Co-operation and Development (OECD) 2018.

15. And Stop Digging in Statism

1. Rogge 1962 (2010), p. 9.

2. Boudreaux 2019.

3. McCloskey 2018d.

4. Schultze 1983, p. 3.

5. Lavoie 1985, p. 4.

6. Gotakanal.se, n.d.

7. Larson 2001.

8. Fogel 1960.

9. Irwin 2017, p. 158.
10. Swanson and Plumer 2018.

16. Poverty Out of Tyranny, Not "Capitalist" Inequality, Is the Real Problem

1. Perry 2018.
2. Sowell 2015, p. 114.
3. Nordhaus 2004.
4. Warren 2001, pp. 129, 351.
5. Lintott 1999; Beard 2015.
6. Twain 1897 (1968), p. 98.
7. Skinner 1969, esp. p. 37, from Wittgenstein.
8. Yet again McCloskey 2018d.
9. Mueller 2006.
10. Lavoie 1985, p. 8.

17. Humane Liberalism Is Ethical

1. Chamlee-Wright and Storr 2010; Storr, Haeffele-Balch, and Grube 2015.
2. New Orleans Times-Picayune 2006; Foster 2006.
3. Stossel and Lott 2018.
4. Scruton 2014, p. 21; compare pp. 79, 109–111.
5. Tyldum 2014.
6. Mencken 1926, p. 153.
7. Quoted in Rimlinger 1968, p. 414.
8. Lippmann 1914 (2015), p. 141; compare p. 138.
9. Mencken 1916, p. 19.
10. Bastiat 1848 ("L'État, c'est la grande fiction à travers laquelle tout le monde s'efforce de vivre aux dépens de tout le monde").
11. Kantor 1976.
12. McCloskey 2018b.
13. Balcerowicz 2017.
14. Smith and Wilson 2018.

18. Liberty and Dignity Explain the Modern World

1. Quoted in Le Roy Ladurie 1978 (1980), p. 332.
2. Mokyr 2010, p. 1.

19. China Shows What Economic Liberalism Can Do

1. Beckert 2014; Mazzucato 2013 (2014).
2. Dumcius 2017.

20. Commercially Tested Betterment Saves the Poor

1. Flaubert 1993, p. 318 ("J'appelle bourgeois quiconque pense bassement").
2. Huizinga 1935 (1968), p. 112.
3. Sombart 1906 (1976), sec. 2.
4. Cowen 2018, pp. 33–34.
5. Hirschman 1977, pp. 56–63.
6. Walzer 2008.

21. Producing and Consuming a Lot Is Not by Itself Unethical

1. Horowitz 1985, p. 166.
2. Horowitz 1985, p. 168.
3. Mingardi 2017, p. 42.
4. Lipset 1961.
5. Douglas and Isherwood 1979, quoted in Staveren 1999, p. 92.
6. Douglas 1975.
7. Chalfen 1987.
8. Sahlins 2003, p. ix.
9. Klemm 2004, p. 232.
10. Bailey 1999, p. 147.

22. Trickle Up or Trickle Down Is Not How the Economy Works

1. Charry 2004, p. 30.
2. Sayers 2004, p. 119.
3. Pope 1731 (1966), lines 169–172.
4. Robert Fogel gives some evidence on the rise and fall of stagnationism in Fogel 2005.
5. Smith 1790 (1976), IV.i.6, p. 180.
6. Smith 1790 (1976), IV.i.10, p. 183. MacIntyre 1999, p. 2, criticizes Smith on similar grounds.
7. Rousseau 1755 (2011), part 2, p. 65.
8. Mandeville 1705, 1714 (1988).
9. Blewhitt 1725, pp. 6–7.

10. Smith 1790 (1976), VII.ii.4.13, p. 313.
11. Smith 1776 (1976), IV.ii.12, vol. 1, p. 457.

23. The Liberal Idea, in Short, Made the Modern World

1. Quoted in Stewart 1795 (1980), p. 322.
2. Rosling, Rosling, and Rönnlund 2018.
3. Collier 2007; or Rosling, Rosling, and Rönnlund 2018 on the bottom of his four stages.
4. Easterly 2001.
5. Jacobs 1984, p. 230.
6. Williamson 2017, p. 181.
7. Bacon 1625.
8. Macaulay 1830 (1881), pp. 186–187.

24. Forced Equality of Outcome Is Unjust and Inhumane

1. Trollope 1867–1868 (1982), vol. 1, pp. 126, 128.
2. Quoted in Kirkland 1986.
3. Wearden 2014 provides the data for the calculation.
4. Cline 2004, p. 255.
5. State of Illinois 1970.
6. Frankfurt 1987, p. 21.
7. Rawls 1985.
8. Iannaccone 2018, personal correspondence with author.
9. Smith 1776 (1976), bk. 1, chp. 2.

26. Europe Should Resist Egalitarian Policies

1. Smith 1776 (1976), IV.vii.c.63, vol. 2, p. 613, my italics.
2. Sumner 1881, p. 256.

27. Piketty Deserves Some Praise

1. Clapham 1922, p. 313.
2. Ellenberg 2014. Something is odd on its face about his calculation, because 26 is 3.8 percent of the pages, even including the index, not 2.4 percent. Ellenberg must be using some smaller number than 26, perhaps some measure of central tendency.

28. But Pessimism About Market Societies Is Not Scientifically Justified

1. Waterman 2012, p. 425. I have slightly modified the punctuation.
2. Clapham 1922, pp. 311, 305, 312.
3. Baran and Sweezy 1966.
4. Harberger 1954; Tullock 1967.
5. Hobsbawm 2011, p. 416.
6. Boudreaux 2018b.
7. Gordon and Ramsay 2017. Admiral Ramsay, in charge of planning and carrying out the seven-thousand-ship armada, was the co-author's father. He would have known Burns's lines, "The best laid schemes o' Mice an' Men / Gang aft agley."
8. McCloskey 1990.
9. Mueller 1999.
10. From Aron's *L'Opium des Intellectuels* (1955), translated and quoted in James 2007, p. 32.

29. The Rich Do Not in a Liberal Society Get Rich at the Expense of the Rest

1. Piketty 2014, p. 558.
2. Aristotle 2015, Book I.
3. Ridley 2014.
4. Nordhaus 2004.
5. Piketty 2014, p. 440.
6. Brennan, Menzies, and Munger 2013.
7. Smith 1776 (1976), I.i.10, p. 22; on the startling fall in family size, Rosling, Rosling, and Rönnlund 2018 throughout.
8. Butler 2018, p. 29.

30. Piketty's Book Has Serious Technical Errors

1. Piketty 2014.
2. On the other hand, the French economist Bernard Guerrien, who inspired the movement, has his own problems with elementary economics. See McCloskey 2006b.
3. Boettke 1997, p. 12.
4. Boettke 1997, p. 13.

31. The Ethical Accounting of Inequality Is Mistaken

1. Clark 1901, p. 1651.
2. Boudreaux and Perry 2013.
3. Fogel 2004.
4. Horwitz 2015, p. 82–83.
5. Horwitz 2015, p. 71.
6. Horwitz 2015, p. 84. Table 5 reports the percentage of poor households with various appliances: in 1971, 32 percent of such households had air conditioners; in 2005, 86 percent did.
7. Klinenberg 2002. The 2003 European heat wave killed 14,800 people in non-air-conditioned France and 70,000 Europe-wide; see Robine and collaborators 2008.
8. Barreca and collaborators 2013 show the very large effect in the United States of air conditioning in reducing excess mortality during heat waves.
9. Reich 2014.
10. Isaacs 2007, quoted in Horwitz 2015, p. 77.
11. Orwell 1937.
12. Saunders 2013, p. 214.
13. Frankfurt 1987, pp. 23–24.
14. Frankfurt 1987, p. 34.
15. Piketty 2014, pp. 577, 480.
16. Margo 1993, pp. 68, 65, 69.
17. Boudreaux 2004.

32. Inequality Is Not Unethical If It Happens in a Free Society

1. Gazeley and Newell 2010, abstract, p. 19, and chart 2 on p. 17.
2. Carnegie 1889 (1901), pp. 19, 21.
3. Piketty 2014.
4. Boudreaux 2014.
5. Ibsen 1878 (1965), p. 132.
6. Peart and Levy 2008a. Kim Priemel of Humboldt University of Berlin suggests to me that "equity" would be a better word for the Scottish concept. But I do not want to surrender so easily an essentially contested concept such as French *égalité*, which indeed in its original revolutionary meaning was more Scottish than what I am calling "French."
7. Smith 1776 (1976), IV.ix.3, pp. 663–664.
8. Butler 2018, p. 15.

9. Baldwin 1949 (1998), pp. 15–16.
10. Whitford 2005.
11. Again see Rosling, Rosling, and Rönnlund 2018.
12. Boudreaux and Perry 2013.
13. Deaton 2013.
14. Sala-i-Martin and Pinkovskiy 2010; Sala-i-Martin 2006. "PPP-adjusted" means allowing for the actual purchasing power of local prices compared with, say, US prices. It has become the standard, an improvement over using exchange rates (which are largely influenced by financial markets).

33. Redistribution Doesn't Work

1. McCloskey 2010.
2. Ogilvie 2019.
3. I thank Greg Mankiw for catching an arithmetical idiocy in an earlier draft and David Wiekliem for catching another one in a published version of the calculation. I often say that the first, crucial step in an economic analysis is getting the accounting straight. Accountant, cure thyself.
4. Colander 2013, p. xi.
5. On 1978, Coase and Wang 2013, p. 37.
6. McCloskey 2006c.
7. Friedman 2005.
8. Lemert 2012, p. 21.
9. Piketty 2014, p. 752.
10. Skwire and Horwitz 2014.

34. The Clerisy Had Three Big Ideas, 1755–1848, One Good and Two Terrible

1. Quoted in Taylor 2016, p. 91.
2. Johnson 1775, p. 89.
3. Quoted in Taylor 2016, pp. 437–438.
4. Smith 1776 (1976), IV.ix.51, p. 687.

35. The Economic Sky Is Not Falling

1. Pagano and Sbracia 2014.
2. Gordon 2012, 2016.
3. Mokyr 2014.

4. Macaulay 1830 (1881), pp. 186–187.
5. Phelps 2013.
6. Perkins and Rawski 2008.
7. Perkins 1995, p. 231.
8. World Bank n.d.

36. The West Is Not Declining

1. Williams 1896; Thwaite 1902.
2. Williams 1896, pp. 10–11.
3. Quoted in McCloskey 1980.

37. Failure Rhetoric Is Dangerous

1. Cannan 1902, p. 470.
2. Landes 1969, chaps. 4 and 5; Landes 1965, pp. 553–584.
3. Landes 1965, p. 553.
4. Landes 1965, p. 563.
5. McCloskey 2018d.
6. Kennedy 2017, p. 299.
7. McCloskey, ed., 1972; McCloskey 1973.

38. The Word "Capitalism" Is a Scientific Mistake

1. Wallerstein 1983 (1995), p. 13.
2. de Soto 1989, 2000.
3. Mises 1956 (2006), p. 24.

39. Marxism Is Not the Way Forward

1. But no women, dears—no Mary or Simone or Hannah or their followers are examined in our book (Strain and Veuger, eds., 2016). For shame.
2. Trevor-Roper 1940 (1962), p. 3.
3. Hand 1944 (1952), p. 190.
4. I recommend for example DeMartino 2011; Amariglio and McCloskey 2008; and Cullenberg, Amariglio, and Ruccio, eds., 2001.
5. Rorty 1983.
6. *National Review,* May 19, 2014, a reproduction of which my brilliant student Graham Peterson gave me once as a Christmas present.
7. Augustine, *De Doctrina Christiana,* book 2, chap. 6.

8. Hobsbawm 2002. I knew Hobsbawm a little while a visiting fellow at his Department of History at Birkbeck College, London, in 1975–1976.
9. Williams 1972 (1993), p. 6.
10. Budziszewski 2010, p. xiv.
11. Hobsbawm 1994.
12. Acemoglu and Robinson 2012, p. 471.
13. Toynbee 1884 (1887), p. 87.
14. Goldstone 2002, abstract.

40. Some on the Left Listen

1. Harvey 2005, p. 2.
2. Brown 2015, p. 10.
3. McCloskey 2012a.

41. But They Have Not Noticed the Actual Results of Liberalism

1. Brecht 1960, p. 293.
2. Venezuelanalysis.com 2007.
3. Paine 1776 (1922), p. 57.
4. *Kelo v. City of New London* 2005.

42. And Are Unwilling to Imagine Liberal Alternatives

1. Smith 1776 (1976), IV.vii.c.63, vol. 2, p. 613.
2. Gerschenkron 1971, p. 655.
3. Schlesinger 1945; Hofstadter 1948; R. McCloskey 1951.
4. McCloskey 2002.
5. McCloskey 2003.
6. McCloskey 1993.
7. Quoted in Boswell 1791 (1833), vol. 2, p. 55.
8. Quoted in Boswell 1791 (1833), vol. 1, p. 509.

43. A Post-Modern Liberal Feminism Is Possible and Desirable

1. Quoted in Clark 1978.
2. McCloskey 1994.
3. Becker 2008, p. 375.
4. Postrel 1998.
5. McCloskey 2012b.

6. Spivak 1990, pp. 118–119.
7. Feinstein 1972, series 21.1 and 21.2 divided by 25.3.
8. Maddison 1989, p. 19; population-weighted figures give about the same result.
9. Lebergott 1993, p. 51, from a little survey by Charlotte Perkins Gilman.
10. Barber 1994, p. 29, quoting the anthropologist Judith Brown.
11. Kolko 1965.
12. Spivak 1990, p. 119.

44. Imperialism Was Not How the West Was Enriched

1. Acton 1906, p. 24.
2. Maddison 1989, p. 96.
3. Spivak 1990, p. 9.
4. Maddison 1989, pp. 75–76.

45. Liberalism Is Good for Queers

1. Bellow 1994, p. 308.
2. Bailey 2003, p. xi.
3. Bailey 2003, p. 164.
4. Derbyshire 2003, p. 52.
5. Carey 2007.

46. The Minimum Wage Was Designed to Damage Poor People and Women

1. Sowell 2009, pp. 26–27.
2. Sellar and Yeatman 1931, pp. 92–93.
3. Leonard 2016, p. 159.
4. Leonard 2016, p. 161.
5. Webb 1912, p. 992.
6. Seager 1913, p. 10.
7. Leonard 2016, p. 85.
8. Leonard 2016, pp. 189, 88.
9. Kocka 2014, personal correspondence with author.
10. Williams 1910, p. 840.
11. Leonard 2016, p. 191.
12. Sowell 2016.

47. Technological Unemployment Is Not Scary

1. McCloskey 2018c; contrast Krugman 2002, who makes heavy weather of it.
2. Cowen 2013, p. 39.
3. Reich 2014.
4. UAW-CIO 1955, p. 6.
5. Reich 2014.
6. As for example in McCloskey 1985, p. 213, fig. 10.33.
7. Boudreaux 2018a.
8. Landsburg 2008.
9. Mill 1859 (2001), pp. 86–87.
10. Boudreaux 2018c.
11. Harsanyi 1955; Buchanan and Tullock 1962; Rawls 1958, 1971.

48. Youth Unemployment Is Scary, and Comes from Regulation

1. Hoffer 1951.
2. International Labor Organization (ILO) 2016, pp. 5, vii.
3. International Labor Organization (ILO) 2016, pp. viii, 5, 18.
4. Organisation for Economic Co-operation and Development (OECD) 2018.

50. Illiberalism, in Short, Is Fact Free, and Mostly Unethical

1. Wilkinson 2012.
2. Anderson 2012; Freeman 2012; Arneson 2012.
3. Wittgenstein 1969, p. 6.

Bibliography

Acemoglu, Daron, and James A. Robinson. 2012. *Why Nations Fail: The Origins of Power, Prosperity, and Poverty*. New York: Crown Business.

Acton, John Edward Emerich, First Baron. 1906. *Lectures on Modern History*. Edited by John Neville Figgis and Reginald Vere Laurence. London: Macmillan.

Agee, James, and Walker Evans. 1941. *Let Us Now Praise Famous Men*. Boston: Houghton Mifflin.

Amariglio, Jack, and Deirdre N. McCloskey. 2008. "Fleeing Capitalism: A Slightly Disputatious Conversation/Interview Among Friends." In *Sublime Economy: On the Intersection of Art and Economics*, edited by Jack Amariglio, Joseph Childers, and Steven Cullenberg, 276–319. London: Routledge.

Anderson, Elizabeth. 2012. "Recharting the Map of Social and Political Theory: Where Is Government? Where Is Conservatism?" *Bleeding Heart Libertarians* (blog), June 12. http://bleedingheartlibertarians.com/2012/06/recharting-the-map-of-social-and-political-theory-where-is-government-where-is-conservatism/.

Aristotle. 1934. *Nicomachean Ethics*. Translated by H. Rackham. Cambridge: Harvard University Press.

Aristotle. 1991. *Rhetoric*. Translated by George A. Kennedy. New York: Oxford University Press.

Aristotle. 2015. *Politics*. Translated by Benjamin Jowett. Adelaide: eBooks@ Adelaide. https://ebooks.adelaide.edu.au/a/aristotle/a8po/book1.html.

Arneson, Richard. 2012. "Free Market Fairness: John Rawls or J. S. Mill?" *Bleeding Heart Libertarians* (blog), June 14. http://bleedingheartlibertarians.com/2012/06/free-market-fairness-john-rawls-or-j-s-mill/.

Aron, Raymond. 1955. *L'Opium des Intellectuels*. Paris: Calmann-Lévy.

Bacon, Francis. 1625. "Of Studies." Website of Steve Draper, Department of Psychology, University of Glasgow. Accessed February 17, 2019. www.psy.gla.ac.uk/~steve/best/BaconJohnson.pdf.

Bailey, J. Michael. 2003. *The Man Who Would Be Queen: The Science of Gender-Bending and Transsexualism*. Washington, DC: Joseph Henry Press.

Bailey, Steve. 1999. "Of *Gomi* and *Gaijin*." In *Japan: True Stories of Life on the Road*, edited by D. W. George and Amy G. Carlson, 147–149. San Francisco: Travelers' Tales.

Bain, Ben. 2018. "Jim Beam Faces SEC Hangover After Bribery Allegations in India." *BloombergQuint*, July 2. www.bloombergquint.com/business /2018/07/02/jim-beam-faces-sec-hangover-after-bribery-allegations-in -india.

Balcerowicz, Leszek. 2017. "Recent Attacks Against Freedom." Future of the Free Society: A Cato 40th Anniversary Online Forum, Cato Institute, Washington, DC, April 25. www.cato.org/publications/cato-online-forum /recent-attacks-against-freedom.

Baldwin, James. 1949. "Everybody's Protest Novel." *Partisan Review*, June 16. Reprinted in *Notes of a Native Son*. Boston, Beacon Press, 1955. Reprinted in *Collected Essays*. New York: Library of America, 1998.

Baran, Paul A., and Paul M. Sweezy. 1966. *Monopoly Capital: An Essay on the American Economic and Social Order*. New York: Monthly Review Press.

Barber, Elizabeth Wayland. 1994. *Women's Work, the First 20,000 Years: Women, Cloth, and Society in Early Times*. New York and London: Norton.

Barnhurst, Kevin G., ed. 2007. *Media/Queered: Visibility and Its Discontents*. New York: Peter Lang.

Barreca, Alan, Karen Clay, Olivier Deschenes, Michael Greenstone, and Joseph S. Shapiro. 2013. "Adapting to Climate Change: The Remarkable Decline in the U.S. Temperature-Mortality Relationship over the 20th Century." NBER Working Paper No. 18692, National Bureau of Economic Research, Cambridge, MA, January. https://www.nber.org /papers/w18692.

Barry, Brian. 1965. *Political Argument*. London: Routledge and Kegan Paul.

Barzel, Yoram. 2002. *A Theory of the State: Economic Rights, Legal Rights, and the Scope of the State*. Cambridge, UK: Cambridge University Press.

Bastiat, Frédéric. 1848. "L'État." *Journal des Débats*, September 25: p. 1, col. 5. https://gallica.bnf.fr/ark:/12148/bpt6k448145j.item.

Bastiat, Frédéric. 1964. *Economic Sophisms*. Edited and translated by Arthur Goddard. Princeton, NJ: Van Nostrand. Reprint, Irvington-on-Hudson, NY: Foundation for Economic Education, 1996.

Bauer, Peter T. 1957. *Economic Analysis and Policy in Underdeveloped Countries*. Durham, NC: Duke University Commonwealth-Studies Center.

Beard, Charles. 1913. *An Economic Interpretation of the Constitution of the United States*. New York: Macmillan.

Beard, Mary. 2015. *SPQR: A History of Ancient Rome*. New York: Norton.

Becker, Howard S. 2008. *Art Worlds*. 25th Anniversary Edition. Berkeley: University of California Press.

Beckert, Sven. 2014. *Empire of Cotton: A Global History*. New York: Alfred A. Knopf.

Beer, Francis A., and Robert Hariman, eds. 1996. *Post-Realism: The Rhetorical Turn in International Relations*. East Lansing, MI: Michigan State University Press.

Bell, Tom W. 2018. *Your Next Government? From the Nation State to the Stateless Nation*. New York: Cambridge University Press.

Bellah, Robert. 2003. *Imagining Japan: The Japanese Tradition and Its Modern Interpretation*. Berkeley and Los Angeles: University of California Press.

Bellow, Saul. 1994. *It All Adds Up: From the Dim Past to an Uncertain Future*. New York and London: Penguin.

Benedict, Ruth. 1946. *The Chrysanthemum and the Sword: Patterns of Japanese Culture*. Reprint, Boston: Houghton Mifflin, 1989.

Berlin, Isaiah. 1958. "Two Concepts of Liberty." From his inaugural lecture. In *Four Essays on Liberty*, 118–172. New York: Oxford University Press, 1969.

Berlin, Isaiah. 2003. *Freedom and Betrayal: Six Enemies of Human Liberty*. Princeton, NJ: Princeton University Press.

Berndt, Ronald M., and Catherine H. Berndt. 1964. *The World of the First Australians*. Sydney: Ure Smith.

Bernstein, Maxine. 2017. "Red Light Camera Critic Says State Board Quashing His Free Speech." *Oregonian*, April 25. https://www.oregonlive.com/portland/index.ssf/2017/04/beaverton_man_claims_oregon_st.html.

Bhidé, Amar. 2017. "Constraining Knowledge: Traditions and Rules That Limit Medical Innovation." *Critical Review* 29, no. 1: 1–33.

Blewhitt, George. 1725. *An Enquiry Whether a General Practice of Virtue Tends to the Wealth or Poverty, Benefit or Disadvantage of a People*. London: R. Wilkin.

Blyth, Mark. 2004. "The Great Transformation in Understanding Polanyi: Reply to Hejeebu and McCloskey." *Critical Review* 16: 117–133.

Boaz, David. 1997. *Libertarianism: A Primer*. New York: Free Press.

Boaz, David. 2015. *The Libertarian Mind*. New York: Simon and Schuster.

Boettke, Peter. 1997. "Where Did Economics Go Wrong? Modern Economics as a Flight from Reality." *Critical Review* 11, no. 1: 11–64.

Boettke, Peter. 2000. *Socialism and the Market: The Socialist Calculation Debate Revisited*. London: Routledge.

Booth, Wayne C. 1974. *Modern Dogma and the Rhetoric of Assent*. Chicago: University of Chicago Press.

Boswell, James. 1791. *The Life of Samuel Johnson, LL.D.* 2 vols. Reprint, New York: George Dearborn, 1833.

Boudreaux, Donald J. 2004. "Can You Spot the Billionaire?" *The Freeman* 54, no. 1 (January/February): 13–14. https://fee.org/media/3086/2004_01.pdf.

Boudreaux, Donald J. 2014. Personal correspondence with the author. June 4.

Boudreaux, Donald J. 2016. "Most Ordinary Americans in 2016 Are Richer than Was John D. Rockefeller in 1916." *Café Hayek* (blog), February 20. https://cafehayek.com/2016/02/40405.html.

Boudreaux, Donald J. 2017a. "Bonus Quotation of the Day. . . ." *Café Hayek* (blog), November 25. https://cafehayek.com/2017/11/bonus-quotation -day-86.html.

Boudreaux, Donald J. 2017b. "Quotation of the Day. . . ." *Café Hayek* (blog), March 5. https://cafehayek.com/2017/03/quotation-of-the-day-2005.html.

Boudreaux, Donald J. 2017c. "Quotation of the Day. . . ." *Café Hayek* (blog), April 10. https://cafehayek.com/2017/04/42587.html.

Boudreaux, Donald J. 2018a. "A Losing Perspective." *Café Hayek* (blog), June 20. https://cafehayek.com/2018/06/a-losing-perspective.html.

Boudreaux, Donald J. 2018b. "Quotation of the Day. . . ." *Café Hayek* (blog), July 3. https://cafehayek.com/2018/07/quotation-of-the-day-2483.html.

Boudreaux, Donald J. 2018c. "And What About Those of Us Who Embrace Freedom?" *Café Hayek* (blog), August 23. https://cafehayek.com/2018/08 /us-embrace-freedom.html.

Boudreaux, Donald J. 2018d. "Quotation of the Day. . . ." *Café Hayek* (blog), October 13. https://cafehayek.com/2018/10/quotation-of-the-day-2582.html.

Boudreaux, Donald J. 2019. "Bonus Quotation of the Day. . . ." *Café Hayek* (blog), February 28. https://cafehayek.com/2019/02/bonus-quotation-of -the-day-269.html.

Boudreaux, Donald J., and Mark J. Perry. 2013. "The Myth of a Stagnant Middle Class." *Wall Street Journal*, January 23.

Bourdieu, Pierre. 1984. *Distinction: A Social Critique of the Judgment of Taste*. Translated by Richard Nice. London: Routledge and Kegan Paul.

Bower, Gordon H. 1992. "How Emotions Affect Learning." In *The Handbook of Emotion and Memory: Research and Theory*, edited by Sven-Ake Christianson, 3–31. Hillsdale, NJ: Erlbaum.

Brecht, Bertolt. 1960. *The Life of Galileo*. Translated by D. I. Vesey. In *Plays*, vol. 1. London: Methuen.

Brennan, Geoffrey, and James M. Buchanan. 1980. *The Power to Tax*. Cambridge, UK: Cambridge University Press. Reprinted as vol. 9 of *The Collected Works of James M. Buchanan*. Indianapolis, IN: Liberty Fund, 2000.

Brennan, Geoffrey, Gordon Menzies, and Michael Munger. 2013. "A Brief History of Inequality." Unpublished paper, Australian National University, Canberra, and University of Technology, Sydney.

Brennan, Jason. 2016. *Against Democracy*. Princeton, NJ: Princeton University Press.

Brennan, Jason, and John Tomasi. 2012. "Classical Liberalism." In *The Oxford Handbook of Political Philosophy*, edited by David Estlund, 115–132. Oxford, UK: Oxford University Press.

Briggeman, Jason. 2015. "Searching for Justification of the Policy of Pre-Market Approval of Pharmaceuticals." PhD diss., George Mason University. http://mars.gmu.edu/handle/1920/9656.

Brooks, David. 2018. "The Rise of the Amnesty Thugs." *New York Times*, June 18.

Brown, Gordon S. 2005. *Toussaint's Clause: The Founding Fathers and the Haitian Revolution*. Jackson, MS: University Press of Mississippi.

Brown, Wendy. 2015. *Undoing the Demos: Neoliberalism's Stealth Revolution*. Brooklyn, NY: Zone Books.

Buchanan, James M. 1990. "The Potential for Politics after Socialism." In *Geschichte end Geset₂, Europäisches Forum Alpbach, 1989*, edited by Otto Molden, 240–256. Vienna: Österreichisches College. Reprinted in *Ideas, Persons, and Events*. Vol. 19 of *The Collected Works of James M. Buchanan*. Indianapolis, IN: Liberty Fund, 2001.

Buchanan, James M. 1991. "The Minimal Politics of Market Order." *Cato Journal* 11, no. 2 (Fall): 215–232. Reprinted in *Choice, Contract, and Constitutions*. Vol. 16 of *The Collected Works of James M. Buchanan*. Indianapolis, IN: Liberty Fund, 2001.

Buchanan, James M., and Gordon Tullock. 1962. *The Calculus of Consent: Logical Foundations of Constitutional Democracy*. Ann Arbor: University of Michigan Press.

Budish, Eric, Benjamin N. Roin, and Heidi Williams. 2015. "Do Firms Underinvest in Long-Term Research? Evidence from Cancer Clinical Trials." *American Economic Review* 105, no. 7: 2044–2085.

Budziszewski, J. 2010. *The Revenge of Conscience: Politics and the Fall of Man*. Eugene, OR: Wipf and Stock.

Burczak, Theodore A. 2006. *Socialism After Hayek*. Ann Arbor: University of Michigan Press.

Burczak, Theodore A. 2018. "Catallactic Marxism: Hayek, Marx, and the Market." In *Knowledge, Class, and Economics: Marxism Without Guarantees*, edited by Theodore A. Burczak, Robert F. Garnett, and Richard P. McIntyre. London: Routledge.

Butler, Eamonn. 2015. *Classical Liberalism: A Primer*. London: Institute of Economic Affairs.

Butler, Eamonn. 2018. *An Introduction to Capitalism*. London: Institute of Economic Affairs.

Butler, Joseph. 1736. *Fifteen Sermons*. Reprinted in *The Analogy of Religion and Fifteen Sermons*, 335–528. London: The Religious Tract Society, n.d.

Caliendo, Lorenzo, Maximiliano Dvorkin, and Fernando Parro. 2015. "Trade and Labor Market Dynamics." Working Paper 2015-009C, Federal Reserve Bank of St. Louis, August.

Cannan, Edwin. 1902. "The Practical Utility of Economic Science." *Economic Journal* 12, no. 48: 459–471.

Caplan, Bryan. 2007. *The Myth of the Rational Voter: Why Democracies Choose Bad Policies*. Princeton, NJ: Princeton University Press.

Carey, Benedict. 2007. "Criticism of a Gender Theory, and a Scientist Under Siege." *New York Times*, August 21.

Carnegie, Andrew. 1889. "The Gospel of Wealth." In *The Gospel of Wealth and Other Timely Essays*, 1–46. New York: Century, 1901.

Castillo, Michelle. 2013. "Bloomberg: Medical Marijuana One of 'Great Hoaxes of All Time.'" *CBS News*, June 3. www.cbsnews.com/news/bloomberg-medical-marijuana-one-of-great-hoaxes-of-all-time/.

Catanese, David. 2013. "Graham's Hawkish Posture Confronts War-Weary Voters in South Carolina." *U.S. News and World Report*, September 5. www.usnews.com/news/articles/2013/09/05/grahams-hawkish-posture-confronts-war-weary-voters-in-south-carolina.

Cather, Willa. 1913. *O Pioneers!* Boston: Houghton Mifflin.

Cather, Willa. 1918. *My Ántonia*. Boston: Houghton Mifflin.

Chalfen, Richard. 1987. *Snapshot: Versions of a Life*. Bowling Green, OH: Bowling Green University Press.

Chamlee-Wright, Emily, and Virgil Storr. 2010. "The Role of Social Entrepreneurship in Post-Katrina Recovery." *International Journal of Innovation and Regional Development* 2, nos. 1/2.

Chapman, Steve. 2019. "Paul's Weak Case Against Mandatory Vaccines Hurts Measles Outbreak Effort." *Chicago Tribune,* March 7.

Charry, Ellen T. 2004. "On Happiness." *Anglican Theological Review* 86 (Winter): 19–33.

Chaudhuri, Nirad C. 1959. *A Passage to England.* London: Macmillan.

Cicero, Marcus Tullius. 1938. *De Amicitia* [Concerning friendship]. Translated by W. A. Falconer. Loeb edition. Cambridge, MA: Harvard University Press.

Clapham, J. H. 1922. "Of Empty Economic Boxes." *Economic Journal* 32: 305–314.

Clark, John Bates. 1901. "The Society of the Future." *The Independent* 53, no. 2746 (July 18): 1649–1651.

Clark, Lindley H., Jr. 1978. "U.S. Monetary Troubles." *Wall Street Journal,* October 13.

Cline, William R. 2004. *Trade Policy and Global Poverty.* Washington, DC: Peterson Institute for International Economics.

Coase, Ronald, and Ning Wang. 2013. *How China Became Capitalist.* Basingstoke, UK: Palgrave Macmillan.

Cohen, Edward. 1992. *Athenian Economy and Society: A Banking Perspective.* Princeton, NJ: Princeton University Press.

Colander, David. 2013. Introduction to *Decline and Economic Ideals in Italy in the Early Modern Era,* by Gino Barbieri. Firenze: Leo R. Olschki Editore.

Collier, Paul. 2007. *The Bottom Billion: Why the Poorest Countries Are Failing and What Can Be Done About It.* Oxford, UK: Oxford University Press.

Constant, Benjamin. 1819. "De la liberté des Anciens comparée à celle des Modernes." In vol. 2 of *Cours de politique constitutionnelle,* 2nd ed., 539–560. Paris: Guillaumin, 1872.

Cosgel, Metin M. 1993. "Religious Culture and Economic Performance: Agricultural Productivity of the Amish, 1850–80." *Journal of Economic History* 53 (June): 319–331.

Cowen, Tyler. 1998. *In Praise of Commercial Culture.* Cambridge and London: Harvard University Press.

Cowen, Tyler. 2013. *Average Is Over.* New York: Dutton.

Cowen, Tyler. 2018. *Stubborn Attachments: A Vision for a Society of Free, Prosperous, and Responsible Individuals.* San Francisco: Stripe Press.

Cox, Harvey. 2016. *The Market as God.* Cambridge, MA: Harvard University Press.

Crandall, Robert W. 1984. "Import Quotas and the Automobile Industry: The Costs of Protectionism." *Brookings Review* 2, no. 4: 8–16.

Cullenberg, Stephen, Jack Amariglio, and David F. Ruccio, eds. 2001. *Postmodernism, Economics and Knowledge*. New York and London: Routledge.

Damasio, Antonio. 1994. *Descartes' Error: Emotion, Reason and the Human Brain*. New York: Grosset/Putnam.

Das, Gurcharan. 2001. *India Unbound: The Social and Economic Revolution from Independence to the Global Information Age*. New York: Random House.

Davies, Stephen. 2018. "You Don't Really Want Smart People Running the World." American Institute for Economic Research, Great Barrington, MA, October 23. www.aier.org/article/you-dont-really-want-smart-people-running-world.

Deaton, Angus. 2013. *The Great Escape: Health, Wealth, and the Origins of Inequality*. Princeton, NJ: Princeton University Press.

DeMartino, George. 2011. *The Economist's Oath: On the Need for and Content of Professional Economic Ethics*. New York: Oxford University Press.

Deneen, Patrick J. 2018. *Why Liberalism Failed*. New Haven, CT: Yale University Press.

Derbyshire, John. 2003. "Lost in the Male." *National Review*, June 30: 51–52.

de Rugy, Veronique. 2018. "The Tyranny of the Administrative State." *Reason*, May 10. https://reason.com/archives/2018/05/10/the-tyranny-of-the-administrative-state.

de Soto, Hernando. 1989. *The Other Path: The Invisible Revolution in the Third World*. New York: HarperCollins.

de Soto, Hernando. 2000. *The Mystery of Capital: Why Capitalism Triumphs in the West and Fails Everywhere Else*. New York: Basic Books.

Diamond, Arthur M., Jr. 2019. *Openness to Creative Destruction: Sustaining Innovative Dynamism*. New York: Oxford University Press.

Dicey, A. V. 1919. *Lectures on the Relation Between Law and Public Opinion During the 19th Century*. 2nd ed. London: Macmillan. http://oll.libertyfund.org/titles/1683#lf1315.

Douglas, Mary. 1975. "Deciphering a Meal." In *Implicit Meanings*, 249–275. London: Routledge and Kegan Paul.

Douglas, Mary, and Baron Isherwood. 1979. *The World of Goods*. New York: Basic Books.

Doyle, Vincent. 2007. "Insiders–Outsiders: Dr. Laura and the Contest for Cultural Authority in LGBT Media Activism." In *Media/Queered: Visibility and Its Discontents*, edited by Kevin G. Barnhurst, 107–124. New York: Peter Lang.

Dumcius, Gintautas. 2017. "Sen. Elizabeth Warren Backs High-Speed Rail Connecting Springfield, Worcester and Boston." *MassLive,* March 16. www .masslive.com/news/index.ssf/2017/03/sen_elizabeth_warren_backs _hig.html.

Dvorkin, Maximiliano. 2017. "What Is the Impact of Chinese Imports on U.S. Jobs?" *The Regional Economist,* Federal Reserve Bank of St. Louis, May 15.

Dworkin, Ronald. 1980. "Is Wealth a Value?" *Journal of Legal Issues* 9: 191–226.

Easterlin, Richard A. 1995. "Industrial Revolution and Mortality Revolution: Two of a Kind?" *Journal of Evolutionary Economics* 5: 393–408. Reprinted in Easterlin, *The Reluctant Economist,* 84–100.

Easterlin, Richard A., ed. 2002. *Happiness in Economics.* Cheltenham and Northampton, UK: Edward Elgar.

Easterlin, Richard A. 2003. "Living Standards." In vol. 3 of *The Oxford Encyclopedia of Economic History,* edited by Joel Mokyr. New York: Oxford University Press.

Easterlin, Richard A. 2004. *The Reluctant Economist: Perspectives on Economics, Economic History, and Demography.* Cambridge, UK: Cambridge University Press.

Easterly, William. 2001. *The Elusive Quest for Growth: Economists' Adventures and Misadventures in the Tropics.* Cambridge, MA: MIT Press.

Economist. 1992. "High-Speed Spending." April 25.

Economist. 2013. "Towards the End of Poverty." June 1. www.economist.com /leaders/2013/06/01/towards-the-end-of-poverty.

Ehrenreich, Barbara. 2001. *Nickel and Dimed: On (Not) Getting By in America.* New York: Henry Holt.

Ehrlich, Paul R. 1968. *The Population Bomb.* New York: Ballantine Books. Reprint, Jackson Heights, NY: Rivercity Press, 1975.

Ekstrom, Karin, and Kay Glans, eds. 2010. *Changing Consumer Roles.* London: Routledge.

Ellenberg, Jordan. 2014. "And the Summer's Most Unread Book is. . . ." *Wall Street Journal,* July 3.

Ellsberg, Robert. 1983. Introduction to *Selected Writings,* by Dorothy Day. Edited by Robert Ellsberg. Maryknoll, NY: Orbis.

Emerson, Ralph Waldo. 1850. "Napoleon; Or, the Man of the World." In *Selected Essays,* 337–359. Edited by L. Ziff. New York: Viking Penguin, 1982.

Engels, Friedrich. 1845. *Die Lage der arbeitenden Klasse in England* [The condition of the working class in England]. Leipzig: O. Wigand.

Epstein, Richard A. 2009. Foreword to *Law, Liberty and the Competitive Market*, by Bruno Leoni. Edited by Carlo Lottieri. New Brunswick, NJ: Transaction.

Erasmus, Desiderius, of Rotterdam. 2001. *The Adages of Erasmus*. Selected by William Barker. Toronto, ON: University of Toronto Press.

Farrell, James T. 1932–1935. *Studs Lonigan*. Reprint, New York: Library of America, 2004.

Feinstein, C. H. 1972. *National Income, Expenditure and Output of the United Kingdom, 1855–1965*. Cambridge, UK: Cambridge University Press.

Field, Alexander J. 2011. *A Great Leap Forward: 1930s Depression and U.S. Economic Growth*. New Haven, CT: Yale University Press.

Fish, Stanley. 1994. *There's No Such Thing as Free Speech . . . and It's a Good Thing, Too*. New York: Oxford University Press.

Flaubert, Gustave. 1867. *Oeuvres complètes et Annexes: Correspondance*. Reprint, Saint Julien-en-Genevois, France: Arvensa Éditions, 2014.

Flaubert, Gustave. 1993. *Gustave Flaubert–Guy de Maupassant Correspondance*. Paris: Flammarion.

Fleischacker, Samuel. 2004. *A Short History of Distributive Justice*. Cambridge, MA: Harvard University Press.

Fodor, Jerry. 1998. "The Trouble with Psychological Darwinism." Review of *How the Mind Works*, by Steven Pinker, and *Evolution in Mind*, by Henry Plotkin. *London Review of Books* 20, no. 2 (January 22): 11–13.

Fogel, Robert William. 1960. *The Union Pacific Railroad: A Case in Premature Enterprise*. Baltimore, MD: Johns Hopkins Press.

Fogel, Robert William. 1999. *The Fourth Great Awakening and the Future of Egalitarianism*. Chicago: University of Chicago Press.

Fogel, Robert William. 2004. *The Escape from Hunger and Premature Death 1700–2100*. Cambridge, UK: Cambridge University Press.

Fogel, Robert William. 2005. "Reconsidering Expectations of Economic Growth After World War II from the Perspective of 2004." NBER Working Paper No. 11125, National Bureau of Economic Research, Cambridge, MA, February. https://www.nber.org/papers/w11125.

Follett, Mary Parker. 1920. *The New State: Popular Organization the Solution of Popular Government*. London: Longmans, Green.

Follett, Mary Parker. 1942. *Dynamic Administration: The Collected Papers of Mary Parker Follett*. Edited by Henry C. Metcalf and L. Urwick. New York: Harper and Brothers.

Foster, Mary. 2006. "New Orleans Police Honor Those Who Stayed." Associated Press, February 22.

Foucault, Michel. 2008. *The Birth of Biopolitics: Lectures at the Collège de France, 1978–1979*. Edited by Michel Senellart. Translated by Graham Burchell. New York: Palgrave Macmillan.

Frank, Robert H. 1985. *Choosing the Right Pond: Human Behavior and the Quest for Status*. New York: Oxford University Press.

Frank, Robert H. 1988. *Passions Within Reason: The Strategic Role of the Emotions*. New York: W. W. Norton.

Frank, Robert H. 1999. *Luxury Fever*. New York: Free Press.

Frank, Robert H. 2004. *What Price the Moral High Ground? Ethical Dilemmas in Competitive Environments*. Princeton, NJ: Princeton University Press.

Frank, Robert H. 2005. "Motives and Self-Interest." In *Business Ethics*, edited by Patricia Werhane and R. E. Freeman, 369f. Vol. 2 of *The Blackwell Encyclopedia of Management*. Oxford, UK, and Malden, MA: Blackwell.

Frank, Robert H., and Philip J. Cook. 1995. *The Winner-Take-All Society: Why the Few at the Top Get So Much More than the Rest of Us*. New York: Penguin Books.

Frankfurt, Harry. 1987. "Equality as a Moral Ideal." *Ethics* 98, no. 1: 21–43.

Frankfurt, Harry. 2004. *The Reasons of Love*. Princeton, NJ: Princeton University Press.

Freeman, Samuel. 2012. "Can Economic Liberties Be Basic Liberties?" *Bleeding Heart Libertarians* (blog), June 13. http://bleedingheartlibertarians.com/2012/06/can-economic-liberties-be-basic-liberties/.

Friedman, Benjamin M. 2005. *The Moral Consequences of Economic Growth*. New York: Knopf.

Friedman, Milton. 1956. "The Relation Between Economic Freedom and Political Freedom." In *Capitalism and Freedom*, 7–21. Chicago: University of Chicago Press, 1962.

Frijda, Nico H. 1994. "Emotions Require Cognitions, Even If Simple Ones." In *The Nature of Emotion: Fundamental Questions*, edited by Paul Ekman and Richard J. Davidson. New York: Oxford University Press.

Fussell, Paul. 1989. *Wartime: Understanding and Behavior in the Second World War*. New York: Oxford University Press.

Gazeley, Ian, and Andrew Newell. 2010. "The End of Destitution: Evidence from British Working Households 1904–1937." Economics Department Working Paper Series No. 2-2010, University of Sussex. www.sussex.ac.uk/economics/documents/wps-2-2010.pdf.

Gerschenkron, Alexander. 1970. *Europe in the Russian Mirror: Four Lectures in Economic History*. Cambridge, UK: Cambridge University Press.

Gerschenkron, Alexander. 1971. "Mercator Gloriosus." *Economic History Review* 24, no. 4: 653–666.

Glare, P. G. W., ed. 1982. *Oxford Latin Dictionary*. Oxford: Oxford University Press.

Goldberg, Jonah. 2018. *Suicide of the West: How the Rebirth of Nationalism, Populism, and Identity Politics Is Destroying American Democracy*. New York: Crown.

Goldstone, Jack A. 2002. "Efflorescences and Economic Growth in World History: Rethinking the 'Rise of the West' and the Industrial Revolution." *Journal of World History* 13: 323–389.

Gordon, Edward E., and David Ramsay. 2017. *Divided on D-Day: How Conflicts and Rivalries Jeopardized the Allied Victory at Normandy*. Amherst, NY: Prometheus Books.

Gordon, Robert J. 2012. "Is U.S. Economic Growth Over? Faltering Innovation Confronts the Six Headwinds." NBER Working Paper No. 18315, National Bureau of Economic Research, Cambridge, MA, August. https://www.nber.org/papers/w18315.

Gordon, Robert J. 2016. *The Rise and Fall of American Growth: The U.S. Standard of Living Since the Civil War*. Princeton, NJ: Princeton University Press.

Gotakanal.se. n.d. "Göta Canal: A Beautiful History." Accessed February 13, 2019. www.gotakanal.se/en/the-gota-canal-history/.

Grace, Francie. 2003. "Salvation Army Shoots Down Donation." *CBS News*, January 2. www.cbsnews.com/news/salvation-army-shoots-down -donation/.

Gray, John. 1996. *Isaiah Berlin*. Princeton, NJ: Princeton University Press.

Greenblatt, Stephen J. 2004. *Will in the World: How Shakespeare Became Shakespeare*. New York: W. W. Norton.

Guthrie, W. K. C. 1971. *The Sophists*. Cambridge, UK: Cambridge University Press.

Hale, Charles A. 1990. *The Transformation of Liberalism in Late 19th-Century Mexico*. Princeton, NJ: Princeton University Press.

Hamburg, Margaret. 2015. "Margaret Hamburg Ends Six-Year Run as FDA Commissioner." Interview by Robert Siegel. *All Things Considered*, National Public Radio, April 1. www.npr.org/2015/04/01/396871346 /margaret-hamburg-ends-six-year-run-as-fda-commissioner.

Hammett, Dashiell. 1929. *The Maltese Falcon*. Vintage edition. New York: Knopf, 1984.

Hand, Learned. 1944. "The Spirit of Liberty." In *The Spirit of Liberty: Papers and Addresses of Learned Hand*. New York: Alfred A. Knopf, 1952.

Hansen, Alvin H. 1939. "Economic Progress and Declining Population Growth." *American Economic Review* 29 (March): 1–7.

Hansen, Alvin H. 1941. *Fiscal Policy and Business Cycles*. New York: W. W. Norton.

Harberger, Arnold C. 1954. "Monopoly and Resource Allocation." *American Economic Review* 44: 77–87.

Harsanyi, John C. 1955. "Cardinal Welfare, Individualistic Ethics, and Interpersonal Comparisons of Utility." *Journal of Political Economy* 63: 309–321.

Hart, David Bentley. 2009. *Atheist Delusions: The Christian Revolution and Its Fashionable Enemies*. New Haven: Yale University Press.

Harvey, David. 2005. *A Brief History of Neoliberalism*. Oxford, UK: Oxford University Press.

Harvey, David. 2014. *Seventeen Contradictions and the End of Capitalism*. London: Profile Books.

Hawking, Stephen. 1988. *A Brief History of Time*. New York: Bantam Books.

Hawley, Ellis W. 2015. *The New Deal and the Problem of Monopoly*. Princeton, NJ: Princeton University Press.

Hayden, Robert. 2013. "Runagate Runagate." In *Collected Poems*, 59–61. Edited by Frederick Glaysher. New York: W. W. Norton.

Hayek, Friedrich A. 1960. *The Constitution of Liberty*. Definitive edition. Vol. 17 of *The Collected Works of F. A. Hayek*. Edited by Ronald Hamowy. Chicago: University of Chicago Press, 2011.

Hayek, Friedrich A. 1973. *Law, Legislation, and Liberty*. Vol. 1, *Rules and Order*. Chicago: University of Chicago Press.

Hayek, Friedrich A. 1979. *Law, Legislation, and Liberty*. Vol. 3, *The Political Order of a Free People*. Chicago: University of Chicago Press.

Hazlett, Thomas Winslow. 2017. *The Political Spectrum: The Tumultuous Liberation of Wireless Technology, from Herbert Hoover to the Smartphone*. New Haven, CT: Yale University Press.

Heilbroner, Robert. 1953. *The Worldly Philosophers: The Lives, Times, and Ideas of the Great Economic Thinkers*. 7th ed. New York: Simon and Schuster, 1999.

Hicks, John R. 1932. *The Theory of Wages*. London: Macmillan.

Higgs, Robert. 1987. *Crisis and Leviathan: Critical Episodes in the Growth of American Government*. New York: Oxford University Press.

Higgs, Robert. 2001. "Unmitigated Mercantilism." *Independent Review* 5: 469–472.

Higgs, Robert. 2008. "Government Growth." Concise Encyclopedia of Economics, Liberty Fund. www.econlib.org/library/Enc/GovernmentGrowth.html.

Higgs, Robert. 2012. "Freedom: Because It Works or Because It Is Right?" *The Beacon* (blog), Independent Institute, December 27. http://blog.independent.org/2012/12/27/freedom-because-it-works-or-because-its-right/. Reprinted in *Taking a Stand*. Oakland, CA: Independent Institute, 2015.

Higgs, Robert. 2018. Facebook post, October 28. www.facebook.com/robert.higgs.568/posts/10156800522539400. In "Bonus Quotation of the Day . . . ," by Donald J. Boudreaux. *Café Hayek* (blog), October 31, 2018. https://cafehayek.com/2018/10/bonus-quotation-day-200.html.

Hill, Christopher. 1940. *The English Revolution 1640: Three Essays*. London: Lawrence and Wishart.

Hinze, Christine Firer. 2004. "What Is Enough? Catholic Social Thought, Consumption, and Material Sufficiency." In *Having: Property and Possession in Religious and Social Life*, edited by William Schweiker and Charles Mathewes, 162–188. Grand Rapids, MI: Eerdmans.

Hirsch, Fred. 1976. *Social Limits to Growth*. Cambridge, MA: Harvard University Press.

Hirschman, Albert O. 1970. *Exit, Voice and Loyalty: Responses to Decline in Firms, Organizations, and States*. Cambridge, MA: Harvard University Press.

Hirschman, Albert O. 1977. *The Passions and the Interests: Political Arguments for Capitalism Before Its Triumph*. Princeton, NJ: Princeton University Press.

Hobsbawm, Eric. 1994. Interview by Michael Ignatieff. *The Late Show*, BBC, October 24.

Hobsbawm, Eric. 2002. *Interesting Times: A Twentieth-Century Life*. London: Allen Lane.

Hobsbawm, Eric. 2011. *How to Change the World: Tales of Marx and Marxism*. New Haven, CT: Yale University Press.

Hobson, John A. 1902. *Imperialism: A Study*. New York: James Pott and Co.

Hoffer, Eric. 1951. *The True Believer: Thoughts on the Nature of Mass Movements*. New York: Harper and Brothers.

Hoffman, Elizabeth, and Matthew Spitzer. 1985. "Entitlements, Rights and Fairness: An Experimental Examination of Subjects' Concepts of Distributive Justice." *Journal of Legal Studies* 14: 259–298.

Hofstadter, Douglas. 1979. *Gödel, Escher, Bach: An Eternal Golden Braid.* New York: Basic Books.

Hofstadter, Richard. 1948. *The American Political Tradition and the Men Who Made It.* New York: Knopf.

Hornby, Nick. 2001. *How to Be Good.* New York: Penguin Putnam.

Horowitz, Daniel. 1985. *The Morality of Spending: Attitudes Toward the Consumer Society in America, 1875–1940.* Baltimore: Johns Hopkins University Press.

Horwitz, Steven. 2015. "Inequality, Mobility, and Being Poor in America." *Social Philosophy and Policy* 31, no. 2 (Spring): 70–91.

Hughes, Langston. 1994. "Let America Be America Again." In *The Collected Poems of Langston Hughes,* edited by Arnold Rampersad, 189–191. New York: Alfred A. Knopf.

Huizinga, Johan H. 1935. "The Spirit of the Netherlands." In *Dutch Civilization in the Seventeenth Century and Other Essays,* 105–137. Edited by Pieter Geyl and F. W. N. Hugenholtz. Translated by A. J. Pomerans. London: Collins, 1968.

Hume, David. 1741–1742. *Essays, Moral, Political and Literary.* Edited by Eugene F. Miller. Indianapolis, IN: Liberty Fund, 1987.

Hume, David. 1751. *An Enquiry Concerning the Principles of Morals.* London: A. Millar.

Hunnicutt, Benjamin Kline. 1996. *Kellogg's Six-Hour Day.* Philadelphia: Temple University Press.

Iannaccone, Laurence. 2018. Correspondence with the author. September.

Ibsen, Henrik. 1878. *A Doll House.* In *Ibsen: The Complete Major Prose and Plays,* 123–196. Edited and translated by R. Fjelde. New York: Penguin, 1965.

Ingersoll, Robert G. 1897. *Great Speeches of Col. R.G. Ingersoll: Complete.* Chicago: Rhodes and McClure.

International Labor Organization (ILO). 2016. *World Employment Social Outlook: Trends for Youth 2016.* Geneva: International Labour Office. www.ilo .org/wcmsp5/groups/public/---dgreports/---dcomm/---publ /documents/publication/wcms_513739.pdf.

Irwin, Douglas. 2017. *Clashing over Commerce: A History of U.S. Trade Policy.* Chicago: University of Chicago Press.

Isaacs, Julia B. 2007. "Economic Mobility of Families Across Generations." Brookings Institution, Washington, DC, November 13. www.brookings .edu/research/economic-mobility-of-families-across-generations/.

Jacobs, Jane. 1984. *Cities and the Wealth of Nations: Principles of Economic Life.* New York: Random House.

Jaeger, Werner. 1939. *Paideia: The Ideals of Greek Culture*. Vol. 1: *Archaic Greece, the Mind of Athens*. Translated by Gilbert Highet. Reprint, New York: Oxford University Press, 1965.

James, Clive. 2007. *Cultural Amnesia: Necessary Memories from History and the Arts*. New York: Norton.

Jameson, Frederic. 2011. *Representing 'Capital': A Reading of Volume One*. London and New York: Verso.

Johnson, Paul. 2002. *Napoleon*. New York and London: Lipper/Viking/Penguin.

Johnson, Samuel. 1775. *Taxation No Tyranny: An Answer to the Resolutions and Address of the American Congress*. 4th ed. London: T. Cadell.

Jones, G. T. 1933. *Increasing Returns*. Cambridge, UK: Cambridge University Press.

Judt, Tony. 2010. *Ill Fares the Land*. London: Penguin.

Kama, Amit. 2007. "Israeli Gay Men's Consumption of Lesbigay Media: 'I'm Not Alone . . . in This Business." In *Media/Queered: Visibility and Its Discontents*, edited by Kevin G. Barnhurst, 125–142. New York: Peter Lang.

Kant, Immanuel. 1781. *Kritik der reinen Vernunft*. 2nd ed. Riga: Hartknoch.

Kantor, Arlene Finger. 1976. "Upton Sinclair and the Pure Food and Drugs Act of 1906." *American Journal of Public Health* 66, no. 12: 1202–1205.

Kaplan, Justin. 1974. *Lincoln Steffens: A Biography*. New York: Simon and Schuster.

Kashdan, Andrew, and Daniel B. Klein. 2006. "Assume the Positional: Comment on Robert Frank." *Econ Journal Watch* 3, no. 3 (September): 412–434.

Kelo v. City of New London. 2005. 545 U.S. 469.

Kennedy, George. 1963. *The Art of Persuasion in Greece*. Princeton, NJ: Princeton University Press.

Kennedy, James C. 2017. *A Concise History of the Netherlands*. Cambridge, UK: Cambridge University Press.

Kennedy, Paul. 1987. *The Rise and Fall of the Great Powers*. New York: Random House.

Kerferd, G. B. 1981. *The Sophistic Movement*. Cambridge, UK: Cambridge University Press.

Keynes, John Maynard. 1937. "Some Economic Consequences of a Declining Population." *Eugenics Review* 29, no. 1 (April): 13–17.

Kibbe, Matt. 2014. *Don't Hurt People and Don't Take Their Stuff: A Libertarian Manifesto*. Now York: William Murrow (HarperCollins).

King, Martin Luther, Jr. 1959. "The Dimensions of a Complete Life." In *The Measure of a Man*. Philadelphia: Christian Education Press.

Kirkland, Richard I., Jr. 1986. "Should You Leave It All to the Children?" *Fortune*, September 29.

Kirzner, Israel. 1979. *Perception, Opportunity and Profit*. Chicago: University of Chicago Press.

Klein, Daniel B. 2017a. "Liberalism 1.0: The Genealogy of Adam Smith's Liberalism." Lecture at Universidad Francisco Marroquín, October 25. https://newmedia.ufm.edu/video/liberalism-1-0-the-genealogy-of-adam-smiths-liberalism/.

Klein, Daniel B. 2017b. "Sentiment, Passive and Active, and Liberalism." Foundation for Economic Education, Atlanta, GA, October 25. https://fee.org/articles/sentiment-passive-and-active-and-liberalism/.

Klein, Daniel B. 2017c. "Beyond Commutative but Not 'Social' Justice." Foundation for Economic Education, Atlanta, GA, June 19. https://fee.org/articles/my-reservations-about-the-concept-of-social-justice/.

Klemm, David. 2004. "Material Grace: The Paradox of Property and Possession." In *Having: Property and Possession in Religious and Social Life*, edited by William Schweiker and Charles Mathewes, 222–245. Grand Rapids, MI: Eerdmans.

Klinenberg, Eric. 2002. *Heat Wave: A Social Autopsy of Disaster in Chicago*. Chicago: University of Chicago Press.

Kling, Arnold. 2018. "The Confusion of the Libertarians." October 15. https://medium.com/@arnoldkling/the-confusion-of-the-libertarians-7f060d4ba844.

Knight, Frank H. 1923. "The Ethics of Competition." *Quarterly Journal of Economics* 37, no. 4 (August): 579–624. Reprinted in *The Ethics of Competition*, 33–67. New York: Harper and Brothers, 1935.

Knight, Frank H. 1929. "Freedom as Fact and Criterion." In *Freedom and Reform: Essays in Economics and Social Philosophy*, 1–18. New York: Harper and Row, 1947. Reprint, Port Washington, NY: Kennikat Press, 1969.

Knight, Frank H. 1934. "Economic Theory and Nationalism." In *The Ethics of Competition*, 268–351. New York: Harper and Brothers, 1935. Reprint, New Brunswick, NJ: Transaction Publishers, 1997.

Knight, Frank H. 1936. "Pragmatism and Social Action." In *Freedom and Reform: Essays in Economics and Social Philosophy*, 35–44. New York: Harper and Row, 1947.

Knight, Frank H. 1944. "The Rights of Man and Natural Law." In *Freedom and Reform: Essays in Economics and Social Philosophy*, 262–300. New York: Harper and Row, 1947.

Knight, Frank H., and T. W. Merriam. 1945. *The Economic Order and Religion*. New York: Harper and Brothers.

Knott, Kim. 1998. *Hinduism*. Oxford, UK: Oxford University Press.

Kocka, Jürgen. 2014. Personal correspondence with the author. November.

Kołakowski, Leszek. 2004. *My Correct Views on Everything*. Edited by Z. Janowski. South Bend, IN: St. Augustine's Press.

Kolko, Gabriel. 1965. *Railroads and Regulation, 1877–1916*. Princeton, NJ: Princeton University Press.

Kropotkin, Prince Pyotr A. 1902. *Mutual Aid: A Factor of Evolution*. London: Heinemann.

Krugman, Paul R. 2002. "Ricardo's Difficult Idea: Why Intellectuals Don't Understand Comparative Advantage." In *The Economics and Politics of International Trade* vol. 2, *Freedom and Trade*, edited by Gary Cook, 22–36. London: Routledge.

Landes, David S. 1965. "Technological Change and Development in Western Europe, 1750–1914." In vol. 6 of *The Cambridge Economic History of Europe*, edited by H. J. Habakkuk and M. Postan, chap. 5. Cambridge, UK: Cambridge University Press.

Landes, David S. 1969. *The Unbound Prometheus: Technological Change and Industrial Development in Western Europe, 1750 to the Present*. Cambridge, UK: Cambridge University Press.

Landsburg, Steven E. 2008. "What to Expect When You're Free Trading." *New York Times*, January 16.

Lange, Oskar, and Fred M. Taylor. 1938. *On the Economic Theory of Socialism*. Minneapolis: University of Minnesota Press.

Langland, Connie. 2001. "Merit Pay Plan Irked Teachers." *Philadelphia Inquirer*, September 6.

Lapore, Jill. 2008. "The Creed: What Poor Richard Cost Benjamin Franklin." *New Yorker*, January 28: 78–82.

Larson, John Lauritz. 2001. *Internal Improvement: National Public Works and the Promise of Popular Government in the Early United States*. Chapel Hill, NC: University of North Carolina Press.

Lavoie, Donald Charles. 1985. *Rivalry and Central Planning: A Re-examination of the Debate over Economic Calculation Under Socialism*. Cambridge, UK: Cambridge University Press.

Lawrence, D. H. 1923. *Studies in Classic American Literature*. New York: Thomas Seltzer.

Lebergott, Stanley. 1966. "Labor Force and Employment, 1800–1960." In *Output, Employment, and Productivity in the United States After 1800,* edited by Dorothy S. Brady, 117–204. New York: National Bureau of Economic Research.

Lebergott, Stanley. 1993. *Pursuing Happiness: American Consumers in the Twentieth Century.* Princeton, NJ: Princeton University Press.

Lefebvre, Georges. 1939. *Quatre-vingt-neuf* [The coming of the French Revolution]. Paris: Maison du Livre Francais.

Leighton, Wayne A., and Edward J. López. 2011. *Madmen, Intellectuals, and Academic Scribblers: The Economic Engine of Political Change.* Stanford, CA: Stanford University Press.

Lemert, Charles. 2012. *Social Things: An Introduction to the Sociological Life.* 5th ed. Lanham, MD: Rowman and Littlefield.

Lenin, Vladimir. 1917. *Imperialism: The Highest Stage of Capitalism* [in Russian]. Petrograd.

Lenin, Vladimir. 1917. "The Higher Phase of Communist Society." In *The State and Revolution,* chap. 5, sec. 4. Reprinted in *Collected Works* vol. 25, edited by Stepan Apresyan and Jim Riordan, 473–479. Moscow: Progress Publishers, 1964. www.marxists.org/archive/lenin/works/1917/staterev/ch05 .htm#s4.

Leonard, Thomas C. 2016. *Illiberal Reformers: Race, Eugenics and American Economics in the Progressive Era.* Princeton, NJ: Princeton University Press.

Leoni, Bruno. 2008. *Law, Liberty and the Competitive Market.* Edited by Carlo Lottieri. New Brunswick, NJ: Transaction.

Le Roy Ladurie, Emmanuel. 1978. *Montaillou: Cathars and Catholics in a French Village, 1294–1324.* Translated by Barbara Bray. London: Scolar. Reprint, London: Penguin, 1980.

Lev, Michael A. 2004. "The Great Migration of China." *Chicago Tribune,* December 27, 28, 29.

Lewis, C. S. 1952. *Mere Christianity.* New York: Macmillan.

Lintott, Andrew. 1999. *The Constitution of the Roman Republic.* Oxford, UK: Oxford University Press.

Lippmann, Walter. 1914. *Drift and Mastery: An Attempt to Diagnose the Current Unrest.* New York: M. Kennerley. Reprint, Madison: University of Wisconsin Press, 2015.

Lipset, Seymour Martin. 1961. "The Conservatism of Vance Packard." *Commentary Magazine,* January: 80–83.

Little, Lester K. 1978. *Religious Poverty and the Profit Economy in Medieval Europe*. Ithaca, NY: Cornell University Press.

Locke, John. 1689. *A Letter Concerning Toleration*. Edited by James H. Tully. Indianapolis, IN: Hackett, 1983.

Lodge, David. 1999. *Home Truths: A Novella*. London: Secker and Warburg. Reprint, London: Penguin, 2000.

London, Jack. 1903. *The People of the Abyss*. London: Macmillan.

Long, Huey. 1934. "Share Our Wealth Speech." February 23. https://www.hueylong.com/programs/share-our-wealth-speech.php.

Lyons, Leonard. 1937. "The Post's New Yorker." *Washington Post*, May 12.

Macaulay, Thomas B. 1830. "Southey's Colloquies." *Edinburgh Review* 50, no. 100 (January): 528–565. Reprinted in *Critical, Historical, and Miscellaneous Essays* vol. 2, 132–187. Boston: Houghton, Mifflin and Co., 1881.

Macfarlane, Alan. 1987. *The Culture of Capitalism*. Oxford, UK: Basil Blackwell.

MacIntyre, Alasdair. 1981. *After Virtue: A Study in Moral Theory*. Notre Dame, IN: University of Notre Dame Press.

MacIntyre, Alasdair. 1999. *Dependent Rational Animals: Why Human Beings Need the Virtues*. London: Duckworth and Co., 1999.

Maddison, Angus. 1989. *The World Economy in the Twentieth Century*. Paris: Organisation for Economic Co-operation and Development.

Maddison, Angus. 2006. *The World Economy*. 2 vols. Paris: Organisation for Economic Co-operation and Development.

Maddison, Angus. 2010. "Historical Statistics of the World Economy: 1–2008 AD." Website of Groningen Growth and Development Centre, University of Groningen. Accessed February 25, 2019. www.ggdc.net/MADDISON/Historical_Statistics/horizontal-file_02-2010.xls.

Madison, James. 1788. "The Structure of the Government Must Furnish the Proper Checks and Balances Between the Different Departments." *Federalist No. 51*. *New York Packet*, February 8. www.congress.gov/resources/display/content/The+Federalist+Papers#TheFederalistPapers-51.

Malkin, Elisabeth. 2017. "Mexico Agrees to Sugar Trade Deal, but U.S. Refiners Remain Unhappy." *New York Times*, June 6.

Mandeville, Bernard. 1705–1729. *The Fable of the Bees: or, Private Vices, Publick Benefits*. 2 vols. Edited by F. B. Kaye. Oxford, UK: Clarendon Press, 1924. Reprint, Indianapolis, IN: Liberty Fund, 1988.

Manzoni, Alessandro. 1827. *I Promessi Sposi*. Livorno, Italy: Pozzolini.

Margo, Robert A. 1993. "What Is the Key to Black Progress?" In *Second Thoughts: Myths and Morals of U.S. Economic History*, edited by Deirdre N. McCloskey, 65–69. New York and Oxford, UK: Oxford University Press.

Marx, Karl. 1867. *Capital: A Critique of Political Economy*. Edited by Friedrich Engels. Translated from the 4th German edition by Ernest Untermann. New York: Modern Library (Random House), 1906.

Marx, Karl. 1885. *Capital: A Critique of Political Economy* vol. 2, *The Process of Circulation of Capital*. Edited by Friedrich Engels. Translated from the 2nd German edition by Ernest Untermann. Chicago: Kerr, 1907. Reprint, Moscow: Progress Publishers, 1956. https://www.marxists.org/archive /marx/works/download/pdf/Capital-Volume-II.pdf.

Marx, Karl. 1894. *Capital: A Critique of Political Economy* vol. 3, *The Process of Capitalist Production as a Whole*. Edited by Friedrich Engels. Translated by Ernest Untermann. Chicago: Kerr, 1909. Reprint, Moscow: Institute of Marxism-Leninism, 1959. www.marxists.org/archive/marx/works /download/pdf/Capital-Volume-III.pdf.

Mauss, Marcel. 1925. *The Gift*. Translated by W. D. Halls. London: Routledge, 1990. Reprint, London: Routledge Classics, 2002.

Mazzucato, Mariana. 2013. *The Entrepreneurial State: Debunking Public vs. Private Sector Myths*. Reprint, London: Anthem Press, 2014.

McClay, Wilfred. 1993. "The Strange Career of 'The Lonely Crowd'; or, The Antinomies of Autonomy." In *The Culture of the Market: Historical Essays*, edited by T. L. Haskell and R. F. Teichgraeber III, 397–440. Cambridge, UK: Cambridge University Press.

McCloskey, Deirdre N. 1970. "Did Victorian Britain Fail?" *Economic History Review* 23 (December): 446–459. Reprinted in *Twentieth-Century Economic History: Critical Concepts in Economics*, edited by Lars Magnusson. London: Routledge, 2010.

McCloskey, Deirdre N., ed. 1972. *Essays on a Mature Economy: Britain After 1840*. Princeton, NJ: Princeton University Press.

McCloskey, Deirdre N. 1973. "New Perspectives on the Old Poor Law." *Explorations in Economic History* 10 (Summer): 419–436.

McCloskey, Deirdre N. 1980. "Magnanimous Albion: Free Trade and British National Income, 1841–1881." *Explorations in Economic History* 17: 303–320.

McCloskey, Deirdre N. 1985. *The Applied Theory of Price*. New York: Macmillan.

McCloskey, Deirdre N. 1990. *If You're So Smart: The Narrative of Economic Expertise*. Chicago: University of Chicago Press.

McCloskey, Deirdre N. 1991. "Voodoo Economics." *Poetics Today* 12, no. 2 (Summer): 287–300.

McCloskey, Deirdre N. 1993. Review of *In Pursuit of the Ph.D.*, by William Bowen and Neil Rudenstine. *Economics of Education Review* 4: 359–365.

McCloskey, Deirdre N. 1994. *Knowledge and Persuasion in Economics*. Cambridge, UK: Cambridge University Press.

McCloskey, Deirdre N. 1998. "Bourgeois Virtue and the History of *P* and *S*." *Journal of Economic History* 58, no. 2 (June): 297–317.

McCloskey, Deirdre N. 2000. "Post-Modern Free-Market Feminism: A Conversation with Gayatri Chakravorty Spivak." *Rethinking Marxism* 12, no. 4 (Winter): 23–37.

McCloskey, Deirdre N. 2001. "Getting It Right, and Left: Marxism and Competition." *Eastern Economic Journal* 27, no. 4: 515–520.

McCloskey, Deirdre N. 2002. "The Insanity of Letters of Recommendation." *Eastern Economic Journal* 28, no. 1: 137–140.

McCloskey, Deirdre N. 2003. "Notre Dame Loses." *Eastern Economic Journal* 29, no. 2: 309–315.

McCloskey, Deirdre N. 2006a. *The Bourgeois Virtues: Ethics for an Age of Commerce*. Chicago: University of Chicago Press.

McCloskey, Deirdre N. 2006b. "A Solution to the Alleged Inconsistency in the Neoclassical Theory of Markets: Reply to Guerrien's Reply." *Post-Autistic Economics Review* no. 39 (October). www.paecon.net/PAEReview/issue39/McCloskey39.htm.

McCloskey, Deirdre N. 2006c. "*Keukentafel* Economics and the History of British Imperialism." *South African Economic History Review* 21: 171–176.

McCloskey, Deirdre N. 2008. "Adam Smith, the Last of the Former Virtue Ethicists." *History of Political Economy* 40, no. 1: 43–71.

McCloskey, Deirdre N. 2010. *Bourgeois Dignity: Why Economics Can't Explain the Modern World*. Chicago: University of Chicago Press.

McCloskey, Deirdre N. 2012a. "What Michael Sandel Can't Buy: Review of Sandel's 'What Money Can't Buy.'" *Claremont Review of Books* 12 (Fall): 57–59. Revised and reprinted as "The Moral Limits of Communitarianism: What Michael Sandel Can't Buy." *ORDO* 64 (Spring 2013): 538–543.

McCloskey, Deirdre N. 2012b. "Sliding Into PoMo-ism from Samuelsonianism: Comment on Ruccio and Amariglio, *Postmodern Moments in Modern Economics*." *Rethinking Marxism* 24, no. 3: 355–359.

McCloskey, Deirdre N. 2016a. *Bourgeois Equality: How Ideas, Not Capital or Institutions, Enriched the World.* Chicago: University of Chicago Press.

McCloskey, Deirdre N. 2016b. "Christian Libertarianism Is What Our Politics Needs." In "Libertarianism, Yes! But *What Kind* of Libertarianism? Virtue vs. Libertinism or, a *Reason* Debate on Liberty, License, Coercion, and Responsibility." Edited by Nick Gillespie. *Reason,* June 9. http://reason.com/archives/2016/06/09/libertarianism-yes-but-what-kind-of-libe/2.

McCloskey, Deirdre N. 2018a. "Why Liberalism's Critics Fail." Review of *Why Liberalism Failed,* by Patrick Deneen. *Modern Age* 60, no. 3 (Summer). https://home.isi.org/why-liberalism%E2%80%99s-critics-fail.

McCloskey, Deirdre N. 2018b. "The Applied Theory of Bossing People Around: Thaler's Nobel." *Reason,* March: 8–9.

McCloskey, Deirdre N. 2018c. "A True but Nonobvious Proposition?" *Reason,* May. https://reason.com/archives/2018/04/03/a-true-but-nonobvious-proposit.

McCloskey, Deirdre N. 2018d. "The Two Movements in Economic Thought, 1700–2000: Empty Economic Boxes Revisited." *History of Economic Ideas* 26, no. 1: 63–95.

McCloskey, Deirdre N. 2019. "Manifesto for a New American Liberalism, or How to Be a Humane Libertarian." In *Economic Freedom and Prosperity: The Origins and Maintenance of Liberalization,* edited by Benjamin Powell. New York: Routledge.

McCloskey, Deirdre N., and Art Carden. n.d. "Leave Me Alone and I'll Make You Rich and Wise: How the Bourgeois Deal Enriched the World." Unpublished manuscript.

McCloskey, Deirdre N., and Santhi Hejeebu. 1999. "The Reproving of Karl Polanyi." *Critical Review* 13 (Summer/Fall): 285–314.

McCloskey, Deirdre N., and Santhi Hejeebu. 2004. "Polanyi and the History of Capitalism: Rejoinder to Blyth." *Critical Review* 16, no. 1: 135–142.

McCloskey, Deirdre N., and Arjo Klamer. 1989. "The Rhetoric of Disagreement," *Rethinking Marxism* 2 (Fall): 140–161. Reprinted in *Why Economists Disagree,* edited by D. H. Prychitko. Albany, NY: SUNY Press, 1998.

McCloskey, Deirdre N., and Arjo Klamer. 1995. "One Quarter of GDP is Persuasion." *American Economic Review Papers and Proceedings* 85, no. 2: 191–195.

McCloskey, Robert Green. 1951. *American Conservatism in the Age of Enterprise: A Study of William Graham Sumner, Stephen J. Field, and Andrew Carnegie.* Cambridge, MA: Harvard University Press.

McNeill, William H. 1974. *Venice, the Hinge of Europe 1081–1797*. Chicago: University of Chicago Press.

Megill, Allan. 2002. *Karl Marx: The Burden of Reason*. Lanham, MD: Rowman and Littlefield.

Meisner, Jason, and Annie Sweeney. 2017. "Landmark Investigation Says Chicago Police Conduct Harms Residents, Endangers Officers." *Chicago Tribune*, January 14.

Melville, Herman. 1856. "Bartleby." In *The Piazza Tales*, 31–108. New York: Dix and Edwards.

Mencken, H. L. 1916. *A Little Book in C Major*. New York: John Lane.

Mencken, H. L. 1922. *Prejudices: Third Series*. New York: A. A. Knopf.

Mencken, H. L. 1926. *Notes on Democracy*. New York: A. A. Knopf. Reprint, New York: Dissident Books, 2009.

Mendelson, Cheryl. 1999. *Home Comforts: The Art and Science of Keeping House*. New York: Scribner.

Midgley, Mary. 1984. *Wickedness: A Philosophical Essay*. London: Routledge and Kegan Paul.

Mielants, Eric H. 2008. *The Origins of Capitalism and the "Rise of the West."* Philadelphia: Temple University Press.

Milanovic, Branko, Peter H. Lindert, and Jeffrey G. Williamson. 2011. "Pre-Industrial Inequality." *Economic Journal* 121: 255–272.

Mill, John Stuart. 1836. "On the Definition of Political Economy; and on the Method of Philosophical Investigation in That Science." *London and Westminster Review*, October: 1–16.

Mill, John Stuart. 1859. *On Liberty*. 2nd ed. London: John W. Parker and Son. Reprint, Kitchener, Ontario: Batoche Books, 2001.

Mill, John Stuart. 1871. *Principles of Political Economy, with Some of Their Applications to Social Philosophy*. Reprint, London: Longmans, Green, 1909.

Mingardi, Alberto. 2017. "Classical Liberalism in Italian Economic Thought from the Time of Unification." *Econ Journal Watch* 14, no. 1 (January): 22–54.

Mises, Ludwig von. 1949. *Human Action: A Treatise on Economics*. New Haven, CT: Yale University Press.

Mises, Ludwig von. 1951. *Socialism: An Economic and Sociological Analysis*. New Haven, CT: Yale University Press.

Mises, Ludwig von. 1956. *The Anti-Capitalistic Mentality*. Princeton, NJ: Van Nostrand. Reprint, Indianapolis, IN: Liberty Fund, 2006.

Mokyr, Joel. 2010. *The Enlightened Economy: An Economic History of Britain 1700–1850*. New Haven, CT: Yale University Press.

Mokyr, Joel. 2014. "What Today's Economic Gloomsayers Are Missing." *Wall Street Journal,* August 8.

Mueller, John. 1999. *Capitalism, Democracy, and Ralph's Pretty Good Grocery.* Princeton, NJ: Princeton University Press.

Mueller, John. 2006. *Overblown: How Politicians and the Terrorism Industry Inflate National Security Threats, and Why We Believe Them.* New York: Free Press.

Murray, John E., and Metin M. Cosgel. 1999. "Between God and Market: Influences of Economy and Spirit on Shaker Communal Dairying, 1830–1875." *Social Science History* 23 (Spring): 41–65.

Nelson, Robert H. 1991. *Reaching for Heaven on Earth: The Theological Meaning of Economics.* Lanham, MD: Rowman and Littlefield.

New Orleans Times-Picayune. 2006. "Commend Center." February 23.

Nordhaus, William D. 2004. "Schumpeterian in the American Economy: Theory and Measurement." NBER Working Paper No. 10433, National Bureau of Economic Research, Cambridge, MA, April. www.nber.org/papers/w10433.

North, Douglass C., John Joseph Wallis, and Barry R. Weingast. 2009. *Violence and Social Orders: A Conceptual Framework for Interpreting Recorded Human History.* Cambridge, UK: Cambridge University Press.

Nozick, Robert. 1974. *Anarchy, State, and Utopia.* New York: Basic Books.

Nozick, Robert. 1981. *Philosophical Explanations.* Cambridge, MA: Harvard University Press.

Nozick, Robert. 1989. *The Examined Life: Philosophical Meditations.* New York: Simon and Schuster.

Nozick, Robert. 2001. *Invariances: The Structure of the Objective World.* Cambridge, MA: Harvard University Press.

Nussbaum, Martha C., and Amartya Sen, eds. 1993. *The Quality of Life.* Oxford, UK: Clarendon Press.

Nye, John V. C. 1997. "Thinking About the State: Property Rights, Trade, and Changing Contractual Arrangements in a World with Coercion." In *The Frontiers of the New Institutional Economics,* edited by John Drobak and John V. C. Nye, 121–142. New York and London: Academic Press.

O'Rourke, P. J. 1988. "What Do They Do for Fun in Warsaw?" In *Holidays in Hell.* New York: Vintage Books.

O'Siadhail, Michael. 2018. *The Five Quintets.* Waco, TX: Baylor University Press.

Ogilvie, Sheilagh. 2019. *The European Guilds: An Economic Analysis.* Princeton, NJ: Princeton University Press.

Organisation for Economic Co-operation and Development (OECD). 2018. "Youth Unemployment Rate (Indicator)." Accessed January 3, 2018. https://data.oecd.org/unemp/youth-unemployment-rate.htm.

Orwell, George. 1937. *The Road to Wigan Pier.* London: Gollancz.

Packer, George. 2013. *The Unwinding: An Inner History of the New America.* New York: Farrar, Straus and Giroux.

Pagano, Patrizio, and Massimo Sbracia. 2014. "The Secular Stagnation Hypothesis: A Review of the Debate and Some Insights." Questioni di Economia e Finanza (Occasional Papers) no. 231, Banca D'Italia.

Paine, Thomas. 1776. *Common Sense.* Reprint, New York: Peter Eckler, 1922.

Paine, Thomas. 1794, 1795, 1807. *The Age of Reason.* Reprint, Indianapolis, IN: Bobbs-Merrill, 1975.

Palmer, Tom G. 2009. *Realizing Freedom: Libertarian Theory, History, and Practice.* Expanded ed. Washington, DC: Cato Institute.

Palmer, Tom G., ed. 2011. *The Morality of Capitalism.* Ottawa, IL: Jameson Books.

Palmer, Tom G. 2013. "Why Be Libertarian?" In *Why Liberty: Your Life, Your Choices, Your Future,* edited by Tom G. Palmer, chap. 1. Ottawa, IL: Jameson Books.

Partridge, H. 1967. "Freedom." In *The Encyclopedia of Philosophy,* edited by Paul Edwards. New York: Macmillan.

Peacock, Alan. 1987. "Economic Freedom." In vol. 2 of *The New Palgrave: A Dictionary of Economics,* edited by John Eatwell, Murray Milgate, and Peter Newman, 88–93. London: Macmillan.

Pearson, James. 2015. "North Korea's Black Market Becoming the New Normal." Reuters, October 28. www.reuters.com/article/us-northkorea-change-insight/north-koreas-black-market-becoming-the-new-normal-idUSKCN0SN00320151029.

Peart, Sandra J., and David M. Levy, eds. 2008a. *The Street Porter and the Philosopher: Conversations in Analytical Egalitarianism.* Ann Arbor: University of Michigan Press.

Peart, Sandra J., and David M. Levy. 2008b. "Denying Human Homogeneity: Eugenics and the Making of Postclassical Economics." In *The Street Porter and the Philosopher,* edited by Peart and Levy, 338–357.

Perkins, Dwight H. 1995. "The Transition from Central Planning: East Asia's Experience." In *Social Capability and Long-Term Economic Growth,* edited by Bon Ho Koo and Dwight H. Perkins, 221–241. Basingstoke, UK: Macmillan.

Perkins, Dwight H., and Thomas G. Rawski. 2008. "Forecasting China's Economic Growth to 2025." In *China's Great Economic Transformation*, edited by Loren Brandt and Thomas G. Rawski, 829–886. Cambridge, UK: Cambridge University Press.

Perry, Mark J. 2018. "Census Data Released Today Show Continued Gains for Middle-Class Americans and Little Evidence of Rising Income Inequality." *AEIdeas* (blog), September 12. www.aei.org/publication/some-charts-from-the-census-data-released-this-week-on-us-incomes-in-2017-showing-impressive-gains-for-americans/.

Persky, Joseph. 1990. "A Dismal Romantic." *Journal of Economic Perspectives* 4, no. 4: 165–172.

Peterson, Christopher, and Martin E. P. Seligman. 2004. *Character Strengths and Virtues: A Handbook and Classification*. Oxford, UK: Oxford University Press.

Pettegree, Andrew. 2014. *The Invention of News: How the World Came to Know About Itself*. New Haven, CT: Yale University Press.

Phelps, Edmund S. 2013. *Mass Flourishing: How Grassroots Innovation Created Jobs, Challenge, and Change*. Princeton, NJ: Princeton University Press.

Piketty, Thomas. 2014. *Capital in the Twenty-First Century*. Translated by Arthur Goldhammer. Cambridge, MA: Harvard University Press. Originally published as *Le capital au XXIe siècle* (Paris: Éditions du Seuil, 2013).

Piller, Charles, and Jia You. 2018. "Hidden Conflicts? An Investigation Finds a Pattern of After-the-Fact Compensation by Pharma to Those Advising the U.S. Government on Drug Approvals." *Science* 361 (July 6): 17–23.

Plato. 1914. *Phaedrus*. In *Plato I: Euthyphro, Apology, Crito, Phaedo, Phaedrus*. Translated by H. N. Fowler. Cambridge, MA: Harvard University Press.

Plato. 1921. *Sophist*. In *Plato VII: Theaetetus, Sophist*. Translated by H. N. Fowler. Cambridge, MA: Harvard University Press.

Plato. 1925. *Gorgias*. In *Plato III: Lysis, Symposium, Gorgias*. Translated by W. R. M. Lamb. Cambridge, MA: Harvard University Press.

Polanyi, Michael. 1951. *The Logic of Liberty*. Chicago: University of Chicago Press.

Pomeranz, Kenneth, and Steven Topik. 2012. *The World That Trade Created*. 3rd ed. Armonk, NY: M. E. Sharpe.

Pope, Alexander. 1731. "Epistle IV to Richard Boyle, Earl of Burlington." In *Pope: Poetical Works*, edited by H. Davis, 314–321. Oxford, UK: Oxford University Press, 1966.

Posner, Eric A. 2018. "The Far-Reaching Threats of a Conservative Court." *New York Times,* October 23.

Posner, Eric A., and E. Glen Weyl. 2018. *Radical Markets: Uprooting Capitalism and Democracy for a Just Society.* Princeton, NJ: Princeton University Press.

Posner, Richard A. 1979. "Utilitarianism, Economics, and Legal Theory." *Journal of Legal Studies* 8: 103–140.

Posner, Richard A. 1985. "Wealth Maximization Revisited." *Notre Dame Journal of Law, Ethics, and Public Policy* 2: 85–105.

Postrel, Virginia. 1998. *The Future and Its Enemies: The Growing Conflict over Creativity, Enterprise, and Progress.* New York: Free Press.

Powers, Kirsten. 2015. *The Silencing: How the Left Is Killing Free Speech.* Washington, DC: Regnery.

Prestona, Stephanie D., and Frans B. M. de Waal. 2002. "Empathy: Its Ultimate and Proximate Bases." *Behavioral and Brain Sciences* 25: 1–72.

Quintilian. 1929. *Institutio Oratia.* Translated by H. E. Butler. Loeb Classical Library. Cambridge, MA: Harvard University Press.

Radford, R. A. 1945. "The Economics of a POW Camp." *Economica* (new series) 12: 189–201.

Rahn, Richard W. 2018a. "The Unthinking and the Unobservant." *Washington Times,* July 2. www.washingtontimes.com/news/2018/jul/2/history -shows-that-socialism-brings-misery-to-nati/.

Rahn, Richard W. 2018b. "Why Some Problems Seem Never to Be Solved." *Washington Times,* July 9. www.washingtontimes.com/news/2018/jul/9 /why-some-problems-seem-never-to-be-solved/.

Rawls, John. 1958. "Justice as Fairness." *Philosophical Review* 67, no. 2: 164–194.

Rawls, John. 1971. *A Theory of Justice.* Cambridge, MA: Harvard University Press.

Rawls, John. 1985. "Justice as Fairness: Political Not Metaphysical." *Philosophy and Public Affairs* 14 (Summer): 223–251.

Reddy, William M. 2001. *The Navigation of Feeling: A Framework for the History of Emotions.* Cambridge, UK: Cambridge University Press.

Reich, Robert B. 1991. *The Work of Nations: Preparing Ourselves for 21st-Century Capitalism.* London: Simon and Schuster.

Reich, Robert B. 2014. "How to Shrink Inequality." *The Nation,* May 6.

Reid, Michael. 2017. *Forgotten Continent: The Battle for Latin America's Soul.* Revised ed. New Haven, CT: Yale University Press.

Reinhart, Carmen M., and Kenneth S. Rogoff. 2011. "Growth in a Time of Debt." NBER Working Paper No. 15639, National Bureau of Economic Research, Cambridge, MA, December. www.nber.org/papers/w15639.

Ridley, Matt. 2014. "Start Spreading the Good News on Inequality." *The Times* (London), June 2. www.thetimes.co.uk/article/start-spreading-the-good -news-on-inequality-nxo3pwjtv6d.

Riis, Jacob. 1890. *How the Other Half Lives: Studies Among the Tenements of New York*. New York: Charles Scribner's Sons.

Rimlinger, Gaston V. 1968. "Social Change and Social Security in Germany." *Journal of Human Resources* 3(4): 409–421.

Robertson, D. H. 1923. *The Control of Industry*. London: Nisbet and Co.

Robine, Jean-Marie, Siu Lan K. Cheung, Sophie Le Roy, Herman Van Oyen, Clare Griffiths, Jean-Pierre Michel, and François Richard Herrmann. 2008. "Plus de 70 000 décès en Europe au cours de l'été 2003." *Comptes Rendus Biologies* 331, no. 2: 171–178.

Rogge, Benjamin A. 1962. "The Case for Economic Freedom." In *A Maverick's Defense of Freedom: Selected Writings and Speeches of Benjamin A. Rogge,* edited by Dwight Lee, 3–9. Indianapolis, IN: Liberty Fund, 2010.

Rönnbäck, Klas. 2009. "Integration of Global Commodity Markets in the Early Modern Era." *European Review of Economic History* 13: 95–129.

Roosevelt, Franklin Delano. 1941. State of the Union Address to Congress, January 6.

Rorty, Amélie Oksenberg. 1983. "Experiments in Philosophical Genre: Descartes' *Meditations*." *Critical Inquiry* 9 (March): 545–565.

Rosling, Hans, Ola Rosling, and Anna Rosling Rönnlund. 2018. *Factfulness: Ten Reasons We're Wrong About the World—and Why Things Are Better than You Think*. London: Hodder and Stoughton.

Rothbard, Murray N. 1982. *The Ethics of Liberty*. Atlantic Highlands, NJ: Humanities Press. Reprint, New York: New York University Press, 1998.

Rousseau, Jean-Jacques. 1755. *Discourse on the Origin of Inequality*. In *Rousseau: The Basic Political Writings,* edited by Donald A. Cress, 25–109. Indianapolis, IN: Hackett, 2011.

Rousseau, Jean-Jacques. 1762. *Du contrat social*. Amsterdam: Marc-Michel Rey.

Rowley, Charles, and Alan Peacock. 1975. *Welfare Economics: A Liberal ReInterpretation*. London: Martin Robertson.

Ruger, William, and Jason Sorens. 2016. "The Case for 'Virtue Libertarianism' Over Libertinism." In "Libertarianism, Yes! But *What Kind* of Libertarianism? Virtue vs. Libertinism or, a *Reason* Debate on Liberty, License,

Coercion, and Responsibility." Edited by Nick Gillespie. *Reason*, June 9. http://reason.com/archives/2016/06/09/libertarianism-yes-but-what-kind-of-libe/.

Rumbold, Richard. 1685. "Speech from the Scaffold." In *The Levellers and the English Revolution*, by Henry Noel Brailsford. Stanford. CA: Stanford University Press, 1961.

Ryan, Alan. "Liberty." 1987. In *The New Palgrave: A Dictionary of Economics*, edited by John Eatwell, Murray Milgate, and Peter Newman. London: Macmillan.

Safi, Michael. 2017. "India Weighs Up the Return on Cash Handouts for the Poorest." *Guardian*, February 6. www.theguardian.com/global-development/2017/feb/06/india-weighs-return-cash-handouts-poorest-universal-basic-income-arvind-subramanian.

Sahlins, Marshall. 1976. *Culture and Practical Reason*. Chicago: University of Chicago Press.

Sahlins, Marshall. 2003. "Preface to New Edition." In *Stone Age Economics*. 2nd ed. London: Routledge.

Sala-i-Martin, Xavier. 2006. "The World's Distribution of Income: Falling Poverty and Convergence." *Quarterly Journal of Economics* 121, no. 2: 351–397.

Sala-i-Martin, Xavier, and Maxim Pinkovskiy. 2010. "Parametric Estimations of the World Distribution of Income." VoxEU.org, Centre for Economic Policy Research, London, January 22. www.voxeu.org/article/parametric-estimations-world-distribution-income.

Sandel, Michael. 2012. *What Money Can't Buy: The Moral Limits of Markets*. New York: Farrar, Straus and Giroux.

Saunders, Peter. 2013. "Researching Poverty: Methods, Results, and Impact." *Economic and Labour Relations Review* 24, no. 2: 205–218.

Sayers, Dorothy L. 2004. "Why Work?" In *Letters to a Diminished Church*, 118–139. Nashville, TN: Thomas Nelson.

Schjeldahl, Peter. 2004. "Dealership: How Marian Goodman Quietly Changed the Contemporary-Art Market." *New Yorker*, February 2: 36–41.

Schlesinger, Arthur M., Jr. 1945. *The Age of Jackson*. Boston: Little, Brown and Company.

Schlesinger, Arthur M., Jr. 1962. *The Politics of Hope*. Boston: Riverside Press.

Schmidtz, David. 1993. "Reasons for Altruism." In *Altruism*, edited by Ellen Frankel Paul, Fred D. Miller, and Jeffrey Paul, 52–68. Cambridge, UK: Cambridge University Press. Reprinted in *The Gift: An Interdisciplinary*

Perspective, edited by Aafke E. Komter, 164–175. Amsterdam: University of Amsterdam Press, 1996.

Schmidtz, David. 2011. "Nonideal Theory: What It Is and What It Needs to Be." *Ethics* 121, no. 4: 772–796.

Schor, Juliet B. 1993. *The Overworked American: The Unexpected Decline of Leisure.* New York: Basic Books.

Schor, Juliet B. 1998. *The Overspent American: Upscaling, Downshifting, and the New Consumer.* New York: Basic Books.

Schor, Juliet B. 2004. *Born to Buy: The Commercialized Child and the New Consumer Culture.* New York: Scribner.

Schultz, Kevin M. 2015. *Buckley and Mailer: The Difficult Friendship That Shaped the Sixties.* New York: W. W. Norton.

Schultze, Charles L. 1983. "Industrial Policy: A Dissent." *Brookings Review* 2 (Fall): 3–12.

Schumpeter, Joseph A. 1942. *Capitalism, Socialism, and Democracy.* 3rd ed. New York: Harper and Row, 1950.

Schumpeter, Joseph A. 1954. *History of Economic Analysis.* Edited by Elizabeth Boody Schumpeter. London: Routledge.

Schuttner, Scott. 1998. *Basic Stairbuilding.* Newtown, CT: Taunton Press.

Scitovsky, Tibor. 1976. *The Joyless Economy: An Inquiry into Human Satisfaction and Consumer Dissatisfaction.* New York: Oxford University Press.

Scruton, Roger. 2014. *How to Be a Conservative.* London and New York: Bloomsbury.

Seabrook, John. 1993. "The Flash of Genius." *New Yorker,* January 11.

Seager, Henry R. 1913. "The Minimum Wage as Part of a Program for Social Reform." *Annals of the American Academy of Political and Social Science* 48 (July): 3–12.

Seaton, James. 1996. *Cultural Conservatism, Political Liberalism: From Criticism to Cultural Studies.* Ann Arbor: University of Michigan Press.

Sellar, Walter Carruthers, and Robert Julian Yeatman. 1931. *1066 and All That: A Memorable History of England.* New York: Dutton.

Sen, Amartya. 1985. *Commodities and Capabilities.* Amsterdam: Elsevier Science.

Sen, Amartya. 1987. *On Ethics and Economics.* Oxford: Blackwell.

Sen, Amartya. 1999. *Development as Freedom.* Oxford: Oxford University Press.

Sender, Katherine. 2007. "Professional Homosexuals: The Politics of Sexual Identification in Gay and Lesbian Media and Marketing." In *Media/Queered: Visibility and Its Discontents,* edited by Kevin G. Barnhurst, 89–106. New York: Peter Lang.

Shilts, Wade. 2007. "Making McCloskey's Rhetoric Empirical: Company Law and Tragedies of the Commons in Victorian Britain." In *Transdisciplinary Readings: Essays in Rhetoric and Economics*, edited by Edward Clift. Lewiston, NY: Mellen Press.

Shlaes, Amity. 2007. *The Forgotten Man: A New History of the Great Depression*. New York: HarperCollins.

Silver, Allan. 1989. "Friendship and Trust as Moral Ideals: An Historical Approach." *European Journal of Sociology* 30, no. 2: 274–297.

Skidelsky, Robert. 2018. *Money and Government: The Past and Future of Economics*. New Haven, CT: Yale University Press.

Skinner, Quentin. 1969. "Meaning and Understanding in the History of Ideas." *History and Theory* 8: 3–53.

Skwire, Sarah, and Steven Horwitz. 2014. "Thomas Piketty's Literary Offenses." *The Freeman* 64 (October): 25.

Smith, Adam. 1762–1766. *Lectures on Jurisprudence*. Edited by R. L. Meek, D. D. Raphael, and P. G. Stein. Oxford, UK: Oxford University Press, 1978.

Smith, Adam. 1776. *An Inquiry into the Nature and Causes of the Wealth of Nations*. 2 vols. Edited by R. H. Campbell and A. S. Skinner. Oxford, UK: Oxford University Press, 1976.

Smith, Adam. 1790. *The Theory of Moral Sentiments*, 6th ed. (1st ed. 1759.) Edited by D. D. Raphael and A. L. Macfie. Oxford, UK: Oxford University Press, 1976.

Smith, Vernon L. 2002. "Constructivist and Ecological Rationality in Economics." Nobel Prize Lecture, December 8. In *Les Prix Nobel: The Nobel Prizes 2002*, edited by Tore Frängsmyr. Stockholm: Nobel Foundation, 2003. www.nobelprize.org/uploads/2018/06/smith-lecture-2.pdf.

Smith, Vernon L., and Bart J. Wilson. 2017. "'Sentiments,' Conduct, and Trust in the Laboratory." *Social Philosophy and Policy* 34, no. 1: 25–55.

Smith, Vernon L., and Bart J. Wilson. 2018. *Humanomics: Moral Sentiments and the Wealth of Nations for the Twenty-First Century*. Cambridge, UK, and New York: Cambridge University Press.

Snyder, Don J. 1997. "Winter Work." In *Survival Stories: Memoirs of Crisis*, edited by Kathryn Rhett, 67–89. New York: Anchor.

Sombart, Werner. 1906. *Why Is There No Socialism in the United States?* Edited by C. T. Husbands. Translated by Patricia M. Hocking and C. T. Husbands. White Plains, NY: Sharpe, 1976. Originally published as *Warum gibt es in den Vereinigten Staaten keinen Sozialismus?* (Tübingen: J. C. B. Mohr).

Sowell, Thomas. 2009. *Applied Economics: Thinking Beyond Stage One.* Revised ed. New York: Basic Books.

Sowell, Thomas. 2015. *Basic Economics.* 5th ed. New York: Basic Books.

Sowell, Thomas. 2016. "Socialism for the Uninformed." Creators, May 31. www.creators.com/read/thomas-sowell/05/16/socialism-for-the-uninformed.

Spencer, Herbert. 1853. "Over-Legislation." *Westminster Review,* July. Reprinted in *The Man Versus the State, with Six Essays on Government, Society, and Freedom.* Edited by Eric Mack. Indianapolis, IN: Liberty Fund, 1981.

Spencer, Herbert. 1891. Introduction to *A Plea for Liberty.* 2nd ed. Edited by Thomas Mackay. London: Murray. Reprint, Indianapolis, IN: Liberty Fund, 1981.

Spivak, Gayatri Chakravorty. 1990. *The Post-Colonial Critic: Interviews, Strategies, Dialogues.* Edited by Sarah Harasym. New York: Routledge.

Stark, Rodney. 2001. *One True God: Historical Consequences of Monotheism.* Princeton, NJ: Princeton University Press.

State of Illinois. 1970. Constitution of the State of Illinois. Accessed February 17, 2019. www.ilga.gov/commission/lrb/conent.htm.

Staveren, Irene van. 1999. "Caring for Economics: An Aristotelian Perspective." PhD diss., Erasmus Universiteit Rotterdam. Delft: Eburon. Republished as *The Values of Economics: An Aristotelian Perspective.* London, Routledge, 2001.

Steinbeck, John. 1939. *The Grapes of Wrath.* New York: Viking Press.

Steinfeld, Robert J., and Stanley L. Engerman. 1997. "Labor—Free or Coerced? An Historical Reassessment of Differences and Similarities." In *Free and Unfree Labour: The Debate Continues,* edited by T. Brass and M. van der Linden. New York: Peter Lang.

Stewart, Dugald. 1795. *Account of the Life and Writings of Adam Smith, LL.D.* In *Essays on Philosophical Subjects,* by Adam Smith, 269–351. Edited by Ian Simpson Ross. New York: Oxford University Press, 1980.

Stiglitz, Joseph E. 2006. *Making Globalization Work.* New York: W. W. Norton.

Stiglitz, Joseph E. 2016. "Is the Euro to Blame for Europe's Problems?" Interview by David Brancaccio. *Marketplace,* National Public Radio, August 18. www.marketplace.org/2016/08/17/economy/stiglitz-euro-globalization-trade.

Storr, Virgil, Stefanie Haeffele-Balch, and Laura E. Grube. 2015. *Community Revival in the Wake of Disaster: Lessons in Local Entrepreneurship.* New York and London: Palgrave Macmillan.

Stossel, John. 2015. "Moving Companies: Who Chooses Who Moves Our Stuff?" *Stossel in the Classroom,* free ed. DVD. Philadelphia: Center for Independent Thought. http://stosselintheclassroom.org/videos/moving _companies/.

Stossel, John, and Maxim Lott. 2018. "Seattle's 'Amazon Tax.'" *Reason.com.* May 15.

Strain, Michael R., and Stan A. Veuger, eds. 2016. *Economic Freedom and Human Flourishing: Perspectives from Political Philosophy.* Washington, DC: Rowman and Littlefield.

Sumner, William Graham. 1881. "The Argument Against Protective Taxes." *Princeton Review,* March: 241–259.

Swanson, Ana, and Brad Plumer. 2018. "Trump Slaps Steep Tariffs on Foreign Washing Machines and Solar Products." *New York Times,* January 22.

Tacitus. 1914. *Dialogus.* In vol. 1 of *Tacitus in Five Volumes.* Translated by William Peterson and Michael Winterbottom. Cambridge, MA: Harvard University Press.

Tanzi, Vito, and Ludger Schuknecht. 2000. *Public Spending in the 20th Century: A Global Perspective.* New York: Cambridge University Press.

Taylor, Alan. 2016. *American Revolutions: A Continental History, 1750–1804.* New York: W. W. Norton.

Taylor, Charles. 1979. "What's Wrong with Negative Liberty." In *The Idea of Freedom: Essays in Honor of Isaiah Berlin,* edited by Alan Ryan, 175–193. Oxford, UK: Oxford University Press.

Taylor, Michael. 1982. *Community, Anarchy and Liberty.* Cambridge, UK: Cambridge University Press.

Thiel, Julia. 2017. "Why Chicago's Once-Promising Food Truck Scene Stalled Out." *Chicago Reader,* March 29.

Thoreau, Henry David. 1849. "Resistance to Civil Government." In *Political Writings,* edited by Nancy L. Rosenblum, 1–21. Cambridge, UK: Cambridge University Press, 1996.

Thurow, Lester. 1985. *The Zero-Sum Solution: Building a World-Class American Economy.* New York: Simon and Schuster.

Thwaite, B. H. 1902. *The American Invasion.* London: Swan Sonnenschein.

Tillich, Paul, and Carl Richard Wegener. 1919. "Answer to an Inquiry of the Protestant Consistory of Brandenburg." Translated by Mrs. Douglas Stange. *Metanoia* 3, no. 3 (September 1971).

Tirole, Jean. 2017. *Economics for the Common Good.* Translated by Steven Rendall. Princeton, NJ: Princeton University Press.

Tocqueville, Alexis de. 1840. *Democracy in America*. Translated by Phillips Bradley. New York: Vintage Books, 1954.

Todorov, Tzvetan. 2000. *Hope and Memory: Lessons from the Twentieth Century*. Translated by David Bellos. Princeton, NJ: Princeton University Press, 2003.

Tomasi, John. 2012. *Free Market Fairness*. Princeton, NJ: Princeton University Press.

Toynbee, Arnold. 1884. *Lectures on the Industrial Revolution in England*. 2nd ed. London: Rivington's, 1887.

Transparency International. 2017. *Corruption Perceptions Index 2016*. Berlin: Transparency International. www.transparency.org/whatwedo /publication/corruption_perceptions_index_2016.

Trevor-Roper, Hugh. 1940. *Archbishop Laud: 1573–1645*. 2nd ed. London: Macmillan, 1962.

Trilling, Lionel. 1948a. "The Princess Casamassima." Introduction to *The Princess Casamassima*, by Henry James. New York: Macmillan.

Trilling, Lionel. 1948b. "Manners, Morals, and the Novel." *Kenyon Review* 10, no. 1: 11–27.

Trollope, Anthony. 1867–1868. *Phineas Finn: The Irish Member*. In *The Palliser Novels*. 6 vols. Edited by Jacques Bertoud. Oxford, UK: Oxford University Press, 1982.

Tronto, Joan. 1993. *Moral Boundaries: A Political Argument for an Ethic of Care*. New York and London: Routledge.

Tucker, Jeffrey A. 2017. *Right-Wing Collectivism: The Other Threat to Liberty*. Atlanta: Foundation for Economic Education.

Tullock, Gordon. 1967. "The Welfare Costs of Tariffs, Monopolies, and Theft." *Western Economic Journal* 5: 224–232.

Tullock, Gordon. 1975. "The Transitional Gains Trap." *Bell Journal of Economics* 6, no. 2 (Autumn): 671–678.

Twain, Mark. 1897. *Following the Equator*, vol. 1. In vol. 5 of *The Writings of Mark Twain*. Reprint, 1968.

Twain, Mark. 1995. *Selected Writings of an American Skeptic*. Edited by Victor Doyno. Amherst, NY: Prometheus Books.

Tyldum, Morten, dir. 2014. *The Imitation Game*. Motion picture. New York: Weinstein Company.

UAW-CIO. 1955. *Automation: A Report to the UAW-CIO Economic and Collective Bargaining Conference Held in Detroit, Michigan, the 12th and 13th of November 1954*. Detroit: UAW-CIO Education Department.

Ulrich, Laurel Thatcher. 1990. *A Midwife's Tale: The Life of Martha Ballard, Based on Her Diary, 1785–1812*. New York: Vintage/Random House.

U.S. Government Accountability Office. 2005. *Understanding the Tax Reform Debate: Background Criteria and Questions*. GAO-05-1009SP. Washington, DC: Government Accountability Office. www.gao.gov/products/GAO -05-1009SP.

Van Doren, Carl. 1938. *Benjamin Franklin*. New York: Viking Press. Reprint, New York: Crown Publishers, 1987.

Veblen, Thorstein. 1899. *The Theory of the Leisure Class*. New York: Macmillan.

Velthuis, Olav. 2007. *Talking Prices: Symbolic Meanings of Prices on the Market for Contemporary Art*. Paperback ed. Princeton, NJ: Princeton University Press.

Venezuelanalysis.com. 2007. "Joseph Stiglitz, in Caracas, Praises Venezuela's Economic Policies." October 11. https://venezuelanalysis.com/news /2719.

Vickers, Brian. 1970. *Classical Rhetoric in English Poetry*. London: Macmillan. Reprint, Carbondale: Southern Illinois University Press, 1989.

Walker, Sheri, and Clark Nardinelli. 2016. "Consumer Expenditure on FDA Regulated Products: 20 Cents of Every Dollar." *FDA Voice* (blog), Food and Drug Administration, Silver Spring, MD, November 1. https://blogs .fda.gov/fdavoice/index.php/2016/11/consumer-expenditure-on-fda -regulated-products-20-cents-of-every-dollar/.

Wallerstein, Immanuel. 1974. *The Modern World-System* vol. 1, *Capitalist Agriculture and the Origins of the European World-Economy in the Sixteenth Century*. New York/London: Academic Press.

Wallerstein, Immanuel. 1983. *Historical Capitalism; with, Capitalist Civilization*. London: Verso. Reprint, London: Verso, 1995.

Walzer, Michael. 2008. "Does the Free Market Corrode Moral Character? Of Course It Does." Templeton.org, John Templeton Foundation. Accessed February 25, 2019. https://web.archive.org/web/20091211111449 /http://www.templeton.org:80/market/PDF/Walzer.pdf.

Warden, Rob. 2007. "Ignoring an Injustice." *Chicago Tribune*, April 29.

Warren, Kenneth. 2001. *Big Steel: The First Century of the United States Steel Corporation 1901–2001*. Pittsburgh, PA: University of Pittsburgh Press.

Wasserstein, Ronald L., and Nicole A. Lazar. 2016. "The ASA's Statement on *p*-Values: Context, Process, and Purpose." *American Statistician* 70, no. 2: 129–133.

Waterman, Anthony M. C. 1991. *Revolution, Economics and Religion: Christian Political Economy, 1798–1833*. Cambridge, UK: Cambridge University Press.

Waterman, Anthony M. C. 2012. "Adam Smith and Malthus on High Wages." *European Journal of the History of Economic Thought* 19: 409–429.

Wearden, Graeme. 2014. "Oxfam: 85 Richest People as Wealthy as Poorest Half of the World." *Guardian*, January 20. www.theguardian.com/business /2014/jan/20/oxfam-85-richest-people-half-of-the-world.

Webb, Sidney. 1912. "The Economic Theory of a Legal Minimum Wage." *Journal of Political Economy* 20, no. 10: 973–998.

Weber, Max. 1922. *Wirtschaft und Gesellschaft*. Tübingen: Mohr.

Weber, Max. 1927. *General Economic History*. Translated by Frank H. Knight. New York: Greenberg. Reprint, New Brunswick, New Jersey: Transaction Books, 1981. Originally published as *Wirtschaftsgeschichte* (Munich and Leipzig: Duncker and Humblot, 1923).

Weber, Max. 1930. *The Protestant Ethic and the Spirit of Capitalism*. Translated by Talcott Parsons, from the 1920 German edition. London: Allen and Unwin. Reprint, New York: Scribner's, 1958. Originally published as *Die protestantische Ethik und der Geist des Kapitalismus* (Tübingen: Mohr, 1904).

White, James Boyd. 1984. *When Words Lose Their Meaning*. Chicago: University of Chicago Press.

White, James Boyd. 1990. *Justice as Translation: An Essay in Cultural and Legal Criticism*. Chicago: University of Chicago Press.

White, Mark D., ed. 2010. *Accepting the Invisible Hand*. New York and London: Palgrave Macmillan.

Whitford, David. 2005. "The Most Famous Story We Never Told." *Fortune*, September 19.

Whitman, Walt. 1855. "Song of Myself." In vol. 1 of *Leaves of Grass: A Textual Variorum of the Printed Poems, 1855–1856*, edited by Sculley Bradley, Harold W. Blodgett, Arthur Golden, and William White. New York: New York University Press, 1980.

Wilkinson, Will. 2012. "Market Democracy and Dirty Ideal Theory." *Bleeding Heart Libertarians* (blog), June 15. http://bleedingheartlibertarians.com /2012/06/market-democracy-and-dirty-ideal-theory/.

Will, George F. 2018. "The Sprawling, Intrusive Administrative State Is Keeping You Unwell." *Washington Post*, August 15.

Williams, Bernard. 1972. *Morality: An Introduction to Ethics.* Canto ed. Cambridge, UK: Cambridge University Press, 1993.

Williams, Ernest Edwin. 1896. *Made in Germany.* London: William Heinemann.

Williams, Henry Herbert. 1910. "Ethics." In vol. 9 of *The Encyclopædia Britannica,* 808–845. 11th ed. New York: Encyclopædia Britannica.

Williamson, Jeffrey G., and Peter H. Lindert. 1980. *American Inequality: A Macroeconomic History.* New York: Academic Press.

Williamson, Oliver E. 2017. *Contract, Governance and Transaction Cost Economics,* ed. Gengxuan Chen. Singapore: World Scientific.

Wilson, A. N. 1988. *Tolstoy.* New York and London: Norton.

Wilson, Edmund. 1940. *To the Finland Station: A Study in the Writing and Acting of History.* New York: Farrar, Straus and Giroux.

Wilson, James. 1791. "Of the Law of Nations." In *The Works of James Wilson,* edited by Robert Green McCloskey. Cambridge, MA: Belknap Press of Harvard University Press, 1967. http://press-pubs.uchicago.edu/founders /print_documents/a1_8_1os5.html.

Winston, Clifford M. 1993. "Economic Deregulation: Days of Reckoning for Microeconomics." *Journal of Economic Literature* 31, no. 2: 1263–1289.

Winston, Kenneth I., ed. 2001. *The Principles of Social Order: Selected Essays of Lon L. Fuller.* Revised edition. Oxford, UK, and Portland, OR: Hart Publishing.

Wittgenstein, Ludwig. 1969. *On Certainty.* Edited by G. E. M. Anscombe and G. H. von Wright. Translated by Denis Paul and G. E. M. Anscombe. Oxford, UK: Basil Blackwell.

Wogaman, J. Philip. 1977. *The Great Economic Debate: An Ethical Analysis.* Philadelphia: Westminster Press.

Wood, Gordon S. 2009. *Empire of Liberty: A History of the Early Republic, 1789–1815.* New York and London: Oxford University Press.

Woolf, Virginia. 1931. *The Waves.* Ware, UK: Wordsworth Editions, 2000.

World Bank. 2013. "Remarkable Decline in Global Poverty, but Major Challenges Remain." Press release. April 17. www.worldbank.org/en/news /press-release/2013/04/17/remarkable-declines-in-global-poverty-but -major-challenges-remain.

World Bank. n.d. "GDP per Capita, PPP (Constant 2011 International $)." Accessed February 19, 2019. https://data.worldbank.org/indicator/NY.GDP .PCAP.PP.KD.

Wright, Richard. 1940. *Native Son.* New York: Harper.

Yeager, Leland. 1976. "Economics and Principles." *Southern Economic Journal* 42: 559–571.

Yeager, Leland B. 2011. "Reclaiming the Word 'Liberal.'" Liberty, March 9. http://www.libertyunbound.com/node/496.

Yeats, W. B. 1928. "Among School Children." In *The Tower*, 55–60. London: Macmillan.

Ziliak, Stephen, and Deirdre N. McCloskey. 2008. *The Cult of Statistical Significance: How the Standard Error Costs Us Jobs, Justice and Lives*. Ann Arbor: University of Michigan Press.

Zola, Émile. 1885. *Germinal*. Paris: G. Charpentier.

Acknowledgments

I am grateful to the publications where the following essays first appeared:

Chapter 17: "Christian Libertarianism Is What Our Politics Needs," from *Reason*, June 2016. Reprinted by permission.

Chapter 18: "Liberty and Dignity Explain the Modern World," from *The Morality of Capitalism*, edited by Tom G. Palmer, Jameson Books, 2011. Reprinted with permission from Atlas Network.

Chapter 19: "An Economist Goes to Shanghai," *Reason*, June 2017. Reprinted by permission.

Chapter 20: "The Great Enrichment Continues," *Current History* 112 (November 2013). Reprinted with permission from *Current History*. © 2019, Current History, Inc.

Chapters 21, 22: Reprinted by permission from Deirdre Nansen McCloskey, *The Bourgeois Virtues: Ethics for an Age of Commerce* (Chicago: University of Chicago Press, 2006), chapter 43. © 2006 by The University of Chicago.

Chapter 23: "Freedom and the Great Enrichment," *Global Perspectives* vol. 1, "The Indigo Era" (September 2016). Reprinted by permission.

Chapter 25: "Interview on Piketty," *EA*, Spring 2016. First published by the Institute of Economic Affairs, London, 2016.

Chapter 26: "Interview on Piketty," *Wprost* [in Polish], August 2015.

Chapters 27 through 33: *Erasmus Journal for Philosophy and Economics*. Reprinted by permission.

Chapter 34: "Nationalism and Socialism Are Very Bad Ideas," *Reason*, February 2017. Reprinted by permission.

Chapter 35: First published by *Prospect* magazine, March 2016. Reprinted by permission.

Chapter 36: First published as Deirdre Nansen McCloskey, "Competitiveness and the Antieconomics of Decline," in *Second Thoughts: Myths and Morals of U.S. Economic History,* edited by Deirdre Nansen McCloskey, pp. 167–173, 1993. Reproduced with permission of Oxford University Press and with permission of the Licensor through PLSclear. © 1993 by Oxford University Press, Inc.

Chapter 37: First published as Deirdre Nansen McCloskey, "Competitiveness and the Antieconomics of Decline," in *Second Thoughts: Myths and Morals of U.S. Economic History,* edited by Deirdre Nansen McCloskey, pp. 167–173, 1993. Reproduced with permission of Oxford University Press and with permission of the Licensor through PLSclear. © 1993 by Oxford University Press, Inc.

Chapter 38: "Against *Capitalism,*" *Reason,* January 2017. Reprinted with permission.

Chapter 39: "Economic Liberty as Anti-Flourishing: Marx and Especially His Followers," from *Economic Freedom and Human Flourishing: Perspectives from Political Philosophy,* edited by Michael R. Strain and Stan A. Veuger (Washington, DC: AEI Press, 2016). https://www.aei.org/publication /economic-freedom-and-human-flourishing-perspectives-from-political -philosophy/. Reproduced with permission of AEI Press. © 2016 by AEI Press.

Chapter 43: "Postmodern Market Feminism: A Conversation with Gayatri Chakravorty Spivak," *Rethinking Marxism* 12, no. 4 (Winter 2000). Available online at: https://www.tandfonline.com/doi/abs/10.1080/08935 690009359022. Reprinted by permission. © 2016. All rights reserved.

Chapter 44: "Postmodern Market Feminism: A Conversation with Gayatri Chakravorty Spivak," *Rethinking Marxism* 12, no. 4 (Winter 2000). Available online at: https://www.tandfonline.com/doi/abs/10.1080/08935 690009359022. Reprinted by permission. © 2016. All rights reserved.

Chapter 45: Republished with permission of Peter Lang Inc., from Deirdre McCloskey, "Introduction: Queer Markets," in *Media/Queered: Visibility and Its Discontents,* edited by Kevin G. Barnhurst (New York: Peter Lang, 2007). © 2007 by Peter Lang Inc. Permission conveyed through Copyright Clearance Center, Inc.

Chapter 46: "The Secret History of the Minimum Wage," *Reason,* July 2016. Reprinted by permission.

Chapter 47: "The Myth of Technological Unemployment," *Reason,* August/ September, 2017. Reprinted by permission.

Index